Leadership Strategies for Global Supply Chain Management in Emerging Markets

Ashish Dwivedi
The University of Hull, UK

Mohammed Saad Alshamrani
King Fahd Naval College, Saudi Arabia

A volume in the Advances in Logistics, Operations, and Management Science (ALOMS) Book Series

IGI Global
PUBLISHER of TIMELY KNOWLEDGE

Published in the United States of America by
IGI Global
Business Science Reference (an imprint of IGI Global)
701 E. Chocolate Avenue
Hershey PA, USA 17033
Tel: 717-533-8845
Fax: 717-533-8661
E-mail: cust@igi-global.com
Web site: http://www.igi-global.com

Library of Congress Cataloging-in-Publication Data

Names: Dwivedi, Ashish N., editor. | Alshamrani, Mohammed Saad, 1976- editor.
Title: Leadership strategies for global supply chain management in emerging markets / Ashish Dwivedi and Mohammed Saad Alshamrani, editors.
Description: Hershey, PA : Business Science Reference, [2020] | Includes bibliographical references and index. | Summary: "This book explores concepts, issues, challenges, innovations, and opportunities covering all aspects of how to create efficient supply chain operations in emerging markets"-- Provided by publisher.
Identifiers: LCCN 2019044087 (print) | LCCN 2019044088 (ebook) | ISBN 9781799828679 (hardcover) | ISBN 9781799828686 (softcover) | ISBN 9781799828693 (ebook)
Subjects: LCSH: Business logistics--Developing countries. | Leadership--Developing countries. | Investments--Developing countries.
Classification: LCC HD38.5 .L399 2020 (print) | LCC HD38.5 (ebook) | DDC 658.7--dc23
LC record available at https://lccn.loc.gov/2019044087
LC ebook record available at https://lccn.loc.gov/2019044088

This book is published in the IGI Global book series Advances in Logistics, Operations, and Management Science (ALOMS) (ISSN: 2327-350X; eISSN: 2327-3518)

British Cataloguing in Publication Data
A Cataloguing in Publication record for this book is available from the British Library.

For electronic access to this publication, please contact: eresources@igi-global.com.

Advances in Logistics, Operations, and Management Science (ALOMS) Book Series

ISSN:2327-350X
EISSN:2327-3518

MISSION

Operations research and management science continue to influence business processes, administration, and management information systems, particularly in covering the application methods for decision-making processes. New case studies and applications on management science, operations management, social sciences, and other behavioral sciences have been incorporated into business and organizations real-world objectives.

The **Advances in Logistics, Operations, and Management Science** (ALOMS) Book Series provides a collection of reference publications on the current trends, applications, theories, and practices in the management science field. Providing relevant and current research, this series and its individual publications would be useful for academics, researchers, scholars, and practitioners interested in improving decision making models and business functions.

COVERAGE

- Finance
- Production Management
- Political Science
- Information Management
- Operations Management
- Services management
- Marketing engineering
- Organizational Behavior
- Networks
- Computing and information technologies

IGI Global is currently accepting manuscripts for publication within this series. To submit a proposal for a volume in this series, please contact our Acquisition Editors at Acquisitions@igi-global.com or visit: http://www.igi-global.com/publish/.

The Advances in Logistics, Operations, and Management Science (ALOMS) Book Series (ISSN 2327-350X) is published by IGI Global, 701 E. Chocolate Avenue, Hershey, PA 17033-1240, USA, www.igi-global.com. This series is composed of titles available for purchase individually; each title is edited to be contextually exclusive from any other title within the series. For pricing and ordering information please visit http://www.igi-global.com/book-series/advances-logistics-operations-management-science/37170. Postmaster: Send all address changes to above address.

Titles in this Series

For a list of additional titles in this series, please visit:
http://www.igi-global.com/book-series/advances-logistics-operations-management-science/37170

Managerial Issues in Digital Transformation of Global Modern Corporations
Thangasamy Esakki (Poompuhar College (Autonomous), India)
Business Science Reference • © 2020 • 270pp • H/C (ISBN: 9781799824022) • US $195.00

Contemporary Approaches to Military Operations Research
Mumtaz Karatas (National Defense University, Turkey) and Hakan Tozan (Istanbul Medipol University, Turkey)
Information Science Reference • © 2020 • 300pp • H/C (ISBN: 9781799844051) • US $195.00

Legal, Safety, and Environmental Challenges for Event Management Emerging Research and Opportunities
Vipin Nadda (University of Sunderland, London, UK) Ian Arnott (University of Westminster, London, UK) and Wendy Sealy (University of Chichester, UK)
Business Science Reference • © 2020 • 158pp • H/C (ISBN: 9781799832300) • US $195.00

Multi-Criteria Decision Analysis in Management
Abhishek Behl (Indian Institute of Technology, Bombay, India)
Business Science Reference • © 2020 • 422pp • H/C (ISBN: 9781799822165) • US $245.00

Handbook of Research on Project Management Strategies and Tools for Organizational Success
Nelson Antonio Moreno-Monsalve (Universidad EAN, Colombia) H. Mauricio Diez-Silva (Universidad EAN, Colombia) Flor Nancy Diaz-Piraquive (Universidad Catolica de Colombia, Colombia) and Rafael Ignacio Perez-Uribe (Universidad EAN, Colombia)
Business Science Reference • © 2020 • 537pp • H/C (ISBN: 9781799819349) • US $285.00

Advancing Skill Development for Business Managers in Industry 4.0 Emerging Research and Opportunities
Sara Fazzin (H-Farm College, UK)
Business Science Reference • © 2020 • 168pp • H/C (ISBN: 9781799820369) • US $185.00

IGI Global
PUBLISHER of TIMELY KNOWLEDGE

701 East Chocolate Avenue, Hershey, PA 17033, USA
Tel: 717-533-8845 x100 • Fax: 717-533-8661
E-Mail: cust@igi-global.com • www.igi-global.com

Table of Contents

Detailed Table of Contents

Victoria Muerza, University of Zaragoza, Spain

Luca Urciuoli, Department of Industrial Economics and Management, KTH Royal Institute of Technology, Stockholm, Sweden & MIT International Logistics Program, Zaragoza Logistics Center, Zaragoza, Spain

E. (Bert) Annevelink, Wageningen Food and Biobased Research, The Netherlands

J.C.M.A (Joost) Snels, Wageningen University & Research, The Netherlands

Jan E. G. van Dam, Wageningen Food and Biobased Research, The Netherlands

This chapter explores the feasibility and advantages of integrated biomass logistics centres (IBLCs). These are centres aiming to collect residues from farming activities and transform these into new intermediate bio-products. Operations in these IBLCs aim to achieve economies of scale through integration of resources and business lines, while creating technical and environmental advantages for firms and societies. The experience from one agro-industry case study in Spain (fodder production) highlights the importance of leadership roles to manage the newly created supply chains, through the identification of strategic objectives and the coordination of operational activities. Hence, the scope of this chapter is to review the concept of IBLCs under the lens of supply chain management leadership. Thereafter, it will discuss the potential to transfer the IBLC concept to emerging markets, with examples for African agricultural crops.

Transport is an important function in the supply chain. This chapter focuses on how to buy a transport service, how to form a transport contract, and how a transparent relationship will influence the risk and the relationship between transport provider and buyer. By developing a decision support tool (DST-model) and calculating the cost and the time parameters, the right price and the cost drivers will appear. The cases described in this chapter are a large Norwegian wholesaler for food, distribution to the retailer, and two Norwegian municipalities collecting household waste. In these cases, the buyer and the provider are acting blind in setting the transport price. This means that there is a huge risk for either a bankruptcy by the transport provider or an overpriced transport for the buyer.

Environmental sustainability and customer response times will continue to remain the vanguard of every business. Being energy efficient is a step towards achieving environmental sustainability. The six-sigma methodology has been adopted by organizations for systematic conservation of energy. Customer responses can be improved by reducing the product supply lead time. The value stream mapping methodology has been used by several organizations to reduce product supply lead time with encouraging results. This chapter describes the use of methodologies such as six sigma and value stream mapping for reducing energy and improving the supply lead time respectively by means of two real life examples. The names of the respective organizations are disguised to protect confidentiality.

Supply chain management (SCM) as a concept first originated in the manufacturing industry from logistics and just-in-time production. Used to successfully utilize SCM elements and diminish lingering issues in construction, its importance lies in the focus that it gives to plan different features of the supply chain by also involving other parties of the chain in the process. SCM in construction supports firms by aiding in the improvement of competitiveness between firms and the increase of the company's profits and control over projects. Although generic supply chains should be simple and linear, the construction sector is much more complex. These problems are present in different parts of SCM due to interdependence in the organization and supply chain. Through a case study analysis and semi-structured interviews,

of the emerging markets of management education. It will enable the management institutes to redesign their strategies to suit the required changes.

This chapter discusses the bullwhip effect performance of serial and divergent supply chains under statistical process control (SPC)-based and order-up-to (OUT) policies. The performance of the supply chains is evaluated in terms of order rate variance ratio and bullwhip slope under four realistic customer demand models such normal, normal with a sudden change in mean, normal with seasonality, and normal with seasonality and a sudden change in mean. The impact of sharing of customer demand among the other members of the supply chain and the introduction of order smoothing parameter on both policies are also studied. The results show that under non-stationary customer demand models the difference in the performance of serial and divergent supply chains is noticeable. The bullwhip slope under OUT policy is significantly differing from the bullwhip slope under the SPC-based policy. OUT policy with order smoothing performs better than the SPC-based policy with order smoothing. This finding provides proper guidelines for a supply chain manager to make a decision in a practical scenario.

The chapter attempts to find out the relationship between the supply chain manufacturing practices (SCMP) and organizational performance, which are identified as financial and market performance. In the context of SCM, the financial and market performance factor is operationalized in terms of market share, return of total assets to firms, profit margin annuals sales growth, frequency of stock out, backorder rate, etc. Multiple regression analysis statistical technique has been used for the analysis of the adoption continuum questions in order to find the predictor variables for various performance measuring variables. The findings suggest that of supply chain manufacturing practices (SCMP) play a crucial role in enhancing the performance of the dairies companies in the form of increase in performance matrix indicators (i.e., level of supplier's defect-free deliveries, inventory turnover, frequency of stock out, backorder rate, sales growth, profit margin, return on investment, return on assets to firm).

Preface

The importance of the emerging markets today cannot be undermined. Historically, emerging markets were only considered to be useful by multinational firms due to wage differentials (i.e., salaries for services and manufacturing being considerably lower in emerging markets vis-à-vis the developed economies). The past trend of multinational firms, using emerging markets as an opportunity to increase profits by benefiting from low salary costs, resulting from being based in emerging economies is no longer the sole attraction. A number of authors have argued that what used to be yesterday's low cost countries are now the current new markets, which have the potential of reaching out to billions of people as customers, and the resulting opportunities for multinational firms is the ability to demonstrate immense growth opportunities their own shareholders by having customers in emerging markets.

However, a key challenge in this context is that multinational firms have to develop customised strategies that enable them to reaching mass markets effectively and this in-turn requires multinational firms to spend time and effort in the development and subsequent optimization of vibrant marketing and supply chain management channels.

The aim of this book is to provide an insight into emerging markets, and provide the readers of this book an understanding of the diversity, challenges and opportunities that multinational firms have in emerging economies, and perhaps to offer an intellectual forum for researchers and practitioners to provide solutions that are likely to be critical to designing efficient supply chain operations in emerging economies.

As editors, we have been fortunate enough to receive several outstanding book proposals. After a great deal of effort, we were able to arrive at twelve book chapters, which we believe present a comprehensive current understanding of supply chain management operations in emerging economies.

The first chapter is entitled "Managing Biomass Supply Chains: The Importance of Strategic Leadership". The authors, Victoria Muerza, Luca Urciuoli, Bert Annevelink, Joost Snels and Jan E.G. van Dam, explain the feasibility and advantages of Integrated Biomass Logistics Centres (IBLCs), in the context of farming activities. The authors conclude that operations in these IBLCs aim to achieve economies of scale through integration of resources and business lines, while creating technical and environmental advantages for firms and societies. The authors conclusions are based on their experience from one agro-industry case study in Spain (fodder production) which they argue has highlighted the importance of leadership roles to manage the newly created supply chains. The use of (inefficient) traditional biomass for cooking substantially reduces the expected gap between per capita figures in high- and low-income countries. This research is extremely important in the context of attempts being made across the world in various initiatives which are focused on reducing energy use and decarbonizing the supply chains of food products. The area of research covered in this book chapter will be of use to those researchers who are considering various combinations of measures which encompass technological measures and behavioural which can drive changes in consumption patterns for firms and societies. This book chapter will also be useful for those researchers who are interested in examining issues relating to food systems and environmental dimensions in Sustainable Development Goals of the United Nations.

The second chapter is entitled “Supply Chain Leadership in Emerging Markets: Understanding the Role of Trust, Information Management, and Collaboration”. The authors, Smitha Girija and Vandana Srivastava argue that the massive growth of emerging economies in last two decades has attracted many global companies to expand their physical presence in these countries. However they point out that not all companies have been able to take advantage of those opportunities as only a few companies have understood the importance of appreciating environmental challenges and complexity of the emerging economies regions region. They go on to argue that in the lexicon of extant literature - substantial focus has been on enhancing supply chain leadership and development of efficient and effective strategies in developed economies only. This has resulted in lack of literature which focuses on emerging economies. In their book chapter - the aim to overcome this drawback and attempt to do so by synthesizing the current literature to understand the phenomenon including its definitions, dimensions and constructs and propose a conceptual model for successful Supply Chain Leadership in emerging markets. The authors discuss the importance of establishing the impact of various factors of Supply Chain Leadership which leads to Sustainable Supply Chain Performance.

The third chapter is entitled “Leadership Strategies for Global Supply Chain Management: The Case of UAE’s Construction Sector”. The authors, Sreejith Balasubramanian and Vinaya Shukla explores the leadership strategies for global supply chain management in the construction sector. The authors take the case of The United Arab Emirates (UAE) construction sector, which has played a pivotal role in transforming UAE to a modern economy from a nomadic one. The authors argue that UAE as a case study is particularly useful, as it is an exemplary case in this study to understand the leadership strategies required for developing ‘globalness’ in their construction supply chain. The authors in the book chapter have used secondary research and interviews with stakeholders in the construction supply chain, and prepare an innovative approach for leadership strategies. The authors argue the importance of focusing on four key areas, namely 1) Policymaking 2) Technology and Innovation 3) Environmental Supply Chain Management, and 4) International Collaboration/Partnerships. This book chapter is particularly useful for practitioners and policymakers as it has the potential in improving the global competitiveness of their construction sector and its supply chain.

The fourth chapter is entitled "Transparency Issues Within a Transport Buyer and Provider Relationship". The author, Eirill Bø notes that Transport is an important function in the supply chain. This chapter focus on developing a decision support tool (DST-model), which includes various key factors such as the cost and the time parameters, the right price and the cost drivers. The cases described in this chapter is a large Norwegian wholesaler for food, distribution to the retailer and two Norwegian municipalities collecting household waste. In both cases, the buyer and the provider are acting blind in setting the transport price. This means that there is a huge risk for either a bankruptcy by the transport provider or an overpriced transport for the buyer. This book chapter is particularly useful for practitioners and policymakers as it has the potential in improving the problems associated with transparency within buyer and provider relationship relationships, which are an area of chronic difficulty for managers.

The fifth chapter is entitled "Methodologies for Achieving Environmental Sustainability and Improving Customer Response". The author, Raj V. Amonkar notes that Environmental sustainability and customer response times will continue to remain the vanguard of every business. This is an important statement as published literature on Environmental sustainability as argued that there is extensive evidence that business organizations, societies, and governments are extremely concerned in the uptake of green operations management. The article adopts six-sigma methodology as a mechanism to examine the use of it by organizations for systematic conservation of energy. This book chapter argues that customer responses can be improved by reducing the product supply lead time. This chapter describes the use of methodologies such as six sigma and value stream mapping for reducing energy and improving the supply lead time respectively by means of two real life examples. This book chapter is particularly useful for practitioners and policymakers as despite the importance of business organizations, societies, and government's efforts to alleviate environmental damages and provide economic benefits to organizations to adopt environmental sustainability strategies -, little is known about the external institutional drivers that enable uptake of environmental sustainability strategies in developing economies.

The sixth chapter is entitled “Challenges and Perspectives of Supply Chain Management in Emerging Markets”. The authors, Eni Ahmeti and Alba Demneri Kruja note Supply chain management (SCM) as a concept first originated in manufacturing industry from logistics and Just-In-Time production. The authors note that SCM in construction supports firms by aiding in improvement of competitiveness between firms, increase of company’s profits and control over projects. The authors argue that although generic supply chains should be simple and linear, the construction sector is much more complex and that these problems are present in different parts of SCM due to interdependence in the organization and supply chain. The authors attempt to provide a resolution to this dilemma by undertaking a case study analysis and semi-structured interviews, to identify and better understand the role of SCM, challenges and complications in different levels of the supply chain, and how firms utilize it to create greater value in construction operations, and specifically in Albania. As such this chapter is going to be of use to practitioners and academic researchers in developing economies, particularly those associated with the construction sector.

The seventh chapter is entitled “Prioritizing the Enablers of Construction Supply Chain in Industry 4.0 Environment”. The authors, Vivek Agrawal, Seemant Yadav, R Mohanty and Anand Agrawal establishing the context further requirement of research studies on the fourth industrial revolution (Industry 4.0) as it has the potential of bringing about a transformation in the construction industry and its connected supply chains. The authors note that construction supply chains (CSCs) have specific characteristics, such as being temporary organizations that require high coordination efforts to align the processes of supply chain actors in Industry 4.0. Construction industry has its own challenges e.g., temporary work and involvement of high coordination among others. The authors argue that to explore the enablers to of construction supply chain in industry 4.0 environment - it is important to use a decision-making technique which makes it possible to explore overcome these issues and prioritize them as these kinds of decisions are more complex if they are intangible, non-expressible, qualitative etc. the authors use AHP to understand 4 enablers and 14 sub-enablers of construction supply chain. E-Supply chain management is ranked first followed by, digitization, tracking and localization, and cloud computing. This chapter is going to be of use to practitioners and academic researchers in developing economies, particularly those associated with the construction sector as it provides a comprehensive understanding of the key influences impacting upon the adaptation of Industry 4.0 technologies for the construction sector. The key part of the originality of this book chapter is that it uses AHP to contribute to the ongoing discussion about how Industry 4.0 technologies act as enablers in construction supply chain in an industry 4.0 environment.

The eighth chapter is entitled "Leadership Model for Supply Chain Management in Business Schools". The author, Ramakrishna Yanamandra observes that Supply chain management has brought sweeping changes in the way organizations achieve profit and competitive advantage in the recent past. But the rapid changes occurring in the business environment due to globalization and emergence of new markets have created many new opportunities as well as challenges for organizations in supply chain. The author further explaining the significance of research in this area by propounding that effectiveness of management institutions can be improved if they focus on changing needs of SCM and provide dynamic leadership in line with the changing needs of students and other stakeholders. The author argues that this created the need for acquiring a completely different kind of supply chain skill sets and competencies among the leaders, of these institutions which they were hitherto unfamiliar with. The significance of this book chapter is particularly important for those practitioners and researchers who are focused on executive education, as a topic like supply chain management, was the potential to serve as an integrator, bringing together academic and non-academic units within an educational institution. The author concludes this chapter by presenting a supply chain leadership model for business schools and management institutions and makes the claim that this model may enable them to align themselves with the changing needs of the emerging markets of management education. This chapter is going to be of use to practitioners and academic researchers in developing economies, particularly those associated with the management institutes in emerging economies.

The ninth chapter is entitled "Bullwhip Effect Performance of Supply Chains Under Statistical Process Control-Based Policy". The authors, Joby George and K. V. Madhusudanan Pillai discuss the bullwhip effect performance of serial and divergent supply chains under Statistical Process Control (SPC)-based and Order-Up-To (OUT) policies. This study is particularly significant as it is known that Inventory control plays an extremely crucial role in supply chain management. Prior research has clearly established that an adequately managed inventory has the potential of ensuring that customers' demands our all was met, and is of particular significance to manufacturing and production firms as it can ensure that there is overall smoothing of the production capacity and also be useful in reducing operational costs. Failure to manage inventory expenses may lead to serious consequences, including bankruptcy. Therefore this chapter which focuses on inventory control and in particular on the bullwhip effect, is an important topic.

The tenth chapter is entitled "Supply Chain Manufacturing Practices (SCMP): An Approach to Become Global Dairy Leader". The author, Rajeev Kumar attempts to find out the relationship between the supply chain manufacturing practices (SCMP) and organizational performance which are identified as financial and market performance. The author findings suggest that supply chain manufacturing practices (SCMP) play a crucial role in enhancing the performance of the dairies companies in the form of increase in performance matrix indicators. This chapter identifies the critical components of product and service aspects of the dairy-food supply chain which required to be strengthened for better supply chain performance. This chapter is going to be of use to practitioners and academic researchers in developing economies, particularly those associated with dairy farmers as it has the potential to provide an understanding to them and how can they build a supply chain that can increase the efficiency of dairy farmers, also collaborate with milk producers who are part of a cooperative supply chain (as is the case of AMUL in an emerging country like India).

The eleventh chapter is entitled “Key Success Factors Facilitating SME E-Commerce in Developing Countries: Literature Review”. The author, Hijrah Saputra This chapter presents a systematic literature review and research agenda regarding key success factors (KSFs) facilitating SME e-commerce in developing countries. The author notes that previous studies have mainly pre-adoption when the Internet and e-commerce were new. However, SMEs have largely been ignored and now that attention has turned to post-adoption issues research is required in SME and developing country contexts due to the worldwide growth of e-commerce. In this book chapter the author presents a structured literature review using Denyer and Tranfield’s context, intervention, mechanisms and outcome (CIMO) criteria for critical analysis to enable the development of future empirical research areas. The KSFs are considered significant and of concern to stakeholders, including inter alia SMEs and governments to encourage SME growth in e-commerce and positively influence SME and overall business performance to meet customer demand.

The twelfth chapter is entitled “Returns Management: An Instrument For Enhancing Customer Service for Indian E-Retail Industry”. The authors, Nikhil Singh and Smriti Asthana report that the e-retail sector of Indian e-commerce industry, despite being a price sensitive market has witnessed an increase in the customers interest and flexibility to compare a product while making a purchase decision through eCommerce platform. The authors point out that the increase in internet penetration and users in India has been facilitated by boost of telecom industry and data penetration from 34% in 2017 to an 60% in 2022 (E). The authors suggest that while some players like Flipkart and Amazon have disrupted the sector with their customer acquisition ratio in the market, other new player Jio mart and Paytm Mall are merely surviving or gearing up to the competition. The cost factor like marketing, forward logistics, inventory and reverse logistics are associated with customer acquisition which the organizations are not able to recover because of low average gross merchandise value (GMV) and high logistics cost to serve the customer. This chapter as per authors depicts the returns management process, which while integrating the forward and the reverse logistics in a supply chain is productive financially and logistically. This chapter is extremely important for researchers and practitioners who are concerned that understanding the interrelationships between supply chain management and returns management. This is because the topic of Returns management is an indispensable part of supply chain management, and it has not received the attention that it deserves. Given that developing economies are likely to see Product returns, as the industry grows in emerging economies - this book chapter provides some pains to put the industry and academic researchers and how can they tackle this dilemma of returns management.

As editors, we have managed to solicit chapters, which discusses how organisations can create innovative solutions for implementing global best practices in supply chain management in emerging markets.

Ashish Dwivedi
The University of Hull, UK

Mohammed Saad Alshamrani
King Fahd Naval College, Saudi Arabia
20 May 2020

Acknowledgment

We are grateful to the reviewers for taking and time and effort to provide their feedback. We are also grateful to Ms Jan Travers of IGI Global for her kind help and assistance.

Chapter 1
Managing Biomass Supply Chains:
The Importance of Strategic Leadership

Victoria Muerza
University of Zaragoza, Spain

Luca Urciuoli
https://orcid.org/0000-0002-9417-9421
Department of Industrial Economics and Management, KTH Royal Institute of Technology, Stockholm, Sweden & MIT International Logistics Program, Zaragoza Logistics Center, Zaragoza, Spain

E. (Bert) Annevelink
Wageningen Food and Biobased Research, The Netherlands

J.C.M.A (Joost) Snels
Wageningen University & Research, The Netherlands

Jan E. G. van Dam
Wageningen Food and Biobased Research, The Netherlands

ABSTRACT

This chapter explores the feasibility and advantages of integrated biomass logistics centres (IBLCs). These are centres aiming to collect residues from farming activities and transform these into new intermediate bio-products. Operations in these IBLCs aim to achieve economies of scale through integration of resources and business lines, while creating technical and environmental advantages for firms and societies. The experience from one agro-industry case study in Spain (fodder production) highlights the importance of leadership roles to manage the newly created supply chains, through the identification of strategic objectives and the coordination of operational activities. Hence, the scope of this chapter is to review the concept of IBLCs under the lens of supply chain management leadership. Thereafter, it will discuss the potential to transfer the IBLC concept to emerging markets, with examples for African agricultural crops.

DOI: 10.4018/978-1-7998-2867-9.ch001

INTRODUCTION

The concern about the environment has boosted the trend towards the circular economy, based on a "recycling society". It has initiated a transformation in different industries and sectors, where residues are used as an input in new processes "closing the cycle" and taking advantage of the existing resources in terms of machinery and knowledge (Geissdoerfer, Savaget, Bocken, & Hultink, 2017). In this context, a new concept has been coined for the agroindustry within the AGROinLOG project: the Integrated Biomass Logistics Centre (IBLC) (Annevelink et al., 2017). IBLCs aim to increase the use of existing facilities of an agroindustry taking advantage of idle periods, allowing a diversification of the business activity.

The feasibility of IBLCs should be studied from a social, environmental and economic standpoint (Muerza, De la Cruz, & Urciuoli, 2019): social viability refers to the creation of employment derived from the diversification of the company's activity. Environmental viability is related to the emissions derived from the collection of the raw material (residues from agribusiness), until the transformation in the IBLC and the distribution in the markets of the new product compared to the reduction of emissions due to the substitution of fossil-based products by biobased products. Economic viability considers the calculation of logistics costs and processing costs, related to the configuration of the supply chain. This strategy is linked to several of the agribusiness leaders' seven top strategic priorities identified in a survey to 200 companies (SpencerStuart, 2015): (i) pursue joint ventures, alliances, acquisitions; (ii) expand presence in international markets; (iii) develop new products; (iv) develop cooperative relationships with farmers, suppliers and customers; (v) develop new sales channels; (vi) build upstream/downstream capabilities to increase vertical integration, and (vii) dramatically reduce costs. Furthermore, the World Council for Sustainable Development system has pointed out the need of deeper collaboration between diverse stakeholders across sectors and the "*use the circular bioeconomy to alleviate resource supply risks, shift from fossil-fuel and non-renewable resources to sustainable, renewable biomass, repurpose agricultural waste and recycle nutrients*" (Morrison, 2019).

Current research is exploring both feasibility and advantages of these IBLCs in three agro-industries in Europe: fodder (Spain), olive oil production (Greece) and cereal processing (Sweden) sectors. The experience from these three demos in Europe highlights the importance of leadership roles in order to manage optimally supply chains, through the identification of strategic objectives and the coordination of operational activities. In this sense, the configuration of the logistics chain must be optimized as it directly impacts on the economic viability of the IBLC (Muerza et al., 2019). The logistic solutions to adopt will depend on the type of final product based on a certain type of residue. The transformation processes will be different both in the IBLC and in terms of supply: raw material size, transport, use of intermediate warehouses, etc.

Leadership in Supply Chain Management (SCM) is of great importance as it affects the optimal integration of people and logistics systems, facing challenges in several stages of the supply chain, e.g. optimal coordination of material and flows in global and uncertain environments (Mentzer et al., 2001). The supply chain leader analyses market trends and selects appropriate information systems, making decisions and promoting innovation to support company growth.

The objective of this chapter is to analyze the concept of Integrated Biomass Logistics Centers under the lens of supply chain management leadership. Main drivers, opportunities and barriers are discussed. In addition, a case study in the fodder sector is presented. Furthermore, the chapter discusses the potential to transfer the IBLC concept from European to emerging markets, including main advantages and disadvantages. Emerging markets are, in principle, appropriate to test the possibilities for the IBLC concept from several perspectives: there is a large access to biomass in developing countries (Faaij & Domac, 2006); for example, Africa owns sustainable forestry products, non-food crops, and food crop residues, including agro-food industry residues, and marine biomass. Crops residues that can be used include sugar crops, carbohydrate crops, oil crops, and bamboo. In addition, production of bioenergy in these countries can benefit local communities and develop further agricultural and forestry sectors (Faaij & Domac, 2006).

The structure of this chapter is the following: it starts by describing the theoretical description of leadership in supply chain management; then it explains the IBLCs concept and the economic implications of integrated biomass centres. Next, by using a case from the feed and fodder sector, it suggests strategic and operational leadership considerations for the implementation of the IBLC concept. Then it describes the potential of biocommodities in emerging markets. Finally, it envisions the implementation of the IBLC concept in emerging markets and discusses leadership implications to manage IBLCs supply chains in emerging countries based on the experience in Europe.

LEADERSHIP IN SUPPLY CHAIN MANAGEMENT

A supply chain consists of a virtual network of organizations that collaborate in order to transform raw materials into finished products to be delivered to final consumers. The network involves value production in form of products and services, involving firms upstream, suppliers, and downstream, distributors (Mentzer et al., 2001). The management of supply chains is a concept that was first identified by Forrester using computer simulation. The model that was developed pointed out the importance to enhance the understanding of interrelationships between company's functions, between companies, markets and national economy. The concepts related to inter-firms relationships, supplier management, integration, partnership, coordination etc. have been transformed into supply chain management theories, applied to current challenges experienced in several stages of the supply chain, e.g. global sourcing, production, transport and distribution in uncertain environments (Mentzer et al., 2001). In essence, companies are stretching their supply chains distances between production and consumption, while coordinating flows of materials optimally. The goal is to manage to deliver the right products to customers in optimal conditions at the right place, in the right quantity and at the right time. Hence, the importance to coordinate flows in complex supply chain networks increases, emphasizing competition not anymore among single entities, but rather among various supply chains. Mentzer et al. (2001) suggest that supply chain management should determine coordination across functions, internally in companies, and externally, across companies. The former implies the understanding of trust commitment and risks, while the latter is about coordination of various third party suppliers, relationships and the feasibility of different supply chain structures (Mentzer et al., 2001).

Leadership is an important characteristic of leaders in order to optimally and effectively navigate teams of people in an uncertain environment. Schoemaker, Krupp, and Howland (2013) state that important traits of leaders include "*the abilities to anticipate, challenge, interpret, decide, align, and learn*". *Anticipate* concern the ability to detect or simply recognize threats or opportunities in advance and steer corporations accordingly. *Challenge* requires a careful analysis of the current status of things or problems and thereby take decisive actions. Leaders could develop solutions to problems in an isolated manner leading to predictable and rarely innovative changes. It is important to discover root causes of problems and dare to embrace basic industry assumptions. *Interpret* is the ability to elaborate complex and conflicting information. Hence, gathering the available information, recognize patterns, remove ambiguity and seek new insights is essential to clean the information and uncover implicit or hidden problems or implications. *Decide*, at some point leaders will have to make decisions and implement them, sometimes with incomplete information and high level of uncertainty. *Align* is the ability to find common ground in different ideas and achieving buy-in from stakeholders with different agendas. *Learn* from failures in a constructive manner and promote a culture to identify lessons learned both from success and failures (Schoemaker et al., 2013).

A sound and effective management leadership is necessary to translate the corporate vision of SCM into strategic plans, short, medium and long-term decision making, processes and operations (Ou, Liu, Hung, & Yen, 2010). A leadership structure is typically determined in a supply chain, defining power, or simply coordination, especially in the downstream market channels (Ellram & Cooper, 1990; Stock &

Lambert, 2001). Leadership is sometimes associated with the size, economic power or the initiation of the inter-firm relationships. When applying the leadership strategic ability to the management of supply chains, it is possible to frame the six abilities defined by Schoemaker et al. (2013): anticipate, challenge, interpret, decide, align and learn (Table 1).

THE IBLC CONCEPT

Introduction

Many European agro-industries are characterized by the fact that capital goods and facilities in these industries cannot be used year-round due to the seasonal availability of the primary feedstocks. The EU project SUCELLOG formed the starting point for the idea to use available agro-industrial capacities as a resource for the processing of biomass for renewable energy (Sucellog, 2017). In AGROinLOG, the project that followed, this idea was defined as Integrated Biomass Logistics Centre (IBLC) concept (Annevelink et al., 2017). The goal of an IBLC is to establish an increased utilization of the facilities of an agro-industry. Alternative non-food feedstocks (e.g. crop residues or non-food crops) could fill the idle periods of, for example, the pre-treatment equipment (e.g. compact, dry, etc.) or of the storage capacity at the facility. Hence, in this situation the underutilization of processing and storage capacity in the middle of the value chain is the main driver for the potential development of an IBLC. However, the drivers of an IBLC could also be considered from two other perspectives, being (i) upstream in the beginning of the value chain: the residues that are not being utilized at the moment and (ii) downstream at the end of the value chain: new biobased products that need clearly defined feedstocks or biocommodities of a specific quality.

Table 1. Leadership strategic ability to manage supply chains (Schoemaker et al., 2013)

Anticipate	**Challenge**
• Establish a closer relationship with both customers and suppliers. Arm's length relationships may not work since 1) suppliers may be reluctant to share internal challenges or likewise 2) buyers/customers could not have resources and managerial setups to engage into better understanding of challenges. Therefore, collaboration/cooperation are to be preferred. • Use market research and simulations to determine competitors' position on the market and detect potential disruptive offerings that could ultimately affect sales. In this aspect, scenario-planning tools could be of great help. • Perform benchmarking of competitors that have been fast growing. • Analyse reasons for customers leaving for competitors. Determine whether changes in the distribution and delivery channels can improve sales and regain loyalty. • Attend conferences and events to determine on-going trends and internalize in upcoming supply chain strategies.	• Focus on root causes of problems in supply chains, e.g. using the five whys of Sakichi. • Discover the long-standing assumptions of a business and its supply chain and question whether they should still hold true. • Encourage open dialogue in meetings, not being afraid of conflicts and welcoming criticism. • Include in meetings people with opposite views, in order to identify and address challenges.
Interpret	**Decide**
• Collect and analyse data to deduct possible explanations for patterns observed. • Search for any missing information, to reject / confirm any hypotheses formulated. • Force and strive to develop the big picture, rather than look at details.	• Frame, weighs and evaluate the options at disposal. • Big decisions related to the whole supply chain, could be broken down into pieces, in order to understand sub-decisions and their implications on the supply chain system. • Diversify short, medium and long-term decisions.
Align (both internally, but also externally with other supply chain companies)	**Learn**
• Improve communication in order to avoid uncertainty and lack of knowledge. • Enhance understanding about on-going coalitions and hidden agendas growing. • Engage in conversations to reduce misunderstanding or resistance to change. Especially reach to resistors to understand their concerns and address them accordingly. • Monitor stakeholders internally and externally during the rollout of any supply chain initiative/ strategy. • Recognize and reward high performing colleagues / supply chain partners.	• Encourage gathering of documentation to review and report lessons learned after major decisions or achieved milestones. Eventually supply chain risk management tools could be exploited. • Examine root causes of failures. Eventually supply chain risk management tools could be exploited. • Establish reward to managers engaging in difficult tasks and failing. In this aspect, the organization should create a culture accepting failures and viewing those as a growing opportunity form lessons learned.

Economic Considerations for an Integrated Biomass System

Previous research has highlighted the importance of integrated biomass systems and their economic significance (Ebadian, Sowlati, Sokhansanj, Stumborg, & Townley-Smith, 2011; Mahmoudi, Sowlati, & Sokhansanj, 2009; Sokhansanj, Kumar, Turhollow, & Bioenergy, 2006). Recent research has emphasized the importance to map processes, activities, and machines in a supply chain and thereby compute and costs-revenues. Urciuoli and Muerza (2018) advance a framework for evaluating costs of IBLCs' supply chains. For each of the actors (i.e. suppliers, focal company (IBLC), distributors), based on the SCOR approach developed by the Supply Chain Council (SCC, 1999), the following activities are distinguished: Source, Make and Deliver. Thereafter, main costs involved in the different parts of the framework are elaborated. Figure 1 shows a summary of the identified costs. The cost to deliver herbaceous biomass varies by feedstock type, location and technologies used for packaging the biomass (An & Searcy, 2012).

Figure 1. Framework for integrated modelling in the agro-food waste and recycle business
Source: Urciuoli & Muerza, 2018

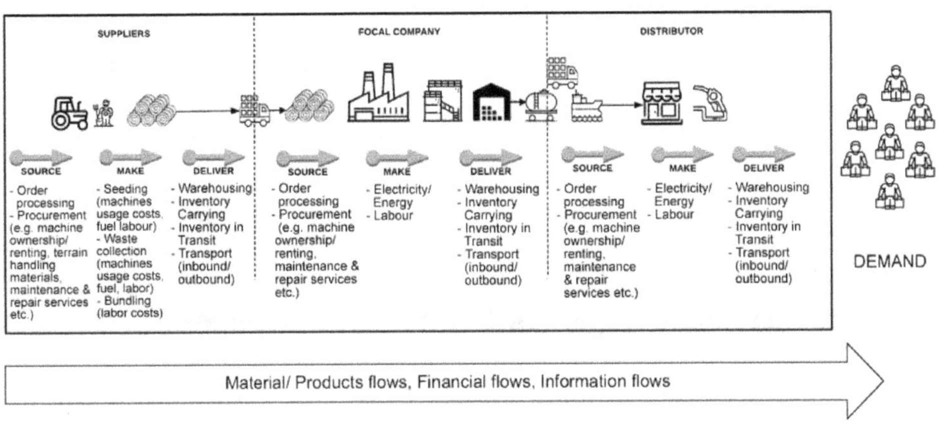

Given the level of uncertainty within biomass supply chains, many authors have been developing simulation tools or mathematical models to evaluate the performance of biomass supply operations (Ho, Hashim, & Lim, 2014; How, Tan, & Lam, 2016; Mitchell et al., 1995). An Integrated Biomass Supply Analysis and Logistics (IBSAL) model was developed that has been applied for different types of feedstocks, e.g. corn grains, wood, wheat etc. (An & Searcy, 2012; Mahmoudi et al.,

2009; Sokhansanj et al., 2006). Ebadian et al. (2011) propose a logistics model and its application to supply a mixture of agricultural feedstocks to a cellulosic ethanol plant. Mitchell et al. (1995) develop a spreadsheet-based decision support system to evaluate integrated biomass systems, focusing on the transformation of biomass into to ethanol schemes. Ho et al. (2014) use mixed integer linear programming (MILP) to compute the cost-effectiveness of an integrated biomass and solar town, where palm kernel, palm oil, food waste, solar radiation and empty fruit bunches are transformed into energy.

These models emphasize the importance of balancing costs and performance / efficiency. An and Searcy (2012) suggest the biomass logistics cost to range between 19.65 \$ Mg^{-1} and 41.26 \$ Mg^{-1} with varying yield levels and transport distances. provide cost components of the logistic system in the Prince Albert region in Canada according to the following logistics operations: square baling, in-field transporting, on-field storage, loading into truck, road transporting, loading into grinder/stacking into at-plant storage, at-plant storage, grinding. How et al. (2016) present a mathematical model to solve the multi-echelon biomass supply chain synthesis problem. The economic performance of the supply chain is based on three components, i.e. annual gross profit, annualized hub investment cost, and annual transportation cost. Mitchell et al. (1995) evaluate the costs of the different technologies to convert raw materials into biomass. Economies of scale are measured as an output on electricity costs when capacity changes (measured in MWe), plantation area (hectares), and cost of delivered fuel (Mitchell et al., 1995). Efficiency is measured as the conversion factor of different technologies, pyrolysis, gas engine, Integrated Gasification Combined Cycle (IGCC) and combustion. Among those IGCC shows the highest overall efficiency of 37.9% (Mitchell et al., 1995). Sokhansanj et al. (2006) measure efficiency in terms of time during which work is done over total time spent in the field.

Integrated Biomass Logistics Centre (IBLC) Concept

An Integrated Biomass Logistics Centre (IBLC) is defined as a business strategy for agro-industries to take advantage of unexploited synergies in terms of facilities, equipment and staff capacities. The strategy aims to diversify regular activity both on the input (food, feed and biomass feedstock) and output side (food, feed, biocommodities & intermediate biobased feedstocks); thereby, enhancing the strength of agro-industries and increasing the added value delivered by those companies. The IBLC concept can be further specified into four separate elements:

Figure 2. Schematic position of an IBLC in value chain

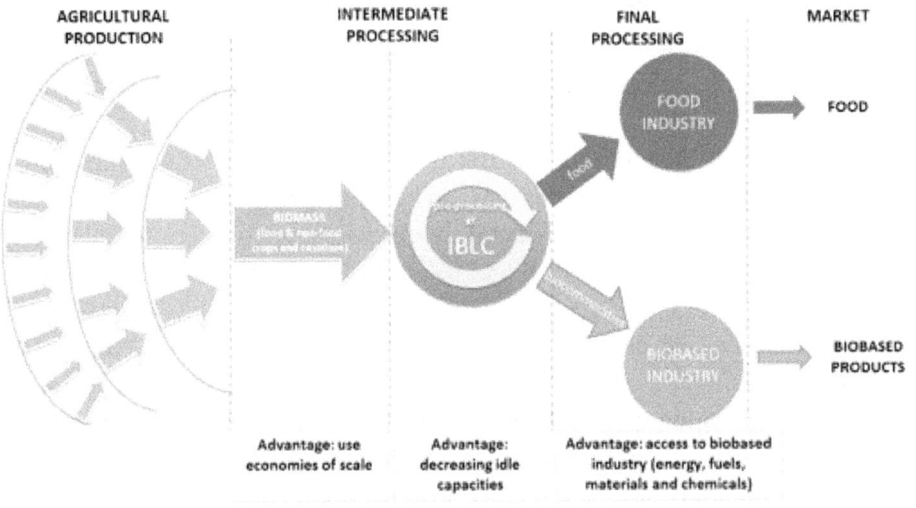

- **Integrated:** Refers to the integration of value adding activities towards food, feed and biobased markets;
- **Biomass:** Refers to biomass that is available in the surrounding region of the agro-industry, that is underutilized or unexploited currently and that has the potential as resource with an added value;
- **Logistics:** Refers to the role of an agro-industry using its available logistics, storage operations and pre-treatment facilities to (i) collect and transport biomass residues, (ii) to pre-treat and transform these residues into food, feed, biocommodities & intermediate biobased products, (iii) to store them and finally (iv) to distribute the biocommodities and intermediate products to industrial processing sites elsewhere;
- **Centre:** Refers to exploiting the central position of the agro-industry in a specific region.

The schematic position of an IBLC within the value chain is presented in Figure 2. Important parts of the value chain are (i) the agricultural production with the suppliers of biomass feedstocks for food and non-food, (ii) intermediate food & biomass pre-treatment / pre-processing industry (IBLC), (iii) final processing by the food and bio-based industry and finally (iv) the markets for food and bio-based products. The advantages of having an integral view on both food and bio-based (non-food) value chains are:

- **Economies of Scale:** Because more biomass feedstocks need to be transported and processed;
- **Decrease idle Capacities:** Because the facilities at an IBLC can be fully used for processing multiple biomass feedstocks for either food, feed or bio-based products;
- **Access to Bio-Based Industry:** Because the IBLC produces not only food or feed but also bio-commodities that can be processed into bioenergy, biofuels, bio-based materials and bio-chemicals for industries further on in the value chain.

The four aspects of an Integrated Biomass Logistics Centre will be further explained below:

An integrated value approach towards food and biobased markets means that both market segments are addressed at the same time by the IBLC. The existing system for supplying food products is combined with supplying bio-based (intermediate) products such as bioenergy (electricity and heat), biofuels, biomaterials and bio-chemicals to new markets. Of course, the availability of profitable new markets for these biobased products is essential for the success of the IBLC concept. A potential biobased market should be analyzed regarding several aspects like size, value, developments, expectations/prognosis, radius for supply, etc. Furthermore, a distinction must be made between three-market types viz. the final consumer market (direct purchasing of final products by households), the business-to-business market (purchasing of intermediate products and bio-commodities by industry) and the public market (direct purchasing by governments). Predominantly the IBLC concept is directed at the business-to-business market. However, the other two markets can also be served if a specific opportunity arises e.g. the case of selling biomass pellets directly from the IBLC to households or municipalities for heating in biomass stoves or boilers.

Regional Availability of Biomass: Nearby locations of agricultural production sites offer easier access to biomass resources (mainly residues) for an IBLC due to the short transportation distances. The technical ability to harvest biomass residues with minimal added costs and without influencing the quality of the primary crop is very important to increase the availability of biomass.

The seasonality of harvesting agricultural crops restricts the availability of biomass residues to a specific period. The time of the season determines the actual ability to harvest a crop residue (e.g. harvesting of maize stalks in November is not always possible because of wet soil).

Easy-to-access biomass residues from the agro-industry's own food or feed production process that do not have a market, could also be an important source for producing biocommodities and intermediate biobased feedstocks. Furthermore, residues from other agro-industries could also be a source of biomass and should be explored when setting up an IBLC.

Logistics, Storage Operations and Pre-Treatment: The availability of existing transport facilities for the collection of biomass residues from the surrounding fields, and the connection with an existing logistic chain are factors that form a stimulating incentive for developing an IBLC. The logistics from harvesting, handling and collection of biomass residues, as well as the transport to the IBLC influence the quality of the end-product and vice versa. In some cases, new transport facilities will be needed to guarantee enough supply of a specified quality. After all, the quality of the end-product will be determined by the type, composition and quality of the biomass that is available, and that will enter the processing stage at the IBLC. The quality and composition specifications of the IBLC's end-product will have to fit with the required technical specs for the processes of the user of the IBLC end-product (e.g. the quality requirements and specifications of agro-pellets for specific biomass stoves or boilers).

Quality requirements of the end-product and microbiological / physiological characteristics of the biomass also affect the storability of biomass residues. Storage facilities for the collected biomass will have to comply with safeguarding enough biomass quality to meet the end-product requirements. Quality and food-safety requirements (originating from the side of the food production) may place limitations to the combination of food and non-food production in the same agro-processing facility.

The input specifications and handling characteristics of collected biomass are the linking pin with available processing capacities in the IBLC. As mentioned, the availability of idle pre-treatment capacity in a certain period is one of the drivers for the IBLC. Therefore, it is important to know the length of the idle period of the facilities, the capacity of these facilities and the way available pre-treatment and storage capacity can be optimally used for biomass processing. In addition, it is very important to assess the technical feasibility of the available capacity, to determine if the capacity is appropriate for processing biomass residues. Furthermore, the available capacity needs to be matched with the volume and timing of the biomass residue availability.

An IBLC can **exploit the benefits of the central geographical position** of the agro-industry in relation to the existing regional biomass sourcing area. The central position of the IBLC reduces the transportation distances and costs in the value chain both from the agricultural production areas to the IBLC and from the IBLC to the industrial processing locations. But also the location of the IBLC relative to the location of the industrial processing facilities that will take product from the IBLC and will supply the market (local, regional, global) with the end-product is something to consider in the design of operations and logistics within an IBLC

(Lamers et al., 2015). The availability of a regional market with enough demand is an advantage for both the IBLC and the industrial processing companies that are in the centre of such a market. However, when the regional biomass is transformed to biocommodities at the IBLC even the national and global markets come within reach.

Main Drivers for Implementing the IBLC Concept

Biomass is an appealing source of energy in the current climate and energy context. Biomass residues will also form an important feedstock in the future to produce biobased products other than solid biofuels. For existing agro-industries there are three important drivers to develop an IBLC:

- Diversification of inputs;
- Optimization of available and new capacity;
- Diversification of outputs.

An existing company could expand its operational activities for value creation in various ways:

- By using extra feedstock types (not only food or feed but also non-food biomass residues) on the input side,
- By optimizing its existing processing capacity that already has fixed (capital) costs or by expanding its processing capacity with extra (pre-treatment) capacity with low additional investment costs,
- By obtaining extra revenues from delivering new output types (e.g. not only food or feed but also biocommodities for the biobased economy).

Opportunities and Barriers for the IBLC Concept

An IBLC can play an important role as a unit for increasing economic, environmental and social sustainability of agricultural production and processing in the region. In addition, the IBLC concept is affected by the governance of the agricultural sector (incl. laws and regulations) as well as by specific policies regarding biomass, waste and valorisation of residues from agriculture into new products. In Table 2, the main opportunities and perceived barriers are listed, categorized by the impact categories (economic, environmental, social, governance and technical).

Table 2. The main opportunities and perceived barriers for the IBLC concept

	Opportunities	Barriers
Economic	• Diversification in feedstocks and end-products: use cheap biomass residues as a resource for bioenergy and biobased intermediate products. • Fixed costs reduction through optimal use of existing agro-industrial facilities (increased return on investment of invested capital). • Diversification of product portfolio to biobased markets.	• Some feedstocks might be too expensive at the gate of the IBLC (including logistical costs) • Lack of experience and knowledge regarding the market potential of bioenergy / biobased products. • Low pricing of fossil product counterparts (oil and gas). • Lack of appropriate technologies for biomass transformation on the market;
Environmental	• GHG reduction (through reduction of the consumption of fossil fuels). • Supply of renewable energy (bio-energy).	• Impact on nutrient cycle. • Impact on soil depletion;
Social	• More employment through increased business activity. • Strengthens the role and function of the agricultural sector and rural areas in the bio-economy.	• Social acceptance / perception of product quality. • Reluctance to change the business as usual in agriculture sector.
Governance, laws & regulations	• Positive contribution to the EU / national goals with reference to the use of biomass for energy and for biobased production. • Current promotion of circular economy needs to be translated into new regulations (in short-term).	• Uncertainty / different interpretation of national legislations what biomass can be used and if it is waste or not. • Limited availability of and access to funding resources. • Unfavourable taxation regimes for raw material, product and fuel.
Technical	• IBLC concepts are suitable to energy integration and hence, energy efficiency optimization within existing facilities. • The equipment is already well known (e.g. dryers, pelletizers, storage facilities, etc.).	• Lack of knowledge on processing (new) types of feedstock (incl. how to deal with variable quality of raw material). • Increased wear and tear of equipment; • Extra cleaning needed between processing of food and non-food feedstocks. • Difficult to meet biomass end-product compatibility / quality requirements.

STRATEGIC AND OPERATIONAL LEADERSHIP CONSIDERATIONS FOR AN IBLC IN THE FODDER SECTOR

The IBLC concept is being applied in a European research project, specifically in three demos in different sectors, feed and fodder in Spain, cereals in Sweden, and olives in Greece (AGROINLOG, 2020). This section presents strategic and operational leadership considerations using data and observations collected in the Spanish demo related to the feed and fodder sector. Focus is on an agroindustry located in Spain whose main activity is the production of dehydrated alfalfa, in the form of bales or pellets (compact granule), intended for direct animal feed or as a raw material for the manufacture of compound feed. Animal feed industries final products are homogeneous mixes of several raw materials (grains, cereals, vegetable and animal by-products) and components (oil and fats, molasses, vitamins and minerals) from which a balanced and nutritious food is achieved, providing a better conversion performance in the animal feeding. Fodder industries process herbaceous matter for better preservation of the nutritious elements contained on it through three different industrial processes: silage, haymaking and dehydration.

The objective is to become and IBLC by optimally designing a new business line taking advantage of the idle period of the equipment in the plant taking place from December to March. During this time, new pellets for two different purposes will be produced: energy use and bio-composite materials. Furthermore, two additional markets will be tackled with these new products: bioenergy and bio-composites. The raw material used to produce the pellets will be cereal straw, maize stalks and Sudan grass to be purchased from the farmers located in the surrounding area. In order to upgrade the quality of the pellet when the goal is to satisfy the energy demands, wood chips will be also acquired.

Leadership strategic ability to design and manage the new supply chain can be discussed in view of the six abilities defined by Schoemaker et al. (2013) as shown in Table 3.

Figure 3. Some logistics solutions to be chosen in the design of the supply chain of an IBLC based on cereal straw

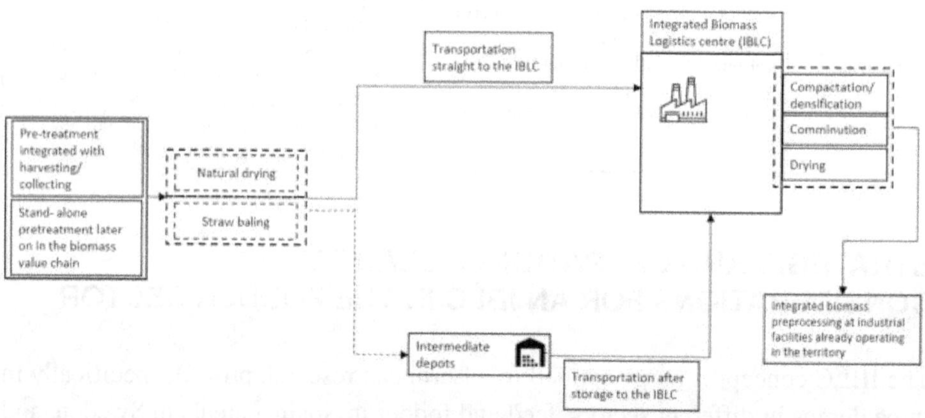

Table 3. Leader strategic abilities for the IBLC in the fodder sector

Anticipate	Challenge
• *Supply chain design.* The configuration of the new business line includes the design of the supply chain. Different logistics solutions and configuration of the supply chain can be adopted depending on the type of final product to be produced from the residue. The transformation processes will be different both in the IBLC and at supply level, e.g. raw material size, transportation mode, use of intermediate warehouses, residues collection technology (see a generic configuration in Figure 3) and directly impact on the feasibility of the IBLC. • *Management of material.* Straw (residue material) storage may be temporarily depending on the sources and period of supply, in the medium-long term in the IBLC itself, in a distribution warehouse, or at the retailer's premises. • *Adapt transport modes.* The mode of transport will depend on the shape of the residue, the quality of the raw material and the distance of transport. Eventually identify existing flows to integrate. • *Relationship management.* A closer relationship with both customers and suppliers must be established. In this sense, the strategy of the company consists of ensuring the supply of small farmers around the company for the main product (alfalfa); acquiring also the straw, they provide (around 20%) to gain loyalty. Agreements with medium and big suppliers are being studied. • *Adapt production lines.* The company has analysed the existing equipment to identify idle time and to include new lines in the production process. In addition, they have studied the possibility to adapt the machinery, and the need for buying new equipment. Feed industries own compatible equipment with the processing of biomass such as pelletizers, silos for storage, screening and chipping machinery, besides of a high degree of staff professionalization and many other valuable assets useful for the biomass processing activities (workforce, means of transport, etc.). Similar to the feed industries, fodder dehydrator industries own pelletizers, silos for storage, screening and chipping machinery compatible with the biomass handling. Besides, the fodder dehydration process requires horizontal rotary dryers to reduce the water content of the fodder, completely suitable for biomass drying in an IBLC. • *Adapt production to electricity tariffs.* An analysis of electricity tariffs from January to December has been carried out. Six electricity tariffs (€/kWhe) have been identified as a function of the month and the hour of the day at which the electricity is consumed. The cheapest tariff is applied from 00:00 to 8:00 a.m. during the whole year. The operation of the new line in the IBLC will consider the operation during the cheapest period time from December to March. • *Identify competitors.* A market analysis before the investment and implementation of a new activity in the IBLC is needed. Main competitors for the new activity are fossil fuel sources, higher quality standard biomass pellets, and similar agro-residues materials. The company has attended to meetings with companies of the sector to explore the possibility to create synergies. • *Assess social impacts.* Surveys are going to be launched to study the social impact of the IBLC in the area. Understanding social impacts can help firms in collaborating with local governments and thereby benefit subsidizes or facilitated procedures. • *Establish relationship with R&D centres.* Technological and research centres in the area are supporting the analysis process in terms of both logistics, design of the installation, and tests and design of the new product, before the launching in the market.	• *Suppliers selection.* Define a strategy of selection of suppliers for the current activity (bales and pellets for the feed industry), mainly based on price and loyalty of small suppliers, and the new activity (pellets for energy market). The strategy should include all stakeholders' standpoint. • *Simulations* to determine quantities of raw (residues) material, and distance-price ratios. Current suppliers are located in a distance of approximately 100 km from the IBLC. • *The equipment* that determine the production timing of the main activity are the dryer and the mill-pelletizer. The challenge is to optimize its use taking into consideration the hours with the cheapest electricity tariffs. Both equipment is needed in the new activity. • *Weather conditions* determine the load of the dryer. Moisture content determine collection and processing. Material can be stocked a maximum of 36 hours (when not baled) due to affections in the quality. Amount to be stored in this format in the IBLC is determined by the space and capacity (around 400 t).
Interpret	**Decide**
• Tests regarding the *size* and *quality* of the new product (in terms of energy) need to be performed. • *Planning tools* are being used. For instance, Value Stream Mapping (VSM) allows an analysis of the material and information flows to optimize the processes (Rother, 1999). Material moved from phase to phase, intermediate inventories, and customer demand are represented. Added value and non-value-added times are calculated. The tool allows the identification of "waste" in the process in terms of material, information and time loses. The interpretation of the VSM is needed to define actuation plans and optimization of resources, stablishing priorities in the activities of continuous improvement and for the integration of the new production line in the company. Figure 4 shows the Value Stream Mapping carried out for the implementation of the new production line considering a pellet with a mix of 60% straw and 40% wood. The non-value-added time is mainly due to the storage times of the material in intermediate points of the manufacturing process.	• The production process is highly influenced by *customer demand.* Decide about the possibility to develop a tool to foresight demand to optimize the integration of the new line. • Value Stream Mapping definition has considered production during the cheapest electricity tariffs. Specifically, from December to February a production of 8 hours/ day, and in March 14 h/ day, and a medium production of 9.5 h/ day (for the 4 months). • Decide about the possibility to operate the new line from October to November as the dryer generally works at 40% of the maximum capacity due to the lower alfalfa yield. • Decide on the quality of pellet for the energy market to be manufactured. Quality is mainly related to the type of biomass used, and the procurement and pre-treatment activities. • *Set the price* for the new product.
Align (both internally, but also externally with other supply chain companies)	**Learn**
• *Set contracts* with suppliers to ensure the supply of the material in the quantity needed. • *Align the actors* of the supply chain: suppliers, IBLC and distributor (Urciuoli & Muerza, 2018). • *Align the strategy of distribution* with the customer demand minimizing transportation costs and environmental emissions. • *Align customer demand and sales channels.* Different strategies may be needed according to the customer typology. • *Develop a good customer service,* including training activities regarding the best use of the product during the first weeks of operation. • *Develop demonstration activities* with potential customers to prove the good operation of a boiler with the pellet developed.	• *Establish reports of* the production activity. • *Encourage feedback* from all stakeholders in the process: design and research, simulation, manufacturing, launching to the market and after sales. • *Examine root causes of failures,* both in the conception of the product (blends and qualities) and the process. • *Learn from key partners in dissemination activities.* Involve agricultural associations, journals in the sector, stakeholders and Administration.

Figure 4. Value stream mapping for the new activity of the companyThe potential of biocommodities in emerging markets

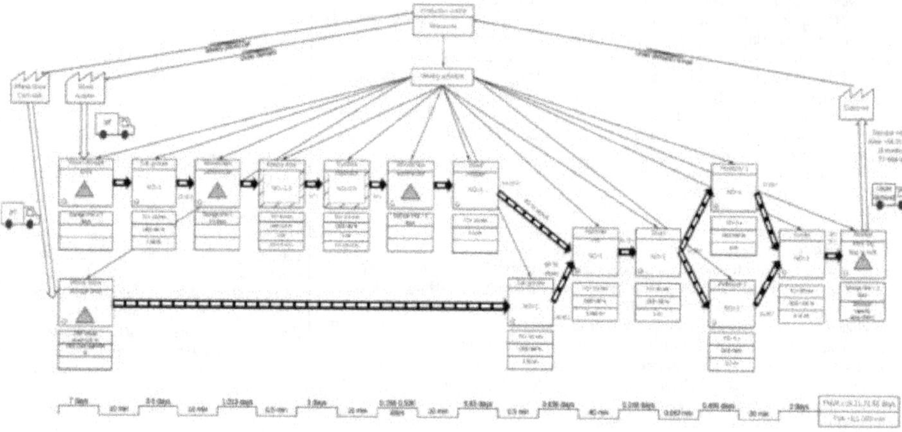

THE POTENTIAL OF BIOCOMMODITIES IN EMERGING MARKETS

One of the few options to combat climate change is to avoid carbon emissions by petrochemical fossil resources and the use of carbon neutral biobased, renewable and circular materials. The resources that potentially can be made available to supply the biobased economy comprise sustainable forestry products, non-food crops, and food crop residues, including agro-food industry residues, besides marine biomass.

Many well-known commodity crops originate from Africa. The indigenous crops that were domesticated in Africa are often drought-resistant crops originating in the savannahs, such as sorghum and (pearl) millet, yams, African rice, baobab, and tamarind. Other crops originating from the forest margins are for example oil palm, cowpea, hyacinth bean, and Bambara groundnut. Kola nut, coffee and malaguete are African forest derived crops. Other crops have been introduced from Eur-Asia or the Americas (Maize, Cassava) in the African agricultural production system.

Bio-Commodities in Africa

The global production volumes and land demands of the major bio-commodity crops are available at the Food and Agriculture Organization of the United Nations (FAO, 2017). The most important nutritious crops that are produced to feed the human population are rich in carbohydrates (sugar, starch) or high yielding oil seeds.

Africa has a significant share in the world sorghum, millet and cassava production. In soybean production, Africa (0.8%) is insignificant on global scale, other Leguminosae such as groundnuts, dry beans, vetches, and Bambara prevail.

From most food crops the foliage and lignocellulose residues are left in the field after harvest, but may find economic value as renewable energy source when collected and properly processed (Jingura & Matengaifa, 2008). Part of the residual biomass is left in the field to compost and considered necessary for maintaining soil carbon and soil fertility. Other part is used as animal fodder. Biomass conversion can be performed by various biorefinery technologies depending on the composition (moisture, energy content) and available supply of biomass volumes for economic plant operation (Figure 5).

Figure 5. Suitability of biomass for biorefinery processing related to the dry-matter content

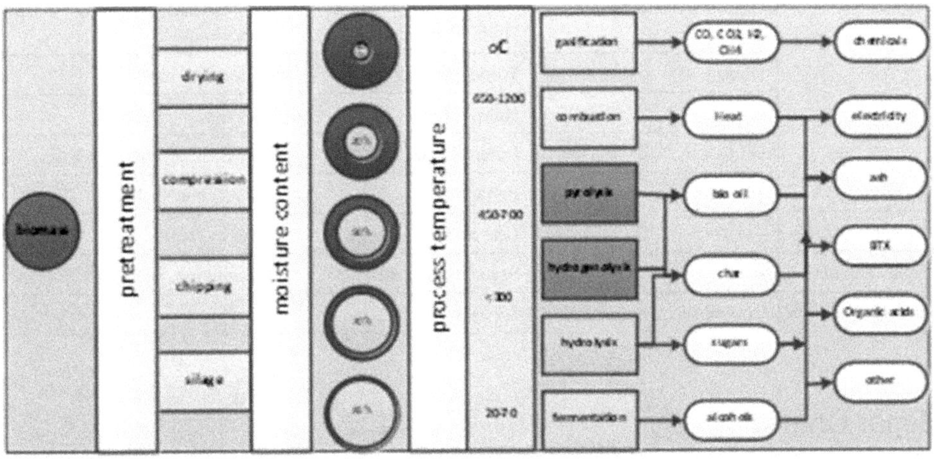

Abundant biomass resources of a wide range of forms (agricultural, municipal and industrial waste, wastewater) can be used in digesters to produce biogas (CH_4). Selection of the optimal biomass feedstock for efficient anaerobic conversion by the various technologies (e.g. floating drum, plug flow, fixed dome, batch and semi-batch) is important for the economics of the process. The variability of feedstock supply can be better controlled when pre-processing and storage capacities can be installed (e.g. IBLC).

Crop Residues Utilization

In the production of food crops significant amounts of biomass residues are produced (Table 4) and left in the field after harvest (primary residues) or liberated at the mill (secondary residues). The degree of utilization differs per crop and per region.

Table 4. Some types of common primary and secondary crop residues

Crops	Example	Primary residues/ by-products	Secondary residues/ by-products
Sugar cane	--	Leaves and tops	Bagasse, molasses filter cake, vinasse
Sugar beet	--	Leaves and tops	Pulp, molasse
Grains	Wheat, corn, rice, barley, millet	Straw (stover), chaff (hulls, husks)	Bran, cobs
Tubers and roots	Potato, cassava, yams	Foliage, tops	Peels, pulp
Oil seeds	Sunflower	Hulls, flower heads	Press cake
	Olive	Wood, pruning	Stones, pomace
	Cocos	Husks, fronts	Shells
	Oil palm	Fronts, stems	EFB, fibre, shells, POME
	Soy, rape, peanut	Foliage	seed coat, shells
Vegetables	--	Leaves, stems, roots	Peelings, skin
Fruits and nuts	--	Seeds, stems, shells	Fruit pulp, peelings
Fibres	Cotton, flax, hemp, sisal	Seeds, stems	Shives, hurts, tow

Sugar Crops

The potential of Africa sugar production is not fully developed due to global protectionism. Sugar beet is found only in North Africa (Egypt/ Morocco). Sugar cane is found widely distributed over Africa, but highest production is found in East Africa. Despite the competitive production of sugar cane (e.g. South Africa, Zambia, Swaziland, Malawi) just 5% of the world sugar cane production is produced in Africa. The African yields stay behind the global average of productivity. The utilization of bagasse, the biomass residue of sugar cane processing, has received much attention as it accumulates at the sugar mills and its use has been demonstrated to produce energy pellets, pyrolysis oil, 2nd generation bioethanol (Leal et al., 2013), and composites (particle boards, fibre boards, fibre cement, etc.) (Verma, Gope, Maheshwari, & Sharma, 2012).

Carbohydrate Crops

Carbohydrate crops in Africa show large regional differences. Wheat production in Africa is only 4.8% of the global production area, with average yields of 75% of the global productivity. Most is produced in the Northern countries (Egypt, Ethiopia, Tunisia, Algeria and Morocco). Rice and millet are mostly produced in West Africa. In some special grains, crops are grown that are only known in Africa such as teff (Eragrostis abyssinica) and fonio (Digitaria exilis). Maize is the largest starch crop and can be found in all regions of Africa. Maize or Corn is primarily produced for its cobs, but also for animal feed in the form of silage and corn. In Africa most biomass residues are used to feed livestock (cattle) (Powell, Pearson, & Hiernaux, 2004).

Maize production is on 20% of the global crop area with strongly varying average yields. In Northern and Southern area, the yields are above average, but in Western, Middle and Eastern Africa the total yields are only 1/3rd of the global average.

The starch from cereal grains are the largest source of carbohydrates for human food production. In the primary production, at the farm, the cereal crops yield as a residue straw and the seed hulls, husks or chaff. The primary crop residues – the biomass left in the field at harvest - from cereals are produced in vast quantities and the worldwide straw production has been estimated for wheat and rice respectively at around 350 and 730 10^6 tons per annum.

Rice and wheat straw burning is a common practice in Africa and give rise to significant air pollution and smog (Mkoma, Kawamura, & Fu, 2013). Attempts to ban these open crop-burning practices are failing and alternative ways of disposal are of interest. Concern about the loss of nutrients and soil carbon when straw is removed from the field should be carefully considered and balanced. The uses of straws include energy and materials. R&D for alternative uses as bioenergy or paper pulp, building materials, particle boards, and 2nd generation bioethanol can be found in the literature (e.g. Batidzirai et al. (2016)).

Electricity and heat can be produced by different technologies such as direct combustion, digestion to biogas, gasification and pyrolysis. Biofuel production from straw, e.g. 2nd generation bioethanol production is still economically hard to achieve if no added value is created for the non-converted residues (unfermented carbohydrates, lignin, and silica).

Oil Crops

Sesame (*Sesamum indicum*) is native to Africa and Tanzania and Sudan are the largest producers. Sesame can grow under harsh conditions and there is a global market for the seeds and oil. The sesame straw that is left after trashing does not find much use as it has low nutritional value.

Karite or shea (*Vittalaria paradoxa* or *Butyrospermum parkii*) is typical from West Africa and yields the much appreciated shea butter, which is in high demand in health food products and cosmetics (NRC, 2006). Smallholder processing of the fruits may be improved to give higher yields and valorisation of the by-products.

Olive trees (*Olea europea*) are found in the Mediterranean countries of North Africa exclusively and the olives are processed similarly to the practice of Southern European producers. The utilisation of residues liberated from olive oil production (pruning, pomace, press cake) as studied in the AGROinLOG project as demonstration for the IBLC concept of can also be implemented in North African olive mills.

Palm oil (*Elaeis guineensis*) originates from West Africa and has evolved from wild harvested oilseeds in the mid-19th century in Ghana to an industrial crop in other continents, for example Malaysia, Indonesia and Colombia. Productivity in Africa of palm oil contributes only 6% to global production on more than 20% of land area covered by Oil Palms. Despite large opportunities of palm oil production in West Africa, conditions of local infrastructure are poorly organized and need improvements. Besides improving institutional conditions for small-scale processors to provide access to international and industrial markets the organization of farmers is important to negotiate better deals (Adjei-Nsiah, Owurak, & Kuyper, 2012).

Coconut (*Cocos nucifera*) is found in tropical coastal areas of both West Africa (Ghana, Nigeria, Ivory Coast) and East Africa (Tanzania, Kenya and Mozambique). African countries account for 10% of the total land area covered by coconut and are producing more than 2 million tons (3.5%) of nuts (FAO, 2017). Many small holder farmers depend on the nuts for their sustenance. Currently the use of the residues (shells, husks, fronts) is limited. Currently in Africa only in Ghana and Ivory Coast, some production of coconut coir is reported. Based on an estimated husk yield of 15% dry matter per coconut the potential production volumes can be estimated per country. The husks commonly are left in the field when the nuts are harvested and transported to the coconut oil mills. Collection and supply of the bulky husk to a pre-processing plant will be essential for implementation of a manufacturing plant, where the dried husks can be converted to building panels or compression moulded forms.

Bamboo

Woody bamboo species are found naturally in many places in sub-Saharan Africa (Bystriakova, Kapos, & Lysenko, 2004) and their hollow stems have traditionally been used for building and construction, fuel, feed and fodder, and to manufacture tools and handicrafts, furniture and many other products (van Dam, Elbersen, & Daza Montaño, 2018). Natural bamboo forests are important for the protection of many endangered species of animals and proper management of the human exploitation of this biomass resource is critical. Bamboo is harvested to produce charcoal or building materials, most often is derived from natural stands.

In the Dutch-Sino East Africa Bamboo Development Programme (INBAR) the options for development of industrial bamboo uses are explored (Mulatu & Kindu, 2010). In Ethiopia, Kenya and Tanzania the industrial production of bamboo show potential for applications such as flooring and furniture, plywood, polymer composites and building materials. Besides the traditional uses of bamboo as charcoal and the tapping of juice to produce bamboo alcohol and vinegar, there is no tradition to harvest edible bamboo shoots. Currently, the industrial production of toothpicks and incense sticks is yielding significant volumes of sawdust, which may be suitable fibres in composite production. The options for bamboo-based pulp and paper industry have been explored in East Africa and is gaining increasing attention in India and China. Because of its rapid growth, bamboo is considered an ideal crop for rural development. The harvest and collection require skilled labour and transportation to pre-processing plants, where the bulky hollow culms can be converted to strips or fibres.

HOW TO APPLY IBLC TO ESTABLISH SCM LEADERSHIP ROLES IN EMERGING COUNTRIES

A leadership function, aiming to setup and run such a supply chain in emerging countries should still build upon on the abilities proposed by Schoemaker et al. (2013): anticipate, challenge, interpret, decide, align and learn. However, the changed contextual factors of two different scenarios, where the IBLC concept is implemented in Europe versus emerging markets, will have to be considered. It can be hypothesized that the following divergences will dawn:

- There is a variety of crop residues that could be utilized in emerging countries like e.g. Africa (see previous section). However, the collection of these residues is still not organized. Therefore, completely new supply chains will need to be designed that cannot build on previous experiences.
- Distances to be covered in the supply chain are often much larger in emerging countries than in the European situation, both from the IBLC to the processing industry and from there to the final market. This will increase transport costs of the raw feedstock. However, it also offers more opportunities for producing high-density intermediates at an IBLC that can be transported at lower costs to a final processing industry at large distance. Hence, supply chain design is crucial for lowering transport costs.

- Less capital might be available in emerging countries to buy extra equipment; hence, more emphasis will be put on utilising the idle time of the equipment that is already available. Therefore, in emerging countries there will be even more need for the IBLC concept than in European countries.
- Optimizing electricity tariffs will only be useful when the really vary. This might not be the case in emerging countries. Security of electricity supply might be a topic that is more relevant in emerging countries, both for the original production and for the new biobased production.
- Storage conditions of raw biomass might be different in emerging countries, e.g. due to climate conditions.
- Competitor analysis will probably be more difficult in emerging countries, nevertheless still very important.
- Social aspects in emerging countries will greatly differ between those countries and from the European situation.
- In emerging countries less relevant knowledge and expertise might have been developed since the concept has not yet been studied locally yet. However, large parts of the European knowledge could serve as a starting point to adopt to the regional situation. In that sense the knowledge base of the AGROinLOG project can be very valuable (http://agroinlog-h2020.eu/en/home/).
- Non-technical issues like rules and regulations will be different in emerging countries. However, this also offers an opportunity to introduce suited new legislation to stimulate the establishment of IBLCs.
- The selection of local suppliers is still very important. However, the type of contact/ business relation between the IBLC and the farmers might be different from the European situation.
- A market analysis will always be needed for each specific country. This will probably lead to different types of products compared to the European situation.

CONCLUSIONS AND DISCUSSIONS

In the agroindustry, the use of residues as an input of new processes has out the basis for the creation of a new concept: The Integrated Biomass Logistics Centre (IBLC). The concept is being tested in three agro-industries in Europe, within the framework of the AGROinLOG project, in terms of both feasibility and advantages: fodder (Spain), olive oil production (Greece) and cereal processing (Sweden). The project aims to align with the growing amount of research and development in the circular economy area, a new sustainability paradigm aiming to conserve our earth's national resources (Geissdoerfer et al., 2017).

While technical innovation has demonstrated pros and cons from the implementation of circular economy principles, it remains unexplored how the related supply chains should be managed and led. This chapter analyse the concept of IBLCs under the lens of supply chain management leadership. By means of a framework proposed by Schoemaker et al. (2013) (anticipate, challenge, interpret, decide, align and learn), leadership abilities to be considered when developing a supply chain management function in these IBLCs are proposed. Thereafter, the potential for applying the IBLCs in emerging market and implications for leadership are discussed.

The following knowledge can be extracted from the analysis:

- A leader should consider that the configuration of the supply chain must be optimized as it directly influences the economic viability of the IBLC. Different storage options should be studied and adapted to climate conditions. In this sense, weather conditions influence moisture content and determine collection and processing.
- The selection of suppliers is fundamental but presents challenges to undertake. Local suppliers should be secured to decrease transport costs and ensure supply. In this aspect, contracting and related legislative frameworks may need to be developed and applied.
- A supply chain manager needs to investigate and use idle time of equipment as an opportunity to activate production of biocommodities. Hence, the idle time of the equipment that is already available should be clearly defined maximizing the use of the existing resources in terms of equipment and resources.
- Perform a competitor and market analysis before making the decision to invest in the new activity in the IBLC. Decide the price for the new product. In particular, the supply chain leader should be able to trade off the costs of production with the potential revenues from sales.
- Production costs and especially utilities costs need to be carefully reviewed. Optimizing electricity tariffs can be challenging in emerging countries where access in rural areas is still limited. This can force the supply chain to move production facilities far away from collection points. Consequences are increased distances and transport costs.
- Rules and regulations will be different in emerging countries. Introducing suited new legislation can be an opportunity to stimulate the establishment of IBLCs.
- Tests are needed to develop the new product in terms of quality and size.
- Develop sales channels. Perform different strategies to introduce the product in the market adapted to the customs and culture.

- Encourage feedback from all stakeholders in the process to learn and align all the needs. Examine cause of failure and apply corrections.
- Involve the community in dissemination activities promoting acceptance.

The main contribution of this research study consists of performing a preliminary analysis to shift the IBLC concept to emerging countries, with a focus on the supply chain management function and its leadership abilities. From a scientific viewpoint, many studies can be found, describing main principles and concepts related to biocommodities supply chains. Nevertheless, there is still very little research defining leadership functions and their main challenges in both developed and developing countries. From a practical viewpoint, supply chain management is a discipline that has not permeated the biocommodities sectors yet. In principle, based on the experience from Europe, it has been discovered that main actors are not able to implement and apply business strategies in the management of their supply chains. Hence, it is of outmost importance to understand how this can be performed to create competitive biocommodities products. At the same, the lessons learned should be moved to developing countries, where the need of sustainable energy supplies is still a problem in many parts of the countries, despite plenty of underutilised resources are available.

The study performed is based on the analysis of data and observations performed in cases respectively in Europe and emerging countries in Africa. The IBLC concept has been developed in the framework of a three years project in Europe. In addition, the senior members of the research team have decade of experience in the topic of biomass supply chains globally. Nevertheless, we acknowledge that the differences highlighted are merely explorative propositions based on the team's expertise. Therefore, further research needs to be developed to ground our preliminary hypotheses in theory and further validate them in a sound confirmatory study.

ACKNOWLEDGMENT

This research has received funding from the European Union's Horizon 2020 research and innovation programme under grant agreement No. 727961.

REFERENCES

Adjei-Nsiah, S., Owurak, S. D., & Kuyper, T. W. (2012). Exploring opportunities for enhancing innovation in agriculture: The case of oil palm production in Ghana. *The Journal of Agricultural Science*, *4*(10), 212–223.

AGROINLOG. (2020). *AGROINLOG, Integrated Biomass Logistics Centres for the agro industry*. Retrieved from http://agroinlog-h2020.eu/en/home/

An, H. J., & Searcy, S. W. (2012). Economic and energy evaluation of a logistics system based on biomass modules. *Biomass and Bioenergy*, *46*, 190–202. doi:10.1016/j.biombioe.2012.09.002

Annevelink, E., van Gogh, B., Nogués, F. S., Espatolero, S., De la Cruz, T., Luzzini, D., . . . Olsson, J. (2017). *Conceptual description of an Integrated Biomass Logistics Centre (IBLC)*. Paper presented at the European Biomass Conference & Exhibition 2017, Stockholm, Sweden.

Batidzirai, B., Valk, M., Wicke, B., Junginger, M., Daioglou, V., Euler, W., & Faaij, A. P. C. (2016). Current and future technical, economic and environmental feasibility of maize and wheat residues supply for biomass energy application: Illustrated for South Africa. *Biomass and Bioenergy*, *92*, 106–129.

Bystriakova, N., Kapos, V., & Lysenko, I. (2004). *Bamboo Biodiversity*. UNEP-WCMC/INBAR.

Ebadian, M., Sowlati, T., Sokhansanj, S., Stumborg, M., & Townley-Smith, L. (2011). A new simulation model for multi-agricultural biomass logistics system in bioenergy production. *Biosystems Engineering*, *110*(3), 280–290. doi:10.1016/j.biosystemseng.2011.08.008

Ellram, L. M., & Cooper, M. C. (1990). Supply chain management, partnership, and the shipper-third party relationship. *International Journal of Logistics Management*, *1*(2), 1–10.

Faaij, A. P., & Domac, J. (2006). Emerging international bio-energy markets and opportunities for socio-economic development. *Energy for Sustainable Development*, *10*(1), 7–19.

FAO. (2017). *Faostat Crops*. Retrieved from http://www.fao.org/faostat/en/#data/QC/visualize

Geissdoerfer, M., Savaget, P., Bocken, N. M., & Hultink, E. J. (2017). The Circular Economy–A new sustainability paradigm? *Journal of Cleaner Production*, *143*, 757–768.

Ho, W., Hashim, H., & Lim, J. (2014). Integrated biomass and solar town concept for a smart eco-village in Iskandar Malaysia (IM). *Renewable Energy*, *69*, 190–201.

How, B. S., Tan, K. Y., & Lam, H. L. (2016). Transportation decision tool for optimisation of integrated biomass flow with vehicle capacity constraints. *Journal of Cleaner Production, 136*, 197–223.

Jingura, R. M., & Matengaifa, R. (2008). The potential for energy production from crop residues in Zimbabwe. *Biomass and Bioenergy, 32*(12), 1287–1292.

Lamers, P., Tan, E. C. D., Searcy, E. M., Scarlata, C. J., Cafferty, K. G., & Jacobson, J. J. (2015). Strategic supply system design–a holistic evaluation of operational and production cost for a biorefinery supply chain. *Biofuels, Bioproducts and Biorefining, 9*(6), 648-660.

Leal, M. R. L. V., Galdos, M. V., Scarpare, F. V., Seabra, J. E. A., Walter, A., & Oliveira, C. O. F. (2013). Sugarcane straw availability, quality, recovery and energy use: A literature review. *Biomass and Bioenergy, 53*, 11–19.

Mahmoudi, M., Sowlati, T., & Sokhansanj, S. (2009). Logistics of supplying biomass from a mountain pine beetle-infested forest to a power plant in British Columbia. *Scandinavian Journal of Forest Research, 24*(1), 76–86.

Mentzer, J. T., DeWitt, W., Keebler, J. S., Min, S., Nix, N. W., Smith, C. D., & Zacharia, Z. G. (2001). Defining supply chain management. *Journal of Business Logistics, 22*(2), 1–25.

Mitchell, C., Bridgwater, A., Stevens, D., Toft, A. J., & Watters, M., & Bioenergy. (1995). Technoeconomic assessment of biomass to energy. *Biomass, 9*(1-5), 205–226.

Mkoma, S. L., Kawamura, K., & Fu, P. Q. (2013). Contributions of biomass/biofuel burning to organic aerosols and particulate matter in Tanzania, East Africa, based on analyses of ionic species, organic and elemental carbon, levoglucosan and mannosan. *Atmospheric Chemistry and Physics, 13*(20), 10325–10338.

Morrison, O. (2019). *Seven ways business leaders can transform the food system.* Retrieved from https://www.foodnavigator.com/Article/2019/10/16/7-ways-business-leaders-can-transform-the-food-system

Muerza, V., De la Cruz, M. T., & Urciuoli, L. (2019). La logística como factor de éxito en los centros logísticos integrados de biomasa. *Revista de Economía Aragonesa, 67*, 107–120.

Mulatu, Y., & Kindu, M. (2010). Status of bamboo resource development, utilisation and research in Ethiopia: A review. *Ethiopian Journal of Natural Resources, 1*, 79–98.

NRC. (2006). Shea. In Lost Crops of Africa (Vol. 2). Washington, DC: The National Academies Press.

Ou, C. S., Liu, F. C., Hung, Y. C., & Yen, D. C. (2010). A structural model of supply chain management on firm performance. *International Journal of Operations & Production Management*, *30*(5), 526–545.

Powell, J. M., Pearson, R. A., & Hiernaux, P. H. (2004). Crop–livestock interactions in the West African drylands. *Agronomy Journal*, *96*(2), 469–483.

Rother, M. (1999). *Learning to See: Value Stream Mapping to Create Value and Eliminate Muda*. The Lean Enterprise Institute.

SCC. (1999). *Supply-Chain Operations Reference-Model: Overview of SCOR Version 3.0*. Pittsburgh, PA: Supply-Chain Council Inc.

Schoemaker, P. J., Krupp, S., & Howland, S. (2013). Strategic leadership: The essential skills. *Harvard Business Review*, *91*(1), 131–134. PMID:23390746

Sokhansanj, S., Kumar, A., & Turhollow, A. F., & Bioenergy. (2006). Development and implementation of integrated biomass supply analysis and logistics model (IBSAL). *Biomass*, *30*(10), 838–847.

SpencerStuart. (2015). *Agribusiness leadership of the future. A Snapshot of Strategic Priorities and Talent Needs in Asia Pacific*. Retrieved from https://www.spencerstuart.com/-/media/pdf-files/research-and-insight-pdfs/agribusiness-leadership-of-the-future_080216.pdf

Stock, J. R., & Lambert, D. M. (2001). *Strategic logistics management* (Vol. 4). McGraw-Hill.

Sucellog. (2017). *Project deliverables*. Retrieved from www.sucellog.eu/en/publications-reports.html

Urciuoli, L., & Muerza, V. (2018). *An integrated Framework for Evaluating Costs of IBLCs' supply chains*. Paper presented at the International Conference on Information Systems, Logistics and Supply Chain, Lyon, France.

van Dam, J. E. G., Elbersen, H. W., & Daza Montaño, C. M. (2018). Bamboo production for industrial utilisation. In E. Alexoupoulo (Ed.), *Perennial grasses for bioenergy and bioproducts* (pp. 175–216). Academic Press.

Verma, D., Gope, P. C., Maheshwari, M. K., & Sharma, R. K. (2012). Bagasse fiber composites-A review. *J. Mater. Environ. Sci*, *3*(6), 1079–1092.

Chapter 2
Supply Chain Leadership in Emerging Markets:
Understanding the Role of Trust, Information Management, and Collaboration

Smitha Girija
SOIL School of Business Design, India

Vandana Srivastava
Christ University (Deemed), India

ABSTRACT

The massive growth of emerging economies in last two decades has attracted many global companies to expand their physical presence in these countries. But the ability to take advantage of those opportunities is only available to companies that appreciate the environmental challenges and complexity of the region. The lexicon of extant literature focuses on enhancing supply chain leadership and development of efficient and effective strategies in developed economies, yet the corresponding literature in emerging economies is very fragmented. The aim of this chapter is to synthesize the current literature to understand the phenomenon including its definitions, dimensions, and constructs and to propose a conceptual model for successful supply chain leadership in emerging markets. The study tries to understand and establish the impact of various factors of supply chain leadership, which leads to sustainable supply chain performance. Collaboration and information management emerge as the major drivers for supply chain leadership in emerging markets and identifies trust as a mediating factor.

DOI: 10.4018/978-1-7998-2867-9.ch002

INTRODUCTION

In the past few years emerging markets have drawn a lot of attention from researchers and practitioners alike due to their sheer size and potential. Large corporations, particularly from developed countries such as the USA, Japan and European countries, have found that globalization is one of the biggest challenges facing them. While on one hand globalization has provided them with a larger customer base, the challenges of doing business with and managing operations in distant locations, not merely in terms of distance, have been immense. As an effect of globalization organizations have been able to leverage the developing or emerging markets to reduce cost of operations and increase profits . Yet, these emerging markets have posed a myriad of challenges in implementation of global strategies. Characterised by institutional voids i.e. absence of specialized intermediaries, contract-enforcing mechanisms and regulatory frameworks (Khanna, Palepu, Sinha, 2005; Silvestre, 2015b), and high environmental turbulence, emerging markets inhibit application of strategies that have successfully been used in developed markets (Accenture Global Operations Megatrends Study, 2014). Moreover, emerging markets vary in terms of political and social systems defined by the many ethnic, regional and linguistic groups and their relationships, a large but heavily segmented population which is difficult of predict due to lack of adequate and authentic data, unavailability of skilled labour and lack of well-regulated capital and financial markets (Khanna et al 2005; Deloitte Report, 2013). Hence, the success of these global organizations depends not just on developing special strategies for emerging markets, but also identifying novel ways of implementing them (Khanna et al, 2005; Krishnan & Jha, 2011).

These challenges of emerging markets extend to supply chain as well. Global outsourcing trends since the early 1990s has reshaped global supply chain systems and have transformed emerging countries into significant players in the global economy (O'Rourke, 2005). Global supply chains are significantly more complex, involving multiple players from emerging and developed economies requiring considerable amount of coordination. Today, a product could be part sourced and manufactured in India, assembled in China and sold in the United States of America. Such movement of goods, material and services across various types of economies raises multiple challenges. Growing economies, complex business environments, and a diverse consumer base make supply chain management a challenge in emerging markets. Supply chains in developing and emerging economies face greater barriers to integration, collaboration, innovation, and sustainability than supply chains operating in developed countries do. Like all other operations, the challenges of lack of infrastructure, high levels of corruption, pressing social issues, and informality affect supply chains in emerging markets making their management difficult (Khanna et al, 2005; Silvestre, 2015a, 2015b). In such a milieu, Supply Chain Leadership (SCL) becomes a critical determinant of success for global organizations.

In this context, we note two pertinent knowledge gaps. First, many studies have focused on supply chain leadership in advanced economies, but much less research has addressed emerging markets. Second, the massive growth of emerging economies attracts many companies to set up manufacturing units despite the potential environmental threats. This calls for extensive study on various sustainable supply chain practicessince the research in this area is fragmented.

This study is an attempt to identify the critical determinants of successful supply chain leadership in emerging markets. It is aimed at addressing the following two main objectives,: (i) to provide a complete review of the current usage and penetration of the SCL concept (including SCL styles, dimensions and influences) based on the existing literature; and, (ii)to set the direction for future research.

This study contributes to the field by synthesizing the current literature to understand the phenomenon including its definitions, dimensions and constructs. and proposing a conceptual model for successful Supply Chain Leadership in emerging markets. We hope to provide a comprehensive, coherent and organised view of the published material that will inform both practitioners and researchers in this field. The findings of this paper can be used by practitioners as a foundation to build a stronger base to understand, define and build sustainable supply chain in the context of emerging markets. Further, an understanding of various factors of SCL would help researchers develop further research questions, empirical investigations and systematically conceptualise this concept in the Supply Chain literature.

The remainder of this paper is organized as follows. In the next section, we present the theoretical background, followed by the Research Methodology in the third section. In the fourth session the conceptual framework and hypothesis for supply chain leadership is presented. Finally, we conclude by discussing the implications of our findings, the limitations of the model, and suggested future research directions

THEORETICAL BACKGROUND

Supply chain management (SCM) involves integration, coordination, and collaboration across organizations and throughout the supply chain. This includes designing, developing, optimizing and managing different components such as material, information and financial flows and distribution of finished products. In other words, it is a way through which products or services are moved (Prajogo & Jan, 2012). According to Doukidis, Matopoulos, Vlachopoulou, Manthou & Manos (2007), SCM is a synthesis of different activities such as inventory management, logistics and distribution of material or finished products. It manages a network of supply chain partners (manufacturers, processors, importers, exporters and retailers) who work together and integrate supply chain activities to achieve certain objectives (Akhtar, Tse, Khan & Rao-Nicholson, 2016).

Conceptualization of Supply Chain Leadership

For centuries, leadership has represented a prolific research stream in the fields of management and organisational behaviour. Most of these have dwelled on individual characteristics of leaders who manage to drive excellence and performance with the scope of influence being limited to the firm where an inspirational figurehead sets the strategic direction of the organization (Sharif & Irani, 2012). However recently, research on leadership has been extended to the interorganisational setting (Müller-Seitz & Sydow, 2012) leading to the emergence of the novel concept of Supply Chain Leadership (SCL), where a firm or focal organization plays a leadership role.

In common management parlance, a system consists of information and analysis, Strategic Planning, Human Resources management and Process management. Leadership has been found to be the most important driver of 'system 'performance. In inherently complex systems such as supply chains (Christopher & Towill 2002) multiple organizations working in the value chain should work in cooperation and coordination to efficiently and effectively fulfill customer needs. Many techniques such as collaboration (Stank, Keller & Daugherty, 2001; Sinkovics & Roath 2004), process integration (Min & Mentzer 2004), information sharing (Sanders & Premus, 2005) have been suggested for achieving supply chain goals. The implementation and acceptance of these techniques across multiple supply chain members requires leadership. Supply chain leadership (SCL), focuses on firms' behaviors and is concerned with the ability of one (or more) firm(s) to influence the actions, behaviors and performance of supply chain members (Defee, Esper & Mollenkopf, 2009; Akhtar et al., 2016; Lockström, Schadel, Harrison, Moser & Malhotra, 2010; Ojha, Acharya & Cooper, 2018).It extends beyond the organization boundaries to encompass the entire supply network to drive strategic supply chain decisions (Lockström & Lei, 2013; Gong, Jia, Brown & Koh, 2018). Greater attention is now being offered to craft appropriate leadership styles that are responsible for sustaining supply chains and, managing their performance and improvement (Robinson & Malhotra, 2005; Li, Ragu-Nathan, Ragu-Nathan & Rao, 2006).An attempt has been made to review existing literature to conceptualize Supply Chain Leadership and a summary is presented in Table 1.

Table 1. Summary of literature on supply chain leadership

References	Supply Chain Leadership
Mokhtar et al., 2019	A set of behaviours exhibited by a firm in influencing and orchestrating the actions and behaviours of its own supply chain partners.
Silvestre, 2015b	Ability of the focal firm to be active and constructive in managing supply chain uncertainty, stimulating knowledge sharing between supply chain partners and enhancing sustainability performance.
Birasnav, Mittal & Loughlin, 2015	A firm that implements transformational leadership style tends to rely on long term relationships and the development of its suppliers while using less control mechanisms
Sharif & Irani, 2012	Have presented the perspective of supply chain leadership as an individual, where individual leadership traits of developing relationships with customers and other chain partners are highlighted.
Lockström et al., 2010	To influence a supplier to achieve a common goal within the supplier's organisation and ability to improve a firm's relational capital including suppliers' commitment and supply chain relationships.
Defee et al., 2009	A relational concept involving the supply chain leader and one or more supply chain follower organizations that interact in a dynamic, co-influencing process.
Hult, Ketchen & Arrfel, 2007	A leading firm acts and behaves in ways that their followers will see them as a role model. Such a firm is required to lead by example, which results admiration, respect and trust from supply chain followers

Sustainable Supply Chain Leadership: Perspective from Emerging Market

Sustainability has today received increasing level of attention at all levels, global or local. Sustainability and Sustainable Supply chain perspectives centre on the notion of the Triple Bottom Line (TBL) which indicates that all three dimensions of performance- economic, social, and environmental- are interconnected and are equally important (Akhtar et al, 2016). As supply chains spread toward emerging economies, the debates about non-financial sustainability issues become increasingly relevant to supply chain and sustainability research (Akhtar et al, 2016).

Sustainable Supply Chain (SSC) is generally deemed as a synergetic blend of corporate social responsibility, environmental management and supply chain management (Linton, Klassen & Jayaraman, 2007). Sustainable business practices can help create wealth for firms and raise the standard of living in emerging markets. To achieve this firms in emerging countries might adapt ecologically friendly strategies and guidelines from their business clients or competitors in more advanced economies. According to Pagell & Wu (2009), sustainable supply chain "is the one that performs well on both traditional measures of profit and loss, as well as on an expanded conceptualization of performance that includes social and natural dimensions". SSC considers the environmental impacts of the production process as goods flow through the supply chain (Hsu, Tan & Zailani, 2016) unlike traditional models. For instance, emerging economies such as Asia and Middle East have gone through rapid economic development (Geng, Sarkis, Ulgiati & Zhang, 2013; Feizpour & Mehrjardi, 2014) in last two decades. These countries are plagued by pressing social and environmental problems (Yawar & Seuring, 2017) amplified by a higher level of complexity and environmental turbulence (Silvestre, 2015b). Environmental concerns have prompted the governments of such emerging economies to regulate business practices and set broad environmental improvement objectives (Child & Tsai, 2005, Tumpa, Ali, Rahman, Paul, Chowdhury & Khan, 2019). Financial constraints, lack of top management commitment, and complexity in supply chain are the most critical barriers for some of the practitioners. These together with low levels of awareness among consumers, economic disparity, lack of promotion of sustainable products, and technical obstructions add to the reluctance to adopting sustainable practices (Ehrgott, Reimann, Kaufmann & Crater, 2013; Tumpa et al., 2019).

Supply chain leaders can play a major role in developing sustainability in such scenarios. Supply chain leaders are distinguished by how well they have been able to extend the sustainability efforts beyond their own operations to those of their suppliers (Porter and Kramer, 2006, Ehrgott et al., 2013). Environmentally sustainable supply chain management extends the responsibility of business organizations from reducing pollution and waste to proactively assuming full responsibility for their products from acquisition of raw materials to the sustainable disposal of the products, not just limited to their operations and strategy but also to the extended organizations (Zailai, Jeyaraman, Vengadasam & Premkumar, 2012; Tumpa et al, 2019). Integration is a key driver of supply chain sustainability performance and facilitates the efficient flow of both material and information (Silvestre, 2015b) by having coordination mechanisms and processes designed to connect supply chain consecutive players (Cagliano, Caniato & Spina, 2006). Technology is a critical driver of relationship management and collaboration (Vachon & Klassen, 2006; Sharfman, Shaft & Anex Jr., 2009; Beske, 2012) and information and communication technologies (ICT) facilitate integration.

Sustainability encompasses social sustainability along with environmental sustainability. Emerging markets are also characterised by varied market segments along with complex social and economic structures. Social sustainability issues related to human rights, work practices and decent work conditions, society, and product-related responsibility hence become important. In a country like India, one the fastest growing and second largest emerging market, social sustainability issues such as labor conditions, child labor, human rights, health and safety, minority development, disabled/marginalized people inclusion and gender (Yawar & Seuring,

2017), philanthropy, health, safety and well-being, equity, ethics and human rights (Mani, Agarwal & Sharma, 2015) have been identified. The role of supply chain leaders in ensuring social sustainability is extremely critical in emerging markets (Morais & Silvestre, 2018). Supply chain leaders who are intrinsically motivated for social sustainability engage through their network of primary stakeholders (i.e. suppliers) as well as secondary stakeholders (such as governmental and non-governmental agencies) (Ehrgott et al., 2013; Morais & Silvestre, 2018). Hsu et al., 2016, have identified eco-reputation and eco-innovation as the strategic orientation factors in deploying sustainable supply chain initiative programs by leaders' firms. Supply chain leaders have been found to be intrinsically motivated i.e. they seem to go beyond to go beyond risk avoidance or monetary opportunities and appear to be linked with organizational values and/or ethical principles. They embrace a wide range of practices such as donations of the profits from specific products for educational programs for communities, and funding social businesses that address social problems such as malnutrition and access to drinking water (Ehrgott et al., 2013; Hsu et al., 2016, Morais & Silvestre, 2018;)

Focal teams have been found to play an active and constructive leadership role in promoting appropriate sustainable policies and practices by coordinating actions of members of the supply chain, managing the escalating ambiguity, stimulating supply chain learning, and promoting innovation with the aim to enhance the sustainability performance (Ehrgott et al., 2013; Gosling, Jia, Gong & Brown, 2017). By playing a motivational role, supply chain leaders encourage and help both upstream and downstream chain members to develop and enforce environmentally and socially sustainable business plans and ensure adherence towards sustainable practices requested by the leader (Zailai et al., 2012; Silvestre, 2015b; Dubey, Gunasekaran, Samar, 2015; Mokhtar, Genovese, Brint & Kumar, 2019).

Table 2. Summary of Literature on Sustainable Supply Chain Leadership in Emerging Markets

References	Sustainable Supply Chain Leadership in Emerging Markets
Tumpa et al., 2019	The major challenges in adoption of Green Supply chain in textile industry of Bangladesh were low customer demand, financial constraints and lack of governmental regulations. Green supply chain strategies addressing these are critical for establishing leadership.
Morais & Silvestre, 2018	Studied the less researched area of Social Sustainability in emerging markets. Focal companies play an important role in leading social sustainability initiatives. Intrinsically motivated leaders lead social sustainability by structural collaborations and involvement with secondary stakeholders such as NGOs and community.
Silvestre, 2015b	Supply chain sustainability performance depends on the supply chain learning and innovation performance. In emerging economies, greater environmental turbulence and weaker institutions increase the importance of focal companies in driving supply chain sustainability through learning and innovation.
Gosling et al., 2017	Have emphasized the role of leadership in sustainable supply chain. Focal companies assume a leadership role (transactional or transformational) to lead sustainable practices in the supply chain by initiating and disseminating learning in the supply chain. The role of the leaders may be transactional in the beginning, but moves to transformations to drive SSCM..
Ehrgott et al., 2013	Have posited that organizational learning and supply chain sustainability are closely related. Environmental supplier development leads to organizational learning and has a positive effect on the buying firm's environmental reputation. This further augments the firm's capability to integrate with supply chain partners from emerging economies.

METHODOLOGY

To answer the research questions this paper reviews the literature on Supply Chain Leadership with a special focus on Emerging Markets .A systematic literature review is useful for locating, selecting, analysing, appraising and evaluating the literature that is relevant to a particular research question and enable the researcher to map and assess the existing intellectual territory to develop the present body of knowledge further (Denyer & Tranfield, 2009). The methodology followed in the present study is a systematic literature review using the four electronic databases: Scopus, Ebsco, Science Direct and Web of Science.

Material Collection

The first stage of the review procedure identified keywords in the literature research around Supply Chain Leadership in Emerging Markets. We focused on the academic articles published in English peer – reviewed journals published between 2005 and 2018.Google Scholar is utilized to search related articles written in English. The selected keywords for our searching are exhibited in Table 1. During the research process, both main keywords and supplementary ones are included to ensure the comprehensiveness and relevance of searching outcomes.

Table 3. The keywords for searching related articles

Main Key Words	Supplementary Keywords
Supply Chain, Leadership	Collaborations
Supply Chain, Emerging Markets	Information Management
Sustainable Supply Chain, Emerging Markets	Data
	Decisions
	Trust
	Systematic Literature Review
	Relationships
	Knowledge

The subsequent filtering of the articles after eliminating duplication was based on the requirement that at least one of the keywords must be used in the title or abstract and it had to demonstrate the orientation of factors of Supply Chain Leadership as clear focus of research. We have excluded studies if the focus of the articles was more on General Leadership, Price, Cost and industry leadership without focusing on Supply Chain Leaderships. By following this procedure, we have selected 63 articles for the review (Table 2). After a thorough analysis of the articles, main trends and factors were determined for Supply Chain Leadership in Emerging Markets. All factors and sub factors were identified and classified to get an overall picture of the research topic.

Table 4. Results of the search and final selection of articles from the databases

Databases	Search Results	Articles Selected
SCIENCE DIRECT	43	28
EBSCO	22	10
SCOPUS	30	17
Web of Science	17	8
Total	112	63

Material Evaluation

Articles selected in the previous stages are crossed-checked with the results in Thomson's Web of Science database to ensure the reliability of the whole process, which means all analyses performed later are based on articles published in SCI indexed journals only. This makes sure the covered articles are from reputable peer refereed sources.

CONCEPTUAL MODEL AND HYPOTHESES FOR SUPPLY CHAIN LEADERSHIP

Based on the review of the background literature, the following conceptual model for Supply Chain Leadership in Emerging Markets emerged (refer Figure 1).

Supply Chain Leaders in Emerging Markets are distinguished by Sustainable Supply Chain Performance where sustainability is defined not just in terms of Environmental and Social Sustainability but also in terms of Financial and Operational Excellence, which result from effective Collaboration and Information Management. The background studies revealed that Collaboration and Information Management are critical for Supply Chain Leadership. Moreover, Trust was identified as mediating factor. A summary of the findings corroborating this and overview of the literature is given below.

Figure 1. Framework of supply chain leadership contributing to sustainability

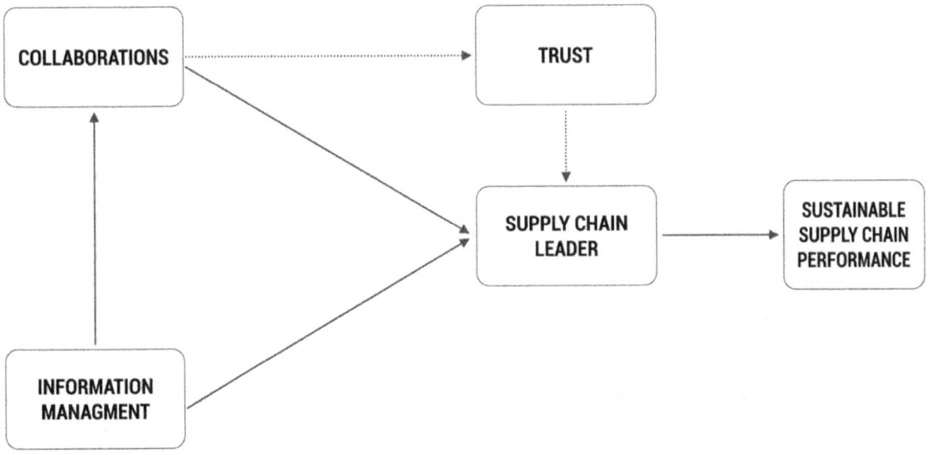

Effect of Collaborations in Supply Chain Leadership

Collaboration in supply chains demands a deliberate effort and "aligned objectives, open communication, sharing of resources, risks and rewards" (Soosay, Hyland & Ferrer, 2008) and allows firms to integrate operations and innovate for increased effectiveness (Soosay et al.,2008; Vachon & Klassen, 2008). The ability of a firm to integrate suppliers, processes and activities is crucial as a supply network will involve several stakeholders with different goals and objectives. Being passive and showing no close interaction with suppliers, means that a firm could experience supply chain disruptions such as communication breakdowns (Harland, Caldwell, Powell & Zheng, 2007) and missing information (Thornton, Autry, Gligor & Brik, 2013). It is generally believed that increased collaboration among supply chain participants leads to lower total cost and enhanced service performance and begins with customers and extends back through the firm from finished goods distribution to manufacturing and raw material procurement, as well as to material and service suppliers.

A supply chain leader works directly with the partners and stakeholders of the supply chain operation. Knowing partners' and stakeholders' core values, interests, strengths and potential enables the leader to integrate these areas into his or her leadership practice. The supply chain leadership has a great role to play in the overall performance of the supply chain members (Silvester 2015b). Supply chain leaders create value not just for themselves but for the other members as well (Gosling et al.,2017). Defee et al. (2009) may be the first to strongly argue that leadership can be applied to supply chain organizations and describe the relationship between a supply chain leader organization and other supply chain member organizations. In a supply chain context, structural elements ensure tighter integration between supply chain members and poor supply chain integration may result in the failure of supply chain leader-member working relationships and hence lead to reduced supply chain performance. The collaborations between the supply chain members are indispensable to ensure that benefits are accrued at each and every point of the value chain (Stank et al., 2001). When the relationship is more informal and people co-mingle, knowledge transfer tends to be more frequent and deeper (Spekman, Spear & Kamauff, 2002).

SCL requires a buying firm to provide care and development to its suppliers, which in return improve members' satisfaction and supply chain relationships (Goffnett & Goswami, 2016). Once a firm is able to control and centralise supply chain activities, the partnership with their suppliers can be enhanced and consensus can be improved (Müller-Seitz & Sydow, 2012). The various value chain members have to collaborate through intelligent business networks which will provide the competitive edge that will enable all the participants in a supply chain to prevail and grow. This is because global markets are growing increasingly efficient and competition no longer takes place between individual businesses, but between entire value chains. And in this, supply chain leadership will play the key role. Collaboration between the supply chain leader and various stakeholders improves service performance by enhancing integration. This relationship may be the key to helping supply chain leaders understand how best to facilitate behavioral change and collaborating with customers and suppliers is a first step in this direction (Stank et al., 2001).

Researchers claim through their empirical findings that as supply chain management facilitates administration of processes across distinct departments, this result in significantly improving an organisation's competitiveness (Robinson & Malhotra, 2005; Li et al., 2006). Another study by Christopher & Towill (2002) shows that mutual co-operation among all partners is required if the system is to succeed in its goal of increasing sales with less inventory in the total system. A successful partnership means higher inventory turns and improved return on investment for each link in the supply chain. Researchers also signify here that overseeing the supply chain connotes administrating effectively operational areas in an organisation and managing communications external to the organisation with stakeholders i.e., customers and suppliers (Li et al., 2006). Several researchers have contributed in the field of supply chain leadership influencing performance by managing relationships with the various stakeholders in the value chain. Successful firms in emerging markets have used a high degree of localization by integration of supply and demand chains (Park, 2014), not just building relations with local suppliers but also with local governmental setups. The literature discussed above shows that Collaboration is one of the are the key determinants of Supply Chain Leadership. Hence, it can be summarized by positing the following hypotheses:

Hypothesis One: Supply Chain Leader's Collaborations with the other members in the value chain have a positive effect on Sustainable Supply Chain performance.

Effect of Information Management in Supply Chain Leadership

The time honoured saying " If you can't measure it; you can't manage it" epitomizes a supply chain reality. Data and Decisions are critical for supply chain; be it for understanding the customer, planning and controlling for operational excellence, integration or knowledge creation. Supply Chain Leaders manage information across the supply chain to understand the markets to spot an opportunity, measure progress, evaluate the accomplishments, and forecast and plan for efficiency and excellence. This becomes even more pronounced in the case of emerging markets as they are intrinsically dynamic, volatile and ambiguous and hence need to be more data-driven and adaptive (Akhtar et al. 2016; AT Kearney and CSCMP Study, 2014). The supply chains of today have become a veritable gold mine of data; as material moves across the supply chain data is captured at each stage. Technologies such as RFID (Radio frequency Identification), Internet of Things (IoT), Social media and cloud computing enable firms to collect vast amounts of data in real time and in myriad forms. These information flows help leaders achieve price competitiveness and time sensitivity while ensuring superior product quality and services (Park, 2014), by providing insights about the market, plan and control operations and hence ensure operational excellence. With the growth in supply chain analytics market, supply chain leaders are distinguishing themselves by embedding data driven intelligence in their supply chain processes to evolve from a tactical level to a strategic transformation agent.

Emerging markets are intrinsically volatile, not just in terms of environment but also in terms of the consumer base. According to AT Kearney and CSCMP Study, 2014, with increasing awareness levels due to education, greater per capita income, online visibility and social media presence, emerging markets are rapidly turning into “buyers markets” from the traditional “sellers markets”. On one hand need for customization and personal product preferences have changed, while on the other hand micro segments are emerging and changing based on income levels, lifestyle choices and value systems which are diverse (Krishnan & Jha, 2011). Also, new segments are emerging in the form of niche segments, the rural urbans, and, mass premium- all with different needs but demanding equal attention (AT Kearney and CSCMP Study, 2014). Knowing the customer, therefore, has become imperative in the such times. Data and new emerging analytics capabilities play a critical role in providing customer insights. Data collected from multiple sources such as point of sales, customer profiles, social networking profiles, orders, market forecasts and geographical schemes can be combined and analyzed using big-data analytics techniques to understand customer sentiments and requirements (Wu & Huang, 2018; Boone, Ganeshan, Jain & Sanders, 2019). These decisions are critical for understanding the market and understand the expectations of customers by anticipating their behaviour (Krishnan & Jha, 2011; Witkowski, 2017; Singh, Shukla & Mishra, 2018).

Management of information across the supply chain has a direct correlation with Operational Excellence. Supply chain leaders are characterized by agility not just in understanding the markets but also ensuring operational excellence. Operational excellence has many connotations, one of them being increased supply chain efficiency. It begins with enhancing basic metrics and reporting. These provide the essential data for performance improvement initiatives and end-to-end visibility of supply chains. Availability of the right data, tools for visualization and interpretation of the data for decision making are the key pillars in monitoring of the key performance metrics of operational excellence. Data Driven and adaptive leadership practices in supply chain have been shown to have a positive and significant relationship (i.e., a correlation, not a causal relationship) with Non-Financial performance measured in terms of environmental, operational and relationship performance (Akhtar et al, 2016). Development models integrated with appropriate information technology infrastructure yield relevant, timely and accurate information about every value-added process and valued relationships. These help build the capabilities that a leader seeks out (Rai, Patnayakuni & Patnayakuni, 2006). Increasing evidences of harnessing technologies for leadership have been evidenced. Singh et al, 2018 have demonstrated the use of advance Data analytics techniques such as Big Data Analytics for monitoring supply chains to facilitating earlier mitigation of issues. Large and global organizations such as DHL have found to use specially designed risk mitigation instruments to achieve customer satisfaction and operational efficiency by providing timely information to customers about potential interference of their respective supply chain (Witkowski, 2017).

According to Deloitte report (2013), management of information across the supply chain is essential for planning and controlling, critical activities for the supply chain. Hence supply chain need control tower like setups to control all functions with the help of a robust technology interface. These when combined with predictive analytics, help monitor real-time critical events and KPIs through multiple touch points. Unbundling information flows from physical flows allows focal firms to share information with their supply chain partners to create information-based approaches for superior demand planning and execution (Rai et al., 2006). Enhanced end -to-end supply chain visibility allows for mitigation of risks, contingency planning and optimization, and identification and propagation of best practices (Sithole, Sergio & Kavelj, 2016). Use of automated tools such as dashboards facilitate real time decision making through modules along with information tracking technologies. IoT, RFID, consumer grade devices such as smart phones, Cloud and Big Data, are increasingly being used to provide operation overview along with other details on a single platform (Sithole et al., 2016; Witkowski, 2017). Instances of strong technology driven supply chain backbone has spelt success for many supply chain leading organizations in emerging economies such as India as it allows leaders to react quickly to real-time data at all points of the supply chain thus helping in planning and control. Use of Big Data analytics has been found to increase operational efficiency through tools that monitor the supply chain in almost real-time (Witkowski, 2017).

The ability to forecast has been traditionally served as a basis for planning, controlling and executing supply chain activities. Volatility and unpredictability of emerging markets make forecasting difficult but critical. While traditional forecasting tools are still being used, forecasting techniques are becoming more technology intensive. A volatile economy creates new challenges for data-based analytics, particularly relative to the availability of representative data. With the availability of varied and voluminous data, a shift from use of traditional statistical data-based demand forecasting models to more big data oriented new predictive analytics approach has been seen (Blackburn, Lurz, Priesea, G¨ob & Darkowa, 2015; Anitha & Patil, 2018; Boone et al, 2019). Large and global organizations such as BASF have used demand forecasting methods based on new predictive analytics approach to combine company data and economic information specifically matched to the market environment of product segments. Evidences of Global retail supply chains using big data analytics to optimize logistics processes, improve customer service have been shown by researchers (Witkowski, 2017; Boone et al., 2019). From the above discussion, the following hypothesis is proposed:

Hypothesis Two: Effective Information Management by Supply Chain Leader have a positive effect on Sustainable Supply Chain performance

Supply chains are inherently complex and dynamic system of flows driven by information and knowledge flow (Pérez-Salazar, Lasserre, Cedillo-Campos & González, 2017). Like other organizations, Supply chains learn and evolve over time. However, their ability to learn and generate knowledge is greatly reduced in turbulent external environments, particularly the type that characterizes emerging economies. This is because the high environmental turbulence and the existence of institutional voids increases the degree of complexity under which supply chains operate, which in turn hinders supply chain learning and innovation performance. Supply chain leaders play a focal role to ensure learning by creating mechanisms for knowledge sharing to increase supply chain capabilities (Silvestre, 2015b). Targeted Supplier Development programs help suppliers without any formal knowledge management systems garner learning necessary to improve their performance, and improve overall efficiency of the supply chain (Silvestre, 2015b). These developmental activities help in relationship building by capturing and sharing knowledge across the supply chain (Ehrgott, et al., 2013; Pérez-Salazar et al., 2017). Hence It is posited that:

Hypothesis Three: Information Management has a positive effect on collaborations that manifests in Sustainable Supply Chain Performance

Trust as a Mediating Factor

Spekman et al. (2002) suggest that "Trust is the belief that one's partner will act in a predictable manner, will keep his/her word, and will behave in a way that will not negatively affect the other". Several informal instruments have been considered and examined in relation to Supply Chain Leadership and trust is regarded as the most prominent mechanisms as it is deemed to have a significant role in improving supply chain performance (Poppo & Zenger, 2002; Ghosh & Fedorowicz, 2008;

Burkert, Ivens & Shan, 2012; Cao & Lumineau, 2015; Liu, Bai, Liu & Wei, 2017). Trust has been facilitating inter-firm relationships (Ireland & Webb, 2007; Panayides & Lun, 2009; Capaldo & Giannoccaro, 2015; Shahzad, Ali, Takala, Helo & Zaefarian, 2018) which leads to numerous benefits in supply chain activities such as encouraging involvement, investment, collaboration, information sharing, sustainability practices and improving performance (Laaksonen, Pajunen & Kulmala, 2008; Nyaga, Whipple & Lynch, 2010; Li, Li & Feng, 2015; Zaefarian, Najafi-Tavani, Henneberg & Naude, 2016;Ramon-Jeronimo, Florez-Lopez & Ramon-Jeronimo, 2017; Kim, Jean & Sinkovics, 2018; Zhao, Pan & Song, 2018). Trust can also help in overall economic benefits (Dyer & Chu, 2003) and leads to the reduction of perceived risks and uncertainty in supply relationships (Yawar & Seuring, 2017; Chen, Yen, Rajkumar, & Tomochko, 2011). To enhance Trust and commitment of supply chain members, Supply Chain Leader will have to involve the members in strategic planning activities such as joint product development, design and production (Lockström & Lei, 2013). Trust is associated with the expectations of supply chain partners who are keen to share something in an optimistic manner and believe in the words and actions of trusted partners (Akhtar et al, 2016). Salamon & Robinson (2008) also believed that trust improves service quality that ultimately affects overall supply chain sustainability. Evidences of use of disruptive technologies such as Blockchain have been found for monitoring as well as trust building. Supply chain leaders are increasingly relying of technological interventions such as Blockchain for increasing traceability of products, ensuring immutability of stored transactional data and sharing of data with supply chain partners (Behnke & Janssen, 2019). For emerging economies their potential is immense in building trust in relationships. However, the adoption of blockchains is country specific and plagued by challenges of inadequate digital infrastructure, low financial literacy and outdated laws that act as impediments to realizing blockchain's potential.

Given the potential direct relationships between Relationship and trust the fourth hypotheses is proposed as:

Hypothesis Four: Trust positively mediates the relationship between Supply Chain Leader and his Collaborations with various stakeholders

To sum up, the theoretical framework shown in Figure 1 depicts the interrelationships discussed in the literature. Effective collaborations and Information Management positively and significantly affects Supply Chain leadership. Trust also affects Supply Chain Leadership and plays the role of a mediator.

Table 5. Summary of framework –related literature

Factors	References
Collaborations	Robinson & Malhotra (2005), Li et al.(2006), Defee et al.(2009), Silvester (2015b), Gosling, et al (2017), Harland (2007), Thornton et al.(2013), Goffnett & Goswami (2016), Soosay et al.(2008), Vachon & Klassen (2008)
Information Management	Akhtar et al. (2016), Rai et al. (2006), Sithole and Sergio (2016), Singh et al. (2018), Witkowski (2017), Anitha & Patil (2018), Blackburn et al. (2015), Sithole et al (2016), Boone et al. (2019), Witkowski (2017), Pérez-Salazar et al. (2017), Silvestre (2015a, 2015b), Wu & Huang (2018), Ehrgott et al. (2013), Krishnan & Jha (2011)
Trust	Ghosh & Fedorowicz (2008), Burkert et al.(2012), Cao & Lumineau (2015), Liu et al. (2017), Capaldo & Giannoccaro, (2015), Shahzad et al. (2018), Kim et al. (2018), Zhao et al. (2018), Ramon-Jeronimo et al. (2017), Zaefarian et al.(2016), Li et al. (2015), Nyaga et al. (2010), Laaksonen et al. (2008), Yawar & Seuring (2017), Chen et al. (2011), Lockström & Lei (2013), Behneke & Janssen (2019)
Sustainability	Zailai et al. (2012), Silvestre (2015b), Tumpa et al.(2019), Morais & Silvestre (2018), Mokhtar et al. (2019); Dubey et al. (2015), Mani et al. (2015), Ehrgott et al. (2013), Hsu et al.(2016), Gosling et al.(2017)

DISCUSSIONS, IMPLICATIONS AND FUTURE RESEARCH DIRECTIONS

The major findings of this study are on the identification of the critical factors to explain the SCL concept in Emerging Markets and its influence towards sustainable supply chain practices. Our findings reveal that the current concept of SCL in the literature is dominated by leadership theory and leaderships styles and there is still a paucity of research in the identification of those factors which can provide insight into leadership capability of the firm which emerges as the Supply Chain Leader. The emergent framework underpinned by the hypotheses offers those seeking to create a leadership capacity within a supply chain context a clearer understanding of the leadership challenges that lie ahead. Literature study leads us to conclude that two major factors which have an effect on the performance of the Supply Chain Leader are Collaboration and Information Management. While collaborating with the other stakeholders in the value chain, Trust also plays an important role. Another noteworthy outcome is the proposed framework which shows the effect of collaboration and Information Management which leads to a Sustainable Supply Chain Performance.

This study makes two major contributions to the theory. First, it contributes to the knowledge on Supply Chain Leadership in the context of emerging countries. While plenty of studies are available in the literature that discuss Leadership in supply chain, only a few researches are conducted in the context of emerging economies.

Since the findings derived from the developed economy cannot be extended to the emerging economy, the findings of our study supplement the inadequacy of research in this area. Second, this research also throws light on the importance of Sustainable practices and the role of Collaboration and Information Management which are identified the key characteristics of Supply Chain Leadership.

Future research could utilize the concepts and framework to develop a detailed conceptualization of Supply Chain Leadership which results in a sustainable supply chain performance. The authors suggest that in extending the work presented in this paper, an empirical study based on chain/logistic scenarios and cases be conducted to deepen and widen the understanding of the topic. It is recommended to extend this study and the theory can further be extended by developing scales. In the present study we have considered only the major elements of Supply Chain Leadership i.e. Collaboration and Information Management. There is further scope to explore more dimensions and sub factors which have an effect on Supply Chain Leadership. In this way, a more detailed investigation can be conducted.

CONCLUSION

It emerged from our study that emerging markets may continue to grow at near double-digit rates and many global companies are seeking to capitalize on the growth by expanding their physical presence there. Though this will result in an inviting opportunity for a large number of corporations, these markets also provide a significant number of risks that many companies may be unaware of and are inadequately prepared to deal with. Notable among them are the host of environmental pollution problems that have arisen and are of serious global concern. There is an increasing interest among scholars on the characteristics of supply chains that operate mainly in developing and emerging economies (Zhu et.al,2008; Linton et al.,2007; Markley and Davis,2007;; Zailani etal.,2012). Most of these studies discussed role of leadership in improving supply chain performance, the literature discussing SCL remains very fragmented. In this study, we sought to improve the understanding and comprehension of the Supply Chain Leadership in Emerging markets. We have accomplished this by introducing a framework to this area of scholarly inquiry. This was done using a thorough analysis of extant literature through a systematic literature review.

Though the paper throws light on the concept of Supply Chain Leadership in Emerging market, this paper suffers some limitations. First, the study is exploratory in nature and draws relevance from literature review. Even though our searching is systematic, manual search method used for retrieving the articles might suffer the risk of excluding or overlooking other relevant articles. Second, this paper only surveys the papers published in SCOPUS and Web of Science. Thus, many related studies are excluded.

REFERENCES

Akhtar, P., Tse, Y.K., Khan, Z., & Rao-Nicholson, R. (2016). Data-driven and adaptive leadership contributing to sustainability: global agri-food supply chains connected with emerging markets. *International Journal of Production Economics*. doi:10.1016/j.ijpe.2015.11.013

Anitha, P., & Patil, M. M. (2018) A Review on Data Analytics for Supply Chain Management A Case study. *International Journal of Information Engineering and Electronic Business, 5*, 30-39. Available at https://business.fiu.edu/centers/ryder/pdf/SCM_in_Emerging_Mkts-Mexico.pdf

Behneke, K., & Janssen, M. F. W. H. A. (2019). Boundary conditions for traceability in food supply chains using blockchain technology. *International Journal of Information Management*. Advance online publication. doi:10.1016/j.ijinfomgt.2019.05.025

Beske, P. (2012). Dynamic capabilities and sustainable supply chain management. *International Journal of Physical Distribution & Logistics Management, 42*(4), 372–387. doi:10.1108/09600031211231344

Birasnav, M., Mittal, R., & Loughlin, S. (2015). Linking Leadership Behaviors and Information Exchange to Improve Supply Chain Performance: A Conceptual Model. *Global Journal of Flexible Systems Managment, 16*(2), 205–217. doi:10.100740171-015-0092-2

Blackburn, R., Lurz, K., Priesea, B., G¨ob, R., & Darkowa, I. L. (2015). A predictive analytics approach for demand forecasting in the process industry. *International Transactions in Operational Research, 22*(3), 407–428. doi:10.1111/itor.12122

Boone, T., Ganeshan, R., Jain, A., & Sanders, N. R. (2019). Forecasting sales in the Supply Chain: Consumer analytics in the big data era. *International Journal of Forecasting, 35*(1), 170–180. doi:10.1016/j.ijforecast.2018.09.003

Burkert, M., Ivens, B. S., & Shan, J. (2012). Governance mechanisms in domestic and international buyer-supplier relationships: An empirical study. *Industrial Marketing Management, 41*(3), 544–556. doi:10.1016/j.indmarman.2011.06.019

Cagliano, R., Caniato, F., & Spina, G. (2006). The Linkage between Supply Chain Integration and Manufacturing Improvement Programs. *International Journal of Operations & Production Management, 26*(3), 282–299. doi:10.1108/01443570610646201

Cao, Z., & Lumineau, F. (2015). Revisiting the interplay between contractual and relational governance: A qualitative and meta-analytic investigation. *Journal of Operations Management, 33-34*(1), 15–42. doi:10.1016/j.jom.2014.09.009

Capaldo, A., & Giannoccaro, I. (2015). Interdependence and network-level trust in supply chain networks. A computational study. *Industrial Marketing Management, 44*(1), 180–195. doi:10.1016/j.indmarman.2014.10.001

Chen, J. V., Yen, D. C., Rajkumar, T. M., & Tomochko, N. A. (2011). The antecedent factors on trust and commitment in supply chain relationships. *Computer Standards & Interfaces, 33*(3), 262–270. doi:10.1016/j.csi.2010.05.003

Child, J., & Tsai, T. (2005). The Dynamic Between Firms' Environmental Strategies and Institutional Constraints in Emerging Economies: Evidence from China and Taiwan. *Journal of Management Studies, 42*(1), 95–125. doi:10.1111/j.1467-6486.2005.00490.x

Christopher, M., & Towill, D. R. (2002). Developing Market Specific Supply Chain Strategies. *International Journal of Logistics Management, 13*(1), 1–14. doi:10.1108/09574090210806324

Defee, C. C., Esper, T., & Mollenkopf, D. (2009). Leveraging Closed-Loop Orientation and Leadership for Environmental Sustainability. *Supply Chain Management, 14*(2), 87–98. doi:10.1108/13598540910941957

Denyer, D., & Tranfield, D. (2009). Producing a systematic review. In D. A. Buchanan & A. Bryman (Eds.), *The SAGE handbook of organizational research methods* (pp. 671–689). Sage Publications Ltd.

Doukidis, G. L., Matopoulos, A., Vlachopoulou, M., Manthou, V., & Manos, B. (2007). A conceptual framework for supply chain collaboration: Empirical evidence from the agri-food industry. *Supply Chain Management, 12*(3), 177–186. doi:10.1108/13598540710742491

Dubey, R., Gunasekaran, A., & Samar Ali, S. (2015). Exploring the relationship between leadership, operational practices, institutional pressures and environmental performance: A framework for green supply chain. trajectories. *International Journal of Production Economics, 160*, 120–132. doi:10.1016/j.ijpe.2014.10.001

Dyer, J. H., & Chu, W. (2003). The role of trustworthiness in reducing cost of improving performance: Empirical evidence from the United States, Japan and Korea. *Organization Science*, *14*(1), 57–68. doi:10.1287/orsc.14.1.57.12806

Ehrgott, M., Reimann, F., Kaufmann, L., & Crater, C. R. (2013). Environmental Development of Emerging Economy Suppliers: Antecedents and Outcomes. *Journal of Business Logistics*, *34*(2), 131–147. doi:10.1111/jbl.12015

Feizpour, M. A., & Mehrjardi, A. S. (2014). Comparative Advantages and Sustainable Development in Iranian Manufacturing Industries. *Indian Economic Review*, *18*(1), 33–52.

Geng, Y., Sarkis, J., Ulgiati, S., & Zhang, P. (2013). Measuring China's circular economy. *Science*, *339*(6127), 1526–1527. doi:10.1126cience.1227059 PMID:23539584

Ghosh, A., & Fedorowicz, J. (2008). The role of trust in supply chain governance. *Business Process Management Journal*, *14*(4), 453–470. doi:10.1108/14637150810888019

Goffnett, S. P., & Goswami, A. (2016). Supply chain transformational leadership, supply chain innovation performance, and satisfaction with relationships and results: Moderating role of supply chain innovativeness. *International Journal of Logistics Systems & Management*, *24*(3), 356–382.

Gong, Y., Jia, F., Brown, S., & Koh, S. C. L. (2018). Supply chain learning of sustainability in multi-tier supply chains: A resource orchestration perspective. *International Journal of Operations & Production Management*, *38*(4), 1061–1090. doi:10.1108/IJOPM-05-2017-0306

Gosling, J., Jia, F., Gong, Y., & Brown, S. (2016). The role of supply chain leadership in the learning of sustainable practice: Toward an integrated framework. *Journal of Cleaner Production*, *137*, 1458–1469. doi:10.1016/j.jclepro.2014.10.029

Harland, C. M., Caldwell, N. D., Powell, P., & Zheng, J. (2007). Barriers to supply chain information integration: SMEs adrift of eLands. *Journal of Operations Management*, *25*(6), 1234–1254. doi:10.1016/j.jom.2007.01.004

Hsu, C., Tan, K., & Mohamad Zailani, S. (2016). Strategic orientations, sustainable supply chain initiatives, and reverse logistics. *International Journal of Operations & Production Management*, *36*(1), 86–110. doi:10.1108/IJOPM-06-2014-0252

Hult, G. T. M., Ketchen, D. J., & Arrfelt, M. (2007). Strategic supply chain management: Improving performance through a culture of competitiveness and knowledge development. *Strategic Management Journal*, *28*(10), 1035–1052. doi:10.1002mj.627

Ireland, R. D., & Webb, J. W. (2007). A multi-theoretic perspective on trust and power in strategic supply chains. *Journal of Operations Management*, *25*(2), 482–497. doi:10.1016/j.jom.2006.05.004

Khanna, T., Palepu, K. G., & Sinha, J. (2005, June). Strategies That Fit Emerging Markets. *Harvard Business Review*, 4–18. PMID:15938439

Kim, D., Jean, R. J. B., & Sinkovics, R. R. (2018). Drivers of virtual interfirm integration and its impact on performance in international customer esupplier relationships. *Management International Review*, *58*(3), 495–522. doi:10.100711575-018-0344-4

Krishnan, R. T., & Jha, S. K. (2011). Innovation Strategies in Emerging Markets: What Can We Learn from Indian Market Leaders. *ASCI Journal of Management*, *41*(1), 21–45.

Laaksonen, T., Pajunen, K., & Kulmala, H. I. (2008). Co-evolution of trust and dependence in customer-supplier relationships. *Industrial Marketing Management*, *37*(8), 910–920. doi:10.1016/j.indmarman.2007.06.007

Li, S., Ragu-Nathan, B., Ragu-Nathan, T. S., & Rao, S. S. (2006). The impact of supply chain management practices on competitive advantage and organizational performance. *Omega*, *34*(2), 107–124. doi:10.1016/j.omega.2004.08.002 PMID:17876965

Li, Y., Li, G., & Feng, T. (2015). Effects of suppliers' trust and commitment on customer involvement. *Industrial Management & Data Systems*, *115*(6), 1041–1066. doi:10.1108/IMDS-11-2014-0351

Linton, J., Klassen, R., & Jayaraman, V. (2007). Sustainable supply chains: An introduction. *Journal of Operations Management*, *25*(6), 1075–1082. doi:10.1016/j.jom.2007.01.012

Liu, W., Bai, E., Liu, L., & Wei, W. (2017). A Framework of Sustainable Service Supply Chain Management: A Literature Review and Research Agenda. *Sustainability*, *9*(3), 421. doi:10.3390u9030421

Lockström, M., & Lei, L. (2013). Antecedents to supplier integration in China: A partial least squares analysis. *International Journal of Production Economics*, *141*(1), 295–306. doi:10.1016/j.ijpe.2012.08.007

Lockström, M., Schadel, J., Harrison, N., Moser, R., & Malhotra, M. K. (2010). Antecedents to supplier integration in the automotive industry: A multiple-case study of foreign subsidiaries in China. *Journal of Operations Management*, *28*(3), 240–256. doi:10.1016/j.jom.2009.11.004

Mani, V., Agrawal, R., & Sharma, V. (2015). Supply chain social sustainability: A comparative case analysis in Indian manufacturing industries. *Procedia: Social and Behavioral Sciences*, *189*, 234–251. doi:10.1016/j.sbspro.2015.03.219

Min, S., & Mentzer, J. T. (2004). Developing and measuring supply chain management concepts. *Journal of Business Logistics*, *25*(1), 63–99. doi:10.1002/j.2158-1592.2004.tb00170.x

Mokhtar, A. R. M., Genovese, A., Brint, A., & Kumar, N. (2019). Supply chain leadership: A systematic literature review and a research agenda. *International Journal of Production Economics*, *216*, 255–273. doi:10.1016/j.ijpe.2019.04.001

Morais, D. O. C., & Silvestre, B. S. (2018). Advancing social sustainability in supply chain management: Lessons from multiple case studies in an emerging economy. *Journal of Cleaner Production*, *199*, 222–235. doi:10.1016/j.jclepro.2018.07.097

Müller-Seitz, G., & Sydow, J. (2012). Manoeuvring between networks to lead: A longitudinal case study in the semiconductor industry. *Long Range Planning*, *45*(2/3), 105–135. doi:10.1016/j.lrp.2012.02.001

Nyaga, G. N., Whipple, J. M., & Lynch, D. F. (2010). Examining supply chain relationships: Do buyer and supplier perspectives on collaborative relationships differ? *Journal of Operations Management*, *28*(2), 101–114. doi:10.1016/j.jom.2009.07.005

O'Rourke, D. (2005). Market movements: Nongovernmental organization strategies to influence global production and consumption. *Journal of Industrial Ecology*, *9*(1-2), 115–128. doi:10.1162/1088198054084608

Ojha, D., Acharya, C., & Cooper, D. (2018). Transformational leadership and supply chain ambidexterity: Mediating role of supply chain organizational learning and moderating role of uncertainty. *International Journal of Production Economics*, *197*, 215–231. doi:10.1016/j.ijpe.2018.01.001

Pagell, M., & Wu, Z. (2009). Building a more complete theory of sustainable supply chain management using case studies of 10 exemplars. *The Journal of Supply Chain Management*, *45*(2), 37–56. doi:10.1111/j.1745-493X.2009.03162.x

Panayides, P. M., & Lun, V. Y. H. (2009). The impact of trust on innovativeness and supply chain performance. *International Journal of Production Economics*, *122*(1), 35–46. doi:10.1016/j.ijpe.2008.12.025

Park, Y. W. (2014). Integration of Supply and Demand Chain in Emerging Markets. *Journal of Business and Economics*, *5*(12), 2282–2293. doi:10.15341/jbe(2155-7950)/12.05.2014/009

Pérez-Salazar, M. R., Lasserre, A. A. A., Cedillo-Campos, M. G., & González, J. C. H. (2017). The Role of Knowledge Management in Supply Chain Management: A Literature Review. *Journal of Industrial Engineering and Management*, *10*(4), 711–788. doi:10.3926/jiem.2144

Poppo, L., & Zenger, T. (2002). Do formal contracts and relational governance function as substitutes or complements? *Strategic Management Journal*, *23*(8), 707–725. doi:10.1002mj.249

Prajogo, D., & Jan, O. (2012). Supply chain integration and performance: The effects of longterm relationships, information technology and sharing, and logistics integration. *International Journal of Production Economics*, *135*(1), 514–522. doi:10.1016/j.ijpe.2011.09.001

Rai, A., Patnayakuni, R., & Patnayakuni, N. (2006). Firm Performance Impacts of Digitally-enabled Supply Chain Integration Capabilities. *Management Information Systems Quarterly*, *30*(2), 225–246. doi:10.2307/25148729

Ramon-Jeronimo, J.M., Florez-Lopez, R. & Ramon-Jeronimo, M.A. (2017). Understanding the generation of value along supply chains: balancing control information and relational governance mechanisms in downstream and upstream relationships. *Sustainability, 9*(8).

Robinson, C. J., & Malhotra, M. K. (2005). Defining the concept of supply chain quality management and its relevance to academic and industrial practice. *International Journal of Production Economics*, *96*(3), 315–377. doi:10.1016/j.ijpe.2004.06.055

Salamon, S. D., & Robinson, S. L. (2008). Trust that binds: The impact of collective felt trust on organizational performance. *The Journal of Applied Psychology*, *93*(3), 593–601. doi:10.1037/0021-9010.93.3.593 PMID:18457488

Sanders, R. N., & Premus, R. (2005). Modeling the relationship between firm IT capability, collaboration and performance. *Journal of Business Logistics*, *26*(1), 1–23. doi:10.1002/j.2158-1592.2005.tb00192.x

Shahzad, K., Ali, T., Takala, J., Helo, P., & Zaefarian, G. (2018). The varying roles of governance mechanisms on ex-post transaction costs and relationship commitment in buyer-supplier relationships. *Industrial Marketing Management*, *71*, 135–146. doi:10.1016/j.indmarman.2017.12.012

Sharfman, M. P., Shaft, T. M., & Anex, R. P. Jr. (2009). The road to cooperative supply-chain environmental management: Trust and uncertainty among pro-active firms. *Business Strategy and the Environment*, *18*(1), 1–13. doi:10.1002/bse.580

Sharif, A. M., & Irani, Z. (2012). Supply Chain Leadership. *International Journal of Production Economics*, *14*(1), 57–68. doi:10.1016/j.ijpe.2012.01.041

Silvestre, B. S. (2015a). A hard nut to crack! Implementing supply chain sustainability in an emerging economy. *Journal of Cleaner Production*, *96*, 171–181. doi:10.1016/j.jclepro.2014.01.009

Silvestre, B. S. (2015b). Sustainable supply chain management in emerging economies: Environmental turbulence, institutional voids and sustainability trajectories. *International Journal of Production Economics*, *67*, 56–169. doi:10.1016/j.ijpe.2015.05.025

Singh, A., Shukla, N., & Mishra, N. (2018). Social media data analytics to improve supply chain management in food industries. *Transportation Research Part E, Logistics and Transportation Review*, *114*, 398–415. doi:10.1016/j.tre.2017.05.008

Sinkovics, R., & Roath, A. (2004). Strategic orientation, capabilities, and performance in manufacturers – 3PL relationships. *Journal of Business Logistics*, *25*(2), 43–55. doi:10.1002/j.2158-1592.2004.tb00181.x

Sithole, B., Sergio, G. S., & Kavelj, M. (2016). Supply chain optimization: Enhancing end-to-end visibility. *Procedia Engineering*, *159*, 12–18. doi:10.1016/j.proeng.2016.08.058

Soosay, C. A., Hyland, P. W., & Ferrer, M. (2008). Supply chain collaboration: Capabilities for continuous innovation. *Supply Chain Management*, *31*(2), 160–169. doi:10.1108/13598540810860994

Spekman, R. E., Spear, J., & Kamauff, J. (2002). Supply chain competency: Learning as a key component. *Supply Chain Management*, *7*(1), 41–55. doi:10.1108/13598540210414373

Stank, T. P., Keller, S. B., & Daugherty, P. J. (2001). Supply chain collaboration and logistical service performance. *Journal of Business Logistics*, *22*(1), 29–48. doi:10.1002/j.2158-1592.2001.tb00158.x

Thornton, L. M., Autry, C. W., Gligor, D. M., & Brik, A. B. (2013). Does Socially Responsible Supplier Selection Pay Off for Customer Firms? A Cross-Cultural Comparison. *The Journal of Supply Chain Management*, *49*(3), 66–89. doi:10.1111/jscm.12014

Tumpa, T. J., Ali, S. M., Rahman, M. H., Paul, S. K., Chowdhury, P., & Khan, S. A. R. (2019). Barriers to green supply chain management: An emerging economy context. *Journal of Cleaner Production*, *236*, 117617. doi:10.1016/j.jclepro.2019.117617

Vachon, S., & Klassen, R. D. (2006). Green project partnership in the supply chain: The case of package printing industry. *Journal of Cleaner Production*, *14*(6), 661–671. doi:10.1016/j.jclepro.2005.07.014

Witkowski, K. (2017). Internet of Things, Big Data, Industry 4.0 – Innovative Solutions in Logistics and Supply Chains Management. *Procedia Engineering*, *182*, 763–769. doi:10.1016/j.proeng.2017.03.197

Wu, P. J., & Huang, P. C. (2018). Business analytics for systematically investigating sustainable food supply chains. *Journal of Cleaner Production*, *203*, 968–976. doi:10.1016/j.jclepro.2018.08.178

Yawar, S. A., & Seuring, S. (2017). Management of social issues in supply chains: A literature review exploring social issues, actions and performance outcomes. *Journal of Business Ethics*, *141*(3), 621–643. doi:10.100710551-015-2719-9

Zaefarian, G., Najafi-Tavani, Z., Henneberg, S. C., & Naude, P. (2016). Do supplier perceptions of buyer fairness lead to supplier sales growth? *Industrial Marketing Management*, *53*, 160–171. doi:10.1016/j.indmarman.2015.07.003

Zailai, S., Jeyaraman, K., Vengadasam, G., & Premkumar, R. (2012). Sustainable supply chain management (SSCM) in Malaysia: A survey. *International Journal of Production Economics*, *140*(1), 330–340. doi:10.1016/j.ijpe.2012.02.008

Zhao, X., Pan, J., & Song, Y. (2018). Dependence on supplier, supplier trust and green supplier integration: The moderating role of contract management difficulty. *Sustainability*, *10*(5), 1673. doi:10.3390u10051673

Chapter 3
Leadership Strategies for Global Supply Chain Management:
The Case of UAE's Construction Sector

Sreejith Balasubramanian
Middlesex University Dubai, UAE

Vinaya Shukla
Middlesex University, UK

ABSTRACT

This chapter explores the leadership strategies for global supply chain management in the construction sector. The United Arab Emirates (UAE) construction sector, which played a pivotal role in transforming UAE to a modern economy from a nomadic one is used as an exemplary case in this study to understand the leadership strategies required for developing 'globalness' in their construction supply chain. Using secondary research and interviews with stakeholders in the construction supply chain, the study proposes leadership strategies in four key areas: 1) policymaking, 2) technology and innovation, 3) environmental supply chain management, and 4) international collaboration/partnerships. The findings are useful for practitioners and policymakers in improving the global competitiveness of their construction sector and its supply chain.

DOI: 10.4018/978-1-7998-2867-9.ch003

INTRODUCTION

The global construction sector is expected to be worth around US$10 trillion in 2021, of which the emerging economies' contribution is expected to be more than 50% (Global Data, 2017). The difference in construction activity between the two economies (emerging and developed) is expected to increase even further in the future as the emerging economies push for rapid urbanisation and modernization. With more than two-thirds of the world's population expected to live in urban areas by 2050, and with most of them living in emerging economies (UN-DESA, 2019), the construction sector would play a critical role in the economic development of these countries (Giang and Pheng, 2011). Governments there are therefore opening up their construction sectors, the goal being to not only attract foreign direct investment but also global talent. Empirical evidence of this is also evident with studies showing significant internationalization of the construction sector, with foreign firms, mostly from industrialized economies entering other countries (Chen et al., 2016).

Though the global orientation of the construction sector is encouraging, it is important that the associated (global) supply chains in the sector are also efficiently and effectively managed. Global supply chains are dynamic worldwide networks where goods and/or services are sourced from global companies, and which require people, information, processes, and resources (CIPS, 2019). While their effective and efficient management is critical for completing construction projects, the challenge (vis-a-vis manufacturing) is that they are highly fragmented which makes integration/coordination and management from suppliers to final consumer much more difficult (Serpell & Heredia, 2004).

The aim of this paper is to understand the contemporary global supply chain strategies used by the construction sector in emerging economies. The focus is on UAE because of its exemplary status in bringing 'globalness' to its local construction supply chain. It has witnessed an unprecedented construction boom in the last decade with the sector playing a key role in transforming UAE to a modern economy (from a nomadic one). Some of the largest construction projects in the world including the tallest structure (Burj Khalifa), the tallest hotel (JW Marriott Marquis), and the largest mall (Dubai Mall) have been executed there recently (Balasubramanian and Shukla, 2017). UAE is also home to some of the most innovative and luxurious skyscrapers and man-made islands; it also hosts the world's first 3D printed building (Dubai Future Foundation, 2019a). The construction sector in UAE has also been growing at more than 9% per year (Construction Week Online, 2015), and is expected to grow 6-10% in 2020 (ME Construction News, 2019a). It accounts for roughly 41% of the total construction projects in Gulf Cooperation Council (GCC) countries (Dubai Metro, 2013) and the sector's net worth is estimated to be US$ 42 billion in 2015 (Arabian Industry, 2015).

Before further exploration of the leadership strategies used in the context of UAE's construction supply chain/sector, it would be pertinent to first provide a background of the construction supply chain itself; also highlight its complexity vis-à-vis those in more commonly understood sectors such as manufacturing.

THE CONSTRUCTION SUPPLY CHAIN

In contrast to the unilateral, long-term transaction relations representative of the manufacturing supply chain, the construction supply chain is highly complex, diverse and fragmented that involves a multitude of stakeholders participating in dyadic relationships (Rezgui and Miles, 2009). The key stakeholders in the construction supply chain are Developers, Architects/Consultants, Main Contractors, Subcontractors and Suppliers. In a large construction project, the number of organizations involved in the supply chain could run into hundreds, if not thousands. Also, the sector is characterized by one-off contracts and a failure to develop longer-term relationships between stakeholders (Dubois and Gadde, 2000; Briscoe et al., 2001). Moreover, the construction supply chain has a reputation for low-trust and adversarial trading relations between supply chain stakeholders (Korczynski, 1996; Akintoye et al., 2000). For instance, Latham (1994) highlighted the adversarial attitudes that commonly exist between main contractors and their suppliers.

Figure 1 shows a typical construction supply chain. The construction supply chain considered in this study includes only the build sector (residential and non-residential buildings). As seen in the figure, the Developer is the one who initiates the project and therefore enjoys a hierarchical position with power in the supply chain to influence the whole project through its decisions on setting up the project and procurement system (Bresnen and Haslam, 1991). For this reason, Developers are considered to be the most important stakeholder in the construction supply chain (Briscoe et al., 2004). Therefore, their strategic decisions play a pivotal role in the behaviour of other downstream supply chain stakeholders. For instance, the developer appoints architects/consultants to be their client representative, to supply both design and any specialist management services such preparation of tender documents, technical

Figure 1. Construction supply chain
Source: Balasubramanian and Shukla, 2017

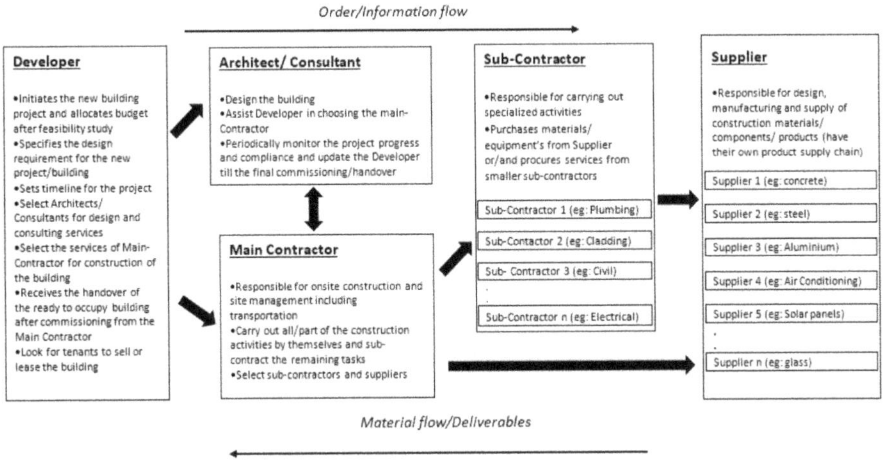

Evaluation of tender bids for the selection of the main contractor and final commissioning of the projects. The main contractor is selected by the developer based on the technical (typically evaluated by the architect/consultant) and commercial proposal (typically evaluated by developer). The main Contractors are responsible for the completion of the project at a pre-determined time, cost and quality. Hence, they play a significant role in the project's success (Hatmoko, 2008). They typically play the role of a `facilitator' to manage demand-side from the Developers/Architects and supply-side from Subcontractors and Suppliers (Cox et al., 2006). Once the main contractor is selected, based on their capabilities, they either carry out the construction activities themselves or hire specialist sub-contractors to perform specific activities such as the installation of building façade, heating, ventilation, and air conditioning (HVAC) systems, building management systems, etc. The Subcontractors, too, play important roles in construction projects. They help the main contractor to carry out specialist works. It is not uncommon for as much as 90% of a construction project to be subcontracted (Matthews et al., 2000) and consequently, subcontractors may contribute as much as 90% of a main contractor's turnover. This shows the important position and contribution of subcontractors in the success of the project. Finally, both the main contractor and sub-contractor will have to rely on several suppliers to provide them with raw materials and equipment to carry out their required activities. Suppliers on the other hand supply materials or components for construction projects in time and at a reasonable cost which can reach a value of as much as 50-60% of the total cost of the project (Stukhart, 1995). They contribute to the project success through shorter cycle time, inventory level reduction and improving service level (Venkataraman, 2007). These aspects justify the importance of selecting and managing environmental conscious suppliers in a construction project.

Regarding material flow/deliverables, the raw materials such as cement, prefabricated components such as glass façade, and systems such as HVAC are processed and assembled onsite by the main/sub-contractors. Upon completion of the building, the final commission of the building will be executed by consultants, and non-compliance (if any) at this stage is reverted to the main contractor to rectify to get the building commissioned. After commissioning, the building is handed over to the developer and is ready for occupation.

Overall, it is apparent that Developers, Architects/Consultants, main Contractors, Subcontractors, and Suppliers have strategic positions in the supply chain and therefore are critical to advancement of construction sector. In addition to the above stakeholders, the government regulatory bodies, and buyer/end-user could also influence the construction sector. Government regulatory bodies worldwide play an important role in enacting policies/ regulations for the construction sector stakeholders to comply (Badi and Murtagh, 2019). The buyer/end-user are either owners or tenants who use the building. Increasing global buyers and increasing customer involvement in the building design coupled with their willingness to pay more for innovative and modern buildings can influence the construction sector to take a global perspective (Xie et al., 2017).

RESEARCH METHODOLOGY

To understand the global supply chain strategies (at strategic, tactical and operational levels) used by UAE's construction sector, a secondary research methodology was used, where relevant data sources such as industry reports, company annual reports and corporate and government websites were utilized. In addition, semi-structured interviews with stakeholders associated with two large construction building projects were also conducted so as to develop a project-level understanding of their strategies.

In terms of sampling, a very stringent purposive or selective sampling, a non-probability sampling technique was used. The goal of purposive sampling is to obtain equal representation of all key stakeholders in the supply chain (i.e. Developers, Architects/Consultants, Contractors/Subcontractors, and Suppliers). Multiple respondents were carefully selected within each stakeholder firm to obtain multiple perspectives. A total of 23 semi-structured interviews with senior professionals (most of whom had more than ten years of experience in the construction sector) were conducted across ten construction firms. Demographic details on the respondents are presented in Table 1.

Table 1. Demographic details of interview respondents

Stakeholders	Interviewee Details	Developer	Architect/ Consultant	Main Contractor	Subcontractor	Supplier
Project -1	Annual Turnover	~$ 825 million	~$ 250 million	~$ 430 million	~$ 160 million	~$ 400 million
	Designation of Interviewee	•Head of sustainability •Senior Vice President-Operations	• Lead Architect • Senior Consultant -Sustainability	• Regional Head -Sustainability • Head of Commissioning	• Technical Manager • Manager-LEED projects •Senior Engineer-MEP & Systems	•Product Specialist •Business Development Manager
Project -2	Annual Turnover	~$ 2.5 billion	~$ 550 million	~$ 900 million	~$ 450 million	~$ 1.8 billion
	Designation of Interviewee	•Head of projects •Director-Sustainability & Commissioning	•Vice President •Senior Architect	• Senior Project Manager • Head of Procurements • Senior Coordinator - Contracts	•Site Engineer •Project Manager	•Divisional Manager •Business Development Manager-MENA •Project Engineer

All interviews were conducted face-to-face at the office of the respondents, though follow-up interviews for clarifications were carried out over the phone. Each interview lasted approximately 45 to 60 minutes.

Most interviews were digitally recorded, and where this was not possible, detailed notes were taken that were later transcribed within one to two days and were also crosschecked with respondents to ensure accuracy.

The next section discusses the key secondary research and interview findings.

FINDINGS AND DISCUSSIONS

The key strategic themes identified in this study that has propelled UAE to become a leading global construction player are discussed in the following sections.

Leadership in Policymaking

The UAE federal government and state governments of individual emirate (e.g. Dubai, Abu Dhabi and Sharjah) have made significant efforts in terms of enacting friendly policies and regulations to encourage foreign direct investments to the country. According to UAE Ministry of Economy, the foreign direct investments to UAE are expected to rise by 20% in 2019 (Gulfnews, 2019a). According to the Global Investment Report 2017, the UAE stands at 9th position as the largest recipient of foreign direct investment (FDI) in Asia and 1st in the region (UNCTAD, 2017). In 2016 alone, the UAE attracted USD 8.9 billion worth of FDI, an increase of 1.7% from 2015. In addition to its political and economic stability, ease of doing business is considered as a reason for this increase in foreign direct investment. According to World Bank Group Doing Business report, UAE is placed relatively high at 26 out of the 192 countries included in the report (WBG, 2017). This is mainly due to factors such as no direct taxation of firms, no limit in the repatriation of funds, and a strong banking and technological infrastructure. Further, the Greenfield Investment statistics of the UAE shows that UAE was the leading country by number of Greenfield FDI projects attracted (302 projects worth USD 13 billion) in the Middle East and North Africa (MENA) region (FDI, 2014).

According to the UAE Bureau of Statistics, the construction sector is the 2nd biggest recipient of FDI after the financial sector in the UAE accounting for roughly 27% of total Greenfield investments (FCSA, 2019). For example, the construction sector contributed $1.6bn (AED6bn) to the foreign direct investment (FDI) recorded by UAE capital Abu Dhabi alone in 2018 (Construction Week Online, 2019a). Similarly, Real Estate and Construction contributes to 13.4% of the GDP for the Emirate of Dubai (DER, 2018).

One of the main initiatives behind the reception of FDIs is the establishment of free zones in the UAE. Free trade zones have special tax, customs, and imports regime. Overall, there are 45 free trade zones in the UAE, mostly in Dubai, with allows 100% foreign ownership of land and commercial facility, 100% import and export tax exemptions, 100% repatriation of capitals and profits, and corporate tax exemptions for 50 years (Edarabia, 2019). As a result, the UAE has been able to attract significant number of foreign construction companies to the country. Also, given the fact that there are no personal income taxes, companies in the UAE including those in construction have been able to attract global talent. For example, in Dubai, the construction and real-estate sector employees 30% of all workers (DER, 2018). Therefore it is imperative that the sector attracts quality yet affordable labour.

Further to attract foreign investors and buyers, UAE has started freehold areas/ properties, in which a foreign national (who doesn't need to be a resident of the UAE) can have 100% ownership on the land and the housing unit on the property (Bayut, 2019). This was able to generate a significant boom in the construction sector. Further, foreigner investors (property owners) including their families in the UAE construction sector are eligible for up to 10-year renewable visa (DER, 2018). Besides, Dubai has announced the launch of "partial" title deeds which will recognize multiple ownerships in a property. This is expected to cover a larger segment of investors, especially smaller ones, both inside and outside the UAE, and allow them to own and sell properties partially in Dubai and benefit from high returns on investments. In other words, it works in the crowd-funding model, and allow those wanting to pool funds and share ownership in a property (Gulfnews, 2019b). The Central Bank of the UAE has already adopted the crowdsourcing technique to enhance the regulatory framework of the UAE financial sector and support the development of financial technology (Fintech) business (Government.ae, 2019).

In addition to government initiatives, Developers in the UAE have also taken initiatives to attract foreign investors and buyers. For instance, Developers in association with Dubai Land Department have launched Rent-to-Own schemes, a first of its kind in the region. They provide an excellent opportunity for both buyers (to affordably become homeowners) and Developers (to sell some of their available, ready stock) (MENA Herald, 2019). For example, Harbour Real Estate has introduced a payment scheme where owners have 20 years to pay off a ready property, which mirrors the time frames many banks offer on mortgages.

According to interviewees on the impact of increasing FDI in the UAE construction sector, competitor pressure from increasing foreign firms and joint-venture firms was highlighted by several respondents as a key factor that is driving innovation and sustainability in the UAE construction sector. For instance, respondents from Developers highlighted their fear of losing competitive advantage and market share as one of their main reasons for implementing environmental practices. In the words of an interviewee (Developer): "*Sustainability is the future, and soon everybody will be talking about it and we need to be ahead of the game*". The need to meet or exceed the practices of competitors has impacted Developers' practices, especially their innovativeness in design and purchasing practices as well as their training and auditing practices. Respondents from Architects/Consultants also reported high competitor pressure because of the increasing number of foreign Architects/Consultants establishing their branch offices in the UAE as well due to increasing overseas consultants bidding for UAE projects. Respondents highlighted their need to be competitive to survive in the market. A similar scenario was found for Contractors as well. The increasing number of foreign and foreign-local joint venture Contractors is highlighted as one of the main factors prompting Contractors, especially local ones, to implement innovative practices. According to a respondent from a local Contractor, increasing numbers of joint venture firms is a major concern as they possess the combined advantage of foreign firms' expertise and local firms' local connections, contacts, and deep understanding of specific conditions of the UAE market. It was also evident from the interviews that firms especially local ones are trying to imitate/mimic the actions of their successful competitors in the industry in order to either follow their success or in an attempt to avoid losing their competitive advantages (DiMaggio and Powell, 1983).

Interviewees also acknowledged the benefits of working with foreign firms in terms of diffusion of innovation. Diffusion of innovation is the process by which an innovation is communicated through certain channels over time among the members of a social system (Rogers, 1963), in this case, through the construction supply chain from large firms to small firms, and from foreign ones to local ones. For example, one of the interviewed local Developer highlighted the benefits of working with a foreign Architect in terms of knowledge transfer.

Leadership in Technology and Innovation

From 3D printing to robotics, technological innovations have the power to shake up the construction industry and improve its productivity, sustainability, and affordability. UAE has been the leader in the regional construction market in terms of technology and innovation. For instance, UAE declared 2015 as the year of innovation as part of its National Innovation Strategy (UAE NIS, 2015). While globally, construction sector has been a laggard, the UAE construction sector has, over the last few years, appeared more responsive to new technology and innovation; their goal in doing so is to not only boost efficiencies and quality but also improve site health and safety (Construction Week Online, 2019b). Some of the key technologies adopted by UAE's construction sector recently include:

3D Printing

Very few technologies have the disruptive power that 3D printing has in the global construction sector. According to studies, the traditional process of construction management will be disrupted and 3D printing technology will deeply influence the architectural design and construction methods in the future (MEED, 2019). While concrete 3D printing is still in its infancy, it is promising in terms of lowering costs, improving sustainability credentials and giving the ability to create more flexible designs; in fact this relatively new technology has virtually unlimited scope for growth worldwide. In the next 5-10 years, 3D printing is expected to merge with traditional construction (MEED, 2019). The 3D concrete printing market, which was valued at $0.3m in 2017 is projected to reach $1.48bn by 2023 – a compound annual growth rate of 317.3% (Markets and Markets, 2019).

UAE construction sector was the first to adopt 3D printing. In fact, UAE hosts the world's first 3D printed building in Dubai (Dubai Future Foundation, 2019a). Dubai Electricity and Water Authority (DEWA) lab is the first 3D-printed laboratory building in the world (DEWA, 2017). DEWA lab will support researchers, designers, and innovators to bring the best minds from around the world, to make Dubai the world's leading 3D-printing hub by 2030. This project will mark the beginning of radical transformations in the world of design and construction, as 3D-printing technology will reduce both cost and time; the two most important elements in construction projects (DEWA, 2017). The DEWA lab is also collaborating with prestigious research centers and universities around the world.

Further, 3D printed molds and formworks are a massive area of opportunity for the construction industry. When it comes to building complex or unique concrete structures and shapes, 3D printed molds provide significant value-add to contractors. For example, Immensa, a UAE based additive manufacturing specialist, collaborated with a number of UAE based contracting companies to test a specific advanced method of producing 3D printed molds (Immensa Technology Labs, 2019).

The emirate of Dubai is determined to ensure that every new building in Dubai in 2025 will have 25% of its structure 3D-printed. The mandate will begin in 2019, starting at 2%, with a gradual increase to achieve this strategic goal (Dubai Future Foundation, 2019b). Also, Dubai has awarded their prestigious projects such as the Dubai Metro extensions and EXPO 2020 sustainability pavilion to Spanish contractor Acciona, who are pioneers in 3D concrete printing technology and has already built the world's first 3D-printed concrete bridge in Madrid, Spain (Construction Week Online, 2018).

The other feature of 3D printing is the scale model making industry in which miniature architectural models of the construction projects can be 3D printed. Architects and Contractors can benefit from this technology and is expected that there will be an increasing number of 3D printed designs and drawings being created in the sector. For example, Dubai based ALEC construction group uses 3D scale models to simulate, test and plan how the building will be constructed onsite (Immensalabs, 2019). In other words, lot of building designs that would have been deemed impractical in the past are now deemed possible with 3D printing (MEED, 2019).

While 3D printing was not found in the two projects considered in the study, interviewees acknowledged the fact they are seriously considering 3D printing for future projects and that they are in the process of monitoring potential partners.

Building Information Modelling (BIM)

Building information modeling is fast becoming the norm in the construction sector. BIM provides tools to tackle inherent challenges such as budget overspend, project delays, and quality control issues, and is transforming the way buildings are designed, built, and operated (Construction Week Online, 2019b). The UAE has already led the way with the Louvre Abu Dhabi's creative use of iterative BIM. The BIM design model was used to create a scale model for physical wave testing that informed the geometry of the perimeter and the position of inlets and concrete breakwaters. UAE based Engineering Contracting Company (ECC) has been at the forefront of using BIM for successful completion of their contracting projects and have been able to complete projects before schedule and on budget using BIM (Construction Week Online, 2019b). It provides greater collaboration and communication between supply chain stakeholders such as Developer, Contractor, and Consultant, greater project visualization, facilitates pre-fabrication, improves safety, and provides superior facility management and handover (Connect and Construct, 2019). Killa Design, a Dubai-based architectural firm behind some of Dubai's most iconic buildings, such as the Museum of the Future uses BIM in their projects (Construction Week Online, 2019b).

It was evident from the interviews that construction firms involved in the projects are using BIM or related tools. For example, the foreign architects/consultants interviewed had access to state-of-the-art 3D modeling software and other tools for innovative design via their headquarters.

Robotics and Drones

Like 3D printing, robots and robotic processes at construction sites are expected to be common by 2025 and in turn be an integral part of the construction process (MEED, 2019). Also, a convergence of robotics and 3D printing is expected soon. UAE construction sector has started using robotics. For example, ALEC, a leading contracting firm is using robotics for plastering and panel installation. The contractor also uses a robotics system to hold façades in place, so workers can fix them from within the building rather than on the outside. This improves safety for laborers and also helps the contractor cut the time required to install an entire floor of façade panels by half (Construction Week Online, 2019c).

Similarly, drones are fast changing the way the construction industry operates. Known also as unmanned aerial vehicles (UAVs), drones are already showing their potential to reduce labour and time in providing accurate surveys, eliminating much of the human error involved in the process (Construction Week Online, 2019b). Also, construction companies are using drones to transport goods aerially thereby enabling difficult transfers.

The drones market in the UAE is currently among the most advanced and developed in the Middle East (Gulfnews, 2017). In the UAE, the Abu Dhabi Municipality rolled out a pilot scheme to use drones for monitoring engineering work on construction sites (Arabian Business, 2019). The drones are fitted with cameras so construction projects can be inspected remotely as it provides live and integrated panoramic images for all construction phases.

While the use of drones and advanced robotics was not evident in the two projects we considered, dependence on automation was evident. Some of the automation used in the projects include concrete mixers, fillers and spreaders and onsite machinery to replace most of the manual works. According to respondents, the use of automation has minimized manual waste and re-works from errors along with significant reduction in project completion time. However, most of the interviewees acknowledged that they are gearing up for more advanced automation using robotics in the near future.

Modular Building

In a similar vein to 3D printing, the field of modular construction has seen greater application in the construction sector. The value of the global modular construction market is estimated to reach US$157.19bn by 2023 (ME Construction News, 2019b). Modular design is a construction methodology by which the building is subdivided into smaller units called modules. Each module is designed and fully manufactured off-site in a factory; modules in various stages of completion will form a production line by which each module will progress from assembly up to complete fit-out. Finished modules will be shipped to the site and joined together at the site, in a Lego look-alike process to form the complete building. To shrink the project delivery timeline, activities are performed in parallel. UAE has been leading in modular building construction as it promises consistent quality with faster construction times than their traditionally built counterparts. For example, DuBox, a Dubai-based modular construction company designs and delivers single or multi-storey concrete buildings, using modular methodologies. It shifts 85 percent of the construction activities off-site and is the first company in the Middle East and North Africa to apply off-site modular manufacturing methods to concrete construction projects (DuBox, 2019). Further, some of the UAE's most iconic projects such as the Dubai Mall and Dubai Opera have used the modular building concept (Construction Week Online, 2019d).

The application of modular design for residential and commercial buildings was also evident from the interviews. Some of the prefabricated components used as part of modular design in the two projects considered in this study include precast facades, staircases, partition walls, semi-precast slabs, and precast bathroom pods. According to respondents, this has reduced onsite construction activities, project completion times, waste and energy consumption, especially in community development projects with several identical buildings. Further, the respondents highlighted that the modular design enabled easy disassembly during the building demolition to maximize recovery and recyclability of materials.

Leadership in Environmental Supply Chain Management

Environmental supply chain management is integrating environmental thinking into supply-chain management, including product design, material sourcing, and selection, manufacturing processes, delivery of the final product to the consumers as well as end-of-life management of the product after its useful life (Srivastava, 2017).

UAE is driven by the need to meet the growing demands of urbanization, while at the same time curtailing its adverse environmental impacts. UAE has the vision to become one of the most sustainable countries by 2021. The significant efforts undertaken by the UAE government and construction firms in recent years have resulted in marked improvements in the environmental aspects in the construction supply chains starting from design to end of life demolition. The introduction of green building regulation in Dubai and Abu Dhabi based on LEED model has ensured 90% of all new buildings in the UAE have to comply with the green building guidelines. This includes the municipal green building regulations in the emirate of Dubai introduced in 2011; the ESTIDAMA pearl rating system for buildings in the emirate of Abu Dhabi introduced in 2010, and the EHS Trakhees in Free Zones introduced in 2006. This is similar to the mandatory green building standards in US and UK. This implies that Developers and Architects have to meet the minimum environmental design standards mentioned in the regulations on aspects such as natural ventilation, lighting, water, and energy consumption and use of renewable energy. Similarly, Contractors must achieve a minimum of at least 50% onsite waste aversion from the landfill.

In addition, Contractors in both Dubai and Abu Dhabi must pay landfill charges (charged for each truckload) and fines for environmental accidents such a spilling of hazardous materials. Although (material) suppliers in the UAE do not face any direct regulatory requirements, they risk exclusion from the project tender if they fail to meet the minimum environmental requirements specified in the regulations. As a result, the number of green buildings in the country has increased. According to Leadership in Energy and Environmental Design (LEED) 2015 statistics (the world's largest green building rating body), the number of LEED-certified projects in the UAE has increased from few in 2011 to close to one thousand in 2015 (LEED, 2015). Also, the per capita carbon emissions have reduced from 23 in 2008 to 18.3 in 2013, UAE is still one of the highest per capita carbon emission countries in the world according to World Bank statistics (World Bank Data, 2019).

In addition, the UAE has also initiated the following initiatives that demonstrate their commitment to environmental protection which has a direct impact on the construction sector:

- The UAE has integrated strategies to reduce energy consumption within the framework for its 2021 vision (SGER, 2016). The UAE Energy Strategy 2050 aims to achieve an energy mix that combines renewable and clean energy sources to balance economic requirements and environmental goals. The UAE will invest AED 600 billion until 2050 to meet the growing energy demand and ensure the sustainable growth of the economy.

- In 2016, UAE established a new ministry called the Ministry of Climate Change and Environment
- The significant strides achieved by the UAE are evident from some of the international recognition it has received for some of their projects. For instance, the Dubai Electricity and Water Authority building, the largest government building in the world to secure a LEED Platinum rating for green buildings, has opened for business. Similarly, the LEED platinum-certified Change Initiative (TCI) building in Dubai has received the award for the "most sustainable" commercial building in the world.
- Within the UAE, Dubai's target (where buildings use 70% of all energy) is to become one of the top 10 sustainable cities in the world by 2020 with targets to cut energy consumption by 20%, water consumption by 15% and GHG emissions by 20% (SGER, 2015).
- Similarly, in Abu Dhabi, Masdar City, when fully completed by 2020 (with a capacity to house around 40,000 people) is expected to become the world's most sustainable low-carbon city and is also a leading centre for sustainable research.
- Mohammed bin Rashid Al Maktoum Solar Park - a leading project that promotes sustainability in the UAE. The capacity of the solar power projects completed at the Mohammed bin Rashid Al Maktoum Solar Park is 413MW. DEWA has other projects under construction at a capacity of 1,550MW and is working on other projects to increase the solar park's capacity to 5,000MW by 2030.
- The Dubai Clean Energy Strategy 2050 aims Dubai to be the city with the lowest carbon footprint in the world by 2050. Initially, it aims to provide 7% of Dubai's total power output from clean energy by 2020. This target will increase to 25% by 2030 and 75% by 2050. Dubai is the only city in the region to have launched such a promising strategy, with set goals and timelines that map the future of energy until 2050.

The focus on promoting environmental supply chain management was evident from the interviews. The interviewed Developers were found to be motivated to go beyond the regulation to achieve LEED certification, which is an internationally recognised green building certificate. This is because these building regulations are modelled around LEED (though not as stringent as LEED), and therefore not too cumbersome to achieve. Also, one of the Developers highlighted that their projects attract significant foreign buyers and investors because of their environmental friendliness.

Further, one of the interviewed Developers was found to be using environmental design competition for Architects to shortlist designs for their projects. In addition, environmental training programs for employees and supply chain partners were also evident from the interviewed firms. Foreign subsidiary firms were found to use their headquarters and online training platforms to run some of the training programs. For example, one of the foreign Contractors interviewed had, as a part of its headquarters policy, imparted training to more than 350 Subcontractors over the previous three years on green/sustainability aspects.

Similarly, both in-house and external environmental auditing was found to be undertaken by the Developers interviewed. These audits (scheduled or unscheduled) were either undertaken themselves or via third-party auditors. Similarly, Contractors were found to conduct random environmental audits of their Subcontractors and Suppliers, including visits to their manufacturing facilities. The consultants, who are responsible for approval of the material/product suppliers in the project, were found to apply stringent auditing checks to ensure products with hazardous materials, low recycled content, and low quality are not approved. The consultants who are also responsible for the final commissioning of the project were found to play an important role in ensuring the building meets the requirements including environmental-related as per the tender, and that non-compliance is reverted to the main Contractor for rectification before commissioning. The stringency in building commissioning was found to ensure Contractors/Subcontractors are not bypassing contractual requirements.

The interviewees also highlighted instances where they asked their suppliers to provide green materials beyond what was necessary for the tender. For example, the foreign contractor interviewed was found to exceed Developer's contractual requirements such as on green material specifications, auditing suppliers and on LEED experience, number of LEED-certified staff in payrolls and ISO 14001 certification when selecting Subcontractors. This is because, in most cases, foreign firms were using their standard global procurement practices. This is because foreign subsidiaries in most cases are required to maintain a common environmental protocol across all branches/subsidiaries operating in different countries (Earnhart et al., 2014). For example, one of the respondents highlighted that their global supply chain/operations are audited, and compliance with regulation is always at the top of the agenda for the auditors. According to one of the foreign Contractors interviewed, in one of their projects, they were able to recycle 50% of the demolition materials including concrete. Similarly a foreign Contractor was found to mandate Subcontractors and Suppliers to sign UN global compact agreement, a commitment to protect the environment, before doing any business.

Leadership in International Collaboration/Partnerships

International collaboration/partnerships between foreign firms and local ones offer scope for technology and knowledge transfer between them. Foreign partners, especially from developed countries could serve as a source of diffusion to local partners in the emerging economy. UAE has been leading in supply chain collaboration/partnering, especially with foreign firms to bring the best technologies, material/equipment, processes, talent, and technical and managerial know-how to its construction sector. Among these, UAE has been in forefront of developing international joint-ventures. A joint venture is an agreement between two or more parties wherein they principally agree on developing a new asset or entity. Given the complexities surrounding construction processes, joint venture, is today one of the most preferred choices globally for construction as it provides flexibility. UAE has been leading the way in terms of international joint-ventures. This is seen across the supply stakeholders. For example, Al Futtaim Carillion LLC is a Dubai-based leading contracting company in the UAE, which is jointly owned by Al Futtaim (Private) Limited of Dubai and Carillion Construction Overseas Limited, the international contracting and services group from the United Kingdom. They have been at the forefront of sustainability and innovation, and have completed prestigious projects such as New York University Abu Dhabi and The Yas Hotel, Yas Island Abu Dhabi (Al-Futtaim Carillion, 2019). Similarly, Al Rostamani Pegel L.L.C. was originally founded in 1998 as a project management company through a partnership between the renowned, UAE-based, Al Rostamani Group and Gustav Pegel & Sohn, a Berlin-based, 145-year-old German construction company. They have won the corporate social responsibility award of Dubai Chamber of Commerce and Industry (Al Rostamani Group, 2019).

Also, joint-venture partnerships are seen for one-off projects. For example, Engineering Contracting Company LLC (ECC), UAE based company in a joint-venture project with McLaren Construction, a UK based company won a multi-storey car park project for Dubai World Trade Centre (Construction Week Online, 2017). Further, Nakheel, a leading Developer in UAE has inked a deal with Germany-based real estate brokerage company Engel and Völkers (E&V), creating a new joint venture firm in Dubai (Nakheel, 2015).

The benefits of international collaboration were evident from the interviews. According to interviewees of joint-venture firms, the joint-venture between local and foreign-subsidiary firms, bring expertise of both firms together and thereby enhance competitive advantage. For example, according to respondents of a foreign subsidiary firm in the UAE, they enjoy access to global tools and expertise of foreign partners' headquarters. This was emphasized by an interviewee from a foreign subsidiary: "The good thing with us [a foreign contractor] is that we have inherited the entire Environmental Management System (EMS) and other systems from our head office." Also, foreign firms were found to use more advanced e-procurement processes and electronic invoicing to encourage greater transparency. Previous studies have highlighted that foreign firms could have better access to external financing, state-of-the-art technologies, and cutting-edge practices (Earnhart et al., 2014). Further, tapping into their headquarters' systems, technologies, and manpower, foreign subsidiary firms are able to reduce their upfront investments (Earnhart et al., 2014; Kim et al., 2016). Further, foreign architects/consultant firms were found to transfer employees from their head office/other branches and thereby easily manage temporary project requirements. In return, the local firm in the joint venture brings significant understanding of the local business environment, local regulations, customs and culture including language which is critical in a competitive setting.

Further, few contractors interviewed were exploring the possibility of joint R&D with Suppliers for developing innovative products. Also, environmental commitment is seen among joint-venture firms, in which the local partner was found to inherit the environmental vision and mission of their foreign partner. Also, it was evident from interviews that foreign subsidiary firms and joint-venture firms were found to additionally develop cross-functional teams between foreign head office (located outside UAE) and the UAE subsidiary. Also that there was a continuous transfer of knowledge, including environment-related from head office to local UAE offices; UAE office employees are also routinely sent to the head office for training. Further, the interviewed firms, especially the foreign firms were found to have strong global partnerships with international suppliers and were found to use the (strong) purchasing power of headquarters to obtain favorable credit terms and delivery schedules from them. They were also found to benefit from economies of scale because of centralized global procurement.

The interviewed Suppliers, both local and foreign had state-of-the-art manufacturing facilities to minimize emissions and waste discharge during the manufacturing process. The heightened use of technology in manufacturing, therefore, was found to reduce manual waste and errors. In fact, one of the glass manufacturers interviewed was able to reduce emission levels by 60% and energy consumption by 30% through such manufacturing facilities.

CONCLUSION

It was evident from this study that the UAE construction sector has undertaken several leadership strategies to become a leading global construction hub. The findings show globalization, liberalization, and foreign direct investment to be not just important for economic development and industrial modernization, but also for environmental protection. Countries looking to improve their construction sector and its supply chain, therefore, should encourage foreign firms, especially from developed countries, to establish subsidiaries there. Additionally, linking up and building relationships between foreign and local firms can help diffuse best practices including environmental practices. Especially with the upcoming new technologies and innovation such as 3D printing, drones, robotics, BIM and modular design, along with others such as blockchain, predictive analytics and artificial intelligence, it is important that construction sector leverage the capabilities of foreign expertise to bring these technologies to the local market, and facilitate diffusion of technology and knowledge transfer from foreign to local counterparts. For instance, policymakers and industrial groups could promote this, for example, through facilitating collaborative partnerships and mentoring opportunities for local firms with foreign firms, or through local-foreign joint ventures. The underlying basis is the diffusion of innovation theory (Rogers, 1962). Previous studies have shown that foreign firms, especially those operating in developing countries, are likely to be proactive agents of change for local firms (Child and Tsai, 2005).

In terms of practical implications, the study provides contemporary strategies for construction firms to benefit from global supply chains. It also provides strategies for governments in other countries on how to attract FDI in the construction sector, and some key policy innovations to achieve sustainable construction sector growth and develop strategies to achieve environmental leadership. For researchers, the study can be used as a starting point to explore further on to develop 'globalness' in their construction supply chain. However, the study has some limitations. The primary research in this study is based only on two case projects. More research is required in UAE and other emerging economies to understand further the leadership strategies used by governments and construction companies to achieve global competitiveness.

REFERENCES

Akintoye, A., McIntosh, G., & Fitzgerald, E. (2000). A survey of supply chain collaboration and management in the UK construction industry. *European Journal of Purchasing & Supply Management*, *6*(3), 159–168. doi:10.1016/S0969-7012(00)00012-5

Al-Futtaim Carillion. (2019). Available at http://www.afcarillion.ae/

Al Rostamani Group. (2019). http://www.alrostamanigroup.ae/sites/en/Pages/SubCompanyDetails.aspx?ItemID=10

Arabian Business. (2018). *Abu Dhabi deploys drones to inspect construction sites.* Available at https://www.arabianbusiness.com/technology/401936-wkd-abu-dhabi-deploys-drones-to-inspect-construction-sites

Arabian Industry. (2015). *UAE construction to grow by 9.3% in 2015.* Available at https://www.arabianindustry.com/construction/news/2015/may/11/uae-construction-to-grow-by-93-in-2015-5036161/

Badi, S., & Murtagh, N. (2019). Green supply chain management in construction: A systematic literature review and future research agenda. *Journal of Cleaner Production, 223*, 312–322. doi:10.1016/j.jclepro.2019.03.132

Balasubramanian, S., & Shukla, V. (2017). Green supply chain management: The case of the construction sector in the United Arab Emirates (UAE). *Production Planning and Control, 28*(14), 1116–1138. doi:10.1080/09537287.2017.1341651

Bayut. (2019). *What's the difference between freehold and free zone areas in Dubai?* Available at https://www.bayut.com/mybayut/freezone-vs-freehold-property-dubai/

Bresnen, M. J., & Haslam, C. O. (1991). Construction industry clients: A survey of their attributes and project management practices. *Construction Management and Economics, 9*(4), 327–342. doi:10.1080/01446199100000026

Briscoe, G., Dainty, A. R., & Millett, S. (2001). Construction supply chain partnerships: Skills, knowledge and attitudinal requirements. *European Journal of Purchasing & Supply Management, 7*(4), 243–255. doi:10.1016/S0969-7012(01)00005-3

Briscoe, G. H., Dainty, A. R., Millett, S. J., & Neale, R. H. (2004). Client-led strategies for construction supply chain improvement. *Construction Management and Economics, 22*(2), 193–201. doi:10.1080/0144619042000201394

Chen, P. H., Ong, C. F., & Hsu, S. C. (2016). The linkages between internationalization and environmental strategies of multinational construction firms. *Journal of Cleaner Production, 116*, 207–216. doi:10.1016/j.jclepro.2015.12.105

Child, J., & Tsai, T. (2005). The dynamic between firms' environmental strategies and institutional constraints in emerging economies: Evidence from China and Taiwan. *Journal of Management Studies, 42*(1), 95–125. doi:10.1111/j.1467-6486.2005.00490.x

CIPS. (2019). *Chartered Institute of Procurement and Supply.* Available at https://www.cips.org/en-ME/knowledge/procurement-topics-and-skills/srm-and-sc-management/global-supply-chains/

Connect and Construct. (2019). *Top 10 Benefits of BIM in Construction*. Available at https://connect.bim360.autodesk.com/benefits-of-bim-in-construction

Construction Week Online. (2015). *UAE construction to grow by 9.3% in 2015*. Available at https://www.constructionweekonline.com/article-33629-uae-construction-to-grow-by-93-in-2015

Construction Week Online. (2017). *ECC awarded joint-venture project with McLaren Construction*. Available at https://www.constructionweekonline.com/article-45480-ecc-awarded-joint-venture-project-with-mclaren-construction

Construction Week Online. (2018). *Acciona unit wins Expo 2020 Dubai Sustainability Pavilion contract*. Available at https://www.constructionweekonline.com/article-50793-acciona-unit-wins-expo-2020-dubai-sustainability-pavilion-contract

Construction Week Online. (2019a). *Construction, building contribute $1.6bn to Abu Dhabi FDI in 2018*. Available at https://www.constructionweekonline.com/business/180938-construction-adds-16bn-to-abu-dhabi-fdi-in-2018

Construction Week Online. (2019b). *How has technology disrupted the Middle East's construction sector?* Available at https://www.constructionweekonline.com/products-services/180835-large-uae-contractors-opt-for-3d-printing-new-tech-to-implement-construction

Construction Week Online. (2019c). *ALEC deploys robotics to build Dubai's $1bn Marina Gate*. Available at https://www.constructionweekonline.com/projects-tenders/168633-uae-contractor-alec-uses-robotics-to-build-dubai-marina-gate-by-select-group

Construction Week Online. (2019d). *Inside a Dubai MEP company's modular design factory in Jebel Ali*. Available at https://www.constructionweekonline.com/products-services/168757-a-look-inside-bk-gulfs-game-changing-modular-construction-mep-factory-in-jebel-ali

Cox, A. W., Ireland, P., & Townsend, M. (2006). *Managing in Construction Supply Chains and Markets: Reactive and Proactive Options for Improving Performance and Relationship Management*. Thomas Telford.

DER. (2018). *Dubai Economic Report 2018*. Available at http://www.dubaided.ae/StudiesAndResearchDocument/Dubai-Economic-Report-2018-Full-Report.pdf

DEWA. (2017). *3D-Printed Lab at Mohammed bin Rashid Al Maktoum Solar Park*. Available at https://www.dewa.gov.ae/en/about-us/media-publications/latest-news/2017/07/he-saeed-mohammed-al-tayer-visits-3d-printed-lab-at-mohammed-bin-rashid-al-maktoum-solar-park

DiMaggio, P., & Powell, W. W. (1983). The iron cage revisited: Collective rationality and institutional isomorphism in organizational fields. *American Sociological Review*, *48*(2), 147–160. doi:10.2307/2095101

Dubai Future Foundation. (2019a). *Office of the Future. The World's First 3D Printed Office*. Available at https://www.dubaifuture.gov.ae/our-initiatives/office-of-the-future/

Dubai Future Foundation. (2019b). *Dubai 3D printing strategy*. Available at https://www.dubaifuture.gov.ae/our-initiatives/dubai-3d-printing-strategy/

Dubai Metro. (2013). *UAE leads GCC with USD1.38trn projects; awaits Expo 2020 win*. Available at http://www.dubaimetro.eu/uae-leads-gcc-with-usd1-38trn-projects-awaits-expo-2020-win/

Dubois, A., & Gadde, L. E. (2000). Supply strategy and network effects—purchasing behaviour in the construction industry. *European Journal of Purchasing & Supply Management*, *6*(3-4), 207-215.

DuBox. (2019). Available at https://www.dubox.me/

Earnhart, D. H., Khanna, M., & Lyon, T. P. (2014). Corporate environmental strategies in emerging economies. *Review of Environmental Economics and Policy*, *8*(2), 164–185. doi:10.1093/reep/reu001

Edarabia. (2019). *45 Free Zones in UAE (All Emirates)*. Available at https://www.edarabia.com/45-free-zones-uae/

FCSA. (2019). *Federal Competitiveness and Statistics Authority*. Available at https://fcsa.gov.ae/ar-ae/Pages/home.aspx

FDI. (2014). *The Foreign Direct Investment Report 2014. Global Greenfield investment trends*. The Financial Times Limited.

Giang, D. T., & Pheng, L. S. (2011). Role of construction in economic development: Review of key concepts in the past 40 years. *Habitat International*, *35*(1), 118–125. doi:10.1016/j.habitatint.2010.06.003

Global Data. (2017). *Global Construction Outlook 2021*. Available at https://www.globaldata.com/store/report/gd-cn0004go--global-construction-outlook-2021/

Government.ae. (2019). *Crowdfunding*. Available at https://government.ae/en/information-and-services/business/crowdfunding

Gulf News. (2019a). *Foreign direct investments to UAE expected to rise by 20% in 2019*. Available at https://gulfnews.com/business/foreign-direct-investments-to-uae-expected-to-rise-by-20-in-2019-1.63143316

Gulfnews. (2019b). *Partial title deeds law opens up investor pools for Dubai*. Available at https://gulfnews.com/business/property/partial-title-deeds-law-opens-up-investor-pools-for-dubai-1.65030251

Gulfnews. (2019c). *UAE is most advanced drones market in Middle East*. Available at https://gulfnews.com/technology/uae-is-most-advanced-drones-market-in-middle-east-1.2104797

Hatmoko, J. U. D. (2008). *The impact of supply chain management practice on construction project performance* (Doctoral dissertation). Newcastle University.

Immensa Technology Labs. (2019). *How 3D printing is impacting the construction industry in UAE and globally*. Available at https://www.immensalabs.com/how-3d-printing-is-impacting-the-construction-industry-in-uae-and-globally/

Kim, N., Moon, J. J., & Yin, H. (2016). Environmental pressure and the performance of foreign firms in an emerging economy. *Journal of Business Ethics*, *137*(3), 475–490. doi:10.100710551-015-2568-6

Korczynski, M. (1996). The low-trust route to economic development: Inter-firm relations in the UK engineering construction industry in the 1980s and 1990s. *Journal of Management Studies*, *33*(6), 787–808. doi:10.1111/j.1467-6486.1996.tb00172.x

Latham, S. M. (1994). *Constructing the team: Final report of the government/industry review of procurement and contractual arrangements in the UK construction industry. HM Stationery Office*. HMSO.

LEED. (2015). *Top 10 countries for LEED in 2015*. Retrieved January 21, 2016, from https://www.usgbc.org/2015top10countries

Markets and Markets. (2018). *3D Concrete Printing Market*. Available at https://www.marketsandmarkets.com/Market-Reports/3d-concrete-printing-market-10362292.html

Matthews, J., Pellew, L., Phua, F., & Rowlinson, S. (2000). Quality relationships: Partnering in the construction supply chain. *International Journal of Quality & Reliability Management*, *17*(4/5), 493–510. doi:10.1108/02656710010371191

ME Construction News. (2019a). *Over half of construction leaders expect 6-10% growth over the next year*. Available at https://meconstructionnews.com/36353/over-half-of-construction-leaders-expect-6-10-growth-over-the-next-year

ME Construction News. (2019b). *Trends in offsite modular construction*. Available at https://meconstructionnews.com/34495/trends-in-offsite-modular-construction

MEED. (2019). *3D printing to take over construction*. Available at https://www.meed.com/3d-printing-take-construction/

MENA Herald. (2019). *Dubai Land Department launches Rent-to-Own Title Deed, first of its kind in the region*. Available at https://www.menaherald.com/en/economy/real-estate-construction/dubai-land-department-launches-rent-own-title-deed-first-its-kind

Nakheel. (2015). *Nakheel and Engel & Völkers sign joint venture agreement*. Available at https://www.nakheel.com/en/media/news/nakheel-and-engel-and-volkers-sign-joint-venture-agreement

Rezgui, Y., & Miles, J. (2009). Exploring the potential of SME alliances in the construction sector. *Journal of Construction Engineering and Management*, *136*(5), 558–567. doi:10.1061/(ASCE)CO.1943-7862.0000150

Rogers, E. M. (1962). *Diffusion of Innovations*. The Free Press of Glencoe.

Serpell, A., & Heredia, B. (2004). Supply chain management in construction: Diagnosis and application issues. *Globalisation and Construction*, 455-466.

SGER. (2015). *State of Green Economy Report.* World Green Economy Submit, Dubai, UAE. Available at https://dcce.ae/state-of-green-economy-report-2015/

SGER. (2016). *State of Green Economy Report. United Arab Emirates Ministry of Climate Change and Environment, Second Edition*. Available at www.moccae.gov.ae/assets/download/40a8d3c1/green-economy-report-2016.aspx

Srivastava, S. K. (2007). Green supply-chain management: A state-of-the-art literature review. *International Journal of Management Reviews*, *9*(1), 53–80. doi:10.1111/j.1468-2370.2007.00202.x

Stukhart, G. (1995). *Construction materials management*. Marcel Dekker Inc.

UAE NIS. (2015). *UAE National Innovation Strategy*. Available at https://government.ae/en/about-the-uae/strategies-initiatives-and-awards/federal-governments-strategies-and-plans/national-innovation-strategy

UN-DESA. (2019). *World Urbanization Prospects 2019: Highlights*. Department of Economic and Social Affairs. Available at: https://population.un.org/wup/Publications/Files/WUP2018-Highlights.pdf

UNCTAD. (2017). *World Investment Report. United Nations Conference on Trade and Development*. United Nations. Available at https://unctad.org/en/PublicationsLibrary/wir2017_en.pdf

Venkataraman, R. (2007). Project Supply Chain Management: Optimizing Value: The way we manage the total supply chain. *The Wiley Guide to Managing Projects*, 621-642.

WBG. (2017). *Doing Business 2017*. World Bank Group Flagship Report, 14th Edition. Available at https://www.doingbusiness.org/~/media/WBG/DoingBusiness/Documents/Annual-Reports/English/DB17-Full-Report.pdf

World Bank Data. (2019). *United Arab Emirates*. Available at https://data.worldbank.org/country/united-arab-emirates?view=chart

Xie, X., Lu, Y., & Gou, Z. (2017). Green building pro-environment behaviors: Are green users also green buyers? *Sustainability*, *9*(10), 1703. doi:10.3390u9101703

Chapter 4
Transparency Issues Within a Transport Buyer and Provider Relationship

Eirill Bø
Norwegian Business School, Norway

ABSTRACT

Transport is an important function in the supply chain. This chapter focuses on how to buy a transport service, how to form a transport contract, and how a transparent relationship will influence the risk and the relationship between transport provider and buyer. By developing a decision support tool (DST-model) and calculating the cost and the time parameters, the right price and the cost drivers will appear. The cases described in this chapter are a large Norwegian wholesaler for food, distribution to the retailer, and two Norwegian municipalities collecting household waste. In these cases, the buyer and the provider are acting blind in setting the transport price. This means that there is a huge risk for either a bankruptcy by the transport provider or an overpriced transport for the buyer.

INTRODUCTION

Transport is an important function in the overall supply chain and stands for a large share of the overall logistics cost. Trends like centralized warehouses and increased globalized purchases has led to longer distances and increased transportation. The complexity in the supply chains has increased (Christopher, 2012), which has led to the need for a new approach for transport cost analysis. Transport is among the largest controllable cost factors in the supply chain. (Bergmann & Rawlings,

DOI: 10.4018/978-1-7998-2867-9.ch004

1998) A traditional view of transportation, by practitioners, is that the cost of transportation is a necessary evil and the only way to reduce cost is by putting pressure on the transport provider to lower the price. . (Morash, 1987) (Bowman, 1994) (Mongelluzzo, 1999) (Hannon, 2005a) (Smyrlis, 2005) (Armstrong, 2006) (Trunic,, 2006.). Competitive pressure is often the drivers of risk. In order to improve competitiveness, reduce costs, and increase or maintain profitability the transport providers are taking a "calculated risk" (Svensson, 2002)in order to get a contract. By academics, there is a new focus and interest on transportation cost and relationships between the transport buyer and provider. (Sahay, Halldórsson, & Skjøtt-Larsen, 2006) (Halldórsson & Skjøtt-Larsen, 2004; Langley, 2007) There is a need to change the traditional practices when buying a transport service from a price focused perspective to a perspective were transportation is seen as a mutual value-adding benefit in the supply chain. (Hannon, 2005a; Harrington, 1997) A new focus on analysing how the transport price can be determined and to visualize the real cost drivers in a transport arrangement has emerged. To be able to analyse the cost and the cost drivers, a transparent approach is necessary. A transparent approach means that all necessary information about both the cost structure and the time parameters in the transport arrangement needs to be visualized. This is often seen as sensitive information from the service provider side, but it is necessary to obtain value creation in the transport arrangement. (Lamming, Caldwell, Harrison, & Phillips, 2001) The relationship between the transport buyer and provider can be characterized as an agency relationship. (Logan, 2000). The transport buyer will act as a principal and the service provider as the agent. Agency theory (Eisenhardt, 1989) tries to solve two problems in an agency relationship; goals of the principal and the agent are in conflict and second it is complicated for the principal to verify the agents actions. The price is the conflict area between the transport buyer and provider, and it is often complicated for the buyer to know the transport providers costs and practical actions in the relationship. An important focus in the principal-agency theory is to set up a contract to share the risk between the partners. (Bergen, Dutta, & O. C. Walker, 1992; Eisenhardt, 1989).

The further discussion in this chapter is based on four articles and one chapter in an academic book within the area of relationship between a transport buyer and provider. An overview of the articles is shown in the table below;

Table 1. List of articles and publications used in this chapter

Author	Publishing journal	Area	Empiri	Theory	Method	Findings
Bø, Hammervold (2010)	*International Journal of Logistics: Research and Applications* Vol. 13, No. 3, June 2010, 197–210	Cost-based pricing of transportation services in a wholesaler-carrier relationship: an MS Excel spreadsheet decision tool	The Norwegian wholesaler Coop and the carrier Harlem transport	Cost based prising	Action research	Developing of a DST tool for both the wholesaler and for the carrier is crucial for keeping track of transport performance
Hammervold Bø (2010)	*European Journal of Marketing Vol. 44 No. 7/8, 2010 pp. 1121-1139*	Shipper-carrier integration Overcoming the transparency problem through trust and collaboration	The Norwegian wholesaler Coop and the carrier Harlem transport	Transparency, trust and communication	Action research	Increased transparency, obtained by means of a decision support tool capturing transportation costs, encourages both parties to manage risk collaboratively
Flygansvær, Bø 2015		Pricing issues in a transport buyer – provider relationship: An empirical evaluation using agency theory	Waste Management in two Norwegian municipalities and their carrier	Prinsipal- agent theory, Cost based prising	Case study	The transport buyer and service provider need to share information to secure symmetry and use a more transparent contract based on flexible pricing.
Bø, Flygansvær, 2015		Decision making and transportation pricing in a complex reverse supply chain	Waste Management in two Norwegian municipalities and their carrier	Cost based prising Decision making	Case study	Decision making complexity in transport arrangements has increased, and that decision makers haven't adjusted their work with decisions accordingly. Decisions due to transport arrangements are based on limited analysis, and decisions makers could improve the quality of their decisions by developing and using a DST
Bø, Grønland 2014	Eirill Bø and Stein Erik Grønland, (2013). "Increased cooperation in the supply chains –how to reduce the need for transportation? Akademika Publishing	Increased cooperation in the supply chains – how to reduce the need for transportation?	9 different cases and a supplementary telephone survey of thirty-nine additional companies		*Survey, interviews and case studies*	The key to an improvement in internal cooperation is in many cases information sharing. The price format for the transport has also a major impact on the capacity utilization achieved.

How can transparency lead to increased efficiency and reduced risk in a transport buyer-provider relationship?

Risk in a transport relationship is for the buyer to pay more than necessary for the transport and for the provider to incur financial losses. (Bø, Flygansvær 2015) The transport price should reflect the actual transport cost including a profit margin to the transport provider but also be based on descent productivity. Productivity in a transport system can be measured as fill rate of the trucks and the total use of the truck during a year. (Hammervoll & Bø, 2010) (Rushton, Croucher, & Baker, 2006). How the relationship between the buyer and seller are organized will influence the risk. The transport buyer might choose to leave the transport planning and organization to the provider. In that sense the provider needs to charge for this administrative work, and consider the transport price based on a possible productivity they think they can obtain. If they manage a higher productivity than calculated in the price, they will increase their profit, but if it is lower, they might incur financial losses. (Flygansvær, Bø 2015) On the other hand, the transport buyer can choose to plan and organize the transport himself or herself, and the transport provider will be dependent on the quality of their planning in pricing the transport. From their survey (Bø, Grønland 2012) they found that 54% of the transport buyers used their provider to do the planning on the transport in from the suppliers and 66% on the planning out to the customers.

A major risk in these relationships depends on the chosen price format. To calculate a transport price you need a total picture of the cost and time parameters. (Somapa, Cools, & Dullaert, 2012) The owner of the transport equipment knows the cost elements, so it is a question whether they are willing to share the information about their costs with the transport buyer. The time processes are often more uncertain before you sign up a contract and the time processes might vary during the year and between different drivers. How to get a right picture of the time parameters is often a challenge. In Norway, the salary share of the transport cost is high because of large driver's salaries. This means that the time processes are very important. For a transport company to offer a transport price, it is necessary to do a detailed calculation and consider the time processes and all the uncertainties. Within a year, the cost uncertainty is mostly tied up to fluctuations in the diesel price and the bank rate. (Bø & Hammervoll, 2010) To cover for the cost uncertainty you either need to calculate with an expected increased price, charge a additional risk fee or make an arrangement in the contract to change (Guajardo, Cohen, Kim, & Netessine, 2011) the price if any cost elements increase during the contract period. For the time processes, it is necessary to define the different processes like loading and unloading time, speed, customer time etc and estimate and / or measure each of them.

(Bø & Hammervoll, 2010) developed a transparent decision support tool, a DST-model for a food wholesaler and their service provider. The model was developed to be a tool to consider whether their transport price was to low or accurate. Their transport arrangement was based on about 30 trucks, and the trucks were only used in this arrangement. By developing a DST model they met challenges in obtaining the exact numbers both cost parameters and time processes. In this arrangement, they had originally agreed on a price per ton for a year at the time. They decided to enter a new transparent focus but they had a lot of discussions to agree on the costs and time parameters. For the cost parameters it was a question whether the transport provider would share information about his costs with the transport buyer, but for the time parameters it was more a lack of measurement, and none of the partners knew the exact time parameters. Through many measurements by participating on the transport trips and a lot of discussions about which parameters to measure, they managed to agree that the model should include sixth different time parameters. They decided to use the following time parameters;

1. Loading time per pallet
2. Unloading time per pallet
3. Driving speed
4. Administrative time per day
5. Fixed time per trip (waiting time)
6. Fixed stop time per customer

By using the DST model, they calculated the price per ton and became aware of the importance of the different parameters in the calculation. They calculated the cost of each trip and then calculated the ton price based on an expected fill rate. (Bø & Hammervoll, 2010) The excepted fill rate in the calculation is essential in a unit price system. None of the partners measured the fill rate. The fill rate is normally based on a forecasted volume. Since the transport price, often is set for a year, it is extremely important for the transport buyer to forecast the volume for the next year right and transport provider to manage the fill rate they put in the calculation. The most common adjustment during a year for a service provider is the change in diesel price. For local distribution, this is a small share of the total transport cost. The unit price, in this case the ton price, was calculated in the following way;

$$Unit\ price = \frac{Trip\ Price}{Fill\ rate * Net\ weight}$$

Figure 1. Graph of price impact of increased weight

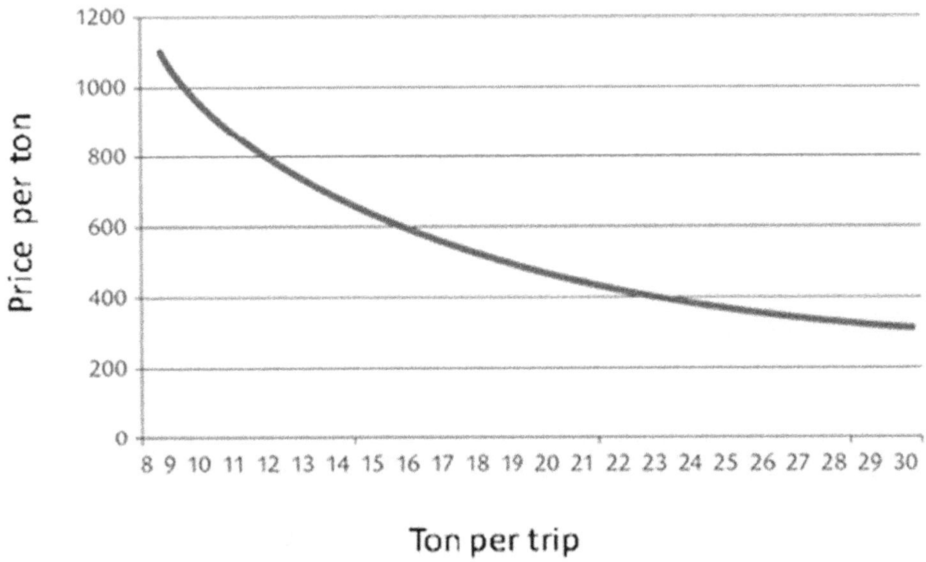

The fill rate has a huge impact on the ton price and to estimate the fill rate for a year is difficult and risky. If it is set to high, the transport provider can go bankrupt and if it is set to low the buyer risks paying more than necessary for their transport. With a ton price, the buyer has no incentives for to increase the productivity. In this case, they wanted to build a totally transparent price model without risk for either parts. To manage this, they decided to measure the actual fill rate averagely every quarter. That meant that they changes the price every third month based on the last quarters fill rate. With this system, the buyer had an incentive to increase the fill rate, higher fill rate lead to decreased prices. For the provider, this reduced his risk of calculating with a too low fill rate; on the other hand, he had no economic incentive to fill up the trucks. In the model, they had calculated with a profit margin and this became more certain with this new system.

From their survey (Bø, Grønland 2012) they asked both the transport buyer and the provider about to what extent they shared forecasts to predict the transported volume. The transport buyers answered that they shared forecast volume in 31% and on the transport out 28%. On the other hand, the providers answered that they received forecasts in 50% in their planning. Anyway, the survey also stated that in the supply chain, 72% of the cargo owners shared forecast with their supplier. The difference in numbers shows that there is still a potential of sharing information also between the transport buyer and the provider. It is also a question of how to use the forecast information and the quality of the information.

With the DST model, the food wholesaler and transport provider were able to simulate on different time parameter and consider the most important ones and again consider the possibility to change and rearrange the transport arrangement. For example, they saw that loading time was a significant cost factor and stood for 4,3% of the total cost. By changing the loading routines, it was possible to reduce the loading time per pallet from 3 to 2 minutes per pallet, and the effect of this reduction was totally 200.000 euro per annum. This number shows the importance of calculating with the right loading time, and the possible economic loss as a risk if they calculate with a too low number. The model also showed the importance of fill rate. By this new and exact insight, especially the wholesaler started to focus on aspect that could influence the fill rate. They identified tree crucial factors that affected the fill rate;

1. Customer service agreement
2. The height of the pallet
3. Fluctuations in demand during the week

For example, they calculated that if the wholesaler could encourage the customer, their own retailers, to avoid large fluctuations in their demand, a possible cost reduction was 24%. They had large fluctuations during a week, and it was possible for the customer to reduce the fluctuation. Especially Tuesday and Wednesday had low volume compared to the rest of the week. If they for example ordered everything within chips and toilet paper on these two days, they could smoothen out demand and increase the fill rate. The problem was that they had no incentives to do so; the transport cost was included in the product price.

To avoid any risk in this arrangement, the food wholesaler and provider decided on a cost based pricing model, a behaviour based contract, for the future. Within all the fluctuations in both cost and productivity, they decided to recalculate the prices every third month based on actual numbers.

Analysis like this is extremely difficult without a DST model. A DST-model can increase the quality of the decision-making. (Guimaraes, 2008). It is important to see the linkage between different decisions and their outcomes and the DST model may serve as a complexity moderator (March & Shapira, 1987) and an ability to use information properly. (Manuj & Sahin, 2011)

(Bø, Flygansvær, 2015) used the same DST-model to calculate the cost and cost drivers for two large Norwegian municipalities in a reverse supply chain picking up waste. Both municipalities had a new situation because they had to sort the waste in four fractions instead of two. Historically the municipalities were used to pick up residual and paper waste but in the new system, the inhabitants also had to sort out plastic and food waste. With this change, they had to develop a new transport collecting system. The new system should give the inhabitants a good service meaning that it should be easy to get rid of the waste. The two factors impacting the perceived service was closeness to the bins and the pick up frequency. At the same time, the municipalities had to keep the transport cost as low as possible and as environmentally friendly as possible. They had to decide on types of trucks, one chamber or two chambers, compression levels and the kerbside system. This was a very complex transport situation and needed a detailed analysis to find the best solution. Unfortunately, they based their decisions on best guesses and choose the lowest transport bid with a limited transport analysis. At the time they choose the new system, they did not use a DST to support their choices, and in 2017, the transport company who won the bin for Oslo municipality went bankrupt. This was after a terrible situation in Oslo with waste all over the city and complaining inhabitants. The researchers used the DST model in their case study after the decision was taken. By using the DST-model, it was possible to analyse both costs and time parameters and different solutions. For example, was loading time per bin an important cost driver. A full truck to pick up waste managed 1100 bins on one trip, in one of the systems. None of the actors, neither the buyer nor the provider, knew in forehand the loading time per bin. This was a very new system for them to separate the waste in four fractions so they just had to estimate the loading time per bin as a best guess system, and it was estimated to be 20 seconds per bin. The problem was that in some places the bins were placed closed to each other and in some places the driver had to walk a distance to pick them up. The calculation showed that a variation of 5 second in loading time per bin resulted in 387 hours per truck per year. By using the model they simulated on different pick up frequencies, different fill rates and on different time parameters. All of them were crucial for the cost. Without this insight, it is hard to consider a transport bid properly.

Within these two examples, it is showed how important it is to do proper decisions based on proper calculations. In classical decision theory, risk is most commonly conceived as reflecting variation in the distribution of possible outcomes, their likelihoods, and their subjective values. (March & Shapira, 1987)

There are many variations within transportation during the year that will influence the outcomes. Both cost and time parameters are uncertain and will vary during a year. In an arrangement when the transport price is set for a year, one part will always carry the risk due to possible productivity depending on the chosen price format. All theories of choice assume that decision makers prefer larger expected returns to smaller ones, based on a constant risk (Lindley & Lindley, 1985). From the two empirical cases above, both the wholesaler and the municipalities, none of them had the perfect insight to actually consider the economical risk.

Figure 2. How contract types impacts the need for information and the risk

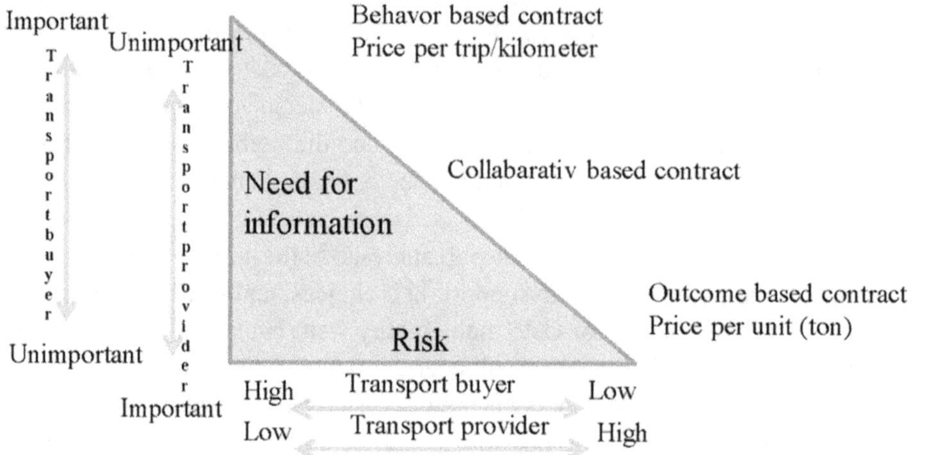

The providers had an overview of the cost parameters but neither the time processes nor the fill rate. From (Bø & Grønland, 2012) survey they measured that only 38% of the transport buyers and only 20% of the providers measured fill rate in their transport arrangements. This shows a low focus on an extremely important risk element in a transport arrangement. This might be a sign of low competence in the transport area and that decision makers have not adjusted their work accordingly with the increased complexity in the supply chain. (Bø, Flygansvær 2015) Too reduce the risk in a transport buyer-provider relationship a transparent relationship is necessary. Transparency leads to proper cost insights and helps the decision maker to make conscious choices.

How can transparency lead to closer collaboration between the transport buyer and provider?

There is a need for a changed relationship between transport buyer and transport provider from a short turn arms length transactions to a long-term relationship. (Harrington, 1997) (Hannon, 2005a) Both parties should be willing to share proper information in order to obtain an effective transport solution and reduce risk for either part. From (Hammervoll & Bø, 2010) the transparent cost model influenced the relationship between the transport buyer and the service provider. The starting point of this development was the statement from the provider that they were unable to make profit unless they received a better price for their services. They claimed that increased costs and reduced productivity was the reason. The provider wonted just to increase the price, but the wholesaler, together with their consultant decided to do a proper analysis of the cost and the transport price. This was in the beginning scaring for the provider because they were not familiar with this kind of calculations. Through the developing period of the DST model, the provider changes their attitude. They saw that the results from the model gave a right picture of the transport situation and found it interesting to simulate on different parameters to see how they affected the ton price. Since they had the best practical picture of the transport situation, they started to suggest new and better ways of solving the transport. They saw for example that they used a lot of time in the grocery stores just to tidy up so it was possible to deliver the goods. In the agreement with the stores, this should not be necessary. By simulating on fixed time per customer in the DST model, they both saw the possible time and cost savings if the stores tided up before deliveries.

They also found it possible to combine inbound and outbound transport on the same trucks, by simulating on the fill rate, they found a huge economic potential to do this, and found practical solutions to be able to do this. It is much more complicated to combine the inbound and outbound transport in the same system, but driven by the huge economical potential, they managed this practical solution together. Based on their survey, (Bø, Grønland, 2012) they found that only 17% of the transport buyers combined inbound and outbound transport on the same truck. This might be a result of lack of knowledge about its potential and the complexity within the decision.

In the situation with the waste transport, the DST model was used after the agreement was signed. The DST model was used to recalculate the prices in research purpose. The transport provider was not very interested in giving the researchers the cost parameters. Anyway, the price was set for a year and any efforts on making a more effective transport would not influence the price.

Effective communication and sharing of information is a question of trust between the partners. (Anderson & Narus, 1990) (Zhou & Benton, 2007) (Gunasekaran, Reichhart, & Holweg, 2007)

The transport buyer have to trust the provider due to the cost parameters, and both need to agree on the time parameters. The provider need to trust the buyer, that all the calculations in the model are correct. Specially in measuring time parameters, it is impossible to cover all aspects. For example, special delays like accidents, weather conditions, closed roads etc is something that is necessary to put into the model and you just have to trust the provider in deciding its meaning.

How can agency theory contribute to a wider understanding of the relationship between transport buyer and the provider?

Transaction cost analysis (Jones, 1983) forms the basis for the decision whether to buy transport services or owning the transport function yourself. The degree of specific investments related to transport arrangement will affect the relationship between the parties. High degree of specific investments, both through investments in equipment as well as through the expertise around the specific arrangement will establish a closer relationship between the parties and they will be more depentant on each other. Transport equipment like waste trucks, with a expensive specialized trailer with two chambers with compression, can hardly be used to anything else than waste transport.

Transport of food are specialized with both a cooler and a freezer part in the trailer, but it is both possible to turn off the cooler and freezer system to use the truck as a command truck, and the total transport marked for food is large. This means that the degree of specific investment is different in a waste transport situation compared with a food transport system and must in some way influence the contract and relationship between the buyer and provider. Research indicates that the more firm specific the outsourced activity becomes, the more difficult it will be to please the customer. (Logan, 2000)

Agency theory is well suited to study supply chain relationship, (Wilding, Wagner, Fayezi, O'Loughlin, & Zutshi, 2012) but little attention has given the relationship between transport buyer and provider. All kind of outsourcing is based on an agency-principal relationship and when outsourcing a transport arrangement, the transport buyer will act as a principal and the provider as the agent. The main focus is how to share the risk between the partners and how this can be set up in a contract. (Bergen et al., 1992; Eisenhardt, 1989) Based on agency theory two contract types are relevant to discuss; 1) a behaviour based contract or 2) an outcome based contract. The choice of the contact type must be based on their insight to information about the transport arrangement and their preferences to risk. Risk aversion by the principal and goal conflict between the principal and agent are negatively related to behaviour based contracts and positively related to outcome based contracts. (Logan, 2000) The question is what kind of information the provider has within the cost and the practical part of the arrangement and to what extent this transport arrangement only is based on one provider or many in the same arrangement. The complexity of getting insights to the arrangement with many providers in one arrangement is much higher and more or less impossible. In those cases an outcome based contact is relevant. In the further discussions, the transport arrangement is based on one agent and one provider. The agency problem arises when the two parties involved have different goals and when it is difficult for the provider to measure the agents' actions. The goal setting in a transport buyer-provider relationship can easily be set as different due to the fact that the buyer wants a low price and the provider wants a high price. Their preferences to risk might also differ in the relationship. The question about in what way it is possible for the provider to measure the agent's actions are more interesting. The agent is operating on behalf of the provider, normally picking up loads one place and delivers to another place. To get insight to the cost and time parameters they need a transparent focus as discussed above. To obtain insight to the cost parameters, it can either be shared between the parties based on the actual numbers or be collected in the open marked. If the agent is not willing to inform the provider about his costs, the provider can get insight to the necessary cost parameters from the marked in general. They have to contact different suppliers on trucks, MRO, diesel etc and try to get a right picture of the cost parameters. The agent might have different prices or might for example have higher discount on diesel than the provider use in their calculations. In a case were the principal and agent have decided not to share this kind of information, this difference is either an extra profit for the agent or a potential loss. On the other hand, if the principal and agent agree on sharing cost parameters and the agent still hides his actual price, for example a very high discount on diesel, he is acting opportunistically. Pre contractual opportunism is hidden information before you sign a contract, for example that the diesel discount is higher than they say. Another situation is that the agent is telling the truth about the diesel price at the moment they sign the contract, but during the contact period they manage to increase the discount with the diesel supplier because of big volumes. If they choose not to tell the provider about this increased discount it is post contractual opportunism. To avoid this problem the provider needs constantly to have attention on the cost development.

The time parameters are more complicated. In an established transport arrangement with a long experience, the numbers are known but not necessary measured in detail. Whether only the agent knows the number or both depends on how the provider measures the transport arrangement. The numbers due to loading and unloading time, speed etc have different meaning in different arrangements. For example, speed is more important on a long distance trip than on a short distance trip and loading and unloading time is the opposite. If the provider wants insight to these numbers, they either can get them from the agent or measure them themselves. If they get them from the agent, they need to be sure that the agent not is acting opportunistically and the relationship must be built on mutual trust. In the interest of the agent, they know that if they can convince the principal that the numbers are higher than they actually are they will increase their income. On the other hand, they know that if the numbers are too optimistically they might incur losses, ref loading example in both cases above. The importance of getting the right information is crucial, and sometimes complicated for both sides. Even for established arrangement, there might be variations in the numbers during a year. The transported volume might vary and there will always be a possibility to do things more effectively. As seen in the two cases above, small changes in the loading routines had a huge influence on the cost. It is hard to get the agent to always inform the provider of new and more effective routines. In new transport arrangement, and especially in the waste transport situation, there are great uncertainties due to the time parameters before a contract is signed. Sometimes it is also impossible to get insights to this numbers before you sign a contract, and the learning curve effect is often high. This means that during the first part of the agreement, the provider will often find new and more effective ways of handling the goods, and this increased efficiency will affect the cost. It could also be the opposite; the calculated efficiency is too high, meaning that the provider is not able to manage within the contract price. To sign a contract based on all this uncertainties includes a lot of risk.

To reduce this risk there are two possibilities; 1) choose the right price format or 2 choose the right contract type. The price format can be either a fixed price per trip/km or a unit price. The risk will shift from one part to the other part due to the price format depending on the fill rate of the trucks.

Table 2. Price format and risk matrix

Risk **Price format**	**Low**	**High**
Trip price	Agent	Principal
Unit price	Principal	Agent

Whatever format you choose, the price must be calculated properly.

Behaviour based or an outcome based contract will also cover the risk differently. In a behaviour based contract all necessary information are shared and any changes during the contract period will affect the transport price. For example an increased diesel price during the year will immediately be updated in the contract and the price adjusted. In an outcome based contract the prices are set for a year, and all possible fluctuations needs to be considered and covered in the price.

Table 3. Contract type and risk matrix

Risk **Contract type**	**Low**	**High**
Behaviour based	Agent- Principal	None
Outcome based	Depending on the price format	Depending on the price format

In the two cases, the food wholesaler and the municipalities they used different contract types. In the food wholesaler situation, they started from scratch and built up a behaviour-based contract. It took them more than a year and it was not easy. In the beginning, the agent behaved very opportunistically and was not at all interested in giving away his numbers. He had to document all his costs and they used a lot of time and effort to agree on the time parameters. The agent in this case had a long experience with transport and during this period the two parts build up tighter relationship built on trust, step by step. The agent saw that this way of working together was very satisfactory and changes his attitude.

In the waste transport situation, the researcher tested the transparent DST-model on the established transport arrangement. Their agreement was based on an outcome based contract with a fixed price per bin set for a year. In this case, they could only advise the municipalities whether the price was accurate, meaning that the price should cover the cost based on a descent productivity. It was very hard to get insight to the information about the cost and time parameters. The municipalities had no information about this numbers; they had negotiated a transport price per bin and did not understand why they should care about this numbers. Even throw they were very helpful to the researcher and gave them a contact person at the agents. The agent were not interested in this research and acted very opportunistically towards the researchers. It was obvious that the numbers they came up with was wrong, and the researchers had to more or less collect the cost data and measure the time parameters themselves. This opportunistically behaviour was probably to hide a high profit, but this was impossible for the researcher to determine because the agreed prices with the municipalities were secret. Due to all the uncertainties in this arrangement, the municipalities should have chosen a behaviour-based contract.

Table 4. Contract comparison between two buyers

	The wholesaler	**The municipality**
Contract type	Behaviour based	Outcome based
Price format	Unit based (NOK/ton)	Unit based (NOK/bin)
Use of DST model	As basis for prising	As a tool for calculating the price
In charge of organizing the transport	The wholesaler	The transport provider
Specific Investment	Partly	Yes
Opportunistically behaviour	Pre opportunistically	Post opportunistically

Both this two transport arrangements are large measured in volume and in kroner. They are also both complex in the sense that there are many possible outcomes due to different variables. The variables are not constant during the year and have important influence on the price. In an outcome based contract you need to cover the risk by charging a risk premium based on an assumption. In a situation with low complexity, small changes during a year and principal has full control of the agents actions an outcome based contract is relevant.

(Bø & Grønland, 2012) did a survey too see how increased cooperation in the supply chain could lead to increased efficiency. They found in their survey that the transport buying companies over estimated their yearly volume by 45% in signing their transport contract in order to obtain a lower price. This meant that the transport companies build up over capacity and were not able to utilize the transport equipment as they planned for and had estimated the price for. In their survey, they also stated that this had no economic consequence for the transport buyer. This is an example of pre contractual opportunism from the provider's side.

To prevent pre contractual opportunism in a transport arrangement a transparency issue must be a part of the specification for bid from the transport buyer. All necessary numbers must be specified in the bid to prevent this action. With todays IT systems it is possible to measure all the time parameter. Mobile IT solution like a PDA connected with GPS makes it possible to follow the moves on a truck. From their survey (Bø, Grønland, 2012) they found out that 60% of the providers can do their own tracing through status and map systems, but they do not use them as a part of the contract with the transport buyer.

FINDINGS

The complexity in the supply chain and transport arrangement has increased and it is therefore a need for a new approach within transport analysis. There is a huge economical risk in signing a transport contract, because of all uncertainties within cost and time parameters. By using a transparent cost model to analyse both the cost and time parameter you are able to visualize the importance of each of them in different transport arrangements. This insight to the variables and its importance gives an opportunity to better know how to increase the transport efficiency. Depending on how you organize the transport and the price format there are different incentives to increase the efficiency. By a totally transparent perspective a collaborative approach is more naturally, the buyers see the potential savings by all actions and the providers will have a constant profit during the year without any concerns about unexpected changes. A transparent approach will reduce opportunistic behaviour and reduce any risk in the relationship. In large transport arrangement, with one buyer and one provider, a behaviour based contract is recommended.

REFERENCES

Anderson, J. C., & Narus, J. A. (1990). A model of distributor firm and manufacturer firm working partnerships. *The Journal of Marketing*, 42-58.

Armstrong, E. (2006). Buying–and selling–transportation. *Paperboard Packaging*, *91*(9), 40–42.

Bergen, M., Dutta, S., & Walker, O. C. Jr. (1992). Agency Relationships in Marketing: A review of the Implications and Applications of Agency and Related Theories. *Journal of Marketing*, *56*(July), 1–24. doi:10.1177/002224299205600301

Bergmann, R., & Rawlings, C. (1998). Transport management. In J. Gattoma (Ed.), *Strategic supply chain alignment: best practice in supply chain management* (Vol. 1, pp. 369–380). Gower.

Bø, E., & Grønland, S. E. (2012). Increased cooperation in the supply chains: how to reduce the need for transportation? In H. C. Dreyer & T. Foss (Eds.), Intelligent goods in transport systems. Trondheim: NTNU, Faculty of Engineering Science and Technology: Akademika Publishing.

Bø, E., & Hammervoll, T. (2010). Cost-based pricing of transportation servies in a wholesaler-carrier relationship: an MS Excel spreadsheet decision tool. *International Journal of Logistics: Research and Applications, 13*(3), 197-210.

Bowman, R. (1994). *Rookie transportation buyers*. Distribution.

Christopher, M. (2012). Managing Supply Chain Complexity: Identifying the Requisite Skills. *Supply chain Forum. International Journal (Toronto, Ont.)*, *13*(2), 4–9.

Eisenhardt, K. E. (1989). Agency Theory: An Assessment and Review. *Academy of Management Review*, *14*(1), 57–74. doi:10.5465/amr.1989.4279003

Guajardo, J. A., Cohen, M. A., Kim, S.-H., & Netessine, S. (2011). Impact of performance-based contracting on product reliability: An empirical analysis. guimaraes, T., Igbaria,M. (2008). characteristics of the research on reverse logistics. *International Journal of Production Research*.

Gunasekaran, A., Reichhart, A., & Holweg, M. (2007). Creating the customer-responsive supply chain: A reconciliation of concepts. *International Journal of Operations & Production Management*, *27*(11), 1144–1172. doi:10.1108/01443570710830575

Halldórsson, A., & Skjøtt-Larsen, T. (2004). Developing logistics competencies through third party logistics relationships. *International Journal of Operations & Production Management*, *24*(2), 192–206. doi:10.1108/01443570410514885

Hammervoll, T., & Bø, E. (2010). Shipper- Carrier Integration - overcomming the transparency problem through trust and collaboration. *European Journal of Marketing*, *44*(7/8), 1121–1139. doi:10.1108/03090561011047553

Hannon, D. (2005a). *Negotiating skills a must for logistics buyers*. Purchasing.

Harrington, L. H. (1997). *The ABC's of Motor Carrier Economics*. Transportation & Distribution.

Jones, G. R. (1983). Transaction costs, property rights, and organizational culture: An exchange perspective. *Administrative Science Quarterly*, *28*(3), 454–467. doi:10.2307/2392252

Lamming, R. C., Caldwell, N. D., Harrison, D. A., & Phillips, W. (2001). Transparency in supply relationships: Concept and practice. *The Journal of Supply Chain Management*, *37*(3), 4–10. doi:10.1111/j.1745-493X.2001.tb00107.x

Langley, C. J. J. (2007). Collaboration: the only way forward. Capgemini, 2007 Third-Party Logistics. Results and Findings of the 12th Annual Study, 44.

Lindley, D. V., & Lindley, D. V. (1985). *Making decisions*. Wiley.

Logan, M. S. (2000). Using Agency Theory to Design Successful Outsourcing Relationships. *International Journal of Logistics Management*, *11*(2), 21–32. doi:10.1108/09574090010806137

Manuj, I., & Sahin, F. (2011). A model of supply chain and supply chain decision-making complexity. *International Journal of Physical Distribution & Logistics Management*, *41*(5), 511–549. doi:10.1108/09600031111138844

March, J. G., & Shapira, Z. (1987). Managerial perspectives on risk and risk taking. *Management Science*, *33*(11), 1404–1418. doi:10.1287/mnsc.33.11.1404

Mongelluzzo, B. (1999). Choose service over lower rates, exporters told. *Journal of Commerce,* (11), 12.

Morash, E. A. (1987). Using transportation intermediaries for industrial purchasing decisions. *Journal of Business and Industrial Marketing*, *2*(4), 15–27. doi:10.1108/eb006039

Rushton, A., Croucher, P., & Baker, P. (2006). *The Handbook of Logistics and Distribution Management* (3rd ed.).

Sahay, B., Halldórsson, Á., & Skjøtt-Larsen, T. (2006). Dynamics of relationship governance in TPL arrangements-a dyadic perspective. *International Journal of Physical Distribution & Logistics Management, 36*(7), 490–506. doi:10.1108/09600030610684944

Smyrlis, L. (2005). Are you employing the right strategies to control rising truck rates? *Canadian Transportation Logistics, 208*(4), 4.

Somapa, S., Cools, M., & Dullaert, W. (2012). Unlocking the potential of time-driven activity-based costing for small logistics companies. *International Journal of Logistics Research and Applications, 15*(5), 303–322. doi:10.1080/13675567.2012.742043

Svensson, G. (2002). A conceptual framework of vulnerability in firms' inbound and outbound logistics flows. *International Journal of Physical Distribution & Logistics Management, 32*(2), 110–134. doi:10.1108/09600030210421723

Trunic, P. A. (2006, Dec.). Price matters. *Logistics Today,* 24–25.

Wilding, R., Wagner, B., Fayezi, S., O'Loughlin, A., & Zutshi, A. (2012). Agency theory and supply chain management: A structured literature review. *Supply Chain Management, 17*(5), 556–570. doi:10.1108/13598541211258618

Zhou, H., & Benton, W. Jr. (2007). Supply chain practice and information sharing. *Journal of Operations Management, 25*(6), 1348–1365. doi:10.1016/j.jom.2007.01.009

Chapter 5
Methodologies for Achieving Environmental Sustainability and Improving Customer Response

Raj V. Amonkar
https://orcid.org/0000-0003-1601-512X
Goa Institute of Management, India

ABSTRACT

Environmental sustainability and customer response times will continue to remain the vanguard of every business. Being energy efficient is a step towards achieving environmental sustainability. The six-sigma methodology has been adopted by organizations for systematic conservation of energy. Customer responses can be improved by reducing the product supply lead time. The value stream mapping methodology has been used by several organizations to reduce product supply lead time with encouraging results. This chapter describes the use of methodologies such as six sigma and value stream mapping for reducing energy and improving the supply lead time respectively by means of two real life examples. The names of the respective organizations are disguised to protect confidentiality.

DOI: 10.4018/978-1-7998-2867-9.ch005

INTRODUCTION

ABC Example

In the past, environmental problems, such as toxic waste, poisoned drinking water, poor air quality, and climate change, were viewed as quality-of-life issues. Now, these are seen as survival issues. Business are increasingly concerned about global warming and pollution. Stringent environmental regulations, particularly in developed nations, are being enforced. Business organizations are under pressure to reduce their carbon footprint (the amount of carbon di oxide generated by their operations and supply chains) and to operate sustainable processes. Sustainability refers to service and production processes, that use resources in ways that do not harm ecological systems that support both current and future human existence. One of the objectives of this chapter is to explain the initiatives taken by ABC India -the Indian arm of ABC's global business of infrastructure and energy solutions, automation and software, and medical imaging equipment- for creating a sustainable environment

XYZ Example

Most businesses realize that, to prosper, they must view customers, suppliers, facility locations, and competitors in global terms. When a firm's operations are scattered globally, customer response times can be longer. Regardless of the area of the world, the challenge is to produce services or products that can compete in a global market, and to design the processes that can make it happen. The other objective of this chapter is to present the ingenuities adopted by XYZ-a leading global provider of traceability systems- to reduce the lead time for supply of its products by improvements in the product design phase.

BACKGROUND

ABC Example

With a focus on electrification, automation and digitalization, ABC India stands for engineering excellence, innovation, and reliability. As one of the world's biggest producers of energy-efficient, resource-saving technologies, ABC is a pioneer in infrastructure and energy solutions, as well as automation and software for industry. The company is also a leader in medical imaging equipment, laboratory diagnostics, and clinical IT. ABC also provides business-to-business financial solutions, rail automation and wind power solutions. ABC India manufactures steam turbines, turbo compressors, high-voltage switchgear (circuit breakers, disconnections and gas-insulated switchgear), switchboards, remote monitoring systems (RMS), fire detectors and suppression systems, motors and generators, relays and Smart Grid systems, transformers, and advanced medical imaging equipment. The factories replicate global, best-in-class manufacturing systems and practices. It also has a facility to overhaul and repair gas turbines, compressor blades and rotors. For over six decades, ABC India has been the preferred technology solutions provider, conceptualizing and implementing various flagship projects in Mobility, Energy Management, Power and Gas, Smart Cities, Intelligent Infrastructure, Industrial Applications, Healthcare and Smart Financing. Sustainability is a key pillar of the corporate strategy at ABC, with the three areas – environment, economy and society – governing all the activities at the organization.

XYZ Example

Founded in 1989, XYZ is a multinational, leading global provider of traceability system practicing responsible human capitalism. The Company's mission is to use its innovative technologies to help create better world. Namely, its renowned solution ensures the quality of consumer health products and help stop counterfeiting of pharmaceuticals and medical devices throughout the world. In addition, XYZ is adapting its technologies to create efficiencies in various other sector - from health-related industries to smart manufacturing and more, all can benefit from global traceability. This coupled with the increased competition due to the increased market size has resulted in further shrinkage of the lead times.

Some of the Current Global Challenges are as mentioned below:

Competition

- Shrinking market share
- Lower margins
- Shorter product life cycles
- Higher variety
- Smaller volumes to depreciate fixed costs
- Globalization is an imperative

Globalization

- Goes beyond imports and exports
- Global markets and global sources
- Potential for increased markets
- Increased potential for lower costs, but increased complexity due to international regulations and other differences

- Greater risk due to currency fluctuations

Customer Preferences

- Must manufacture what customer wants.
- Need to reduce response and lead times
- Logistics needs to be better integrated with the entire supply chain
- Need to keep a tight control on costs
- Need to bring new products to the market faster

Technology

- Technology has to be harnessed. Don't let it control you
- Inefficient utilization of technology is expensive
- Technology includes approaches such as TQM, VSM, TPS, TPM, Six Sigma etc.

Government Regulations

- Within a country, there may be laws pertaining to inter-state commerce
- Environmental responsibility – green production
- Labor laws
- Customs and other duties
- Tax laws
- Currency exchange rates
- Drug Regulation

Uncertainty

- Growing uncertainty in the global market with greater access to information
- Uncertainty has an impact on production and delivery schedules and on the inventory levels
- Some of the uncertainty is due to increased climatic events, tsunamis, earthquakes, etc.
- There is also a growing threat due to the increased incidence of terrorism and piracy
- Logistics systems need to be able to respond to changing situations and conditions

Environmental Concerns

- Reverse logistics is assuming greater importance as part of a company's logistical activities

- Fuel emissions and spills and leaks in the ocean are receiving more focus
- Companies are assuming a more responsible position in regard to the environment
- Better planning, measurement (emissions), control and use of sustainable technologies will have an impact on logistics

MAIN FOCUS OF THE CHAPTER[1]

Issues, Controversies, Problems

ABC Example

ABC has put in place various initiatives for creating a sustainable environment. This includes not only making employees, suppliers, business partners and customer's environmentally-conscious but also encouraging all stakeholders to choose approaches that support sustainable environment which includes being energy efficient. These approaches are consistent with contemporary best practices (Olatz, Beatriz, & Javier, 2019), (Rajagopalan, Andamon, & Moore, 2019), (Danish, Senjyu, MatinIbrahimi, Ahmadi, & Howlader, 2018). ABC set norms for energy consumption across its various manufacturing units globally. It was found that the energy (electricity) consumption in Example of one of its unit was higher than the stipulated norms. It was imperative for ABC to address this issue pertaining to one of its unit.to determine the major consumers of energy and look for opportunities to reduce consumption of energy. In September 2015, ABC announced its intention to cut the carbon footprint of its operative business to half by 2020 and to become climate neutral by 2030.

XYZ Example

In light of global competition, XYZ experienced several challenges due to customer preferences such as the need to reduce response time and lead time by bring new products faster to the market. XYZ envisaged several non-value adding activities in the design or product development phase of its business process. Therefore, XYZ decided to work on a focused project in 2019 to improve the product development or design stage of its business process. The importance of product development from the point of view of response time is underpinned by extant literature (Sivakumara & Fengb, 2019), (Thornton, Henneberg, Leischnig, & Naudé, 2019), (Horvat, Behdani, Fogliano, & Luning, 2019).

SOLUTIONS AND RECOMMENDATIONS

ABC Example

ABC's intent to reduce energy and consequently cut the carbon footprint in a time bound manner needed a disciplined, data-driven, and statistics- based approach. The six-sigma methodology is often used for systematic resolution of issues pertaining to energy consumption (Razali & Afthanorhan, 2014), (Yuvamitra, Guiberteau, & Kozman, 2014). The six-sigma methodology was therefore used by ABC for one of its manufacturing units. to resolve the issues of energy consumption This methodology comprises of five stages which are Define, Measure, Analyze, Improve, and Control (DMAIC) (refer Appendix 1 for details of DMAIC) The methodology used is further described as follows:

Define

The main objective was to reduce the electrical consumption in the manufacturing unit. Based on process mapping shown in Figure 1, the government electricity board is the supplier of electricity to ABC's unit. The electricity usage involves Process 1, Process 2, Process 3, Chiller and Office.

Measure

The objective was to evaluate the electrical component that has the highest electrical consumption. For this purpose, an energy audit was carried out which entailed an energy balance and data collection in terms of energy consumption for the three time zones in light of the differential tariff fixed by the government electricity board for the three time zones. The data are shown in Table 1 and Table 2. The details of the process used for energy balance is shown in Appendix2.

From the data in Table 1, it is found that the Chiller is the major consumer of electricity. It was also evident from Table 2 that the major consumption of electricity was during Zone A and that there was an opportunity to transfer some of the operations from Zone A to Zone C which was the minimum tariff Zone.

Analyze

The objective was to analyze the Chiller operation in detail and identify opportunities for reduction in Chiller energy consumption.

Figure 1. Process map for electricity supply and consumption

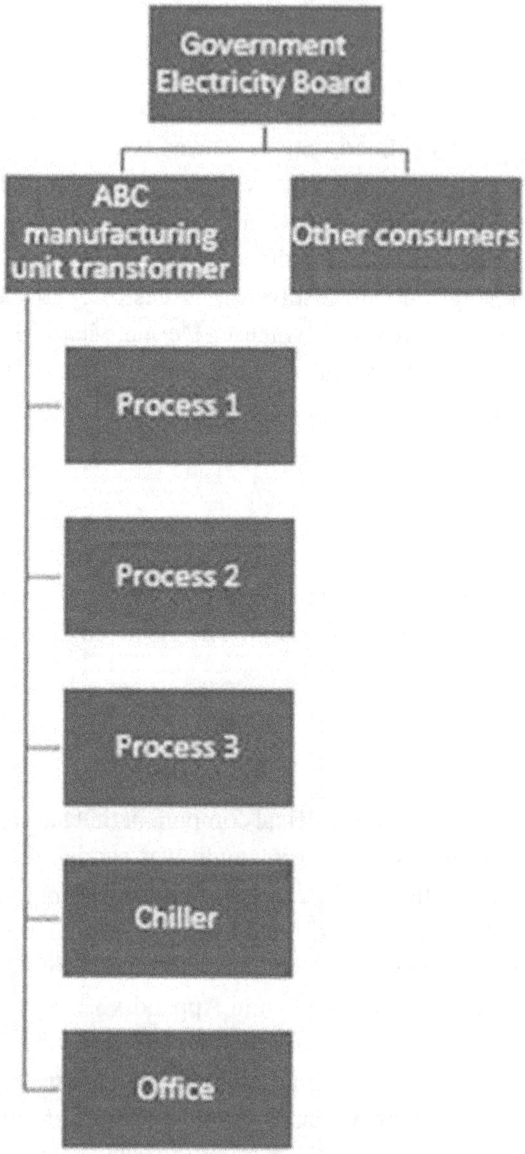

The data of energy consumption based on daily operation of the Chiller during the three time zones was obtained. The data is reproduced in Table 3 a,3b and 3c.

Based on the analysis of the data in Table 3a, Table 3b, and Table 3b it is found that the major energy consumption is during Zone A and that there was room for improvement in terms of shifting the operation to Zone C.

Table 1. Energy balance

	kWh (3 hours log)	%
Energy supply	1951.37	100%
Energy consumption		
Process 1	313.9	16%
Process 2	277.69	14%
Process 3	148.51	8%
Chiller	667.42	34%
Office	371.08	19%
Unaccounted Energy Consumption	162.41	9%
Total Electrical Consumption	**1951.37**	**100%**

Table 2. The tariff for electricity purchased

Time of the day	Tariff (INR per kWh)
6:00am-6:00pm (A-Zone)	4.30
6:00pm-11:00pm (B-Zone)	5.16
11:00pm-6:00am (C-Zone)	3.87

Table 3a. Chiller daily energy consumption during Zone A

CURRENT CHILLER SYSTEM:

FOR ZONE - A : 6.00 AM to 6.00 PM

Months	Avr. Load	% of load	Peak Load	TOTAL TRH	Power Consumption		Unit Rate	Total Amount
	In TRH		1877.28		IKW/TR	Total KWH	In Rs.	In Rs.
16-Oct	117.0	0.75	1408	43647	1.54	67216	4.3	289029
16-Nov	113.0	0.72	1360	40795	1.54	62824	4.3	270143
16-Dec	113.0	0.72	1360	42155	1.54	64918	4.3	279148
17-Jan	112.0	0.72	1348	41782	1.54	64344	4.3	276677
17-Feb	111.0	0.71	1336	37401	1.54	57598	4.3	247671
17-Mar	132.0	0.85	1588	49242	1.54	75833	4.3	326084
17-Apr	145.0	0.93	1745	52347	1.54	80615	4.3	346643
17-May	156.4	1.00	1883	58360	1.54	89874	4.3	386459
17-Jun	124.3	0.80	1496	44874	1.54	69106	4.3	297157
17-Jul	128.6	0.82	1547	47963	1.54	73863	4.3	317611
17-Aug	125.0	0.80	1504	46616	1.54	71789	4.3	308693
17-Sep	121.0	0.78	1456	43683	1.54	67272	4.3	289268
	YEARLY TOTAL - ZONE A			548865		845251		3634581

Table 3b. Chiller daily energy consumption during Zone B

FOR ZONE - B : 6.00 PM to 11.00 PM

Months	Avr. Load In TRH	% of load	Peak Load 580	TOTAL TRH	Power Consumption IKW/TR	Total KWH	Unit Rate In Rs.	Total Amount In Rs.
16-Oct	87.0	0.75	435	13485	1.40	18879	5.16	97416
16-Nov	84.0	0.72	420	12600	1.40	17640	5.16	91022
16-Dec	84.0	0.72	420	13020	1.40	18228	5.16	94056
17-Jan	83.0	0.72	415	12865	1.40	18011	5.16	92937
17-Feb	83.0	0.72	415	11620	1.40	16268	5.16	83943
17-Mar	98.0	0.84	490	15190	1.40	21266	5.16	109733
17-Apr	108.0	0.93	540	16200	1.40	22680	5.16	117029
17-May	116.0	1.00	580	17980	1.40	25172	5.16	129888
17-Jun	92.0	0.79	460	13800	1.40	19320	5.16	99691
17-Jul	96.0	0.83	480	14880	1.40	20832	5.16	107493
17-Aug	93.0	0.80	465	14415	1.40	20181	5.16	104134
17-Sep	90.0	0.78	450	13500	1.40	18900	5.16	97524
	YEARLY TOTAL - ZONE B			169555		237377		1224865

Table 3c. Chiller daily energy consumption during Zone C

FOR ZONE - C : 11.00 PM to 6.00 AM

	Months	Avr. Load In TRH	% of load	Peak Load 812	TOTAL TRH	Power Consumption IKW/TR	Total KWH	Unit Rate In Rs.	Total Amount In Rs.
	16-Oct	87.0	0.75	609	18879	1.40	26431	3.87	102286
	16-Nov	84.0	0.72	588	17640	1.40	24696	3.87	95574
	16-Dec	84.0	0.72	588	18228	1.40	25519	3.87	98759
	17-Jan	83.0	0.72	581	18011	1.40	25215	3.87	97584
	17-Feb	83.0	0.72	581	16268	1.40	22775	3.87	88140
	17-Mar	98.0	0.84	686	21266	1.40	29772	3.87	115219
	17-Apr	108.0	0.93	756	22680	1.40	31752	3.87	122880
	17-May	116.0	1.00	812	25172	1.40	35241	3.87	136382
	17-Jun	92.0	0.79	644	19320	1.40	27048	3.87	104676
	17-Jul	96.0	0.83	672	20832	1.40	29165	3.87	112868
	17-Aug	93.0	0.80	651	20181	1.40	28253	3.87	109341
	17-Sep	90.0	0.78	630	18900	1.40	26460	3.87	102400
		YEARLY TOTAL - ZONE C			237377		332328		1286109
	Additional Yearly Cost of DG operation - D								2000000
A	YEARLY OPERATING COST OF CONVENTIONAL SYSTEM (A+B+C+D)				955797		1414956		8145555

Improve

The objective was to make improvements based on the prior analysis. ABC installed a Thermal Energy Storage System (TES) so that the Chiller operated during Zone C when the tariff is low and the energy stored in the TES was used for cooling purpose during Zone A and Zone B. The resultant savings are shown in Table 4. The details of TES and TES project implementation plan are shown in Appendix 3 and Appendix 4 respectively. The project commenced in April 2018 and was completed in September 2018. The annual energy consumed by the chiller could be reduced by around 35%.

Table 4. Savings due to installation of the TES

FOR ZONE - C : 11.00 PM to 6.00 AM (Chiller Operation for Cooling : 80 TR)

	Months	Avr. Load In TRH	% of load	Peak Load 812	TOTAL TRH	Power Consumption IKW/TR	Power Consumption Total KWH	Unit Rate In Rs.	Total Amount In Rs.
	16-Oct	87.0	0.75	609	18879	0.70	13215	3.87	51143
	16-Nov	84.0	0.72	588	17640	0.70	12348	3.87	47787
	16-Dec	84.0	0.72	588	18228	0.70	12760	3.87	49380
	17-Jan	83.0	0.72	581	18011	0.70	12608	3.87	48792
	17-Feb	83.0	0.72	581	16268	0.70	11388	3.87	44070
	17-Mar	98.0	0.84	686	21266	0.70	14886	3.87	57610
	17-Apr	108.0	0.93	756	22680	0.70	15876	3.87	61440
	17-May	116.0	1.00	812	25172	0.70	17620	3.87	68191
	17-Jun	92.0	0.79	644	19320	0.70	13524	3.87	52338
	17-Jul	96.0	0.83	672	20832	0.70	14582	3.87	56434
	17-Aug	93.0	0.80	651	20181	0.70	14127	3.87	54670
	17-Sep	90.0	0.78	630	19530	0.70	13671	3.87	52907
	YEARLY TOTAL - ZONE C (Chiller Cooling)				**238007**		**166605**		**644761**
B	**YEARLY OPERATING COST OF TES SYSTEM /Optimized Chiller**				**956447**		**741357**		**2869053**
C	**YEARLY SAVING BY TESS and Optimized chiller for Night Load (11.00pm-6.00am)**						**673599**		**5276502**

Control

The objective was to regularly monitor and control energy consumption. ABC installed a Building Management system (BMS) to continuously monitor all the parameters of the Chiller control the parameters through sensors, pressure transmitters and automatic actuator valves.

The system generated dashboards to enable the operators to perform analysis on day to day basis and to track the Chillier performance. A typical dashboard is shown in Figure 2.

Figure 2. Typical Dashboard from the BMS

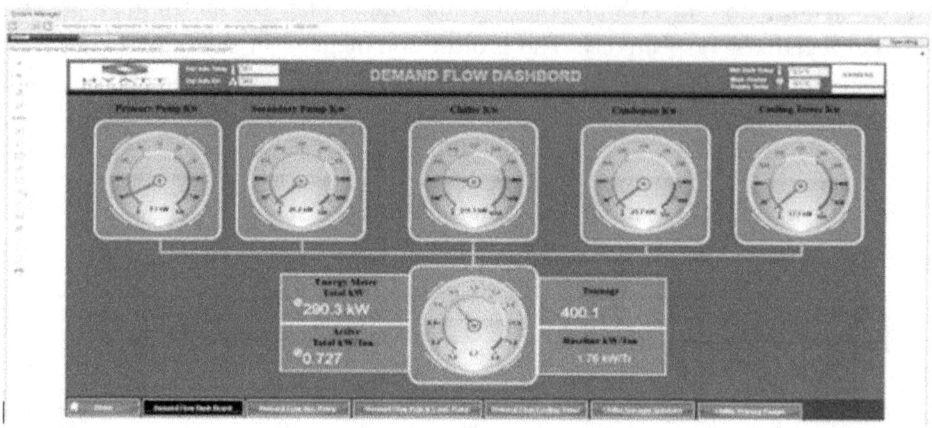

XYZ Example

Value stream mapping (VSM) is a powerful tool to identify non-value adding activities. It is based on a lean-management method for analyzing the current state and designing a future state for the series of events that take a product or service from its creation to its final delivery to the customer (refer to Appendix 5 for details of value stream mapping). It employs a flow diagram documenting in high detail every step of a process. It is a fundamental tool to identify waste, reduce process cycle times, and implement process improvement (Deokar, Raj, Jayakrishna, & Abdul Zubar, 2019). The tool results in significant cost reduction and quality improvement (Dhingra, Kumar, & Singh, 2019). XYZ therefore found VSM apt for its project to improve the design or product development phase of its business.

Current State

An overview of the existing delivery process followed at XYZ is show in Figure 1.

The delivery process activates the ensemble of the operational procedures to allow for the delivery of a system to the customer based on the customer's statement of requirements. The process then starts with the assessment of an opportunity following the discussions engaged between the sales team and the customer concerning the customer's operational and functional needs. The delivery process consequently covers all the stages up to the startup of the system integrated to the customer's operational systems.

Figure 3. Overview of the delivery process

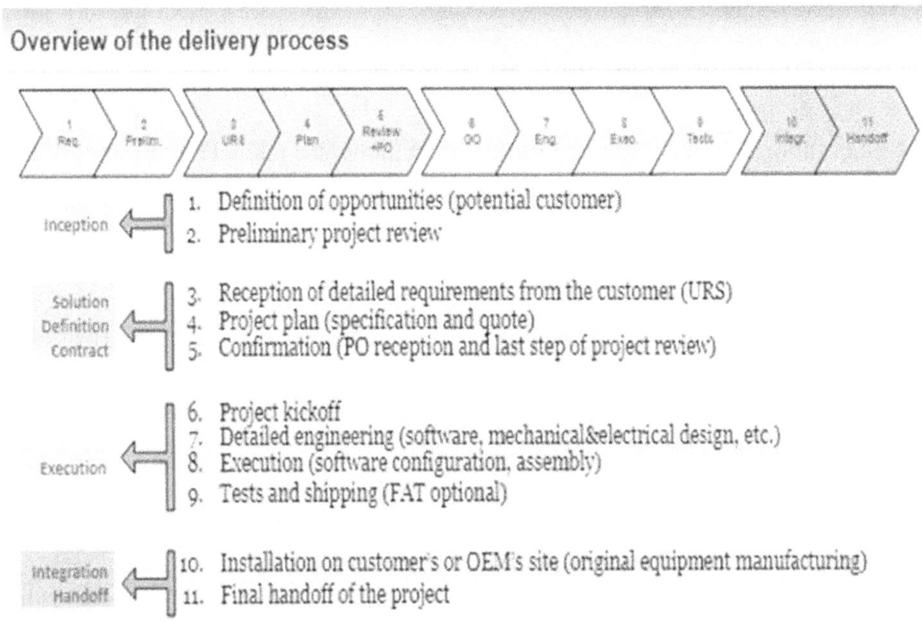

Delivery Process of a solution in accordance with the customers specification, cost and lead times, include 11 stages prior to transfer to the customer service (Stage 12). These stages can be grouped in four major delivery blocks:

Inception (Gates 1 and 2)
Solution Definition Contract (Gates 3,4 and 5)
Execution (Gates 6,7,8 and 9)
Integration & Handoff (Gates 10 and 11)

Inception (Gates 1 and 2)

This includes Gate1 (Opportunities Management) and Gate 2 (Project Review). As soon as the customer's intentions become reality for the sales team, this cycle can begin, allowing to suggest avenues and options to the customer, to clarify the delivery criteria as well as to establish the budgets, the lead times and high-level solutions. This cycle also allows for the customer to decide on these elements and to engage internal budgets. This cycle directs the costlier and more detailed subsequent stages. This cycle must not engage in intense analysis efforts since it is used to point the customer towards a main solution and to put aside hazardous avenues. At this stage, the customer's intention as well as its internal master plan (profitability analysis) is still being elaborated.

Solution Definition Contract (Gates 3, 4 and 5)

The elaboration of the contractual project plan includes Gate 3 (Requirements and Specifications Definition), Gate 4 (Project Plan) and Gate 5 (Confirmation). These Gates are crucial to clarify what will be delivered to the customer. A vague command opens the door to equivocation, functional and financial risks and to customer's concerns in the course of the execution and the delivery of the final solution. At Gate 3, it is important to clarify with the customer, the user requirements specifications, and the acceptance and satisfaction criteria. At Gate 4, a project plan is written by the team containing five aspects on which a solid contractual agreement will be based. The five aspects are as follows:

1. A specifications document that demonstrates the relevant covering of the user requirements specifications document elements.
2. A project planning document clearly indicating each critical stage and the critical milestone dates.
3. A communication plan to determine the communication mode, the frequency, the roles and responsibilities of the parties involved in the project and the decision chain.
4. A contractual design explaining the engineering design rationale, this is essential to control the risks and to satisfy the customer (not applicable to a preconfigured solution).
5. A final quote including an explanation of the costs per stage and for the delivered product securing a reasonable profit margin for Optel, the Optel and customer responsibilities as well as the conditions of the payment, service, penalties, etc.

Gate 4 generally requires customer samples analysis and can require an engineering visit to the customer's site. At Gate 5, a contractual review is performed. If all contractual agreement elements are accepted by both parties (XYZ and the customer), the management can therefore confirm the project execution dates and notify the different teams of the moment the work can begin. Also, at this Gate, the management must make official the gross margin objectives, the dates for the following stages and thc number of hours for the project.

Execution (Gates 6, 7, 8 and 9)

The delivery sprints include Gate 6 (Project kick-off), Gate 7 (Detailed Engineering), Gate 8 (Execution) and Gate 9 (Testing and Shipping). These Gates are planned in order to give an easily controllable execution rhythm with concrete deliverables. These steps constitute more than 50% of the time and material costs and require tight coordination by the project management team and by the supervisors. The work performed prior to Gate 4 and the care taken to perform the detailed design review at Gate 7 contribute to avoiding costly problems during the subsequent stages. Gate 6 allows for confirming the project by executing the required verification following the purchase order receipt. Gate 7 allows for the performance of the detailed engineering and for the detailed design review, mainly of the non-standard aspects. This is a key Gate since it comprises of the following critical design related processes:

Solution Design (SD)

SD validates if the information received is correct and confirms to the Project Manager (PM) regarding start of the process (Day 0).

SD/PM: Take Conference Call with customer to clarify the solution and start the work. Supervisors receive an email to assign resource, PM creates a team in Microsoft Teams and adds each resource.

PM/SD: Receive deliverables from different teams (approx. 4-7 days) and present them to the customer.

If the solution is more expensive then the new price is reconfirmed with the customer.

Software Engineering

Based on the Pre-Design meeting solution proposed, Software will have to estimate the hours required for the project configuration from scratch. Same applies for Software Vision Engineer.

In the timeline provided software engineer has to provide the configuration modelling of the project to present in the design review meeting.

Once in Design review meeting modelling is approved then initial software for the project needs to be released & simulated before using it on machine.

Vision software engineer has to complete vision study of the camera to be used for perfect inspection of the customer product based on customer samples received.

Mechanical Engineering

Based on the Vision study prepared by Vision software engineer, mechanical has to provide mechanical draft for the project.

Apart from this all other layout for the project needs to be given for customer for approval based on the customer layout on plant.

Mechanical has to complete all the drawing so that the Bill of Material load can be loaded.

Electrical Engineering

For Software Engineer to begin their work, Electrical Engineer should provide electrical layout to understand the signal exchange between XYZ & Customer system.

Once Mechanical has completed the mechanical drawing, electrical will load the Bill of Material.

Validation Specialist

Based on the above, the Validation Specialist provides test strategy for the project.

Gate 8 mainly covers the parts purchasing, reception and inspection, the system manufacturing, the software configuration, as well as the preparation of the necessary documentation. Gate 9 covers the final system testing and the system release and the shipping.

Integration and Handoff (Gates 10 and 11)

The integration and project handoff include Gate10 (Installation) and Stage 11 (Handoff). Gate 10 consists of installation of XYZ's systems at the customer's site as well as to train the future system administrators and operators. Gate 11 allows for the last corrections and updates in order to close the project. This stage also allows for the assessment of what happened in the project in order to improve the processes and future projects.

Based on the above the Current State Map is as shown in Figure 2.

It transpired from the above Current State Map that there is idle time and wastage of resources at a Gate if the process at the preceding Gate is not yet complete. It was also evident that as the project moves from Gate4 to Gate8 it takes around 80days, before project goes in execution stage. XYZ experienced problems in the processes pertaining to detailed engineering as described earlier. Inadequate or improper understanding of customer requirements by the various Departments was found as a potential cause for these problems and hence there was a need to redesign the current processes.

Figure 4. Current state map
**Average number of working days*

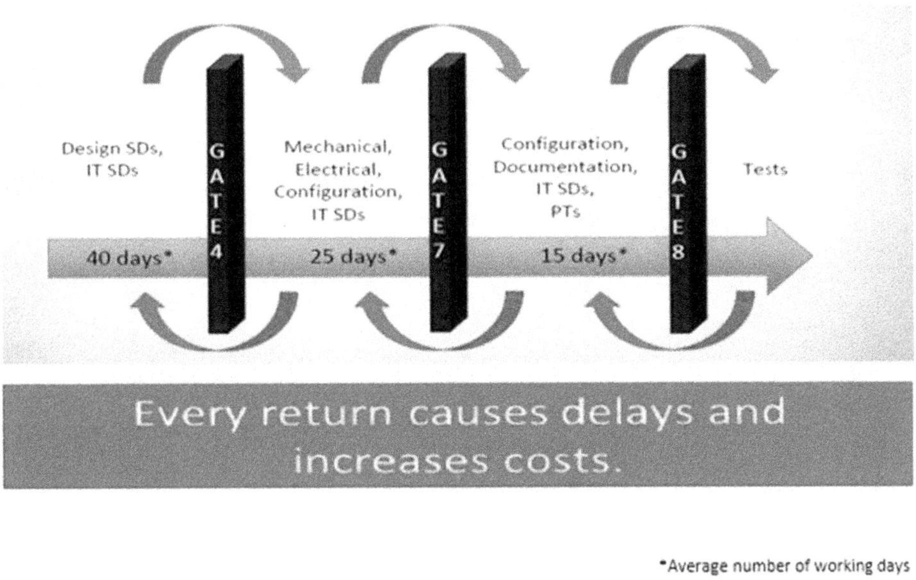

Future State

XYZ adopted Concurrent Engineering as a means of overcoming problems with the existing process. By this means Gate5, Gate6 and Gate7 are started at same time (project requirement/specification is known to each resource simultaneously) to start and complete their respective work at same time. The resultant Future State Map is as shown in Figure 3.

With reference to the Future State Map, at Day0, all the information required to start the Concurrent Engineering process for a project is available. Solution designer will provide SOD (Solution Design overview) and Project notes to respective Design cell assigned to execute the project. Between Day3 to Day7 there will be a Pre-Design meeting scheduled for the Design Cell assigned for the project. In Pre-Design meeting entire project scope, requirement and specification will be explained by Solution Designer.

From Day7 to Day20, all the resources will work to provide their respective draft copy, so that it can be presented to customer for approval, like mechanical, electrical, Software, vision & validation draft. At around Day20, there will be design review meeting in which each resource from Design cell will present their draft, here it will be a test of each resource if they have understood the project and made their draft accordingly. If required the draft can be reviewed by their respective peers.

Figure 5. Future state map

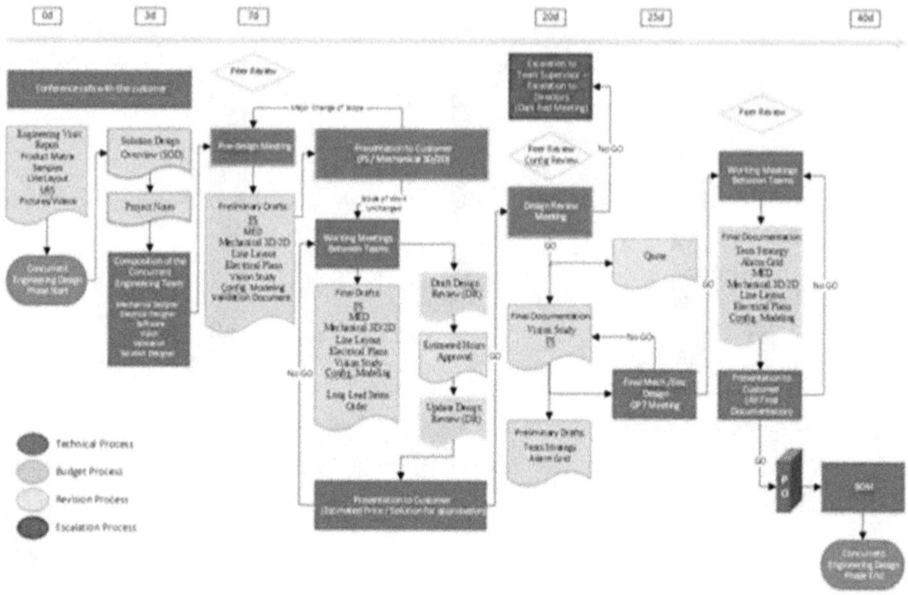

Based on the Design review meeting all the resources will work to provide final draft which will be sent to customer as final documentation, once final drafts are completed with customer review there is no scope for change in those. Based on the final approval, PO will be received & BOM will be loaded. Once BOM is loaded in SAP system, this marks end of Gate 7, i.e. Design Phase.

This future state map is drawn based on the information/data collected for a complex project when we start everything from scratch. The project is completed in December, 2019 with the potential for reducing the duration of the design phase by around 50%.

FUTURE RESEARCH DIRECTIONS

The ABC Example illustrated the use of the use of six sigma methodology for reduction in the energy consumed. The Example focused on energy savings due to the selective operation of a chiller during the time zone when the tariff is relatively lower. The use of the six-sigma methodology can be extended for use of the six-sigma methodology for further optimization of chiller operation. For instance, the incorporation of a Variable Frequency Drive in the chiller can be explored. The XYZ Example demonstrated the use of value stream mapping for reducing response time to the customer. The study focused on the product development process. The use of value stream mapping can be explored for other aspects of the business process such as after sales service.

CONCLUSION

Business are increasingly concerned about creating a sustainable environment. This is forcing organizations to adopt methodologies that support sustainable environment which includes being energy efficient. The ABC Example illustrates use of the six- sigma methodology for reducing energy consumption. By using the define, measure, analyze, improve, and control technique of the six-sigma methodology, ABC identified the major consumer of electricity (the chiller) and found that by selective operation of the chiller during the time zone when the tariff was on the lower side, the energy consumed by the chiller could be reduced by around 35%.

When a firm's operations are scattered globally, customer response times can be longer. Regardless of the area of the world, the challenge is to produce services or products that can compete in a global market, and to design the processes that can make it happen. The XZZ Example demonstrates use of value stream mapping to reduce the lead time for supply of by improvements in the product design phase. Based on the value stream mapping methodology, XYZ analyzed the Current State of the product development processes and formulated the Future State whereby there is potential to reduce the lead time by around 50%.

REFERENCES

Danish, M., & Senjyu, T., MatinIbrahimi, A., Ahmadi, M., & Howlader, A. (2018). A Managed Framework for Energy-efficient Building. *Journal of Building Engineering*.

Deokar, A., Raj, S., Jayakrishna, K., & Abdul Zubar, H. (2019). *Implementation of Lean Concepts Using Value Stream Mapping in Automotive Firm*. Advances in Manufacturing Technology. doi:10.1007/978-981-13-6374-0_17

Dhingra, A., Kumar, S., & Singh, B. (2019). Cost reduction and quality improvement through Lean-Kaizen concept using value stream map in Indian manufacturing firms. *International Journal of Systems Assurance & Engineering Management*.

Horvat, A., Behdani, B., Fogliano, V., & Luning, P. (2019). A systems approach to dynamic performance assessment in new food product development. *Trends in Food Science & Technology*, *91*, 330–338. doi:10.1016/j.tifs.2019.07.036

Olatz, P., Beatriz, R., & Javier, N. (2019). Life cycle thinking toward sustainable development policy-making:The Example of energy retrofits. *Journal of Cleaner Production*, 267–281.

Rajagopalan, P., Andamon, M., & Moore, T. (2019). Energy Performance in the Australian Built Environment. In P. Rajagopalan, M. Andamon, & T. Moore (Eds.), *Green Energy and Technology*. Springer.

Razali, N., & Afthanorhan, W. (2014). Improving Energy Conservavtion Using Six Sigma Methodology at Faculty of Computer & Mathematical Sciences (FSKM), Universiti Teknologi Mara Shah Alam. *Asian Journal of Economic Modelling*, 52-68.

Sivakumara, K., & Fengb, C. (2019). Patterns of product improvements and customer response. *Journal of Business Research*, *104*, 27–43. doi:10.1016/j.jbusres.2019.06.044

Thornton, S., Henneberg, S., Leischnig, A., & Naudé, P. (2019). It's in the Mix: How Firms Configure Resource Mobilization for New Product Success. *Journal of Product Innovation Management*, *36*(4), 513–531. doi:10.1111/jpim.12489

Yuvamitra, J., Guiberteau, K., & Kozman, T. (2014). Six-Sigma Approach to Energy Management Planning. *Strategic Planning for Energy and the Environment*.

APPENDIX 1

DMAIC

DMAIC is a data-driven quality strategy used to improve processes. It is an integral part of a Six Sigma initiative, but in general can be implemented as a standalone quality improvement procedure or as part of other process improvement initiatives such as lean.

WHAT DOES DMAIC STAND FOR?

DMAIC is an acronym that stands for Define, Measure, Analyze, Improve, and Control. It represents the five phases that make up the process, including the tools to use to complete those phases shown in Figure 1:

1. **Define** the problem, improvement activity, opportunity for improvement, the project goals, and customer (internal and external) requirements.
    - Project charter to define the focus, scope, direction, and motivation for the improvement team
    - Voice of the customer to understand feedback from current and future customers indicating offerings that satisfy, delight, and dissatisfy them
    - Value stream map to provide an overview of an entire process, starting and finishing at the customer, and analyzing what is required to meet customer needs
2. **Measure** process performance.
    - Process map for recording the activities performed as part of a process
    - Capability analysis to assess the ability of a process to meet specifications
    - Pareto chart to analyze the frequency of problems or causes
3. **Analyze** the process to determine root causes of variation and poor performance (defects).
    - Root cause analysis (RCA) to uncover causes
    - Failure mode and effects analysis (FMEA) for identifying possible product, service, and process failures
    - Multi-vary chart to detect different types of variation within a process
4. **Improve** process performance by addressing and eliminating the root causes.
    - Design of experiments (DOE) to solve problems from complex processes or systems where there are many factors influencing the outcome and where it is impossible to isolate one factor or variable from the others
    - Kaizen event to introduce rapid change by focusing on a narrow project and using the ideas and motivation of the people who do the work

5. **Control** the improved process and future process performance.
    - Quality control plan to document what is needed to keep an improved process at its current level
    - Statistical process control (SPC) for monitoring process behavior
    - 5S to create a workplace suited for visual control
    - Mistake proofing (poka-yoke) to make errors impossible or immediately detectable

Figure 6. The DMAIC methodology

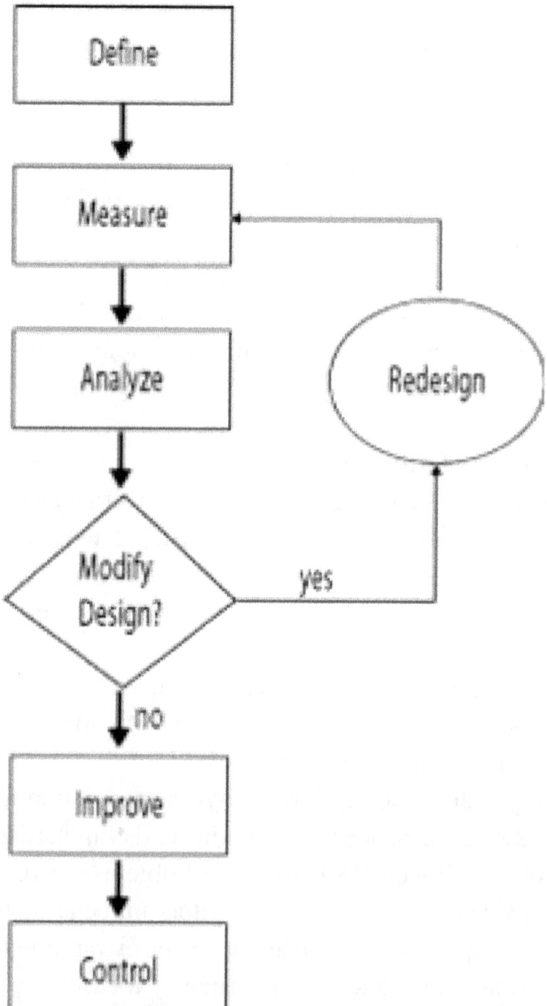

APPENDIX 2

Energy Balance Audit Steps

Step 1

1. Identify the unknown electrical load distribution.
2. Study of Single Line Diagram (SLD) of Electrical Distribution System. If required generation of SLD of entire plant from transformer to last distribution board and switches.
3. Load profile and other electrical parameters on transformers of above-mentioned factories for 24-hour cycle.
4. Running load of all equipment at outgoing feeders. Preparing energy balance.
5. Study of metering and monitoring and recommendations for Energy Management System.
6. Study of reactive power management and solutions.
7. Thermal Imaging of all electrical switch-gear level along-with digital photography.
8. Study of Harmonics and solutions for mitigation of Harmonics.
9. Study of Power Quality where non-linear loads are expected.
10. Analysis of electricity bills and recommendations on Tariff Management.
11. Action plan for optimization of electrical distribution system for energy saving.

Step 2

1. Analysis of 12-month data of DG set's operation, power generation and monthly fuel consumption.
2. Working out average load and specific power generation (kWh/Ltr).

Step 3

1. Study of each Chiller will be undertaken.
2. 72-hour data logging for running –load and temperature difference between inlet and outlet of evaporator will be undertaken. Primary flow will be measured with ultrasonic flow meter. This will be used to calculate trend of load on all Chillers (TR) and its specific power consumption (KW/TR).
3. Following Parameters will be logged Simultaneous for 72 hours: Power, Evaporator Flow, Evaporator inlet and outlet temperature, Condenser inlet

and outlet temperature, Ambient Temperature (Dry Bulb, Wet Bulb), bypass temperatures before and after valve.

4. Study of Air Handling Units (AHU) with respect to load, chilled water flow, control valves, header and sub headers. Also, air-flow of AHU filters will be measured. Performance and load of AHUs will be compared with their design parameters. 25% of select Critical AHUs will be undertaken for this detailed study. Effectiveness of All the AHU coils
5. Opportunities for system improvement and Energy Conservation will be explored in Chillers, Pumps (Generation-side) and AHUs (User-side).
6. Identify the split, packages AC units and quantify the tonnage and electrical load. Study the possibility of converting to Chilled water system including existing Air-cooled chiller. Preparing the BOQ for the same.

Step 4

1. Thermal imaging to identify any major leakages through Air conditioning areas.

APPENDIX 3

Details of TES

- Ice Storage System catering to the cooling requirements for the EA factory between 6.00 am and 11.00 pm reducing the dependency on the electricity grid and the DG system during the period.
- Ice storage tank will be charged during the night between 11.00 pm and 6.00 am taking advantage of the low tariff rates during this time zone.
- During night, A 80 TR chiller will provide the required cooling for the EA factory.
- 350 TR Brine water cooled chiller will be installed to charge the TES tank during the night.
- Location for a mini plant room to cater to the water- cooled chiller and its related accessories have been identified.
- The chiller plant will be further optimized to deliver performance by providing VFD's on the primary pumps and high accuracy sensors and transmitters.
- 38% energy saving for the plant from its existing consumption.
- Performance of the Chiller plant will be monitored through both BMS and Navigator.

Figure 7.

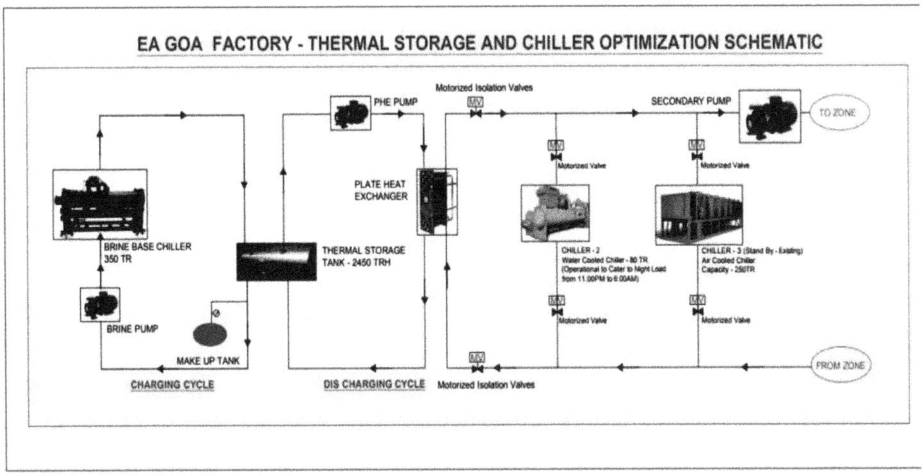

- Replacement of existing belt driven blowers for 8 Air handling units with EC fans / Plug Fans.
- latest product in energy efficient air movement technology
- EC stands for Electronically Commutated which basically means it is a fan with a brushless DC motor.
- DC motors are around 30% more efficient than AC motors.
- 43% energy saving for the plant from its existing consumption.

APPENDIX 4

TES Project Implementation Plan

ABC implement the project for installation of the TES by using standard project management practices and project management knowledge areas detailed as follows:

SCOPE: Installation and commissioning of TES plant which includes procurement as per technical tender documents prepared by Design team as per site conditions and desired parameters, civil foundation, mechanical coupling with existing system, and Electrical and instrumentation connectivity with existing system, training is in scope

Table 5.

	PROJECT SCHEDULE	WEEKS																											
SR NO	ACTIVITY	W1	W2	W3	W4	W5	W6	W7	W8	W9	W10	W11	W12	W13	W14	W15	W16	W17	W18	W19	W20	W21	W22	DURATION WEEKS	ES	EF	LS	LF	SLACK
1	Define Broad scope of work																							1	0	1	0	1	0
2	Approval from the management																							1	1	2	1	2	0
3	Project team formation																							1	2	3	2	3	0
4	Appointing consulatant for detailed engineering																							1	2	3	2	3	0
5	Detail engineering with design basis,BOQ,PID,costing etc																							3	3	6	3	6	0
6	Approval from the management for design and budget																							1	6	7	6	7	0
7	Procurement-selection of vendor																							2	7	9	7	9	0
8	Receipt of various equipments,chiller,pumps,pipes,electrical and instruments,mechanical and civil material																							6	9	15	9	15	0
9	cicil foundation																							3	9	12	12	15	3
10	Installation of chiller																							2	15	17	15	17	0
11	Installation of pumps																							2	15	17	15	17	0
12	Installation of cooling tower																							2	15	17	15	17	0
13	Installation of AHU's																							2	15	17	15	17	0
14	Pipeleine job																							2	15	17	15	17	0
15	AHU ducting job																							2	15	17	15	17	0
16	Electrical panel instalation and cabling																							1	17	18	17	18	0
17	Instruments fixing and caliobration																							1	17	18	17	18	0
18	BMS installation and conevting field devices																							1	18	19	18	19	0
19	Testing and comissioning of the system																							1	19	20	19	20	0
20	Trial run monitoring for performance check																							1	20	21	20	21	0
21	Project closure-Handing of documents,and system handover																							1	21	22	21	22	0

The designing of the TES plant is not in scope.

TIME: The Gantt Chart and Network diagrams are shown in the following Figures.

Activity 9 is only having a slack of 3 weeks, rest all activities are having 0 Slack and hence are on the critical path.

Altogether there are 24 critical paths all with duration of 22 weeks. Hence the project duration is 22 weeks.

Figure 8.

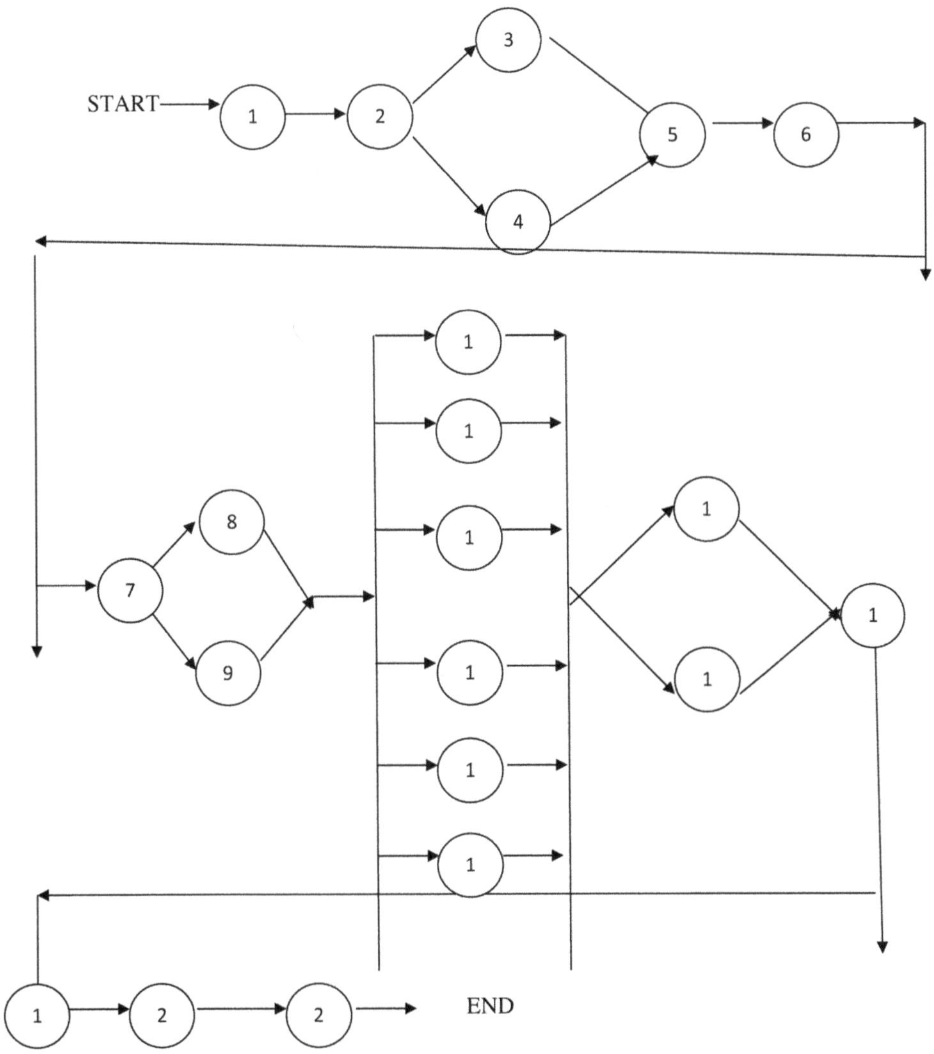

COST

Table 6.

	COSTING FOR NEW CHILLER AND TES SYSTEM						
Sr	Description	Unit	Qty	Supply Unit Rate (INR)	Supply Amount (INR)	Installation Unit Rate (INR)	Installation Amount (INR)
1	Upgradation of Central Monitoring Station	Nos	1	101,818	101,818	685	685
2	Upgradation of BMS Software Desigo CC	LOT	1	178,675	178,675	13,699	13,699
3	Interface controller required for System Upgrade	Nos	1	40,178	40,178	8,219	8,219
4	3rd. Party Integration required for System Upgrade	LOT	1	242,247	242,247	13,699	13,699
5	DDC Controllers required for System Upgrade	LOT	1	477,636	477,636	93,151	93,151
6	Temperature Transmitter	Nos	28	7,474	209,279	2,466	69,041
7	Differential pressure transmitter	Nos	8	28,359	226,869	10,959	87,671
8	Outside Temperature & Rh Sensor	Nos	1	18,188	18,188	685	685
	Isolation Valves and Actuators required for System Upgrade	LOT	1	1,364,198	1,364,198	170,548	170,548
9	Variable Frequency Drives (kW)) required for System Upgrade	LOT	1	482,119	482,119	16,438	16,438
10	VFD Panels required for System Upgrade	LOT	1	351,341	351,341	16,438	16,438
11	Mechanical Modification	Nos	1	16,000	16,000	35,714	35,714
12	Electrical Modification	Nos	1	16,000	16,000	35,714	35,714
13	Cables & Conduits required for System Upgrade		1	367,835	367,835	-	-
14	Energy meters	Nos	6	13,684	82,106	3,425	20,548
15	Replacement of 250TR with 350TR water cooled screw chiller	Nos	1	5,364,183	5,364,183	171,233	171,233
16	New Water cooled chiller of 80 TR	Nos	1	1,524,437	1,524,437	34,247	34,247
17	Thermal Storage Tank required for 350TR WC Chiller - 2450 TR-HR	Nos	1	9,048,735	9,048,735	136.986	136,986
18	Primary Pumps for New Chillers	Nos	2	168,248	336,496	68,493	136,986
19	Heat Transfer Media required for 350TR WC Chiller	Nos	1	935,886	935,886	136,986	136,986
20	For conversion from air cooled to water cooled - Cooling tower for 350TR Water Cooled Chiller	Nos	1	808,885	808,885	68,493	68,493
21	Cooling tower for 80TR Water Cooled Chiller	Nos	1	205,581	205,581	68,493	68,493
22	Upgaradtion of Condenser Water Pumps for 350TR chiller	Nos	2	236,978	473,955	68,493	136,986
23	Condenser Water Pumps for 80TR chiller	Nos	1	100,114	100,114	68,493	68,493
24	Modification & Upgradation of MS Piping with Insulation	Nos	1	1,493,326	1,493,326	68,493	68,493
25	Upgradation of Electrical Panel for Chiller , Pumps, CT	Nos	1	767,119	767,119	136,986	136,986
26	Upgradation of Power Cable -Chiller , Pumps, CT	Nos	1	151,351	151,351	68,493	68,493
27	Manual butterfly valve for system upgrade	Nos	12	12,274	147,287	3,425	41,096
28	Modification/ Upgradation in Structure & Civil Work for Chiller Plant	Nos	1	1,196,103	1,196,103	399,873	399,873
29	Upgradation of AHU with Adibatic Solutions	Nos	3	2,724,693	8,174,078	6,849	20,548
30	Energy Audit Fees as per EEP2 Guideline + Cloud Based Navigator M&V Tool with Periodic Report Generation and Data Analysis, Remote Monitoring	Nos	1	-	-	3,233,649	3,233,649
31	Performance Assurance (One Year) includes Measurement & Verification, Monthly Report Generation and Savings Establishment	Nos	1	-	-	1,050,000	1,050,000
	Sub Total				34,902,025		6,560,293
	Total (BT Order Value)						41,462,318

QUALITY

Chiller installed should be able to maintain temperature from 18 Deg C to 25 Deg C and RH between 45% to 65% and deliver the guaranteed Specific energy consumption in KW/Tons of refrigeration in order to deliver performance and also the Energy savings.

Table 7.

Sl. No.	Quality Checks	Quality Goals	Acceptance Criteria	Status
1.	Design Qualification	Machine Design specification should be verified physically.	Machine Design specification should be as per Design qualification documentation as supplied by OEM.	Checked & found OK
2.	Installation Qualification	Specification for machine installation should be verified.	Installation specification should be as per Installation parameters defined by OEM	Checked and found to be OK.
3.	Operational Qualification	Machine operational parameters after start-up should be checked.	Machine operational should be as per operational parameters as per OEM	Checked and found OK.
4.	Performance Qualification	User achieved parameters as defined in design & agreed by OEM to be verified – e.g. Chilled water Temperature – 6 to 8 Deg. C	Machine performance to be as defined in design and agreed by OEM	Checked and found to be OK. Temperature and RH maintained as per design details.

HUMAN RESOURCE

Organogram

Figure 9.

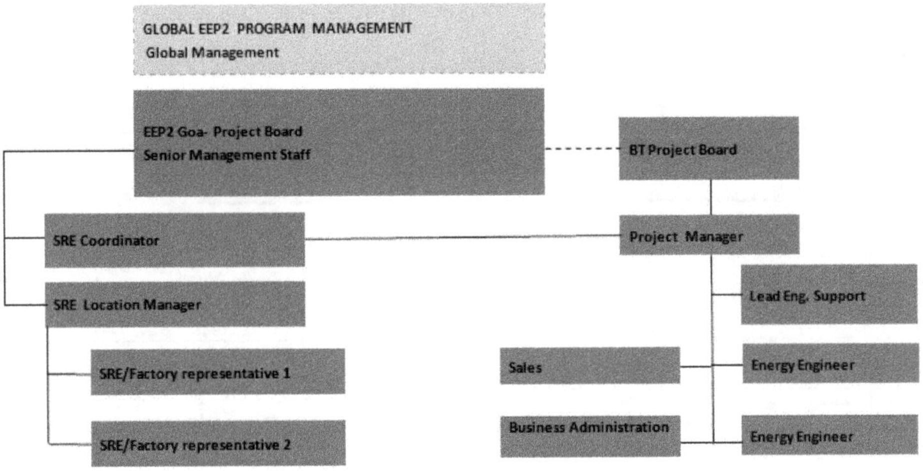

Training

Table 8.

S. No.	Designation	Name of the Training	Mode of Training	Phase / Training Time lines
1	Operators	Operation of chiller	Utilities section	After Implementation
2	Maintenance officers	Attending breakdown/ Trouble shooting on chiller	Utilities section	After Implementation

PROCUREMENT

Vendor Evaluation for Chiller

Criteria for Vendor Evaluation

- Chiller capacity to be match with the load requirement.
- Quality of the chiller and its full load running capacity.
- Timely delivery of Equipment.
- Maintenance support during breakdowns and service calls.
- Technical competency of the service team to execute work.
- Rating on 0 to 5 Scale (0 Being poor and 5 being V Good)

Table 9.

TECHNICAL COMPARISON SHEET - CHILLED WATER PLANT 350 TR

		YORK		RATING FOR YORK	TRANE	RATING FOR TRANE
Sr. No.	Specifications	YEW325	YEWS350		350TR	
TECHNICAL COMPARISON						
	General					
1	Capacity (TR)	350	350		350	
2	Model selected	YEWS325	YEWS350		RTHD	
3	Chilled water temp. (In/Out)	12/7 DegC	12/7 DegC		12/7 deg C	
4	Refrigerant	R-134a	R-134a		R134a	
5	Refrigerant Quantity (Kgs)	200	260		283 kgs	
	Type of cooling	Water	Water		Vapour compression cycle	
	Capacity control	Stepless	Stepless		Stepless	
a	Compressor					
	Type	Twin Screw Rotary Screw Type	Twin Screw Rotary Screw Type	4	Semi-hermetic screw	5
	No. of compressors	2	2		1	
	Compressor RPM	2975	2975		2980 RPM	

COMMUNICATION

Table 10.

Stakeholders	Contact Person	Contact Details	Nature of Liaison/ Interface
GHQ	ABC	XXXXXXXXXX	Personal Interaction
Senior management staff	ABC	XXXXXXXXXX	Personal Interaction
SRE Location Manager	ABC	XXXXXXXXXX	Personal Interaction
SRE Factory Representative	ABC	XXXXXXXXXX	Personal Interaction
BT project Board	ABC	XXXXXXXXXX	Personal Interaction
Project Manager	ABC	XXXXXXXXXX	Personal Interaction
Lead Engineering support	ABC	XXXXXXXXXX	Personal Interaction
Energy Engineer	ABC	XXXXXXXXXX	Personal Interaction
Sales	ABC	XXXXXXXXXX	Personal Interaction
Business Administration	ABC	XXXXXXXXXX	Personal Interaction

Table 11.

Stake holder name	Nature/details of collaboration	Information needs	Format of the communication	Phase in which interaction takes place
GHQ	Initiation	Entire Project Details, profits to company	Face to Face	Initiation
Energy Engineer	Requirement Gathering	Energy Audit	Face to Face, Documentation	Initiation, Planning
Project Manager/ Energy Engineer	Requirements, Planning	Technology, Optimization Strategy	Face to Face, Documentation	Initiation, Planning, Implementation, Monitoring and Control
Business Administration	Procurement & Process Optimization	Material Management, Quality Standards, Order Details	Face to Face, Documentation	Initiation, Planning, Implementation, Monitoring and Control
Location Manager	Integration with the existing facility	Material delivery, site team, schedule, shutdown details	Face to Face, Documentation	Planning, implementation, Execution at site

RISK

Table 12.

Identified Risk	Owner of the Risk	Impact of Risk	Risk Priority (High/ Medium/Low) and probability	Risk Mitigation Plan
Delay in planned activities	Project Manager	Delay in planned activities in line with project schedule	Impact: High Likely hood: Low	Daily meeting and update regarding the project progress
Delay in receiving Chiller and other critical material required	Procurement Department	Delay in completion of project	Impact: High Likely hood: Low	Continuous follow up with vendor and procurement team, to give delivery date 2 week before the actual requirement
Accident during work execution	Project Manager	Damage/harm to Machine/Man	Impact: High Probability: Medium	All safety measures to be followed, strict action to be taken against any unsafe actions
Manpower shortage	HR department	Delay in activities planned	Impact: Medium Likelihood: High	Backup Manpower to be kept on rolling on other non-critical work in plant so in Example of urgency man power can be diverted.
Unavailability of plant shutdown during planned work	User Dept. / Management	Delay in Completion of project.	Impact: High Likelihood: Low	Prior intimation regarding shutdown requirement to be mailed to all Stakeholder. Mail approval to be taken.

INTEGRATION

The Existing 250 TR chiller will be removed and new 350 TR along with 80 TR and TES system will be integrated with the existing BMS.

This includes the entire piping, electrical and instrumentation integration.

The schematic of new integrated system is as shown below.

Figure 10.

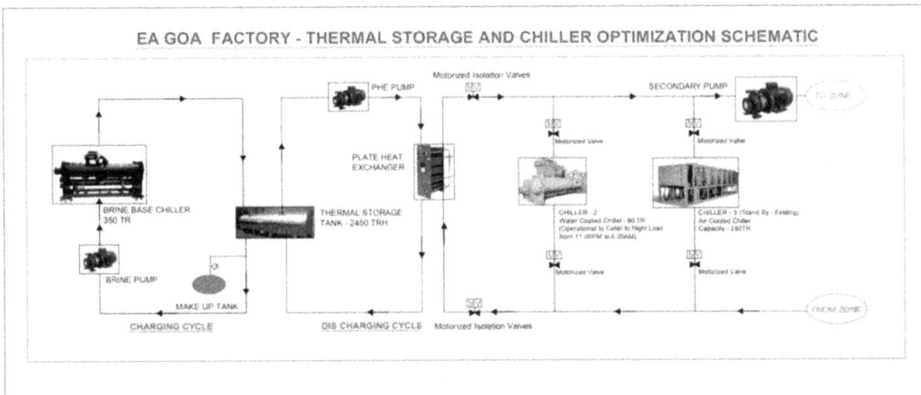

APPENDIX 5

Value Stream Mapping

Value stream mapping (VSM) is a lean-management method for analyzing the current state and designing a future state for the series of events that take a product or service from its beginning through to the customer. It employs a flow diagram documenting in high detail every step of a process. It is a fundamental tool to identify waste, reduce process cycle times, and implement process improvement. Once wastes are identified, the appropriate Lean Manufacturing technique is used to meet specific improvement metrics. These techniques include visual systems, 5S, TPM, cellular layout, work balancing, JIT, etc.

Value Stream Mapping Purpose

Provide optimum value to the customer through a complete value creation process with minimum waste in:

- Design (concept to customer)
- Build (order to delivery)
- Sustain (in-use through life cycle to service)

Why Value Stream Mapping

Many organizations pursuing "lean" conversions have realized that improvement events alone are not enough. Improvement events create localized improvements, value stream mapping & analysis strengthens the gains by providing vision and plans that connect all improvement activities.

Value stream mapping & analysis is a tool that allows you to see waste, and plan to eliminate it.

Key Elements of a Value Stream

- Specify what does and what does not create value from the customer's perspective
- Identify all the steps necessary to order, design and produce across the entire value stream to highlight non-value-added wastes
- Make those activities that create value flow without interruption, detours, backflows waiting or scrap
- Only make what is pulled by the customer just-in-time
- Create a dynamic transparency of strategies, costs and information in the value stream
- Address competitive advantage at the value stream network level, moving past simple buyer/supplier partnership rhetoric
- Use value stream mapping for analysis, diagnosis and implementation of change
- Focus on key processes, not just separate business departments
- Address the entire supply chain over time rather than on short-term improvement of individual facilities
- Strive for perfection by continually removing successive layers of waste as they are uncovered

Value Stream Mapping Process

Figure 11.

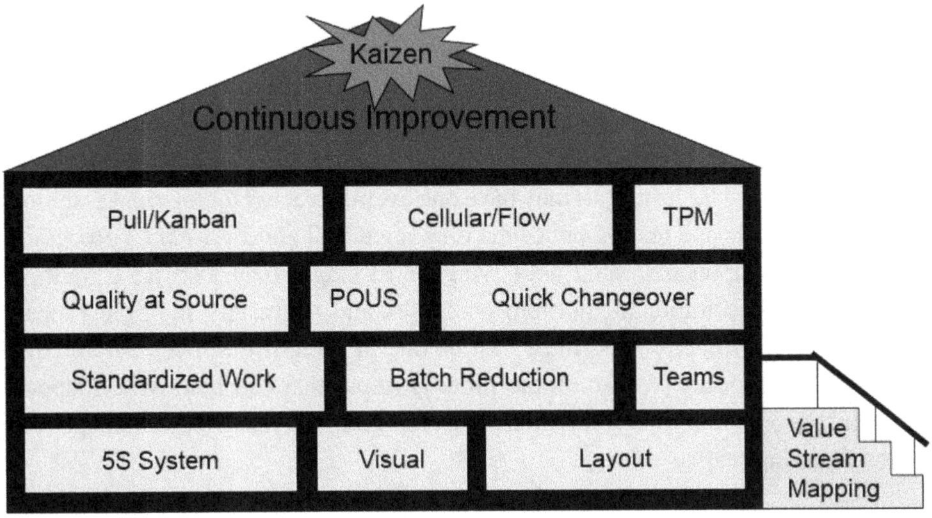

Figure 12.

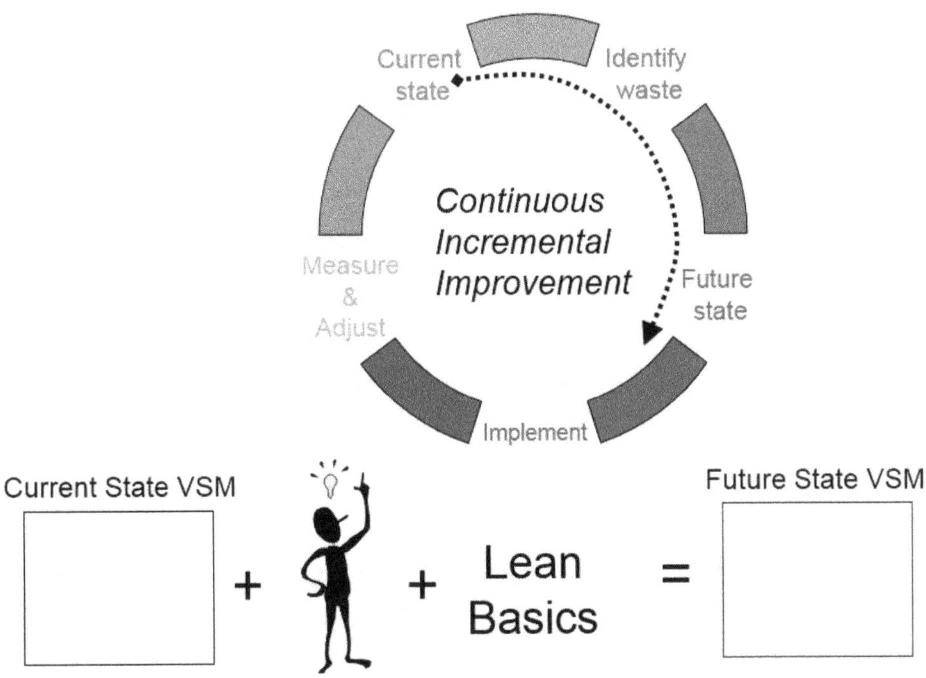

THE PROCESS OF VALUE STREAM MAPPING CAN BE REDUCED TO 6 GENERAL STEPS

1. Determine the appropriate process to improve.

In any normal manufacturing environment there can exist many individual processes. Many individual products contain multiple processes, of which each process is further subdivided into multiple process steps (operations). An example of manufacturing a large aircraft may have one overall process for the final assembly of the components and testing but each component will have individual processes. Each of the components, such as a wing or fuselage, may also have multiple subcomponents resulting in multiple processes and ultimately multiple process steps. The appropriate process must first be one in need of improvement and also be of a single process (with multiple process steps) that can readily be mapped. The selection of this process involves research and analysis by the management and engineering teams.

2. Create the current state map of the process.

Once a process has been selected, the detailed mapping can begin. The initial effort is too simple, and generally, determine process steps and map them in the order of the process flow. The mapping requires a vast amount of information on each and every step in the process. Examples of the required information may include (but not limited to):

Pre-manufacturing:
Order entry time, Raw material delivery time, Incoming inspection time

Process steps:
Cycle time, Setup time, Number of operators required, Batch (lot) sizes,
Equipment uptime, Quality rating (defect rate), Idle time, WIP (work in process)

Post manufacturing:
Final inspection time, stocking time, Loading time, Delivery time

All of this information is gathered and displayed in order to get the 'big picture" of the process. The process of mapping starts with the customer and ends with the customer.

3. Determine the appropriate metric for improvement or Identify wastes that must be eliminated.

When a current state map is produced, it usually becomes evident that there are many opportunities for improvement. Unfortunately, there are times when multiple improvements can result in cancelling each other out; ending with an unimproved process. Metrics for manufacturing process improvements can generally be divided into 3 categories; those that reduce inventory, increase throughput, or reduce operational expenses. Inventory metrics may include quantity, quality, and obsolete product; turn over frequency, space, labor, location, etc. Typical metrics for throughput includes cycle times, order size, batch size, setup times, equipment uptime, material availability, available labor, labor skills, scheduling, etc. Operational expenses include overhead costs, material costs, labor costs, transportation cost, quality costs, or any other cost associated with production. The selection of the proper metric will determine the improvement path taken for the process, so it is very important that the correct metric is selected and that a realistic metric value is also determined. An improvement metric of increasing throughput by reducing the cycle time by 95% is admirable, but may not realistic nor obtainable. An unobtainable goal is a sure-fire way to sabotage the improvement effort. Why should an improvement team attempt the impossible knowing that they will fail to achieve an acceptable result?

4. Create the future state map of the process.

When a realistic metric and metric value (i.e. improve quality rate on part XYZ by 15%) has been determine, the future state map can be created. During this exercise, the processes are redrawn in such a way as to include the metric improvement (i.e. quality rate).

5. Implement future state map by doing improvements and reducing/eliminating waste

It is at this point that the engineering minds are challenged. Contemplating methods to improve a process from the current state to the future state can be difficult. Typical methods include brainstorming, and 'fish-bone" analysis in a group environment. Of the many possible solutions to the problem, several would be chosen and reviewed in depth until a single solution emerges. From this unique solution, the method of implementing it can be determined and detailed.

6. **Measure and adjust the output as required per standard**

Chapter 6
Challenges and Perspectives of Supply Chain Management in Emerging Markets:
A Case Study Approach

Eni Ahmeti
Epoka University, Albania

Alba Demneri Kruja
https://orcid.org/0000-0002-6902-1489
Epoka University, Albania

ABSTRACT

Supply chain management (SCM) as a concept first originated in the manufacturing industry from logistics and just-in-time production. Used to successfully utilize SCM elements and diminish lingering issues in construction, its importance lies in the focus that it gives to plan different features of the supply chain by also involving other parties of the chain in the process. SCM in construction supports firms by aiding in the improvement of competitiveness between firms and the increase of the company's profits and control over projects. Although generic supply chains should be simple and linear, the construction sector is much more complex. These problems are present in different parts of SCM due to interdependence in the organization and supply chain. Through a case study analysis and semi-structured interviews, this chapter aims to identify and better understand the role of SCM, challenges and complications in different levels of the supply chain, and how firms utilize it to create greater value in construction operations, and specifically in Albania.

DOI: 10.4018/978-1-7998-2867-9.ch006

INTRODUCTION

Albania has experienced a major transformation over the last quarter century, emerging from a particularly isolated form of communism in the early 1990s to face the substantial challenges of forming a responsive, democratic system of government and developing a modern economy (O`Brien et al., 2017). Universities' role in the socio-economic development is important as they improve and diffuse scholarly knowledge (Kruja, 2013, p.14).

Albania is a country dominated by trade sector, providing the highest number of established enterprises, employment and turnover too (Kruja, 2020). Even though construction sector is one of the most important sectors of Albanian economy and it has undergone a significant increase since 2002 (instat.gov.al). It has greatly contributed to the development and modernization of the country through improved technology and infrastructure.

A significant impact in improvement of construction sector has been made by the implementation of Supply Chain Management (SCM). Essentially, SCM is the planning and management of all activities from sourcing to logistics activities. In addition, it coordinates the organizations involved in the chain such as suppliers, service providers and customers.

A proper management of materials and information flows are two very important aspects for construction companies. By doing so, they are provided with significant benefits and can offer their clients greater value in what they purchase. In this regard, SCM is a very useful approach. Because construction operations are characterized by high degrees fragmentation, coordination and management of the supply chain, it has to be accurately managed so that good results can be obtained.

However, practitioners have noticed that SCM application in construction operations has brought up underlying issues and challenges in different stages of the supply chain. Vrijhoev and Koskela (2000) claim that these problems are caused from myopic control. Another factor is that the nature and fragmentation of the sector itself may be an indicator for them. Nevertheless, construction firms aim to utilize supply chains to measure their performance, create competitive advantage and maximize customer satisfaction.

This research aims to identify the role of SCM in construction operations in Tirana, capital city of Albania, identify the problems that arise from its application and explore the opportunities of gaining competitive advantage and achieving customer satisfaction through its use. Based on these objectives, this study seeks to answer the following questions:

R1: What is the role of SCM in construction operations?
R2: What are the problems that arise from SCM application?
R3: How do firms use supply chain to gain competitive advantage and achieve customer satisfaction?

THEORETICAL BACKGROUND

During the recent years, SCM is used as a tool by companies in order to improve their overall performance and gain competitive advantage in the market. Even more important is its presence in construction operations. Through this theoretical background, we will gain insight about supply chain networks, supply chain management, what are its characteristics and role in construction operations and the problems present in it.

Supply Chain Management

SCM, as a concept, was initiated in manufacturing industry. The first signs were noticeable in the JIT delivery system, a system used by Toyota which aimed to adjust supplies to the factory in the right amount, in the right time (Vrijhoev and Koskela, 2000). Its goal was to lower levels of inventory and improve suppliers' relation with the production processes.

However, SCM today has different definitions by different authors. In order to define what supply chain management is, some authors first give a definition to "supply chain".

A supply chain is an integer of firms or organizations that pass the materials forward in the chain. Several firms are included in the manufacturing of a product – raw material producers, component producers, assemblers, wholesalers, retailers and transportation companies (La Londe and Masters, 1994, as cited by Mentzer et al., 2001). All of them are part of a supply chain in which the final customer is also included. On the other hand, Pryke states that supply chain is a network of relationships within which organizations are positioned. It is the focus for ways which are more effective in value creation for the customer; a tool for innovation and continuous improvement, and integration system (Pryke, 2009). For a supply chain to be effective, it needs to have the support of all linkages of exchange, expand beyond them so that it can create value for in every link. Just as individuals seek out other individuals with skills and attributes that they don't possess themselves, firms aim to create collaborative relationships with firms that possess attributes or resources that fulfill and compliment the first firm (Pryke, 2009). These collaborations enable the firm to avoid isolation in the business and failure. Instead, it gives them market power.

The term supply chain implies a linear process (Pryke, 2009) and it is such abstractly. However, at an applied level, because of the nature of supply management and depending on the industry, supply chains become more complex, and work as a cohesive, singularly competitive unit (Pryke, 2004; Wisner et al., 2012). Thus, Mentzer et al. (2001), identified three cases of supply chain complexity:

1. A direct supply chain, which consists of a company, a supplier and a customer.
2. An extended supply chain, which includes suppliers of suppliers and clients of clients.
3. An ultimate supply chain that includes all organizations and firms in the flow of products, information, services and finances.

The difference between supply chain as a phenomena and supply chain management consists in the fact that the former exists, while management of supply chain is done through management efforts by the firms within it.

The Council of Supply Chain Management Professionals defines SCM as: "the planning and management of all activities that are involved in sourcing and procurement, conversion, and all logistics management activities. It also includes coordination and collaboration with channel partners which can be suppliers, third party service providers and customers. In essence, it integrates supply and demand management within and across companies" (cscmo.org).

Furthermore, in literature SCM is defined as a management philosophy (Mentzer et al., 2001). When considered as a philosophy, SCM views the supply chain as a single entity rather than a fragmented piece of a chain. It extends the concept of integration into a bigger organizational effort to manage the flow of goods and information from the supplier to the client. For one of the objectives of SCM is to create costumer value, SCM philosophy suggests the integration of all functions of the firm and the supply chain to achieve strategic advantage, and customer value and satisfaction (Mentzer et al, 2001; Serpell and Heredia, 2004). In other words, it pushes members of supply chain to be oriented towards the customer (Mentzer et al, 2001).

One of the aims of management of supply chains is to synchronize customer requirements with material and information movement in the network, so that it can maintain a balance between customer satisfaction and cost. It consists of coordination of all the activities in which supply chain members participate, to satisfying the client by knowing production requirements, to reduce costs of the organization and to deliver products of greater value (Serpell and Heredia, 2004). Supply chain management is about economic value added (Aneesa et al., 2005).

Supply Chain Management in Construction

The application of SCM mostly in manufacturing, has been successful and beneficial. Some of these benefits are competitive advantage, cost reduction, improvement in productivity, better relationships with partners. Seeing the success in manufacturing industry, the need for significant improvement in project performance and profits eventually appeared in construction. Its implementation is suggested as a way to improve construction operations by the integration of the supply chain so that it can give the customer a greater (Latham, 1994; Egan, 1998; Strategic Forum, 2002, as cited by Aneesa et al., 2015).

However, SCM initiatives have not given the results desired as there is observed a deficiency of effectiveness. Vrijhoef and Koskela (2000) state that there is only fragmented application, as management is focused on different areas depending on circumstances; the focus may fall on the supply chain, other times on the construction site and some focus on both of them.

According to Aloini et al. (2012), SCM is heavily affected by the characteristics of the construction industry which has its own distinctive features:

- Production systems – construction is a project production industry and it operates in an environment where complexity and uncertainty are present (Fearne and Fowler, 2006, as cited by Aloini et al., 2012).
- Customer influence – customers have a great influence on the final product regarding its physical aspects as the project is adapted to their needs and demands.
- Fragmentation – market and process fragmentation.
- Number and type of stakeholders – a network involves multiple firms and relationships, including the flow of supplies, services and information as well as finances.
- Temporary arrangement – temporary projects require temporary organization. Thus, relationships are created on short term thinking where parties involved try to make the most out of their contract. Consequently, opportunism prevails in the environment (Cox and Thompson, 1997; Kamann et al., 2006; as cited by Aloini et al., 2012).

These aspects make SCM application crucial as it views production as a flow and as a generation of value (Aloini et al, 2012) and indicates that construction supply chain is complex and dynamic.

As mentioned in the sections above, supply chains can have a complex nature, and they do in the majority of the cases. In construction, supply chains can be very complex depending on the project. This complexity is credited to the range of firms (sub-contractors and suppliers) required for a construction project; the more parties are involved the more compounded is the project. Al-Werikat (2017) states that there is a correlation between the growing scope of the project and the complication of the supply chain, because a greater manpower and more parties are needed for its completion. Therefore, one of the main characteristics is that the degree of complexity varies in relation to the project. Construction supply chains are converging, fragmented, temporary and make to order (Vrijhoev, 1998 as cited by Al- Werikat. 2017).

1. Converging supply chains means that operations meet at one point. Normally in construction project materials, equipment, documents, operation capacity and so on are delivered and brought together in the construction site by the supplier and under the supervision of the main contractor.
2. Fragmented supply chain is the type of supply chain where sub-contractors, suppliers and other participants are active in different stages, and the responsibility and authority distribution changes during the project.
3. Temporary supply chain is a short-term partnership where all the parties involved are dismissed upon having fulfilled their duties. However, because of its nature it may cause difficulties and instabilities in the firms' performance and productivity.
4. In make to order supply chains, it is the client that initiates the creation of the projects. The initiative is taken, and the construction project is started, thus the client is involved in the whole process.

Al-Werikat (2017) pointed out that construction supply chains can also be categorized in:

1. Primary supply chain. It delivers materials that are integrated in the final stage of the process such as raw materials, mechanical and electrical equipment, other components and assemblies.
2. The support supply chain. It is responsible for providing assistance along the process, expertise and support through scaffolding, excavation or other technicalities.
3. Human resource supply chain. It is responsible in supply labor force such as: supervisory staff or work force for the construction process.

Construction involves incorporating materials and components designed and produced by several suppliers, working in a variety of disciplines, services and technologies, in order to create the "built environment" (Burtonshaw-Gunn and Ritchie, 2004). Consequently, it can be viewed as a complex of manufacturing and services (Aneesa et al, 2015) as there are operations involved in manufacturing that are similar with those in construction projects such as: procuring materials and assembling them in a product.

Role of SCM in Construction Operations

Construction supply chain management offers new tactics in cost reduction and increase of reliability and operation's speed in construction (O'Brien, 1999). It seeks optimization by taking into consideration production activities of independent production units such as suppliers. Furthermore, it gives insight and consideration of the firm's production cost and capabilities. That being said, it provides a coherent source to improve coordination and project control.

Vrijhoev and Koskela (2000) conclude in their research that that SCM roles in construction are vital and of importance. They claim that there are 4 major roles of SCM in construction, which can be identified based on industry concerns either about the construction site or supply chain or both. It offers guidelines which can be used to analyze, properly coordinate and continuously improve the complete construction supply chain, by resolving basic problems and mismanagement that may be present in the supply chain Vrijhoev and Koskela, 2000).

The main areas that are impacted to SCM application are cost reduction (mostly logistical costs) lead-time and inventory in the supply chain (Vrijhoev and Koskela, 2000). This is an appropriate focus considering how fragmented and complex construction projects are. Another factor effecting those areas is that construction supply chains are at two levels: firm level and project level. Supply chains of firm level can provide long term and stable support, meanwhile project level supply chain is temporary because of their fixed duration.

Secondly, the focus may fall on the impact of supply chain on construction site activities. SCM ensures an undisturbed material and labor flow to the site, where it aims to reduce site costs and duration (Vrijhoev and Koskela, 2000). Because project level supply chains are temporary, and depending on the complexity of a project design, a smooth material and information flow is vital to the completion of the project.

When focusing on transferring activities form the site to other upstream stages of the supply chain (Vrijhoev and Koskela, 2000), by avoiding any inferior conditions of the site, again total cost and duration are reduced. However, it may be difficult or not possible, because of the many technical dependencies in the site (Vrijhoev and Koskela, 2000). Nevertheless, in practice, these areas are interconnected. In order to improve dependability of different parts of the supply chain, the total supply chain has to be addressed.

The need for improvement in performance and profit enabled the entry of SCM in construction. However, SCM initiatives did not make the desired breakthrough in the industry because of a lack of effectiveness and slow implementation (Aloini et al, 2012). Specialists have realized instead a partial implementation and focus on different areas depending on circumstances (Vrijhoev and Koskela, 2000). In particular obstacles are faced because of difficulties in managing networks of multiple parties involved, supplying materials, components and services (Aloini et al, 2012).

Problems in construction supply chain can also be explained by the fragmented structure that characterizes construction industry, a structure indicated in the aforementioned sections. That being said, in this context Al-Werikat (2017) mentions three issues. First, a fragmented industry refers to the various sizes and number of construction companies, diversity in trends and professionals and the fact that sub-contractors themselves sub-contract other firms to carry out work. Untrained and non-professional sub-contractors lead to emerge of problems along operations and in later stages of the supply chain. This explains why the industry's structure is fragmented. Second, poor management of site or company activities can decrease any positive outcome of SCM implementation. This may occur at construction site, company level or a mismanagement from the sub-contractor's side which may lead to low performance levels. Third, an inadequate investment in training causes a lack of research and development in the construction industry. Furthermore, it may lead to negative influence on the client and contractor, and the procurement process in general.

Waste and problems can be found present in construction supply chains because of myopic control (Vrijhoev and Koskela, 2000). They are present due to interrelationship connected to other stages in the supply chain. Some of these problems, according to Serpell and Heredia (2004), are:

- Materials and components of poor quality.
- Constant changes and inconsistent information in project design.
- Poor communication and information transfer between main contractor and sub-contracts.
- Lack of coordination, cooperation and commitment form actors within the supply chain.
- Mismanagement within the supply chain, mainly in regard to planning and control.
- Supplier, sub-contractors and work force not trained enough.
- Ineffective methods for performance measurement not only form the firm, but also from other parties within the supply chain.

METHODOLOGY

Case Study Research for SCM In Construction Operations

The construction sector is on the most important sectors of the economy. It makes up for approximately 20% of our GDP. There has been a continuous increase since 2002. This increase can be indicated by the rise in building permits, about 11.2%, and the increasing number of populations employed in the construction sector, 42,661 employees in 2017 (instat.gov.al).

The majority of the building permits were given in Tirana, the capital of Albania, 120 permits in 2018. Because it is the capital, it is the metropolis and greatest economic and political center of the country, and also the target of migration from other parts of Albania. Thus, in recent years it is noticed the need to expand, so that the city can accommodate the increasing population. This expansion is done through the improvement of infrastructure, public spaces and new residential buildings.

The main focus of this research is to identify the role of SCM in construction operations, identify their challenges and explore the opportunities of gaining competitive advantage through SCM implementation. In 2017 there were about 3500 enterprises operating in construction sector and the number has increased since then. From this range it is decided that the firm Kontakt ShPK, with their approval, is treated as a case study for this paper. The firm was selected based on their performance in the market and customer satisfaction, and the complexity of the implemented projects. In order to answer the research questions, two specialists from the firm were interviewed, Mr. Ardit Bektashi – civil engineer, and Ms. Eralda Konomi – Accounting and Logistics specialists. Their knowledge and expertise were found extremely useful during this research.

Research Design and Data Collection

The research methodology is based on qualitative research and exploratory research design to collect primary data. Qualitative data was found more suitable for this research as it provides access to deeper exploration and understanding of the answers. Duriau, et al. (2007) emphasise that exploratory and interpretive research is more likely to rely on primary data such as interviews, field notes, or open-ended questions to surveys. It gives more insight and is more flexible. Quantitative researchers often fail to understand the usefulness of studying small samples (Marshall, 1996).

Primary and secondary data are used to compile this research. Primary data is collected through semi-structured interview with key informants, specialists from a construction firm in Albania, Kontakt ShPK. The said construction company is used as a case study regarding the application of SCM in Albanian construction firms.

Therefore, case study method is used as a research design. According to Marshall (1996) an appropriate sample size for a qualitative study is one that adequately answers the research question. The interviewees are a civil engineer, Mr. Ardit Bektashi, and Ms. Eralda Konomi, logistics specialist. Their experience in the field was found valuable for the purpose of this research.

RESULTS

Construction sector is one of the pillars of Albanian economy, which contributes approximately 25% of our GDP. There has been a continuous increase throughout the years since 2002. The main contributors to this increase are from infrastructure, hydropower stations and house-build construction. The latter one has expanded massively all through the country. This expansion is indicated by an increase in building permits, as shown in the graph below.

The data for this research was collected from an interview session with two specialists of a construction firm Kontakt Shpk. The firm was specifically selected because of the degree of complexity of projects they implement and their performance. They have a 20-year experience in residential and non-residential construction. From project implementations through the years, they have faced obstacles and problems which are considered normal to the construction sector.

According to the firm, logistics plays a major role in project design and implementation. Because their main goal is to construct a building within 12 months, they employee temporary and fragmented supply chains as it is also a characteristic to the nature of the sector. The temporary supply chain is created from the moment of project design until the construction of the building. Long-term supply chain has proven not to be effective. The reason is the increase in material price, which in turn increases purchasing cost of the company. Furthermore, every year newer supplying firms enter the market and offer lower prices; thus, they create a competitive advantage over existing firms. In turn this prolongs the tendering process done by the firm.

Secondly, the supply chain has a greater impact in inventory management and material handling. Practice has shown that proper forecasting has effectively decreased costs in inventory and ordering. More precisely, close partnering and legal binding with sub-contractors enables the firm to return any extra material from the site. Consequently, inventory levels are decreased and supplies, and machineries are used to their full capacity.

The majority of the impact is in the construction site, where the company employs primary, secondary and human resource supply chain. The firm itself acts as the supervisor who makes sure that the flow of information, materials, services and finances is as smooth as possible, so no complications arise. Yet, there have been instances of misunderstanding from the sub-contractors. This has created delays in other stages of construction operations ex. delays in concreting by 4 weeks.

Nevertheless, being that the supply chain is characterized by a temporary nature, the firm does not see any necessity in building long-time relationships with its sub-contractors. However, there are few instances where the company has sub-contracted foreign firms, a decision driven from the better quality offered, despite the increase in logistics costs. Not only materials, the firm also sub-contracts foreign design studios. Architecture graduates in Albania are not specialized in designing big residential complexes.

Another aspect is how the firm utilizes the supply chain. In order to finish a project within the time frame, the supply chain is coordinated to operate several activities simultaneously but in different stages. That being said, in the site while the masonry of the fourth floor is being done, they start plastering the first floor, while the supply chain is engaged in supplying and transporting materials, machinery and workforce. Therefore, by engaging the supply chain in every part of the process they manage to create long-lasting buildings.

DISCUSSION

Through this research it was aimed to identify the role of SCM in construction operations, identify their challenges and explore the opportunities of gaining competitive advantage through SCM implementation.

The implementation of SCM in construction operations, has proven in practice to improve overall performance and create customer value.

In literature supply chains are thought to be linear but depending on the industry their complexity is more apparent. In the case of construction, supply chains take characteristics form the sector it is applied in. Supply chains in construction operations are complex, they include many parties such as sub-contractors of sub-contractors and customers of customers. Depending on the project they can be long-term (on company level), but mostly they are short-term (project level, construction site).

The main areas affected by the supply chain are cost reduction, inventory and lead time. In practice, the temporary nature of the supply chain affects the cost reduction. New firms entering the market, offer lower prices for materials, thus the firm decreases ordering costs.

In addition, SCM implementation has decreased inventory costs and levels because of the better practices.

Overall, SCM provides the construction sector with openings to diminish myopic control, increase profit and reduce time, costs and waste on site. There is a great impact on waste reduction, by using recycling machines. Thus, not only are they maintaining the construction site, they are also preserving the environment and our resources.

The downfall is that there is a misconception that supply chain management and logistics are the same concept. This has caused a shift of attention form relationships with other parties in the supply chain, to logistic activities. Even though construction site supply chains are temporary, the lack of attention to the relation with sub-contractors could rise challenges in the future for the firm. The more time it spends looking for suppliers, the longer the construction operations will be delayed.

That being said, there is still room from improvement when it comes to successfully applying SCM in construction.

CONCLUSION

Supply chain management plays an important role in any industry it is applied. However, in the case of Albanian construction sector and Kontakt, it is noticed that there is not a proper implementation. Problems or obstacles are noticed in management levels of the company and in the architecture educational institutions. What could bring improvement forward, is a partnership between universities, construction firms and the government. This model is "Triple Helix" and it is a model regarding interactions between university, industry and government. The triple helix message is that universities, firms and governments assume some of the capabilities of the other, even as each maintains its primary role and distinct identity (Kruja, 2013, p.13).

In this case a partnership between the university and industry could result in the transfer of knowledge, practice and experience. Kontakt outsources human labor when it comes to complex projects because of lack of education from our graduates. A close partnership between them would enable engineering and architect graduates to see in real practice what goes on in a construction site. It would give a chance to logistics graduates to see the application of SCM and logistics in a construction firm. In the other hand, the educational formation from proper methodologies and research would aid firms on how to properly implement SCM. In the end, the construction sector will recognize economic growth and a minimization of problems

When it comes to the government, its current relations to the university are not strong because of the independency of educational institutions form government. However, if university departments are offered funds to further conduct their researches, government institutions can create closer ties to higher education. Another point is that the government can create possibilities for the industry to fully utilize what universities offer.

This partnership would ensure a future where the newly graduates are more skilled and knowledgeable about the industry, in turn construction firms will decrease costs as they won't have to outsource anymore but employee capable, local workforce. It may open opportunities in creating effective management systems which in the long run will be incredibly beneficial. In the end the construction sector itself will recognize economic growth.Even though it may seem difficult to implement, trainings, workshops and practices can be a good start towards the implementation of this model. The long-term outcomes will be valuable and incentive for further integration of these elements.

REFERENCES

Akintola Akintoye, G. M. (2000). A survey of supply chain collaboration and management in construction industry. *European Journal of Purchasing & Supply Management*, 159-168.

Al-Werikat, G. (2017, March). Supply Chain Management in Construction; Revealed. *International Journal of Scientific & Technology Research*, *6*(3), 106–110.

Alfredo Serpell, B. H. (2004). Supply chain management in construction: Diagnosis and application issues. *Globalisation and Construction*, 455-466.

Alma Spaho, T. M. (2012). Supply Chain Management in Albania: An Empirical Study. *EuroEconomica,* (1), 17-24.

Andrew, R. J., & Dainty, G. H. (2001). Subcontractor perspectives on supply chain alliances. *Construction Management and Economics*, *19*(8), 841–848. doi:10.1080/01446190110089727

Benton, J. A. (2010). *Construction Purchasing & Supply Chain Management.* McGraw-Hill.

Burtonshaw-Gunn, S. A. R. L. (2004). Developments in Construction Supply Chain Management and Prime Contracting. In *1st International SCRI Symposium*, (pp. 334-347). Academic Press.

Christopher, M. (2005). *Logistics and Supply Chain Management: Creating Value-Adding Networks* (3rd ed.). Pearson Education.

CSCMP. (2019). Retrieved from Council of Supply Chain Management Professionals: https://cscmp.org/CSCMP/Academia/SCM_Definitions_and_Glossary_of_Terms/CSCMP/Educate/SCM_Definitions_and_Glossary_of_Terms.aspx?hkey=60879588-f65f-4ab5-8c4b-6878815ef921

Davide Aloini, R. D. (2012). Supply chain management: A review of implementation risks in the construction industry. *Business Process Management Journal, 18*(5), 753–761. doi:10.1108/14637151211270135

Davis, T. (1993). Effective Supply Chain Management. *Sloan Management Review*, 35–46.

Duriau, V. J., Reger, R. K., & Pfarrer, M. D. (2007). A content analysis of the content analysis literature in organization studies: Research themes, data sources and methodological refinements. *Organizational Research Methods*, *10*(1), 5–34. doi:10.1177/1094428106289252

Hartmut Stadtler, C. K. (2005). *Supply Chian Management and Advanced Planning* (3rd ed.). Springer. doi:10.1007/b106298

Instat. (2019). Retrieved from Instituti i Statistikes: http://www.instat.gov.al/al/temat/industria-tregtia-dhe-sh%C3%ABrbimet/nd%C3%ABrtimi/#tab2

John, T., & Mentzer, W. D. (2001). Defining Supply Chain Management. *Journal of Business Logistics*, *22*(2), 1–24. doi:10.1002/j.2158-1592.2001.tb00001.x

Kruja, A. (2013). Entrepreneurship and knowledge-based economies. *Revista Românească pentru Educaţie Multidimensională, 5*(1), 7-17.

Kruja, A. D. (2020). *Enterprise Investments, Innovation and Performance: Evidence from Albania* (Vol. 11). International Journal of Innovation in the Digital Economy.

Marshall, M. N. (1996). Sampling for qualitative research. *Family Practice*, *13*(6), 522–525. doi:10.1093/fampra/13.6.522 PMID:9023528

Martha, C., & Cooper, D. M. (1997). Supply Chain Management: More Than a New Name for Logistics. *International Journal of Logistics Management*, *8*(1), 1–13. doi:10.1108/09574099710805556

Mulla Aneesa, I. A. K. (2015, March). Supply Chain Management: Effective Tool in Construction Industry. *International Journal of Novel Research in Engineering and Science*, *2*(1), 35–40.

O'Brien, T., Nedelkoska, L., & Frasheri, E. (2017). *What is the Binding Constraint to Growth in Albania*. Center for International Development at Harvard University.

O'Brien, W. J. (1999). *Construction Supply-Chain Management: A Vision for Advanced Coordination, Costing, and Control.* NSF Berkley - Stanford Construction Research Workshop 6.

Pryke, S. (Ed.). (2009). *Construction Suply Chain Management: Concepts and Case Studys*. Wiley-Blackwell. doi:10.1002/9781444320916

Ruben Vrijhoev, L. K. (2000, December). Roles of Supply Chain Management in Construction. *European Journal of Purchasing & Supply Management*, *6*(3-4), 69–178. doi:10.1016/S0969-7012(00)00013-7

Thunberg, M. (2016). *Developing a Framework for Supply Chain Planning in Construction* (Doctoral thesis). Linkoping Studies in Science and Technology, Linkoping.

William, J., & O'Brien, K. L. (2004). Construction Supply Chain Modeling: a research review and interdisciplinary research agenda. *ICAF Journal of Operations Management, 3*(3), 64-84.

KEY TERMS AND DEFINITIONS

Construction Supply Chain Management: Seeks optimization by taking into consideration production activities of independent production units through offers new tactics in cost reduction and increase of reliability and operation's speed in construction by providing a coherent source to improve coordination and project control.

Supply Chain Management (SCM): A management philosophy focusing on planning and managing effectively and efficiently in collaboration with suppliers and customers all the activities involved in the sourcing, procurement and conversion of materials to final products.

Triple Helix Model: Is a model of continuous interaction between university-industry-government through assuming some of the capabilities of the other as each maintains its primary role and distinct identity.

Chapter 7
Prioritizing the Enablers of Construction Supply Chain in the Industry 4.0 Environment

Vivek Agrawal
GLA University, Mathura, India

Seemant Kumar Yadav
Institute of Business Management, GLA University, Mathura, India

R. P. Mohanty
SOA University, Bhubaneswar, India

Anand M. Agrawal
https://orcid.org/0000-0002-1740-0292
GLA University, Mathura, India

ABSTRACT

Industry 4.0, the fourth-generation industrial revolution, is not only changing the manufacturing industry but others also, like the construction industry and the related supply chain issues. The construction industry has its own challenges (e.g., temporary work and involvement of high coordination, among others). This study is an attempt to explore the enablers to overcome these issues and prioritize them. Decisions are more complex if they are intangible, non-expressible, qualitative, etc. To overcome this problem in the present study, AHP technique is used. With the help of AHP, 4 enablers and 14 sub-enablers of construction supply chain are prioritized. E-supply chain management is ranked first followed by digitization, tracking and localization, and cloud computing. In the case of sub-enablers, web service technology comes at first rank whereas management information system comes at 14th rank. This study will help the managers and professionals in construction organizations in building a good setup by focusing on these explored enablers.

DOI: 10.4018/978-1-7998-2867-9.ch007

INTRODUCTION

First industrial revolution began in 1800s with the emphasis on mechanization and generation of mechanical power. It involved the transition from manual to manufacturing. The second industrialization in 1900s began with the use of electrification, resulting in mass production followed by third industrial revolution. The third phase of revolution started in 1960s with the use of digitization, use of microelectronics which facilitates the flexible production (Man and Strandhagen, 2017) with different production line controlled by programmable machines (Rojko, 2017). Such production systems still do not have flexibility regarding to the quantity.

In today's era, due to the development of information and communication technology, industry is compressed with increasing competition and fast changing consumers preferences. Moving ahead from Industry 3.0 which utilizes ICT tools to bring competitiveness the next revolution is being notified as Industry 4.0

This industrial revolution is termed as fourth generation revolution (Industry 4.0) (Gertler, 2003). Which emphasizes on functioning of smart factories with the help of Internet of Things (IOT), Cyber-Physical system and Big data. This concept comes from Germany which involves the decentralized control of manufacturing processes with advanced connectivity features and smart automation. Industry 4.0 organizations are not only limited to the use of advanced technology but also the decreasing cost, fast production and better quantity. According to Industry 4.0 organization could result in reduction of production, quality management and logistics cost up to 30%, 20% and 30% respectively. Additionally Industry 4.0 will also be beneficial in terms of shorter supply time, mass production, more human friendly work environment, and effective utilization of resources (Kagermann et al., 2013).

Despite the ever increasing application of Industry 4.0, the companies from the field of construction are not able to integrate these practices to keep pace with the counterparts like automotive and electronic sector (Hampson & Sanchez, 2014). One of the reasons could be attributed to the nature of industry itself. As, the construction value system is the result of collaboration of sub-contractors, unorganized workers and customers itself hence it is difficult to make of them innovative and tech savvy. Numerous interrelated processes and sub-processes, construction at different locations makes the construction industry more complex (Dubois and Gadde, 2002; Arayici and Goates, 2012).The output in the form of unique project requires high degree of customization, limited time, face locational challenges, coordination among the small and medium suppliers (Dubois and Gadde, 2002). Supply chain management playing an important role in increasing the productivity of construction industry (London, 2004; Prakash and Mohanty, 2014).

In spite of the fact that the construction procedure is extraordinary, SCM can be helpful and successful in construction. The SCM in construction includes a number of internal and external parties which work in coordinated manner to get the work done within the stipulated time interval. The SCM can play a significant role to achieve integration between internal and external suppliers, designers, contractors, subcontractors etc.

In view of that a number of researchers have reported the various factors affecting the efficiency and effectiveness of SCM in the field of construction. Some of them includes Lack of coordination, Design problems, Poor quality of materials, poor planning and control Akintoye et al., (2000), Ofori, (2000).

To get the winning edge of the SCM at global level it is important to design and implement a highly coordinated supply chain at global level to get the competitive advantage. While that all sounds great, the greatest obstacle to finishing this change is that a large number of the supply chain managers as of now in administration positions are not set up to bridle the capacities of this new transformed coordinated supply chain network. One of the biggest reason attributed to this may be that they have not been officially prepared in to process of developing a leadership position while managing the supply chain at global level.

Insight taken from literature it is observed that little attention has been paid to supply chain in construction supply chain to describe the current existence (Ali et al., 2010; Bassioni et al., 2004).

In this regard, this study is an attempt;

1. To explore the enablers in construction supply chain management to overcome these challenges.
2. To prioritize the explored enablers of construction supply chain management.

BACKGROUND

Small construction companies have limited competencies to invest in innovative practices and advanced technology (Kraatz, 2014). Only limited numbers of companies are fully using the advanced technologies and digital planning tools. To overcome these issues, automation, digital access, connectivity and digital data are the four keys seen (Oesterreich and Teuteberg, 2016).

Other associated concepts like cost reduction can be possible by using automatic work flow and robotics (Oesterreich and Teuteberg, 2016) through industry 4.0. Material cost can be reduced by use of automatic tracking system (Sardroud, 2012). Big data analytics can be used to support the decision makers to make more effective decision through increased access to information (McMalcolm, 2015).

Insights taken from the literature about different enablers in construction supply chain in Industry 4.0 to overcome the challenges are documented in Table 1.

Table 1. Enablers in construction supply chain management (related to industry 4.0)

SN	Enabler	Sub enabler	Reference from Literature
1	E-Supply chain management	E-Business	Zou and Seo, 2006; Zhang et al., 2009; Aziz and Ahmad, 2011
		Extranet	Pala et al., 2016
		Web portal	Chenga, 2011; Pinho et al., 2008; Cheng et al., 2010
2	Cloud computing	Collaboration technology	Singleton and Cormican, 2013; Gong and Azambuja, 2013
		Web services technology	Das et al., 2015
		Mobile internet based CSCM	Shi et al., 2016
3	Digitization	Intelligent transportation system	Zhou, 2008; Moon et al., 2017
		Management information system	Zhou, 2008; Moon et al., 2017
		3D printing	Kothman and Faber, 216
		Real time SCM	Min and Bjornsson, 2008; Dallasega et al., 2016
4	Tracking and Localization	Geographical Information System	Irizarry et al., 2013; Majrouhi and Limbachiya, 2010
		Decision Support	Bao and Jin, 2014
		Monitoring CSC	Irizarry et al., 2013; Getuli et al., 2016
		SC Performance Improvement	Dike and Kapogiannis, 2014; Azambuja et al., 2012

E-Supply Chain Management

Supply chain management involves the product flow, information flow and financial flow. Now-a-days construction industry is using the e-portals for supplying the information to their end users. They are using the web portals, because web portals are able to manage information, documents, stock etc (Ajam et al., 2010). Construction companies also using the web portals to control their fleet through controlled hubs with information technology. TenderSpace is an example of online hub, which help in construction supply chain openly, transparently and fairly to avoid conflict.

E-Business

E-business is the integration between internet and supply chain. It is transforming many processes from procurement to product design and customer management. It is establishing a new rules of competition for established businesses in a miraculous way (Amit & Zott, 2001). As per the definition of e-commerce, a company who earn at least 10% of its revenue from internet transactions can be referred as a e-business firm. But as construction supply chain is consisting of many small and medium sized firms, these SMEs deals with their niche market hence they do not feel to have a global connectivity via internet. Also due to issue related to the online payment security and lack of necessary IT skilled human resource it is very rare to have e-business in construction sector.

Extranet

A type of private network, which use the internet, telecommunication system, and technology to share part of information with vendors, suppliers, partners, customers or with other business securely.

Web Portal

A web portal is a customized private website. To assess this login details are required.

Cloud Computing

The use of cloud computing and information technology has significantly transformed the construction supply chain management. It indicates a fundamental change of utilizing the information and communication technology (ICT).Due to real time access of information is available to the organization from any location (www.xperiencedynamics.com, Madas, 2017). Cloud computing is improving the collaboration (Madhukar, 2017) in construction supply chain.

Cloud computing is beneficial to business owners as it reduces the requirement for users to plan for future, and allows companies to initiate from the least and increase resources utilization. However, despite the fact that cloud computing provides great benefits the IT industry; the development of cloud computing technology in sector like construction is at its early phase.

Cloud computing represents a concurrence of two major components (1). IT efficiency and (2). Business flexibility .The IT efficiency represents the situation where the modern computers are utilized with more efficiency using a competitive hardware and software components and business agility reflects a platform of competitive tool by adopting rapid improvements in various business processes which are important for the fulfillment of customers request effectively and efficiently in real time.

Collaboration Technology

In this data can be merged which is collected from different sources. This merged data can be assessed by different parties and supply chain status can be visualized. It diminishes the risk of out dated and incorrect information.

Web Services Technology

This incorporates SC professionals; those are using web portal. Through this information can be access, integrate, retrieved into a supply chain.

Mobile Internet Based CSCM

Mobile internet based CSCM is helping in sharing the real time information, improve material flow, technology support, safety issues (Shi et al., 2016). The mobile terminal device and mobile terminal enabling technology can be used mutually with Radio-frequency Identification on construction sites to improve the material control.

Digitization

This factor address the issues related to information, information network, logistics and traffic management. The first framework for digitization is proposed by Zhou (Zhou, 2008). Digitization can improve the coordination among different construction organization. Now a day's customers are expecting excellent quality products and services but many organizations are not able to meet these expectations. To do so it is inevitable that companies need to go for digitization. Digitization brings transparency and coordination in the systems which assist in boosting the business performance.

The incremental growth of existing business can be boosted with the help of digitization and related issues like big data analytics. Because the ever increasing process of digitization dramatically reduces the concerned transaction costs related to the collecting information and other controlling activities. Digitization also reduces the overall manufacturing cost as it has been observed that labor costs would comprise an ever smaller component of manufacturers' cost structures as IT developments and automation progressed (Ford 2009).

Intelligent Transportation System

It is an advanced application which provides innovative services related to the traffic management and modes of transport. Due to this users are well informed and make proper coordination with other.

Management Information System

Due to this information can be flow faster than before in more accurate manner at lower cost. By considering this factor the efficiency of construction organization will definitely improved.

3D Printing

Also known as additive manufacturing and it is impacting supply chain. It is a process of constructing a physical thing from a three-dimensional model, by using many thin layers in chain.

Real Time SCM

The real time information in construction industry is very important. With the assess of real time information a reliable demand forecasting can be obtained.

Tracking and Localization

Many tracking and localization technology are available for the construction organization and they will be benefitted by using these. Some are global positioning system, automated material locating and tracking technology etc.

Geographical Information System

This is a system which stores all the geographical information. It helps in understanding of what belongs where.

Decision Support

Decision support system is very helpful in taking decisions. It also stores the different information which helps the professionals in taking decision optimally in adverse situations, which reduce the risk and diminishes the cost also.

Monitoring CSC

In this different systems are integrate in to a special unique system. With this integrated model supply chain professionals in construction industry track of the status of supply chain and to ensure the delivery of materials, warning signals can be provided.

SC Performance Improvement

This can be done regardless the type software application. Information and data can be mutually browsed without focusing to the companies. In this data can transfer and share by the standard data exchanges languages.

MAIN FOCUS OF THE CHAPTER

Indian construction market is expected to be US$180billlion by 2020. With emergence of nuclear families and urbanization the demand of houses are increased. By 2020 more than 70% of GDP is contributed by Urban areas, out of this 11% will be contributed by housing sector by 2020 (www.ibef.org).

The Union Cabinet of India approved 100 Smart City Projects in August 2015. The Indian government also raised limited for FDI to 100%, and offered different schemes in Union Budget 2018-19 with near about US $9.97 billion. This will boost the construction industry in India. But the companies can get full advantages of this by construing more and more projects. For speed up of these projects, it is necessary that construction companies should focus on supply chain management enablers.

Supply chain management enablers in construction industry in industry 4.0 environment are playing an important role now-a-days. Without focusing the different enablers, the advantage of Industry 4.0 cannot be taken by construction industry. Some of the challenges in the construction industry are (Riddell, T. 2016)

- Shortage of qualified workers
- Generational Differences
- Technology adoption
- Environmental sustainability
- Project complexity

Such challenges can be overcome by use of fourth generation industrial revolution. But most of the companies do not understand the power and real potential of fourth industrial revolution. For example companies are doing enough to satisfy the government norms but others very little. The technique of Building Information Modeling (BIM) is much more than the digital plan and apprehension – its full continuum should perceive the built asset through to ongoing, in-life servicing and maintenance. In other words Building Lifecycle Management (Stokoe, 2017).

The use of prefabrication or offsite, modular construction, with components being produced in automated factories, shows signs of revolutionizing the housing market, enabling relatively rapid construction of low cost but high quality housing to meet social demand. By the use of digital technology, companies have potential to build more energy efficient, intelligent and sustainable building. Few companies in India, using this style of construction policy for cost cutting and time saving. While the interaction with seven senior managers (production) at Delhi based construction companies, it has been analyzed that, professionals in construction industry are aware with the industry 4.0. They are aware with the benefits of Industry 4.0 revolution, but they are not able make the priority of different enablers in industry 4.0 environment in their different construction projects.

RESEARCH METHODOLOGY

Decisions are more complex, if it is based on multi criterion. Generally these criteria are intangible, non-expressible, qualitative, and subjective. Quantification is typical. Analytical Hierarchy Process (AHP) is a technique which can be used in such situations for decision making (Saaty, 1980). AHP converts the qualitative values into metric values which enable the decision makers to evaluate the weights and make the preferences (Saaty, 1980, 1982, 2008) through a series of pair wise comparisons. AHP provides the relative importance of the criterions which help in giving better decisions. The basic structure of AHP Model (Figure 1), start with the goal at the top that segregate into sub parts which are helping in achieving the goal (Saaty, 1980, 1982, 2008).

Figure 1.

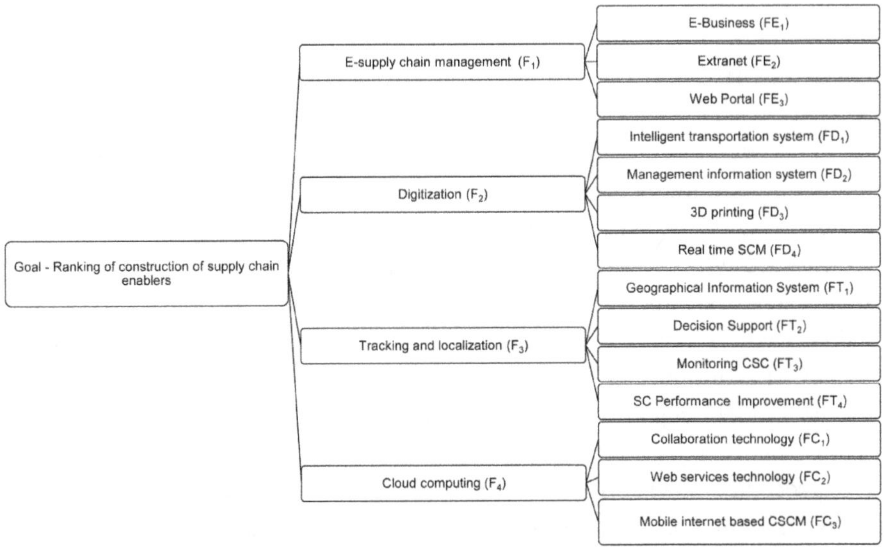

Analysis

The Analytic Hierarchy Process (AHP), was introduced by Thomas Saaty (1980). It deals with the complex decision making situations where the decision maker set priorities and expected to take best possible course of action. AHP reduces these complex scenarios into to a series of pairwise comparisons, and then integrating the output.

In AHP, according to Dağdevirena et al., (2009), initially hierarchy structure is developed for the decision problem similar to a family tree (Albayrak and Erensal, 2004).The following procedure is referred for the formation of the problem given by Mohanty (1992):

- The structure of the problem should be decomposable into hierarchical structure; hence structure of any problem is more important than solution of this problem.
- Structuring can be attended by only few experts. They use their skills, knowledge, facts, documents etc.
- The experts are expertise in assigning the weights to the different criteria of the structure.

In the present study 4 enablers and their 14 sub enablers were considered on the recommendation of 5 experts' opinion. These enablers are important because they can help the construction companies in facing the challenges and take the advantage of Industry 4.0. By using AHP, following the discussed steps above the pair comparison tables are prepared with the help of 5 expert opinions (1 academician and 4 from industry).

Expert Profile

Two experts were more than 55 years of age; one fell in the age group of 45–55 years and two experts fell in the age groups of 35–45 years. Since this study is associated with the construction industry, experience in construction industry is also considered while selection of the experts. No expert selected had experience less than five years. Among the experts selected, two had experience of 6–10 years with Construction Company engaged in supply chain and rests were having an experience of more than 10 years. Four experts out of five are post graduate and one expert (academician) is post doctorate degree. All the experts are of engineering background in their graduation.

In the second step criterions or alternatives are compared. At each level of the hierarchy structure the criterions are compared pair wise. Each pair consists of two criteria. In AHP all the pairwise comparison is based on a comparison scale consisting of nine levels (Saaty, 1980, 1982, 2008). The steps for AHP analysis are as follows:

Step 1: Make the initial pairwise comparison matrix (from Table 6 to 8) for all the pairs of criterion on the basis of scale shown in Table 2.

Table 2. Saaty's 9-point scale

Scale	1	3	5	7	9	2,4,6,8
Compare factor	Equally important	inadequately important	Strongly important	Very strongly important	exceptionally important	middle value

Step 2: Calculate the sum for each column $\sum_{i} C\,ij$

Step 3: Standardized each cell by $Xij = \dfrac{Cij}{\sum_{i} Cij}$

Step 4: Calculate the row sum by using the formula $Ri = \sum_{i} X\,ij$ and Weights by

$$Wi = \frac{Ri}{N},$$

Step 5: Calculate vector for priority by using Vi = A. Wi where i = 1,2,3,.........., N

Step 6: Calculate $\lambda i = \dfrac{Vi}{Wi}$ and calculate λmax by averaging the λi's.

Step 7: Calculate consistency index and consistency ratio

$$C.I. = \frac{»max - n}{N - 1}$$

$$C.R. = \frac{C.I.}{R.I.}$$

(should be < 0.10, where R.I. means random Index)

Table 3. R. I. (Saaty, 1980)

Matrix	1,2	3	4	5	6	7	8	9	10	11
Random Index	0	0.52	0.89	1.12	1.26	1.36	1.41	1.46	1.49	1.52

From the above the value of C.R. is less than 0.10, which is an allowable value. Hence, matrix is found to be acceptable due the consistency in the judgments which is in the acceptable range.

Step 8: Repeat step 1 to step 7 for each expert and check the consistency ratio for each case.

SOLUTIONS AND RECOMMENDATIONS

Calculations for the given problem on the basis of expert score are presented from Table 4 to 8.

From the table 4 it is observed that E-supply chain management is very important enabler for in construction supply chain management, followed by digitization, tracking and localization, and cloud computing.

E-supply chain management is consisting E-business, extranet, and web-portal as sub enablers. Out of these extranet is the most important sub-enabler with highest priority score i.e. 2.0617 (Table 5) which followed by E-business and web portal. Construction Company should focus on extranet and need more investment in e-business and their web portal for making more effective supply chain.

Second enabler Digitization consisting of intelligent transportation system, management information system, 3D printing and real time SCM. The real time SCM is the most important sub-enabler out of the four, which followed by 3D printing, intelligent transportation system, and management information system.

Tracking and digitization is at third rank as per the priority score (Table 6) which consist of geographical information system, decision support, monitoring, and SC performance improvement as sub enablers. In this SC performance improvement is the most important sub-enabler and proper care is required to this by construction organization. Monitoring, geographical information system and decision support comes at second, third and fourth rank respectively as per the priority scores (Table 7).

Cloud computing consisting collaboration technology, web service technology, and mobile internet based CSCM. Out of these, web service technology is most important sub-enabler followed by mobile internet based CSCM and collaboration technology.

Table 4. Priority score of enablers

Initial Matrix							
	F1	**F2**	**F3**	**F4**			
F1	1	3	8.6	9			
F2	0.33	1	5.8	8.2			
F3	0.114	0.176	1	3			
F4	0.11	0.122	0.33	1			
	1.554	4.298	15.73	21.2			
Sensitize Matrix							
	F1	**F2**	**F3**	**F4**	**Prioritized Vector (PV)**		
F1	0.6435	0.6980	0.5467	0.4245	0.5782		
F2	0.2124	0.2327	0.3687	0.3868	0.3001		
F3	0.0734	0.0409	0.0636	0.1415	0.0798		
F4	0.0708	0.0284	0.0210	0.0472	0.0418		
Reachability matrix							
	F1	**F2**	**F3**	**F4**	**Prioritized Vector (PV)**	**Weighted Vector**	**Eigen Value**
F1	1.0000	3.0000	8.6000	9.0000	0.5782	2.5417	4.3961
F2	0.3300	1.0000	5.8000	8.2000	0.3001	1.2971	4.3216
F3	0.1140	0.1760	1.0000	3.0000	0.0798	0.3241	4.0587
F4	0.1100	0.1220	0.3300	1.0000	0.0418	0.1684	4.0258
				N	4.0000		
						Average Lambda	4.2005
						CI	0.0668
						RI	0.9000
						CR	0.0743

Table 5. Priority score of sub enablers of E-supply chain Management

Initial Matrix						
	FE1	**FE2**	**FE3**			
FE1	1	0.2	1.4			
FE2	5	1	3			
FE3	0.8	0.33	1			
	6.8	1.53	5.4			
Sensitize Matrix						
	FE1	**FE2**	**FE3**	**Prioritized Vector (PV)**		
FE1	0.1471	0.1307	0.2593	0.1790		
FE2	0.7353	0.6536	0.5556	0.6481		
FE3	0.1176	0.2157	0.1852	0.1728		
Reachability matrix						
	FE1	**FE2**	**FE3**	**Prioritized Vector (PV)**	**Weighted Vector**	**Eigen Value**
FE1	1.0000	0.2000	1.4000	0.1790	0.5506	3.0759
FE2	5.0000	1.0000	3.0000	0.6481	2.0617	3.1810
FE3	0.8000	0.3300	1.0000	0.1728	0.5299	3.0661
			N	3.0000		
					Average Lambda	3.1076
					CI	0.0538
					RI	0.5800
					CR	0.0928

Table 6. Priority score of sub enablers of digitization

Initial Matrix							
	FD1	**FD2**	**FD3**	**FD4**			
FD1	1	3	1	0.33			
FD2	0.33	1	0.2	0.14			
FD3	1	5	1	0.33			
FD4	3	7	3	1			
	5.33	16	5.2	1.8			
Sensitize Matrix							
	FD1	**FD2**	**FD3**	**FD4**	**Prioritized Vector (PV)**		
FD1	0.1876	0.1875	0.1923	0.1833	0.1877		
FD2	0.0619	0.0625	0.0385	0.0778	0.0602		
FD3	0.1876	0.3125	0.1923	0.1833	0.2189		
FD4	0.5629	0.4375	0.5769	0.5556	0.5332		
Reachability matrix							
	FD1	**FD2**	**FD3**	**FD4**	**Prioritized Vector (PV)**	**Weighted Vector**	**Eigen Value**
FD1	1.0000	3.0000	1.0000	0.3300	0.1877	0.7631	4.0656
FD2	0.3300	1.0000	0.2000	0.1400	0.0602	0.2405	3.9981
FD3	1.0000	5.0000	1.0000	0.3300	0.2189	0.8834	4.0349
FD4	3.0000	7.0000	3.0000	1.0000	0.5332	2.1742	4.0777
				N	4.0000		
						Average Lambda	4.0441
						CI	0.0147
						RI	0.9000
						CR	0.0163

FUTURE RESEARCH DIRECTIONS

Since this study considers the enablers from the literature, future study can be conducted for exploring the enablers by conducting the interviews of the expert. Only 5 experts were considered for the analysis, other can do this study by taking more responses so that validity can be improved.Discuss solutions and recommendations in dealing with the issues, controversies, or problems presented in the preceding section.

Table 7. Priority score of sub enablers of tracking and localization

Initial Matrix							
	FT1	FT2	FT3	FT4			
FT1	1	2.6	1	0.33			
FT2	0.464	1	0.2	0.14			
FT3	1	5	1	0.33			
FT4	3	7	3	1			
	5.464	15.6	5.2	1.8			
Sensitize Matrix							
	FT1	**FT2**	**FT3**	**FT4**	**Prioritized Vector (PV)**		
FT1	0.1830	0.1667	0.1923	0.1833	0.1813		
FT2	0.0849	0.0641	0.0385	0.0778	0.0663		
FT3	0.1830	0.3205	0.1923	0.1833	0.2198		
FT4	0.5490	0.4487	0.5769	0.5556	0.5326		
Reachability matrix							
	FT1	**FT2**	**FT3**	**FT4**	**Prioritized Vector (PV)**	**Weighted Vector**	**Eigen Value**
FT1	1.0000	2.6000	1.0000	0.3300	0.1813	0.7493	4.1322
FT2	0.4640	1.0000	0.2000	0.1400	0.0663	0.2690	4.0559
FT3	1.0000	5.0000	1.0000	0.3300	0.2198	0.9084	4.1332
FT4	3.0000	7.0000	3.0000	1.0000	0.5326	2.2001	4.1312
				N	4.0000		
						Average Lambda	4.1131
						CI	0.0377
						RI	0.9000
						CR	0.0419

CONCLUSION

Supply Chain is a finished procedure that begins from the crude materials and the inbound coordination right to the outbound coordination and expediting the thought the table. Without a proficient production network, there would be a ton of bottleneck associated with the association.

Table 8. Priority score of sub enablers of cloud computing

	Initial Matrix					
	FC1	**FC2**	**FC3**			
FC1	1	0.2	1			
FC2	5	1	3			
FC3	1	0.33	1			
	7	1.53	5			
	Sensitize Matrix					
				Prioritized Vector (PV)		
	FC1	**FC2**	**FC3**			
FC1	0.1429	0.1307	0.2000	0.1579		
FC2	0.7143	0.6536	0.6000	0.6560		
FC3	0.1429	0.2157	0.2000	0.1862		
	Reachability matrix					
	FC1	**FC2**	**FC3**	**Prioritized Vector (PV)**	**Weighted Vector**	**Eigen Value**
FC1	1.0000	0.2000	1.0000	0.1579	0.4752	3.0105
FC2	5.0000	1.0000	3.0000	0.6560	2.0038	3.0548
FC3	1.0000	0.3300	1.0000	0.1862	0.5605	3.0105
			N	3.0000		
					Average Lambda	3.0253
					CI	0.0126
					RI	0.5800
					CR	0.0218

Supply chain in construction industry is an important concept. With the development of Industry 4.0 the construction company should use the features and those enablers which can reduce the different type of cost and ultimately the production cost of a project or a unit. This study is an attempt to explore those enablers which can overcome the challenges in construction supply chain management. From the limited available study, the different enablers; E-Supply chain management, Digitization, Tracking and Localization, and Cloud computing and their 14 sub enablers are explored. With the help of AHP all the enablers were prioritized. E-Supply chain management is ranked at one with score 0.2809 followed by, Digitization, Tracking and Localization, and Cloud computing with priority score 0.1919, 0.0499, 0.0439 respectively (Table 6). Sub enablers are also ranked on the basis of their priory score. Web service technology comes at first rank whereas management information system comes at fourteenth rank.

The companies are required to put enormous focus on the improvement of supply chain performance. Companies can make their supply chain either responsive or efficient with the help of developing an appropriate supply chain capability. These capabilities are very important as far as gaining the competitive advantage is concern. The techniques like digitization cloud computing big data can add more value to the supply chain performance as they all integrates the various cross functional activities and not only integrate they in fact play the role of driver in bringing the coordination among the members of supply chain. The resultant enablers like Monitoring, geographical information system and decision support system web service technology, mobile internet based CSCM and collaboration technology all are proven to be significant predictor of supply chain performance. The application of these outcome no doubt will help construction companies to bring a consistency between their competitive strategy and supply chain strategy so that they can get their strategic fit. For that purpose not it is upto the construction companies that in which form they are expected to design their supply chain so that the objective of supply chain strategies can be aligned well with the strategies of gaining the competitive advantage.

This study will help the managers and professionals in construction organizations in building a good setup by focusing on these explored enablers. They can be more focused on those enablers and sub-enablers who come at the highest priority. All the factors are important but some needs more focus due to their benefits. For example: E-supply chain management can help the professionals for strengthening their SCM using electronic solution and information technology for coordination and building relationship between supplier and contractors. By the use of cloud computing construction organizations can control on duplication of data or data conflicts. It can integrate the data from contractors, suppliers, and carriers. It also provides, up to date real time information. With the help of digitization, inventory can be tracked on real time basis, traffic condition can be analyzed, by which one can control the lead time. By using the technology for tracking and localization, construction organization can reduce the experience on material stock, reduce the task duration, and also reduce the labor cost by optimum utilization of them.

The proper management of these supply chain enablers are related to the acquisition of skills to acquire as a leadership position in global supply chain management. The key skills for the purpose includes, the supply chain manager's ability to negotiate with different stakeholders, high degree of flexibility in supply chain designing and implementation and a proactive approach to mitigate the risk associated with the supply chain management. The supply chain enablers like E-supply chain management significantly contributes in supply chain negotiation with vendors, the enabler like cloud computing and digitization provides a platform for bringing flexibility in supply chain and the supply chain enabler tracking and localization recues the supply chain risk and improves its performance. As the result the ultimate goal of supply chain enablers is to assist the supply chain in making it more competitive and flexible at every level. In addition, the famous 3Cs of supply chain leadership strategies i.e. Communicate, Collaborate and Change cannot be exercised without the successful implementation of these enablers.

To some things up the successful implementation of these supply chain enablers can be considered as the building blocks of leadership strategies for making supply chain more flexible, competitive, efficient and effective.

REFERENCES

Ajam, M., Alshawi, M., & Mezher, T. (2010). Augmented process model for e-tendering: Towards integrating object models with document management systems. *Automation in Construction*, *19*(6), 762–778. doi:10.1016/j.autcon.2010.04.001

Akintoye, A., McIntosh, G., & Fitzgerald, E. (2000). A survey of supply chain collaboration and management in the UK construction industry. *European Journal of Purchasing & Supply Management, 6*(3-4), 159-168.

Albayrak, E., & Erensal, Y. C. (2004). Using analytic hierarchy process (AHP) to improve human performance: An application of multiple criteria decision making problem. *Journal of Intelligent Manufacturing*, *15*(4), 491–503. doi:10.1023/B:JIMS.0000034112.00652.4c

Ali, A. S., Mohd-Don, Z., Alias, A., Kamaruzzaman, S. N., & Pitt, M. (2010). The performance of construction partnering projects in Malaysia. *International Journal of Physical Sciences*, *5*(4), 327–333.

Amit, R., & Zott, C. (2001). Value creation in e-business. *Strategic Management Journal*, *22*(6-7), 493–520. doi:10.1002mj.187

Arayici, Y., & Coates, P. (2012). A system engineering perspective to knowledge transfer: a case study approach of BIM adoption. In *Virtual Reality-Human Computer Interaction*. InTech. doi:10.5772/51052

Azambuja, M., Alves, T., Leite, F., & Gong, J. (2012). Leveraging building information models to support supply chain decisions in construction projects. In *Construction Research Congress: Construction Challenges in a Flat World* (pp. 747-756). 10.1061/9780784412329.076

Aziz, N. A., Ahmad, R., & Durai, D. D. (2012, January). B2B collaboration method through trust values for e-supply chain integrator: a case study of Malaysian construction industry. In *Fourth International Conference on Machine Vision (ICMV 2011): Computer Vision and Image Analysis; Pattern Recognition and Basic Technologies* (Vol. 8350, p. 835031). International Society for Optics and Photonics. 10.1117/12.920549

Bao, J., Su, Z., & Jin, S. (2014). Building and Operation of Construction Supply Chain Information Integration Management Mode Based on Building Information Model. In *Proceedings of the 18th International Symposium on Advancement of Construction Management and Real Estate* (pp. 467-476). Springer. 10.1007/978-3-642-44916-1_46

Cheng, J. C., Law, K. H., Bjornsson, H., Jones, A., & Sriram, R. (2010). A service oriented framework for construction supply chain integration. *Automation in Construction, 19*(2), 245–260. doi:10.1016/j.autcon.2009.10.003

Chenga, J. C. (2011). A web service framework for measuring and monitoring environmental and carbon footprint in construction supply chains. *Procedia Engineering, 14*, 141–147. doi:10.1016/j.proeng.2011.07.016

Dağdeviren, M., Yavuz, S., & Kılınç, N. (2009). Weapon selection using the AHP and TOPSIS methods under fuzzy environment. *Expert Systems with Applications, 36*(4), 8143–8151. doi:10.1016/j.eswa.2008.10.016

Dallasega, P., Marcher, C., Marengo, E., Rauch, E., Matt, D. T., & Nutt, W. (2016). *A decentralized and pull-based control loop for on-demand delivery in ETO construction supply chains.* International Group for Lean Construction.

Das, M., Cheng, J. C., & Law, K. H. (2015). An ontology-based web service framework for construction supply chain collaboration and management. *Engineering, Construction, and Architectural Management, 22*(5), 551–572. doi:10.1108/ECAM-07-2014-0089

de Man, J. C., & Strandhagen, J. O. (2017). An Industry 4.0 research agenda for sustainable business models. *Procedia CIRP, 63*, 721–726. doi:10.1016/j.procir.2017.03.315

Dike, I. U., & Kapogiannis, G. (2014). A conceptual model for improving construction supply chain performance. *Proceedings of the 30th Annual Association of Researchers in Construction Management Conference (ARCOM 2014).*

Dubois, A., & Gadde, L. E. (2002). The construction industry as a loosely coupled system: Implications for productivity and innovation. *Construction Management and Economics*, *20*(7), 621–631. doi:10.1080/01446190210163543

Gertler, M. S. (2003). Tacit knowledge and the economic geography of context, or the undefinable tacitness of being (there). *Journal of Economic Geography*, *3*(1), 75–99. doi:10.1093/jeg/3.1.75

Getuli, V., Ventura, S. M., Capone, P., & Ciribini, A. L. (2016). A BIM-based construction supply chain framework for monitoring progress and coordination of site activities. *Procedia Engineering*, *164*, 542–549. doi:10.1016/j.proeng.2016.11.656

Gong, J., & Azambuja, M. (2013). Visualizing construction supply chains with google cloud computing tools. In *ICSDEC 2012: Developing the Frontier of Sustainable Design* (pp. 671–678). Engineering, and Construction.

Hampson, K., Kraatz, J. A., & Sanchez, A. X. (2014). The global construction industry and R&D. In *R&D Investment and Impact in the Global Construction Industry* (pp. 42–61). Routledge. doi:10.4324/9781315774916

Heidelberg.Bassioni, H. A., Price, A. D., & Hassan, T. M. (2004). Performance measurement in construction. *Journal of Management Engineering*, *20*(2), 42–50. doi:10.1061/(ASCE)0742-597X(2004)20:2(42)

Irizarry, J., Karan, E. P., & Jalaei, F. (2013). Integrating BIM and GIS to improve the visual monitoring of construction supply chain management. *Automation in Construction*, *31*, 241–254. doi:10.1016/j.autcon.2012.12.005

Kagermann, H., Helbig, J., Hellinger, A., & Wahlster, W. (2013). *Recommendations for Implementing the Strategic Initiative INDUSTRIE 4.0: Securing the Future of German Manufacturing Industry, acatech*. Irizarry.

Kothman, I., & Faber, N. (2016). How 3D printing technology changes the rules of the game: Insights from the construction sector. *Journal of Manufacturing Technology Management*, *27*(7), 932–943. doi:10.1108/JMTM-01-2016-0010

Kraatz, J. A., & Sanchez, A. X. (2014). R&D Investment and Impact in the Global Construction Industry. Routledge.

London, K. (2004). *Construction Supply Chain Procurement Modelling* (PhD thesis). The University of Melbourne.

Madas, M. (2014). *Building on ICT to Connect SMEs in the Digital Construction Supply Chain, Information Systems & e-Business Lab*. Available: http:// www.iseb.gr/blog/building-ict-connect-smes-digital-construction-supply-chain

Madhukar, B. A. (2017). *Construction Supply Chain Management. For Reeingeneering Construction Industry*. Available: http://www. builtconstructions.in/OnlineMagazine/Bangalore/Pages/Construction-Supply-Chain-Management-0114.aspx

MajrouhiSardroud, J., & Limbachiya, M. C. (2010). *Integrated advance data storage technology for effective construction logistics management*. Academic Press.

Min, J. U., & Bjornsson, H. C. (2008). Agent-based construction supply chain simulator (CS 2) for measuring the value of real-time information sharing in construction. *Journal of Management Engineering*, *24*(4), 245–254. doi:10.1061/(ASCE)0742-597X(2008)24:4(245)

Mohanty, R. P. (1992). Project selection by a multiple-criteria decision-making method: An example from a developing country. *International Journal of Project Management*, *10*(1), 31–38. doi:10.1016/0263-7863(92)90070-P

Moon, S., Han, S., Zekavat, P. R., Bernold, L. E., & Wang, X. (2017). Process-waste reduction in the construction supply chain using proactive information network. *Concurrent Engineering*, *25*(2), 123–135. doi:10.1177/1063293X16667451

Oesterreich, T. D., & Teuteberg, F. (2016). Understanding the implications of digitisation and automation in the context of Industry 4.0: A triangulation approach and elements of a research agenda for the construction industry. *Computers in Industry*, *83*, 121–139. doi:10.1016/j.compind.2016.09.006

Ofori, G. (2000). Greening the construction supply chain in Singapore. *European Journal of Purchasing & Supply Management*, *6*(3-4), 195–206. doi:10.1016/S0969-7012(00)00015-0

Pala, M., Edum-Fotwe, F., Ruikar, K., Peters, C., & Doughty, N. (2016). Implementing commercial information exchange: A construction supply chain case study. *Construction Management and Economics*, *34*(12), 898–918. doi:10.1080/01446193.2016.1211718

Prakash, A., & Mohanty, R. P. (2015). Understanding construction supply chain management for road projects. *International Journal of Logistics Systems and Management*, *22*(4), 414–435. doi:10.1504/IJLSM.2015.072747

Riddell, T. (2016). *Top 5 issues facing the construction industry in 2017*. Available at: https://esub.com/top-issues-facing-the-construction-industry-2017/

Rojko, A. (2017). Industry 4.0 concept: Background and overview. *International Journal of Interactive Mobile Technologies*, *11*(5), 77–90. doi:10.3991/ijim.v11i5.7072

Saaty, T. (1980). *The Analytic Hierarchy Process*. McGraw-Hill.

Saaty, T. (1982). *Decision-Making for Leaders*. Wadsworth.

Saaty, T. L. (2008). Decision making with the analytic hierarchy process. *International Journal of Services Sciences*, *1*(1), 83–98. doi:10.1504/IJSSCI.2008.017590

Sardroud, J. M. (2012). Influence of RFID technology on automated management of construction materials and components. *Scientia Iranica*, *19*(3), 381–392. doi:10.1016/j.scient.2012.02.023

Shi, Q., Ding, X., Zuo, J., & Zillante, G. (2016). Mobile Internet based construction supply chain management: A critical review. *Automation in Construction*, *72*(82016), 143–154. doi:10.1016/j.autcon.2016.08.020

Shi, Q., Ding, X., Zuo, J., & Zillante, G. (2016). Mobile Internet based construction supply chain management: A critical review. *Automation in Construction*, *72*, 143–154. doi:10.1016/j.autcon.2016.08.020

Singleton, T., & Cormican, K. (2013). The influence of technology on the development of partnership relationships in the Irish construction industry. *International Journal of Computer Integrated Manufacturing*, *26*(1-2), 19–28. doi:10.1080/0951192X.2012.681907

Stokoe, J. (2017). *The construction industry – a leader or a follower in the fourth industrial revolution?* Available at: https://blogs.3ds.com/uk/construction-industry-revolution/

Xperiencegroup. (2016). *Five Ways to Improve Construction Supply Chain Management*. Available: http://xperiencedynamics.com/blog/30/five-ways-toimprove- construction-supply-chain-management/

Zhang, M., Wang, J., & Zhang, J. (2009, October). Research on construction supply chain management in e-business environment. In *Industrial Engineering and Engineering Management, 2009. IE&EM'09. 16th International Conference on* (pp. 1565-1568). IEEE. 10.1109/ICIEEM.2009.5344374

Zhou, J. (2008, October). The optimization mode for construction supply chain management based on information techniques. In *Service Operations and Logistics, and Informatics, 2008. IEEE/SOLI 2008. IEEE International Conference on* (Vol. 1, pp. 1054-1058). IEEE.

Zhou, J. (2008). The optimization mode for construction supply chain management based on information techniques. *SOLI 2008, IEEE International Conference on Service Operations and Logistics, and Informatics*, 1054–1058. 10.1109/SOLI.2008.4686554

Zou, P. X., & Seo, Y. (2006). Effective applications of e-commerce technologies in construction supply chain: Current practice and future improvement. *Journal of Information Technology in Construction, 11*(10), 127–147.

ADDITIONAL READINGS

Bogoviz, A. V. (2019). Industry 4.0 as a new vector of growth and development of knowledge economy. In *Industry 4.0: Industrial Revolution of the 21st Century* (pp. 85–91). Springer. doi:10.1007/978-3-319-94310-7_8

Büchi, G., Cugno, M., & Castagnoli, R. (2020). Smart factory performance and Industry 4.0. *Technological Forecasting and Social Change, 150*, 119790. doi:10.1016/j.techfore.2019.119790

Frank, A. G., Dalenogare, L. S., & Ayala, N. F. (2019). Industry 4.0 technologies: Implementation patterns in manufacturing companies. *International Journal of Production Economics, 210*, 15–26. doi:10.1016/j.ijpe.2019.01.004

Lasi, H., Fettke, P., Kemper, H. G., Feld, T., & Hoffmann, M. (2014). Industry 4.0. *Business & Information Systems Engineering, 6*(4), 239–242. doi:10.100712599-014-0334-4

Olsen, T. L., & Tomlin, B. (2020). Industry 4.0: Opportunities and Challenges for Operations Management. *Manufacturing & Service Operations Management, 22*(1), 113–122. doi:10.1287/msom.2019.0796

Oztemel, E., & Gursev, S. (2020). Literature review of Industry 4.0 and related technologies. *Journal of Intelligent Manufacturing, 31*(1), 127–182. doi:10.100710845-018-1433-8

Popkova, E. G. (2019). Preconditions of formation and development of industry 4.0 in the conditions of knowledge economy. In *Industry 4.0: Industrial Revolution of the 21st Century* (pp. 65–72). Springer. doi:10.1007/978-3-319-94310-7_6

Tortorella, G. L., Vergara, A. M. C., Garza-Reyes, J. A., & Sawhney, R. (2020). Organizational learning paths based upon industry 4.0 adoption: An empirical study with Brazilian manufacturers. *International Journal of Production Economics*, *219*, 284–294. doi:10.1016/j.ijpe.2019.06.023

Xu, L. D., & Duan, L. (2019). Big data for cyber physical systems in industry 4.0: A survey. *Enterprise Information Systems*, *13*(2), 148–169. doi:10.1080/17517575.2018.1442934

KEY TERMS AND DEFINITIONS

3D Printing: Also known as additive manufacturing and it is impacting supply chain. It is a process of constructing a physical thing from a three-dimensional model, by using many thin layers in chain.

Cloud Computing: The use of cloud computing and information technology has significantly transformed the construction supply chain management. It indicates a fundamental change of utilizing the information and communication technology (ICT).

Collaboration Technology: In this data can be merged which is collected from different sources.

Decision Support: Decision support system is very helpful in taking decisions.

Digitization: This address the issues related to information, information network, logistics and traffic management.

E-Business: E-business is the integration between internet and supply chain. It is transforming many processes from procurement to product design and customer management.

E-Supply Chain Management: Supply chain management involves the product flow, information flow and financial flow.

Extranet: A type of private network, which use the internet, telecommunication system, and technology to share part of information with vendors, suppliers, partners, customers or with other business securely.

Geographical Information System: This is a system which stores all the geographical information. It helps in understanding of what belongs where.

Industry 4.0: This concept comes from Germany which involves the decentralized control of manufacturing processes with advanced connectivity features and smart automation. Industry 4.0 organizations are not only limited to the use of advanced technology but also the decreasing cost, fast production and better quantity.

Intelligent Transportation System: It is an advanced application which provides innovative services related to the traffic management and modes of transport.

Management Information System: Due to this information can be flow faster than before in more accurate manner at lower cost. By considering this factor the efficiency of construction organization will definitely be improved.

Mobile Internet-Based CSCM: Mobile internet based CSCM is helping in sharing the real time information, improve material flow, technology support, safety issues.

Monitoring CSC: In this, different systems are integrated into a special unique system.

Real-Time SCM: The real time information in construction industry is very important. With the assess of real time information a reliable demand forecasting can be obtained.

Tracking and Localization: Many tracking and localization technology are available for the construction organization and they will be benefitted by using these.

Web Portal: A web portal is a customized private website.

Web Services Technology: This incorporates SC professionals; those are using web portal.

Chapter 8
Leadership Model for Supply Chain Management in Business Schools

Ramakrishna Yanamandra
https://orcid.org/0000-0001-9101-6072
School of Business, Skyline University College, Sharjah, UAE

ABSTRACT

Supply chain management has brought sweeping changes in the way organizations achieve profit and competitive advantage in the recent past. But the rapid changes occurring in the business environment due to globalization and emergence of new markets have created many new opportunities as well as challenges for organizations in supply chain. Effectiveness of management institutions can be improved if they focus on changing needs of SCM and provide dynamic leadership in line with the changing needs of students and other stakeholders. This created the need for acquiring a completely different kind of supply chain skill sets and competencies among the leaders of these institutions, which they were hitherto unfamiliar with. This chapter attempts to develop a supply chain leadership model for business schools and management institutions to align themselves with the changing needs of the emerging markets of management education. It will enable the management institutes to redesign their strategies to suit the required changes.

DOI: 10.4018/978-1-7998-2867-9.ch008

INTRODUCTION

During the last two decades extensive research has been done on Supply Chain Management (SCM) and its positive influence on organizations. Though SCM is found to be applicable for both manufacturing and service industry, most of the supply chain (SC) related developments took place in manufacturing sector and little less in wholesaling and retailing, the downstream aspect of it and practically very less in service sector, especially in the management education sector (Cláudia S. Sarrico et al., 2016; Govindaraju Basu, 2016). SC concepts, frameworks, strategies, and models are found to be providing positive results in manufacturing, service industry and also in educational sector (Gopalakrishnan, 2015; Govindaraju Basu, 2016; Ramakrishna Yanamandra, 2018). But, to achieve positive outcomes in education sector, especially, the management institutes, the SC leadership strategies of these institutions should play a major role. Effectiveness of education sector can be improved if these institutions focus on SCM and provide dynamic leadership in line with the changing needs of students and other stakeholders (Mason, 2008; Mourshed et al., 2012; Snyder, 2013). The leadership styles, competencies, traits and skills required for SC leaders in general and in management educational institution, in particular, are fundamentally different compared to SC leadership in business (Marion Spendlove, 2007).

Management institutions and educators in management education face several challenges today due to changing institutional environment (Granit Almog-Bareket, 2012), increasing competition (Lorange, 2002), changing needs of management students and placement companies, attitude and behaviour of present generation of students, emergence of online technologies, availability of knowledge through online resources etc. All these factors have totally redefined the way the management education is taught in B-Schools and other management institutions. In addition to these factors, other factors like globalization, scarcity of talented management faculty, mushrooming of management institutes, emergence of online management programs and provision of equal rigor for those programs has also impacted the way management is taught (Granit Almog-Bareket, 2012; Pallabi Pal Sarkar & Rajendra Prasad, 2015; Govindaraju Basu, 2016).

Inspite of a dynamic global education environment and the presence of challenges mentioned above, a management institute can be managed successfully, if the SC leadership of institution is more dynamic and possesses the commitment to provide a long-term, stakeholder oriented strategy (Granit Almog-Bareket, 2012). Also, the SC leadership team of institutions should focus on developing a new set of competencies aligning with these changing trends. To develop new competencies, these institutions like any other business organization, need to modify their existing HR policies and incorporate innovative HR aspects like HR flexibility and Stress

Management (Maku, T.C 2005; Mangan, J et al., 2005; Kumar, V. A et al, 2017). Thus, there is a need to understand and analyze the SC leadership of management institutes and their strategies for nurturing and developing future-ready managers by overcoming the existing challenges, through the implementation of SC leadership concepts (Granit Almog-Bareket, 2012). But, the focus on this aspect is found to be limited and there are no studies related to this area precisely (Eugene H. Pfeiffer, 2014). Therefore, this chapter attempts to develop a SC skill / competency model for a typical B-School / Management Institute to enable the SC leadership of these institutes to achieve positive outcomes in this emerging market of management education.

The broad objectives of this research are,

- To study the SC leadership strategies, practices and competencies of business organizations
- To study the SC leadership strategies, practices and competencies of leadership in B-Schools / Management Education Institutions.
- To develop a SC leadership skill / competency model for B-Schools / Management Education Institutions.

BACKGROUND AND LITERATURE REVIEW

SC Leadership Skills and Competencies

Irrespective of sector, there is a great shortage of availability of talented people in SC area in the recent past, which resulted in enormous focus of organizations on developing this talent (Clearspider, 2019). Another major reason for this increased interest of organizations on SC talent is due to the transformation of modern supply chains from a tactical aspect to a strategic aspect. Therefore, while being technological savvy (technology integration, big data analytics, artificial intelligence etc.), there is a need for SC leaders to develop critical thinking and problem solving skills too (Melnyk S. A., 2017).

Many studies found that supply chain leaders should possess several competencies in order to develop both these skills. As studied by Barlow Risk Dana, (2015), a progressive SC leader should possess competencies like perseverance, persistence, creativity, flexibility, collaborative skills, trust level, risk taking attitude, ability to communicate in order to build strong relationships, ability to think differently about current problems and solutions, realistic understanding of current SC situation to identify its weaknesses, ability to embrace change, possess a big picture mind-set, and a committed curiosity.

This view was supported by Becky Partida, (2019), who found that in the era of globalization, changing business dynamics and emerging markets, the role of SC has increased multi-fold and its effective implementation takes place only by the display of the above mentioned wide range of leadership competencies and skills. Companies achieve greater results and sustainable outcomes due to the unique styles of leaders, their innovative strategies and inherent traits. However, at the same time, lack of visionary leadership for implementing SC strategies has resulted in failure of supply chains. There is a need for all SC managers to visualize the future and sharpen their talent to make themselves the futuristic leaders, not just managers. This need is more prevalent in business schools due to the pressing demands of corporate world and the changing attitudes of young generation of talented students. Considering this background, this chapter attempts to develop a conceptual SC leadership competency model for business schools and management institutes. The published research in this area of SC is very limited and lacks identification of leadership best practices in management of supply chains in business organizations (Eugene H. Pfeiffer, 2014) and in management institutions too. Therefore, in order to identify the aspects related to SC leadership, a systematic literature review is conducted as presented in the forthcoming sections of the chapter.

SC leaders are supposed to link the company with its customers through effective resource utilization, relationship development, improved product design, in-time delivery of goods, providing services, creating value addition to customers and identification of future of SCM (Melnyk et al., 2009). For achieving effective SCM, it's important to take and rational and timely decisions by the leaders (Tate, Dooley & Ellram, 2001). But, it is found that there is a lack of information on SC leadership, best practices, innovative skills (Chakravarthy and Lorange, 2008; Melnyk et al. 2009; Zacharia et al., 2011). In the studies conducted till now, on what type of skills and competencies should a SC leader possess, there is still no consensus among the authors.

Supply chain leaders must attempt to understand the complicated interrelationships between organizations in supply chains (Deshpande, 2012) if the leaders of supply chains are to realize their potential benefits. Eugene H. Pfeiffer (2014), identified the best practices in supply chain leadership using a Delphi study as i) Institute the use of cross-functional steering teams, ii) Establish a position for a dedicated entrepreneur-manager, iii) Add experienced knowledge managers, iv) Appoint a Chief Relationship Officer to the C-suite, v) Institute collaborative planning vi) Institute sustainability initiatives and improve strategic leadership.

The future of every supply chain organization depends on developing and retaining good leaders (APICS, 2015). The best practices of a supply chain leader are found to be i) understanding the vision of the organization, ii) attracting people for implementation of vision, and iii) explore opportunities to realize the set vision

(APICS, 2015). The supply chain leadership consists of areas like relationships, data and decision-making (Ramakrishna, Y. 2016, APICS, 2015).

A mix of hard and soft skills such as i) focus on results, ii) working in teams, iii) collaborative working, iv) listening, v) strategic planning, vi) adaptability, vii) focus on cost reduction, viii) knowledge and application of analytics, and ix) knowledge sharing are the most important leadership skills for supply chain employees (Becky Partida 2019). The influence of supply chain leader is across the entire chain and a continuous interaction with all major members of this chain is the primary role of this leader. Additionally, they also possess competencies like influence management and development of team. Five traits and competencies like i) influencing others, ii) developing people to leaders, iii) customer focus, iv) focusing on results, and v) emotional resilience are found to be required for best supply chain leaders (Tim Stratman, 2010). Supply chain leaders have to be elevated to executive level in organizations and they should focus on strategies by looking beyond just cost-control and they should work closely with finance managers for achieving value-based customer focus (Michael Schiller, 2017).

A supply chain leader should possess a set of characteristics like, i) leads the change and improvement, ii) increases performance and productivity through change in all areas of the supply chain, from design to processes, iii) helps the supply chain adopt new patterns of operation by improving relationships and trust between people, and innovation in processes, iv) overcomes the doubts of others through good performance, insight, careful planning, good timing and growing team loyalty, v) prioritizes the mission of the organization, vi) uses available resources, talent and opportunity to execute the organization's mission and vii) is accountable for the vision and its execution (APICS, 2015). The supply chain leader should be i) metrics driven, ii) should possess a holistic view of organization and a global understanding, iii) Understand the influence internal and external factors, iv) Motivating skills, v) technical knowledge, vi) flexibility and ability to change based on customer requirements, and vii) ability to develop network of connections (Clearspider, 2019).

In the past, SC leader was a tactical position – one with specific expertise on things such as warehousing equipment, shipping routes, and fuel costs. Today, the profile of a SC leader is vastly different. SC leaders are strategic, focusing on the overall company, not just their part of it. With organizations spending large amount of money on their supply chains, the need for smart, strategic supply chain leaders is crucial. Whether it is gathering business intelligence to help make better decisions, or building relationships with suppliers and stakeholders, SC leaders require a new set of skills above and beyond logistical knowledge (Michael Schiller, 2017). Today's SC leaders need to have business skills in order to drive results and accelerate revenue for their respective companies. They must view the SC end – to – end, not just their individual part in it. This requires a more strategic approach, and a more strategic mindset from the SC leaders. Some new characteristics which a SC leader must possess are, i) business acumen, ii) global mindset, iii) leadership, iv) analysis, v) relationship building (Sam Mikles, 2016). Information Technology and Automation Knowledge, familiarity with enterprise software applications like ERP, a grasp of economics and market dynamics, understanding cost-to-serve, skill of flexibility, project management skills, and the ability to get the best from the people are the six major competencies for supply chain leaders to achieve the 3Cs of supply chains, i.e., Communication, Collaboration and Change (Rob O'Byrne, 2016).

From a research conducted on professionals belonging to operations and management industries, the core skills of SC leadership are found to be, i) Applying certainty to uncertain situations affecting others, such as in forecasting or decision making, ii) Balancing risk and reward in careful analysis using hard and soft skills, iii) Aligning tactics to strategy in planning and harmony with organizational culture, iv) Maintaining and improving relationships of SC partners and v) -- Satisfying competing priorities and stakeholders on an ongoing basis (APICS, 2015).

Supply Chain Management in future will no longer be a process, managing all activities from 'raw material' to 'consumer' (Eric Lange, 2018). Artificial Intelligence, Power of Big Data, Block chain, Robotics, and 3D printing will influence the way SC is managed along with the people who manage it. Organizations need to react quickly to make effective and value-based decisions. This requires the active involvement of key people and their competencies managing them. While possessing communication and collaborative skills, these people should balance their business and technical skills. They also need to influence their internal business heads and external partners with their interactive skills and business acumen. SC technologies are managed through people's skills and competencies. Therefore, the SC leader in emerging markets has to be digital savvy and people friendly (Eric Lange, 2018).

Summary of views of several Global leaders in supply chain is presented here to understand the importance of future supply chain leaders. Frank Jones, Vice President of the Technology and Manufacturing Group at Intel Corp., opined that Intel achieved implementation of new supply chain through a steady vision and a sweeping cultural change to dramatically improve the company's speed, agility and cost competitiveness through a transformation process which is a multi-front battle that can be won, even without a crisis. Brian Tobey, former corporate VP of Microsoft, opined that supply chain talent development is a lifetime achievement (Kewin O'Marah, 2018).

Supply Chain Leadership in Management Institutions

Many authors have attempted to map the SC leadership skills and competencies of organizations as discussed in the previous section to the SC leadership in educational institutions as discussed in this section. Educational Supply Chain has gained momentum in the research world during the recent past (Govindaraju Basu, 2016). The concept of 'adding value', derived from the business and service organizations is equally applicable in higher education institutions too as they work closely with industry and collaborate with other institutions for providing internships, placements, exchange programs, consultancies and for pursuing collaborative research. Therefore, application of supply chain management concept for educational institutions is termed as 'Educational Supply Chain' (O'Brien, E.M., & Deans, K. R., 1996).

Education belong to Service Supply Chain. Ellram et al. (2004) define supply chain management as the management of information, processes, goods and funds from the earliest supplier to the ultimate customer, including disposal and conclude that a common theme in services is that human labor is a significant element of the total value delivered. This applies to all institutions in education sector and especially to management institutions.

A management institute closely works with many partners like other institutions and colleges from where it procures its students for management education. It also works closely with its existing students, alumni, industry, publishers, consultants, academicians, government, society, corporate employees, vendors and other regulatory agencies. Satisfying all these stakeholders of education supply chain is a very important and at the same time a challenging task (O'Brien, E.M., & Deans, K. R., 1996; Govindaraju Basu, 2016). The leader of the institute manages the upstream and downstream members of education supply chain as any other leader of a typical business organization. A two-way communication process for information sharing, mutual coordination and integration of processes with all these stakeholders of the institute is an essential requirement in developing strategic relationships with them for shaping the direction of the institute towards providing quality management education and achieving sustainability (Westbrook & Frohlich, 2001). The practices of SC are clearly evident in management institutions and leaders who manage them, play a pivotal role.

For a management institution, one of the primary suppliers of process inputs is customers (students) themselves, who provide their bodies, minds, belongings, or knowledge as inputs to the service processes. This concept of customers being suppliers is recognized as 'customer-supplier duality' and it implies that service supply chains are bi-directional (Sampson, 2000). The service SCM concept may be applicable to the academia as well (Sampson, 2000). The ITESCM (Integrated Tertiary Educational Supply Chain Management) model developed by Habib and Jungthirapanich (2008) identifies the multi-tier suppliers, multi-tier customers, service provider (university) and the consumer. It demonstrates how each party that has been identified plays its role in this integrated supply chain to finally deliver valuable graduates to the society. Academic Credibility (reputation, respect), Experience,

People skills/human aspects (negotiation, delegation, motivating, mentoring, monitoring, team building and communication) are found to be the most important competencies for academic leaders (Marion Spendlove, 2007).

A framework of competencies for effective academic leadership using three broad categories, i.e., attitudes, knowledge and behaviour (Marion Spendlove, 2007) identified flexibility, openness, honesty, outgoing, acceptability, sensitive to others' views, academic knowledge, process awareness, broad thinking, people skills, negotiation skills, communication skills, team playing skills, delegating skills and mentoring skills as the major competencies.

An estimate of Intelligence Leadership in universities by studying four types of academic leadership, i.e., i) Rational, ii) Emotional, iii) Spiritual and Collective leadership with different indicators for each type (Keikha A., et al., 2017) resulted in diverse results and application of Heiftez's adaptive leadership model on two academic institutions revealed that there is a greater potential for successful change initiatives through this model (Randall et al., 2007). Habib, M., and Jungthirapanich, C. (2009) developed an integrated educational SCM model for the universities which consists of three levels of decision-making, strategic, planning and operational. The model also classifies the SCM processes in universities as suppliers, service providers (university), customers and society.

Though, the concept of SC leadership is known to many institutions and SCM is taught as a subject in many management institutions across the world, it's implementation is found to be below the expected level and the leadership of these institutions is not clear about the competencies and skills required to manage SC effectively (Govindaraju Basu, 2016). Development of right SC skills and competencies improves the student satisfaction, employee satisfaction and provides a way for the achievement of sustainability of educational institutions (Govindaraju Basu, 2016).

Govindaraju Basu, (2016) and Ramakrishna, Y. (2016) identified five distinct dimensions, which include strategic supplier partnership, customer relationship, level of information sharing, quality of information sharing and innovation, for measuring SCM practices in Private Universities These five constructs covered upstream (Strategic Supplier Partnership) to downstream (Customer Relationship) sides of education supply chain network and found how integrated operations with the external suppliers and customers with the central university operations have enabled the achievement of good outcomes.

Further, Ang, D., (2010) identified the effective use of relevant and timely information by all functional elements within the supply chain as a key competitive and distinguishing factor. Use of information technology for delivery of services and accomplishment of institutional mission (Green, KI, 2007) leads to development of innovative education facilities, programmes and maintenance of quality in all aspects of managing the institution (Utterback, J. M., & Abernathy, W. J., 1975). Besides that, Erwin Danneels (2002) also noted that innovation will take place when organizations have competences relating to technologies and customers. It is obvious that SCM practices will have a significant impact on university's performance.

Line management ability (ability to manage day-to-day supply chain operations), problem solving ability (ability to anticipate and diagnose problems), project management ability (ability to structure and manage projects designed to improve SC processes) and people management skills (ability to lead and motivate all employees for improving their technical and management skills) are essential SC leadership skills and competencies (Kisperska-Moroń D., 2013). To achieve a higher level of performance, higher education institutions should focus on reducing waste, increasing efficiency and engaging in good communication internally and externally. SC integration is a process of interaction and collaboration across firms that incorporate customers and suppliers into a cohesive supply network (Govindaraju Basu et al., 2016; Ming C. H., et al., 2014).

An interactionist model of leadership (Kets de Vries, 2006) proposed four key leadership characteristics: hope, humanity, humility and humour focusing on leadership characteristics, followers, leadership styles, and situation. While mentioning that the studies in leadership in business schools and management institutes are limited, a stronger focus on the development of personal and communication skills was recommended and further research in the areas of leadership characteristics, leadership roles and change and leadership training was suggested (Howard Thomas & Lynne Thomas, 2011).

Though the management institutions face various challenges (Pallabi Pal Sarkar & Rajendra Prasad, 2015; Govindaraju Basu, 2016), the number of studies specific to SC leadership in management education is relatively less (Baltacioglu et al., 2007; Habib et al., 2008; Howard Thomas & Lynne Thomas, 2011; Govindaraju Basu, 2016) The existing models (Habib et al., 2008; Habib et al., 2009; Govindaraju Basu et al., 2016) focused only on supply chain integration for achieving sustainability. The present model therefore, is an extension of the existing ones which includes the SC leadership competencies and their 'enablers' in addition to the supply chain operations of a management institution. Therefore, the present study would contribute to the existing body of knowledge in educational supply chain with special reference to management education / B-Schools.

MAIN FOCUS OF THE CHAPTER

Issues, Controversies, Problems

An educational institution, especially a management institute very closely works with many stakeholders in its day-to-day functioning. These stakeholders consist of suppliers of all equipment and infrastructure developers, students, parents of students, employees, corporate executives, HR managers of recruiting agencies and companies, society, government, regulatory authorities and the alumni of the institute. The biggest issue that a management institute faces is managing the institute by balancing the interests of all these stakeholders (O'Brien, E.M., & Deans, K. R., 1996; Govindaraju Basu, 2016). Generally, the leader of the institute manages most of these stakeholders at different stages. Concepts and strategies of SC leadership play an enormous role in this balancing act.

But, though the management institutes are well aware of SC as a concept and a subject area in their programs, it's application and implementation is found to be below the expected level and the leadership of these institutions is not clear about the competencies and skills required to manage SC effectively (Govindaraju Basu, 2016). This is a controversy as well as a problem in many management institutes and B-Schools across the world. It is found that those institutes which developed appropriate SC skills and competencies among the employees, have achieved positive results in terms of student and employee satisfaction (Govindaraju Basu, 2016). Also, another controversy and problem is related to the leadership styles of top level employees of management institutions. The leadership styles, competencies, traits and skills required for SC leaders in general and in management educational institution, in particular, are fundamentally different compared to SC leadership in business (Marion Spendlove, 2007). Due to some of the dynamic aspects like globalization, changing educational environment in the world, changing attitudes and demands of present generation students, dearth of talented faculty members, increasing requirement of diverse set of skills in placement companies, increased cost of education, emergence of online management programs, many management institutes face several challenges these days (Lorange, 2002; Granit Almog-Bareket, 2012).

All these factors have totally redefined the way the management education is taught in B-Schools and other management institutions. In addition to these factors, other factors like globalization, scarcity of talented management faculty, mushrooming of management institutes, emergence of online management programs and provision of equal rigor for those programs has also impacted the way management is taught (Granit Almog-Bareket, 2012; Pallabi Pal Sarkar & Rajendra Prasad, 2015; Govindaraju Basu, 2016).

Though the management institutions face various challenges (Pallabi Pal Sarkar & Rajendra Prasad, 2015; Govindaraju Basu, 2016), the number of studies specific to SC leadership in management education is relatively less (Baltacioglu et al., 2007; Habib et al., 2008; Howard Thomas and Lynne Thomas, 2011; Govindaraju Basu, 2016). The existing models (Habib et al., 2009; Govindaraju Basu et al., 2016) focused only on supply chain integration for achieving sustainability.

Therefore, the main focus of this chapter would be identify the SC leadership strategies for management institutes / business schools and develop a supply chain leadership model by plugging the weaknesses in the existing models for enabling the leaders of management institutes to implement SC model for managing successfully to achieve positive outcomes.

METHODOLOGY ADOPTED

A systematic literature review has been done to achieve the objectives of this chapter. This review is done with multiple objectives of studying the SC leadership strategies, practices and competencies of business organizations, and in B-Schools / Management Education Institutions and finally for developing a SC leadership skill / competency model for B-Schools / Management Education Institutions. The key words used for the purpose of this literature review are 'supply chain management', 'supply chain leadership', 'supply chain strategies', 'supply chain leadership models', 'supply chain skills and competencies', 'management institute leadership', 'b-school management strategies', 'b-school leadership' and other combinations comprising similar terminology have been used. Articles published in leading online journal databases of ProQuest and EBSCO were reviewed.

The research gaps were identified based on the literature review. An analysis of these gaps in the existing research works was done to develop a model a leadership model for supply chain management in Business Schools.

SOLUTIONS AND RECOMMENDATIONS

An analysis of research works from the literature review reveals that there is a gap as far as studies related to leadership in management institutes / business schools. Also, there is a very limited research on supply chain skills and competencies required for the top leadership to manage a business schools (Eugene H. Pfeiffer, 2014).

Considering these gaps in the existing body of knowledge, the chapter attempts to develop a leadership model for SCM in business schools as a solution to resolve some of their issues, challenges and problems and also to fill the gap in the research area.

DEVELOPMENT AND DISCUSSION OF SUPPLY CHAIN LEADERSHIP MODEL

Though it is accepted by researchers that supply chain management practices will improve the overall effectiveness of a management institute / business school, lack of awareness about SC leadership competencies and skills may hinder its successful implementation. In this backdrop, by considering the gaps in the existing models, a supply chain leadership has been developed as shown in Fig.1.

Figure 1. Supply Chain Leadership Model for Business Schools

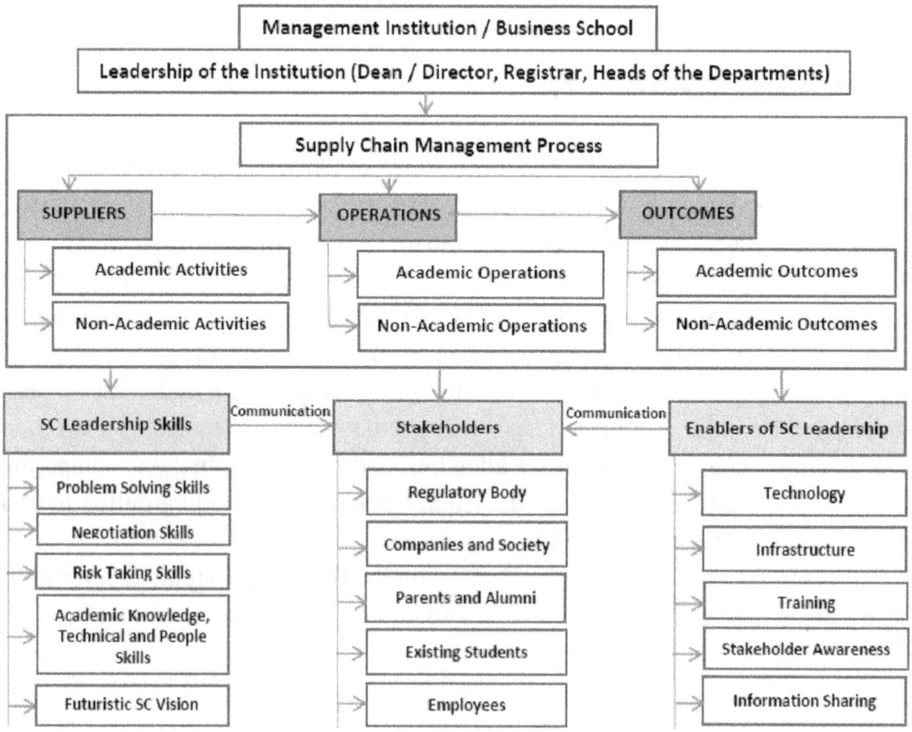

The core leadership team of every management institution generally consists of Deans, Directors, Registrar and Heads of Departments. This team drives down the core values of the institute and develops strategies supply chain strategies by synchronizing them with the vision, mission and objectives of the institute. The supply chain management process of a management institute consists of managing the activities related to suppliers, management of operations / processes and achieving positive outcomes. In the present model, all these three are categorized into academic and non-academic in nature as both of them are important for the effective implementation of supply chain.

Based on discussions in the literature review, SC leadership competencies and skills are categorized into problem solving, negotiation, risk-taking, people and futuristic vision skills. The SC leadership 'communicates' with the stakeholders of the institute through these skills which are 'enabled' by technology, training, infrastructure, customer awareness and information sharing. Therefore, stakeholders are mentioned in the middle portion of the model.

In a management institute, suppliers are required for two types of activities, i) academic and ii) non-academic. Suppliers supplying books, research publications like journals, magazines, newspapers (both online and physical copies), Software for teaching purpose and software for other academic purposes, all types of fittings in class rooms (the academic environment), library furniture, and computers / laptops for faculty and students are categorized as academic suppliers. Whereas, suppliers of general furniture, equipment and items related to the infrastructure of the institute, recruitment and internship providing agents, rules, guidelines and norms (regulatory bodies), stationery items, canteen items, security systems, sports equipment, sports grounds, all other contractors (cafeteria, housekeeping, security, transportation, elevator systems, fire safety etc.), drinking water, web site maintenance, software like ERP and LMS, all types of promotional material (flyers, pamphlets, brochures, manuals, handbooks etc.) and gardening and landscaping are categorized as suppliers for non-academic activities.

The second component of the model, operations is also categorized into academic and non-academic operations. Teaching, research, communication to students about academic processes, operations and information, assessments, information about grades and their criteria, uploading of faculty teaching material, teaching blogs, case studies, videos etc. are categorized as academic operations. Whereas, student admission, registration, student services, display of schedules, behavioral norms, grievances, ethical code of conduct, safety and security, risk management, sports, competitions, institute events, community service etc. are categorized as non-academic operations.

Outcomes of the institute are also categorized into two, i) academic outcomes and ii) non-academic outcomes. Performance of an academic institute is measured on majorly in terms of academic outcomes, whereas, the non-academic outcomes are also very important for the SC leadership and the stakeholders of the institute. Faculty research and publications, consultancies, number of management and executive development programs, students' performance in terms of grades, distinction and number of students successfully completing the programs are considered to be the academic outcomes. Whereas, number of students securing placements, range of their salaries, accreditation, ranking, commitment towards society, supplier satisfaction, stakeholder satisfaction, prizes won by students in various competitions, representation of the institute in various events locally and globally are categorized to be non-academic outcomes.

The SC leadership of the management institute provides a strategic direction to the supply chain management process of the institute. For this purpose, the leadership should possess the skills as mentioned above and in the model in the emerging markets of management education.

The model also includes the 'enablers' of SC leadership. In a traditional management institute, most of the communication to the stakeholders happens to be through a one-to-one correspondence. Whereas, in the changing management education environment, the traditional approaches no longer achieve the purpose of satisfying all the stakeholders. Therefore, the management institutes need to develop certain enablers as mentioned in the model. Technology is the most important enabler among all of them for communication with stakeholders. Today's students in the global business and education environment expect technology-based teaching, learning and communication. Hence the institute should have a mechanism to satisfy them through appropriate technological environment (Rob O'Byrne, 2016). Technology is supported through physical environment of the institute, the second enabler. Third most important enabler is 'training'. Provision of high-end technology and infrastructure in a management institute will not yield any positive outcomes unless all users are appropriately trained on its usage.

Management institutes need to create awareness among all stakeholders about the operations of the institute, services provided, and how to use technology to get most of the services using the 'online' facility. Most of the services can be provided 'online' to the students, suppliers, regulatory bodies, companies, society and all employees of the institute. This will reduce the overall cost of operations of the institute and increases the convenience to the students. For example, modern B-Schools provide the video recorded version of a professor's lecture in case the student wants to go through it or in case of student's absence to the lecture on a particular day. This requires the supply chain process of 'integration' to be effective and timely through the usage of technology enabler. Similarly, all the other services like declaration of results, grades, registration and re-registration, payment of fee, students' and faculty attendance can be integrated to the technology. The SC leadership of the institute should create awareness to the stakeholders about all these services through training and competency building activities to them.

The model considers 'information sharing' as another important enabler (Westbrook & Frohlich, 2001; Govindaraju Basu, 2016). Traditional management institutes used to maintain confidentiality in most of the academic and non-academic operations and transparency in certain aspects related to the stakeholders was considered to be a weakness of the institute. But, in today's globalized supply chain and digitized academic environment, 'information sharing' is considered to be one of the best practices to achieve greater stakeholder satisfaction. Therefore, the SC leadership should focus on 'information sharing' to communicate with the stakeholders using its problem solving skills.

SC Leadership skills are identified to be i) Problem Solving Skills, ii) Negotiation Skills, iii) Risk Taking Skills, iv) People Skills, and v) Futuristic SC vision.

The SC leadership of a management institute encounters several situations which require the display of problem-solving skills (Melnyk S. A., 2017). These situations are related to the overall strategic problems of the institute, decisions related to expansion (addition of programs, courses, branches and number of institutes), faculty related problems, student related problems, supplier related problems, performance related problems and any other problems related to any of the stakeholder. Acquaintance of Problem solving skills by the leadership enables them to anticipate the problems and provide amicable solutions.

A second important skill of SC leadership is categorized as negotiation skills. The leadership of management institute frequently needs to display these skills due to their nature of occurrence. In a management institute, negotiations take place with suppliers (academic and non-academic activities), other partnering institutes (collaborative skills), companies, student and faculty exchange institutes, parents, and sometimes with the students. Therefore, negotiation skills are highly essential for SC leadership in emerging education market (Deshpande, 2012).

Today, management institutes encounter with several internal and external risks due to various uncontrollable factors. SC leadership of the institute should be risk taking (Barlow Rick Dana, 2015) and develop a 'risk management plan' by identifying, analyzing, assessing and devising means to mitigate the risks. Academic Knowledge, Technical and People skills such as delegation, motivating, mentoring, monitoring, listening, team building are the most important skills for academic leaders in today's management education environment of changing attitudes and expectations of students, employees, parents and other stakeholders of the institute (Marion Spendlove, 2007; Tim Stratman, 2010; Becky Partida, 2019).

Management institutes have been facing severe competition and several challenges due to many changes in global business environment (Granit Almog-Bareket, 2012). Therefore, based on the above discussion of SC model, it is recommended that the top management and other leadership related employees of the management institutes and business schools develop the competencies among them by implementing the above model for successful implementation of SC.

It is also recommended that SC leadership of the institute should develop a long-term futuristic vision (Melnyk et al., 2009; APICS, 2015; Becky Partida 2019) to keep pace along with changes in the management education by anticipating the opportunities. Therefore, the model lays emphasis on 'futuristic SC vision' for SC leadership.

IMPLICATIONS OF SC LEADERSHIP MODEL

Leadership in management institutes provides growth and direction for growth and sustainability. These institutes can achieve positive outcomes, if their leadership shifts their existing strategies and focus towards SCM by providing a dynamic leadership in line with the changing needs of students and other stakeholders (Mason, 2008; Mourshed et al., 2012; Snyder, 2013) by identifying and acquiring the SC leadership skills and by developing the competencies. Also, it is found that leadership styles, competencies, traits and skill required for management institutes are quite different from those required for business organizations. (Mario Spendlove, 2007).

Therefore, the present model would provide a direction to understand and analyze the leadership of all management institutes and business schools. The model provides a link between SC leadership skills, Stakeholders and Enablers. The focus should be on developing the enablers and leadership skills to communicate with effectively with the stakeholders which keep the supply chain processes align with each other. Implementation of this model equips the SC leadership of a management institute / business school to manage its supply chain process more effectively in the emerging competitive markets of management education.

CONCLUSION

Effective implementation of supply chain management practices in management institutes and business schools has the ability to provide positive outcomes and sustainable direction. This implementation is possible only when the SC leadership develops the SC talent in these institutes. Understanding and analysing the process of SC is an important pre-requisite for developing SC talent. The SC leadership of the institutes are found to be lacking the futuristic skills and competencies which are required in this dynamic management education environment. The process of SC consists of suppliers, operations and outcomes in every management institute. Analysis and interpretation of results of this research identified very interesting aspects about SC leadership skills and its enablers.

Problem solving, Negotiation, risk taking, academic and technical knowledge, people skills and futuristic vision are found to be SC leadership skills required for the leadership of management institutes. These skills are required to communicate with the stakeholders of the institute through enablers like technology, infrastructure, training, stakeholder awareness and information sharing. It is concluded that implementation of this model by managing the enablers would provide the management institute with adequate opportunities for effective communication with all types of stakeholders of the institute.

Therefore, to conclude, management institutes can achieve positive outcomes, if their leadership shifts their existing strategies and focuses towards SCM by providing a dynamic leadership in line with the changing needs of students and other stakeholders (Mason, 2008; Mourshed et al., 2012; Snyder, 2013) by identifying and acquiring the SC leadership skills and by developing the competencies.

FUTURE RESEARCH DIRECTIONS

An analysis of results of the present research revealed interesting facts about supply chain leadership in business schools and management institutes. The research also provided a tangible output by developing a SC leadership model. Validating this model by conducting an empirical survey of different management institutes and business schools would be the future topic for research. Also, the model can be expanded with more number of competencies and enablers for increasing its scope for implementation in future.

REFERENCES

Almog-Bareket, G. (2012). Visionary leadership in business schools: An institutional framework. *Journal of Management Development*, *31*(4), 431–440. doi:10.1108/02621711211219086

Ang, D., Griffin, T., Goodson, J., & Ho, J. (2010). Enterprise System Education through Supply Chain Management. *Contemporary Management Research*, *6*(1), 3–10. doi:10.7903/cmr.2666

APICS. (2015). *Next Generation Supply Chain Leader.* APICS SCC Report.

Baltacioglu, K., Yurt, O., & Kaplan, C. (2007). A New Framework for Service Supply Chain. *Service Industries Journal*, *27*(2), 105–124. doi:10.1080/02642060601122629

Barlow Rick Dana. (2015). What ignites a progressive supply chain leader? *Healthcare Purchasing News*, *39*(7), 10-13.

Basu, & Jeyasingam, & Habib. (2016). Education Supply Chain Management Model to Achieve Sustainability in Private Universities in Malaysia: A Review. *International Journal of Supply Chain Management*, *5*(4), 24–37.

Chakravarthy, B., & Lorange, P. (2008). Driving renewal: The entrepreneur-manager. *Journal of Business Strategy, 29*(2), 14-21. doi:10.1108%2F02756660810858116

Danneels, E. (2002). The Dynamics of Product Innovation and Firm Competences. *Strategic Management Journal*, *23*(12), 1095–1121. doi:10.1002mj.275

Deshpande, A. (2012). Supply chain management dimensions, supply chain performance and organizational performance: An integrated framework. *International Journal of Business and Management*, *7*(8), 2–19. doi:10.5539/ijbm.v7n8p2

Ellram, L. M., Tate, W. L., & Billington, C. (2004). Understanding and managing the services supply chain. *The Journal of Supply Chain Management*, *40*(4), 17–32. doi:10.1111/j.1745-493X.2004.tb00176.x

Gopalakrishnan. (2015). How to apply academic supply chain management: The Case of an International University. *Management, 20*(1), 207-221.

Green, K. (2007). *Analytics and Assessment: A New Imperative for Campus and IT Services*. Edu Connection, Sun Microsystems.

Habib, M., & Jungthirapanich, C. (2009). Research framework of education supply chain, research supply chain and educational management for the universities. *International Journal of the Computer, the Internet and Management, 17*(24), 1-8.

Habib, M. M., & Jungthirapanich, C. (2008). An integrated framework for research and education supply chain for the universities. *Proceedings of 4th IEEE International Conference on Management of Innovation and Technology*, 1027-1032. 10.1109/ICMIT.2008.4654509

Keikha, A., Hoveida, R., & Yaghoubi, N. M. (2017). The Development of an Intelligent Leadership Model for State Universities. *Foresight and STI Governance*, *11*(1), 66–74. doi:10.17323/2500-2597.2017.1.66.74.

Kets de Vries, M. (2006). *The Leadership Mystique*. Pearson.

Kisperska-Moroń, D. (2013). Required Skill Set for the Supply Chain Manager in Changing Economic Reality. *Journal of Economics & Management*, *11*, 34–48.

Kumar, V. A., & Rai, S. (2017). Role of human resource flexibility in Organizational performance: A study of Indian IT firms. *International Journal of Indian Culture and Business Management*, *14*(3), 306–325. doi:10.1504/IJICBM.2017.083236

Lange, E. (2018). The Supply Chain leader of the future. *Anaplan blog*. https://www.anaplan.com/blog/supply-chain-leader-future/

Lorange, P. (2002). *New Vision for Management Education: Leadership Challenges*. Elsevier.

Maku, T. C., Collins, T. R., & Beruvides, M. G. (2005). The impact of human interaction on supply chain management practices. *Performance Improvement*, *44*(7), 26–33. doi:10.1002/pfi.4140440708

Mangan, J., & Christopher, M. (2005). Management development and the supply chain manager of the future. *International Journal of Logistics Management*, *16*(2), 178–191. doi:10.1108/09574090510634494

Mason, M. (Ed.). (2008). *Complexity Theory and the Philosophy of Education*. Wiley-Blackwell. doi:10.1002/9781444307351

Melnyk, S. A. (2017). The emergence of the strategic leader. *Supply Chain Management Review*. https://www.scmr.com/article/the_emergence_of_the_strategic_leader

Melnyk, S. A., Lummus, R. R., Vokurka, R. J., Burns, L. J., & Sandor, J. (2009). Mapping the future of supply chain management: A Delphi study. *International Journal of Production Research*, *47*(16), 4629–4653. doi:10.1080/00207540802014700

Mikles, S. (2016). Characteristics of a Supply Chain Leader. *Flash Global Blog*. https://flashglobal.com/blog/characteristics-supply-chain-leader/

Ming, C. H., Ghi, F. Y., & Tzu, C. L. (2014). Re-examining supply chain integration and the supplier's performance relationships under uncertainty. *Supply Chain Management*, *19*(1), 64–78. doi:10.1108/SCM-04-2013-0114

Mourshed, M., Farrell, D., & Barton, D. (2012). Education to Employment: Designing a System that Works. *McKinsey Centre for Government*. Available at: www.mckinsey.com/mcg

O'Brien, E. M., & Deans, K. R. (1996). Educational supply chain: A tool for strategic planning in tertiary education? *Marketing Intelligence & Planning*, *14*(2), 33–40. doi:10.1108/02634509610110787

O'Byrne. (2016). 6 Key Supply Chain Leaders Skills and why you need them? *Logistics Bureau Blog*. https://www.logisticsbureau.com/6-key-supply-chain-leaders-skills-and-why-you-need-them

O'Marah. (2018). Lessons in Excellence from Five Supply Chain Leaders, SCM world learning engine. *SCM World*. https://www.forbes.com/sites/kevinomarah/2018/05/30/lessons-in-excellence-from-five-supply-chain-leaders/#403559551545

Partida, B. (2019). Using Dynamic Leadership to Prepare for the Future. *Supply Chain Management Review*. https://www.scmr.com/article/using_dynamic_leadership_to_prepare_for_the_future

Pfeiffer. (2014). *Lessons learned in Supply Chain Leadership: A Delphi Study* (PhD dissertation). University of Phoenix.

Ramakrishna, Y. (2016). Supply Chain Management: Large vs. Small and Medium Enterprises (SMEs). In A. Dwivedi (Ed.), *Innovative Solutions for Implementing Global Supply Chains in Emerging Markets* (pp. 141–151). IGI Global. doi:10.4018/978-1-4666-9795-9.ch009

Randall, L. M., & Lori, A. (2007). Applying adaptive leadership to successful change initiatives in academia. *Leadership and Organization Development Journal*, *28*(4), 325–335. doi:10.1108/01437730710752201

Sampson. (2000). Customer-supplier duality and bidirectional supply chains in service organizations. *International Journal of Service Industry Management*, *11*(4), 348-364.

Sarkar & Sharma. (2015), Challenges Faced by Educators in Management Education. *Parikalpana, KIIT Journal of Management*, *11*(1), 74-87.

Sarrico, C. S., & Rosa, M. J. (2016). Supply chain quality management in education. *International Journal of Quality & Reliability Management*, *33*(4), 499–517. doi:10.1108/IJQRM-11-2014-0181

Schiller, M. (2017). Looking beyond cost control – a new role for strategic supply chain leaders. *Healthcare Financial Management*. https://www.hfma.org/topics/article/55362.html

Snyder, S. (2013). *The Simple, the Complicated, and the Complex: Educational Reform Through the Lens of Complexity Theory*. OECD.

Spendlove, M. (2007). Competencies for effective leadership in higher education. *International Journal of Educational Management*, *21*(5), 407–417. doi:10.1108/09513540710760183

Stratman. (2010). Are Supply Chain leaders ready for Supply Chain Management Review? *Supply Chain Management Review*. https://www.scmr.com/article/are_supply_chain_leaders_ready_for_the_top1

Tate, W. L., Dooley, K. J., & Ellram, L. M. (2011). Transaction cost and institutional drivers of supplier adoption of environmental practices. *Journal of Business Logistics*, *32*(1), 6–16. doi:10.1111/j.2158-1592.2011.01001.x

Thomas, H., & Thomas, L. (2011). Perspectives on leadership in business schools. *Journal of Management Development*, *30*(5), 526–540. doi:10.1108/02621711111133037

Utterback, J. M., & Abernathy, W. J. (1975). A dynamic model of process and product innovation. *Omega*, *3*(6), 639–656. doi:10.1016/0305-0483(75)90068-7

Westbrook, R., & Frohlich, M. (2001). Arcs of integration: An international study of supply chain strategies. *Journal of Operations Management*, *19*(2), 185–200. doi:10.1016/S0272-6963(00)00055-3

Yanamandra, R. (2018). Development of an integrated healthcare supply chain model, *Supply Chain Forum. International Journal (Toronto, Ont.)*, *19*(2), 111–121. doi: 10.1080/16258312.2018.1475823

Zacharia, Z. G., Sanders, N. R., & Nix, N. W. (2011). The emerging role of the third party logistics provider (3PL) as an orchestrator. *Journal of Business Logistics*, *32*(1), 40–54. doi:10.1111/j.2158-1592.2011.01004.x

KEY TERMS AND DEFINITIONS

Business School: A high-level educational institution in which students study subjects relating to business and commerce, such as economics, finance, and management.

Educational Supply Chain: Application of supply chain management practices to an educational institution.

Leadership Competency: Leadership competencies are leadership skills and behaviors that contribute to superior performance. By using a competency-based approach to leadership, organizations can better identify and develop their next generation of leaders.

Service Supply Chain: A process of managing all the activities related to providing services at different stages and levels of supply chain for effective delivery of products to customers. It also includes services involved in order management, provision of timely and accurate information to the customer, management of delivery and returns, repair and maintenances.

Stakeholder: In education, the term stakeholder typically refers to anyone who is invested in the welfare and success of a school and its students, including administrators, teachers, staff members, students, parents, families, community members, local business leaders, and elected officials such as school board members, city councilors, and state representatives.

Supply Chain Leader: A responsible manager, generally at a top-level position in the hierarchy of organization, who develops the vision and commits to implement it through leadership skills and competencies.

Supply Chain Management: The design, planning, execution, control, and monitoring of supply chain activities with the objective of creating net value, building a competitive infrastructure, leveraging worldwide logistics, synchronizing supply with demand, and measuring performance globally.

Chapter 9
Bullwhip Effect Performance of Supply Chains Under Statistical Process Control-Based Policy

Joby George
https://orcid.org/0000-0002-9922-2353
Amal Jyothi College of Engineering, Kanjirappally, India

V. Madhusudanan Pillai
https://orcid.org/0000-0001-6702-7994
National Institute of Technology Calicut, India

ABSTRACT

This chapter discusses the bullwhip effect performance of serial and divergent supply chains under statistical process control (SPC)-based and order-up-to (OUT) policies. The performance of the supply chains is evaluated in terms of order rate variance ratio and bullwhip slope under four realistic customer demand models such normal, normal with a sudden change in mean, normal with seasonality, and normal with seasonality and a sudden change in mean. The impact of sharing of customer demand among the other members of the supply chain and the introduction of order smoothing parameter on both policies are also studied. The results show that under non-stationary customer demand models the difference in the performance of serial and divergent supply chains is noticeable. The bullwhip slope under OUT policy is significantly differing from the bullwhip slope under the SPC-based policy. OUT policy with order smoothing performs better than the SPC-based policy with order smoothing. This finding provides proper guidelines for a supply chain manager to make a decision in a practical scenario.

DOI: 10.4018/978-1-7998-2867-9.ch009

INTRODUCTION

Nowadays in the emerging global market, the competition is not between the companies but between the supply chains. Hence, the best performing supply chains may survive over a long period. In a supply chain, the increase in demand variability from downstream stage to upstream stage, namely bullwhip effect creates an adverse impact on the performance of the supply chain (Lee, Padmanabhan, & Whang, 1997). Previous studies confirmed that the bullwhip effect cannot be eliminated from a supply chain, but can be reduced or controlled (Chen, Drezner, Ryan, & Simchi-Levi, 2000). The common methods to mitigate the bullwhip effect in supply chain are: avoid multiple demand forecast updates; break order batches; stabilize prices; eliminate gaming in shortage; reduce lead time and adapt strategic partnerships (Lee, Padmanabhan, & Whang, 1997), implement appropriate co-ordination mechanism (Disney, Lambrecht, Towill, & Van de Velde, 2008), share information (Chen, Drezner, Ryan, & Simchi-Levi, 2000), select proper inventory policy (Gaalman, 2006; Pillai, Talari, & Elluri, 2013), use smoothened inventory policy (Dejonckheere, Disney, Lambrecht, & Towill, 2004; Kim & Springer, 2008), use better forecasting method (Wright & Yuan, 2008), and reduce variability in lead time (Boute, Disney, Lambrecht, & Van Houdt, 2007). Inventory policy has a vital role in a supply chain and is one of the contributory factors to the bullwhip effect in the supply chain. The selection of appropriate inventory policies is often quoted as the effective means of achieving better supply chain performance and alleviating overall supply chain cost. Hence, the challenging role of a company manager is to keep inventory cost as least as possible by choosing an appropriate inventory policy in consideration with inventory policies chosen by other members of the same supply chain. The industrially popular periodic review inventory policy is Order-Up-To (OUT) policy. The OUT policy and its variants cause bullwhip generation in a supply chain, where the order variance amplification is more under OUT policy than its variants (Dejonckheere, Disney, Lambrecht, & Towill, 2003; Dejonckheere, Disney, Lambrecht, & Towill, 2004). However, in the present competitive market, an inventory policy that adjusts with the market trend may perform better in terms of bullwhip effect (T C Pamulety & Pillai, 2011). Control charts used for process control uses current information to indicate the latest status of a process. The concept of control charts is used for developing a Statistical Process Control (SPC)-based inventory policy.

This chapter discusses the bullwhip effect performance comparison of serial and divergent supply chains under an SPC-based and OUT policies. For this purpose, the concepts of the SPC-based policy proposed by Costantino, Di Gravio, Shaban, & Tronci (2014a, 2014b, 2015a, 2015b) are adapted. The bullwhip effect measures used are the order rate variance ratio and the bullwhip slope. The analysis is carried out under different customer demand patterns such as normal, normal with a sudden change in mean, normal with seasonality (Dominguez, Cannella, & Framinan, 2015; watts, Zhou, & Disney, 2007), and normal with seasonality and a sudden change in mean. The supply chain's bullwhip effect performances are evaluated under SPC-based and OUT policies and then the performances are compared. The impact of sharing of customer demand among the members of the supply chain is also studied. Besides, order smoothing parameter is introduced in both policies and the bullwhip effect performance of the supply chains is evaluated. All these performance evaluations are carried out using simulation models developed in Scilab 5.5.0.

BACKGROUND

Earlier studies reported in the literature show that the SPC-based policy performs better than the other policies which could not adjust to changes in the present competitive market. Watts, Hahn, & Sohn (1994) initiate the application of the control chart concept for inventory control. The researchers used control charts to monitor and diagnose the performance of a reorder point inventory system. Pfohl, Cullmann, & Stolzle (1999) developed an SPC-based inventory control system using the concepts of Shewart control chart. This SPC-based inventory control system determines replenishment orders by adjusting dynamically to the variation in inventory and demand data. Various demand and inventory rules are used for determining the replenishment orders in the SPC-based policies reported in the literature, and the results show the dominating nature of SPC-based policy over the traditional policies. Lee & Wu (2006) evaluated the performance of a two-stage serial supply chain under two traditional ((s, S) and (s, Q)) and one SPC-based inventory control policies. Cheng & Chou (2008) modified the SPC-based inventory control policy of Pfohl, Cullmann, & Stolzle (1999) and proposed an auto-regressive moving average control chart to monitor the demand data. The decision rules for framing the policy are adapted from Western Electric Handbook published in 1956. Pamulety & Pillai (2011) proposed an SPC-based inventory control policy by applying control chart concepts to historical inventory data. The historical data were generated using OUT inventory control policy at each stage in a four-stage serial supply chain. Three sets of decision rules (namely, decision rule-1, decision rule-2, and decision rule-3) were developed under SPC-based inventory control policy, and their performance was evaluated under a serial supply chain. The performance of SPC with decision rule-3 was found to be better than the other two sets of rules. Kurano, McKay, & Black (2014) developed an inventory control system based on control charts for the mitigation of supply chain risk in a three-stage serial supply chain. Here, the risk occurs due to the amplification of disruption such as stock-out through the supply chain. Costantino, Di Gravio, Shaban, & Tronci (2014a, 2014b, 2015a, 2015b) developed an SPC-based policy with two types of rules, namely, demand rules and inventory rules which were derived from demand and inventory control charts, respectively. The performance of a four-stage serial supply chain was evaluated in terms of average service level, bullwhip effect, and inventory variance ratio. The supply chain performance under the proposed SPC-based policy is compared with the performance under OUT policy. The summary of the literature that proposed and analysed the control chart concept for inventory control in supply chains is given in *Table 1*.

Table 1. The summary of the literature that used control chart concept for inventory control in supply chains

Author (Year)	Supply chain model			Methodology	Performance measures	Demand model
	Structure	Stage(s)	Environment			
Watts, Hahn, & Sohn (1994)	-	1	-	Simulation	Inventory costs	Normal
Pfohl, Cullmann, & Stolzle (1999)	-	1	-	Simulation, Empirical study	Inventory costs, Service level	Real data
Lee & Wu (2006)	Serial	2	Traditional	Simulation	Number of back orders, Average inventory	Poisson
Cheng & Chou (2008)	-	1	-	Simulation	Service level, Inventory level, Stockout	Normal, Auto regressive
Pamulety & Pillai (2011)	Serial	4	Traditional, Information sharing	Simulation	Fill rate, Bullwhip effect, Inventory costs	Normal
Kurano, McKay, & Black (2014)	Serial	3	Traditional	Simulation	Inventory level, Stockout	Normal
Costantino, Di Gravio, Shaban, & Tronci (2014a)	Serial	4	Traditional	Simulation	Service level, Bullwhip effect, Inventory variance ratio	Normal
Costantino, Di Gravio, Shaban, & Tronci (2014b)	Serial	4	Traditional	Simulation	Service level, Bullwhip effect, Inventory variance ratio	Normal
Costantino, Di Gravio, Shaban, & Tronci (2015a)	Serial	4	Traditional, Information sharing	Simulation	Service level, Bullwhip effect, Inventory variance ratio	Normal, Auto regressive, Normal with seasonality
Costantino, Di Gravio, Shaban, & Tronci (2015b)	Serial	4	Traditional	Simulation	Bullwhip effect, Inventory variance ratio	Auto regressive

The literature review provided in Table 1 confirms that in almost all studies using the SPC-based policy focus on serial supply chains. Also, in most of the literature, the business environment is traditional, simulation methodology is used for analysis, bullwhip effect is used as a performance measure, and the supply chains are evaluated under normal demand model. This literature review shows that studies based on SPC-based policies in a complex supply chain structure are absent. It may be noted that the complexity of structure affects the bullwhip effect performance of the supply chain (Paik & Bagchi, 2007; Bottani, Montanari, & Volpi, 2010; Dominguez, Cannella, & Framinan, 2015).

MAIN FOCUS OF THE CHAPTER

The main focus of the chapter is the evaluation of the bullwhip effect performance of serial and divergent supply chains under OUT and SPC-based policies. In this section, we provide a basic understanding of the supply chain structures considered for the study, inventory policies considered for the study and development of simulation models that are relevant to this chapter.

Supply Chain Structures Considered for the Study

Four-stage serial and divergent supply chain structures are considered for the study. *Figure 1* shows the supply chain models considered for the study with order and shipment flows. The total number of members in the divergent supply chain is 15 (the members are 8 retailers, 4 wholesalers, 2 distributors and 1 factory). A single item moves through the supply chains. The serial supply chain comprises four stages, and the members are retailer, wholesaler, distributor and factory. The serial supply chain model is similar to that of Chatfield, Kim, Harrison, & Hayya (2004), which is one of the main studies on bullwhip effect quantification. For similarity and to compare with the serial supply chain, the divergent chain also has four stages.

To compare the bullwhip effect performance based on supply chain structures, (Dominguez, Framinan, & Cannella, 2013; Dominguez, Cannella, & Framinan, 2014) have used serial and divergent structures with four stages. So, similar structures with 4- stages are used in this study also. Each stage serves as either customer or supplier to the other. Factory gets an item from the production area. Each member supplies the quantity against the order received based on the availability of stock. The supplied quantity is equal to the order size if sufficient stock is available; otherwise, it is equal to stock available at that point in time. The order placed by a member of the stage (i) reaches the associated supplier stage ($i + 1$) after a fixed interval of time called order lead time, k. The quantity supplied by a member in stage (i) reaches the associated downstream stage (i - 1) after a fixed period called delivery lead time, L. In the divergent supply chain, at any period, the available stock of a member in a stage may not be sufficient to meet the demand of its downstream stage members. In such situations, the proportional allocation rule (Duan & Liao, 2013) is used to allocate the available inventory among the associated members in the downstream. The sequence of inventory distribution events occurring in each member, j, in each stage, i, at the time, t, is shown as a flow diagram in *Figure 2*.

Figure 1. Serial and divergent supply chain structures with order and shipments flows

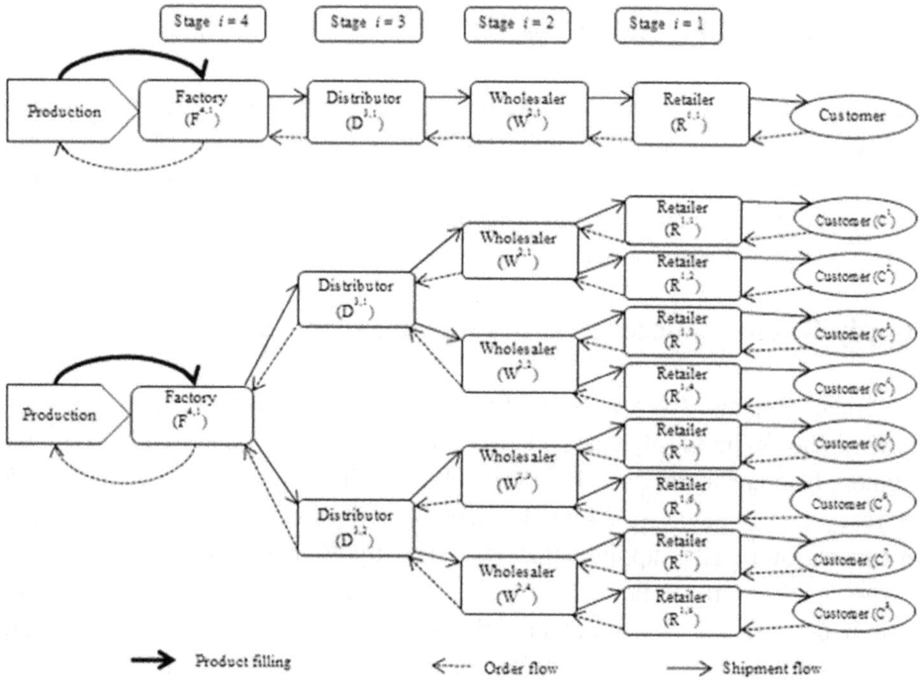

The sequence is as follows:

1. Receives the shipment quantity from the associated member in supplier stage (i + 1), if any, and update the on-hand inventory.
2. Receives the orders from the associated member of the stage (i – 1) (retailer stage receives customer demand as per the demand pattern).
3. Transports the quantity from the available inventory against the order received and updates the inventory status. Unmet quantity is backlogged.

4. Decides the order size and place the order to the associated member in $(i + 1)$ stage. While factory stage issues production orders. The order size is based on SPC-based policy.

Figure 2. Flow diagram of inventory distribution events in a member of stage i

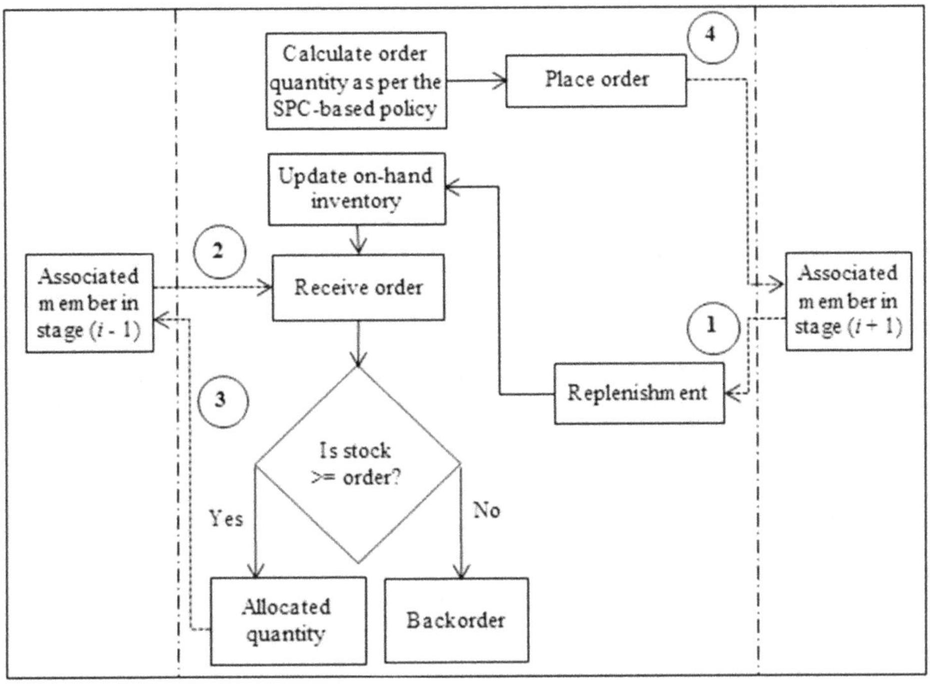

Inventory Control Policies Considered for the Study

Order-Up-To (OUT) Policy

In this policy, an order is placed at each review point so that the sum of the inventory position and the order placed in that period must be equal to the order-up-to level. The order quantity is determined using Equation (1).

$$O_t^{i,j} = \begin{cases} 0, & if \quad \left(IP_t^{i,j} \geq S_t^{i,j}\right) \\ S_t^{i,j} - IP_t^{i,j}, & if \quad \left(IP_t^{i,j} < S_t^{i,j}\right) \end{cases} \tag{1}$$

where,

$O_t^{i,j}$ - Size of an order placed by member j in stage i at period t

$S_t^{i,j}$ - Order-up-to level of member j in stage i at period t

$IP_t^{i,j}$ - Inventory position of member j in stage i at period t

Statistical Process Control (SPC)-Based policy

The order size under the SPC-based policy is determined by applying control chart concepts proposed by Costantino, Di Gravio, Shaban, & Tronci (2014a, 2014b, 2015a, 2015b). The control chart technique involves the calculation of mean, standard deviation, upper control limit and lower control limit. The control parameter is within the upper control limit and lower control limit when the process is in control. Two control charts, namely demand control chart and inventory position control chart are prepared. The order quantity includes two parts: base order quantity and inventory balance. The base order quantity is determined using the demand control chart, and the inventory balance is determined using the inventory position control chart. Three demand rules are prepared based on demand control chart. Similarly, three inventory rules are prepared based on the inventory position control chart.

1. **Demand Control Chart:** For a member j in stage i, based on the demand control chart, the centre line is estimated using Equation (2), and dynamic control limits such as upper control limit and lower control limit are estimated using Equations (3) and (4) respectively. The various demand rules are shown in *Figure 3*.

$$\text{Centerline } (CL_{t,D}^{i,j}) = \frac{1}{a^{i,j}} \sum\nolimits_{t-a^{i,j}+1}^{t} D_t^{i,j} \quad \forall i, \forall j \tag{2}$$

$$\text{Upper control limit } (UCL_{t,D}^{i,j}) = CL_{t,D}^{i,j} + 3\sigma_{t,D}^{i,j} \tag{3}$$

$$\text{Lower control limit } (LCL_{t,D}^{i,j}) = CL_{t,D}^{i,j} - 3\sigma_{t,D}^{i,j} \tag{4}$$

where,

$CL_{t,D}^{i,j}$ - Centre line for a member j in stage i at period t based on demand control chart

$\sigma_{t,D}^{i,j}$ - Standard deviation for a member j in stage i at period t based on demand control chart

$D_t^{i,j}$ - Demand arose at member j in stage i at period t

$a^{i,j}$ - Number of demand periods considered to estimate centre line for member j in stage i

Figure 3. Various demand rules based on demand control chart (q = 4)

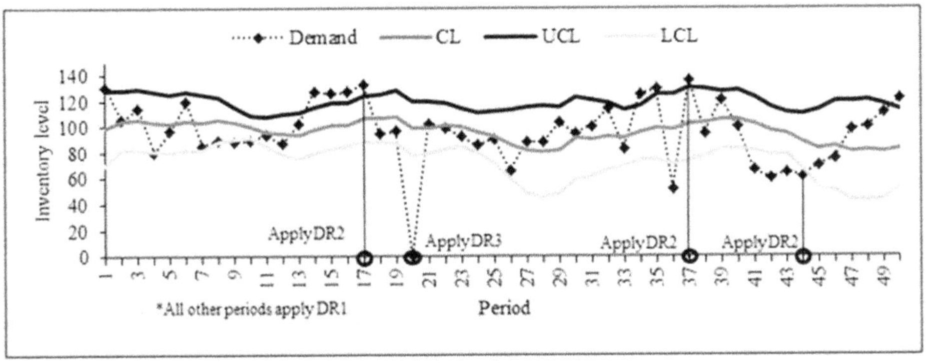

- **Demand Rule 1 (DR1):** For a member j in stage i, if the last consecutive $q^{i,j}$ data points of orders of associated downstream members are within the control limits, $CL_{t,D}^{i,j} + K_D^{i,j}\sigma_{t,D}^{i,j}$ and $CL_{t,D}^{i,j} - K_D^{i,j}\sigma_{t,D}^{i,j}$, then the base order quantity is the centerline of the control chart, where $K_D^{i,j}$ represents the number of $\tilde{A}_{t,D}^{i,j}$ taken to define control limits in demand control chart. Base order quantity is estimated using Equation (5).

$$BOQ_t^{i,j} = CL_{t,D}^{i,j} = \frac{1}{a^{i,j}}\sum_{t-a^{i,j}+1}^{t} D_t^{i,j} \quad \forall i, \forall j \tag{5}$$

- **Demand Rule 2 (DR2):** For a member j in stage i, if the last consecutive $q^{i,j}$ data points of orders of associated downstream members are either above or below the control limits $CL_{t,D}^{i,j} + K_D^{i,j}\sigma_{t,D}^{i,j}$ and $CL_{t,D}^{i,j} - K_D^{i,j}\sigma_{t,D}^{i,j}$ then the base order quantity is the average of last $q^{i,j}$ data points.
- **Demand Rule 3 (DR3):** If the order from the associated downstream member is zero, then the order placed by a member j in stage i is zero. So $BOQ_t^{i,j} = 0$.

2. **Inventory Position Control Chart:** For a member *j* in stage *i*, based on the inventory position control chart, the centre line is estimated using Equation (6), and dynamic control limits such as upper control limit and lower control limit are estimated using Equations (7) and (8) respectively. The various inventory rules are shown in *Figure 4*.

$$\text{Centerline } (CL_{t,IP}^{i,j}) = CL_{t,D}^{i,j}(k^{i,j} + L^{i,j} + L_s^{i,j}) \tag{6}$$

$$\text{Upper control limit } (UCL_{t,IP}^{i,j}) = CL_{t,IP}^{i,j} + 3\sigma_{t,IP}^{i,j} \tag{7}$$

$$\text{Lower control limit } (LCL_{t,IP}^{i,j}) = CL_{t,IP}^{i,j} - 3\sigma_{t,IP}^{i,j} \tag{8}$$

where,

$CL_{t,IP}^{i,j}$ - Centre line for a member *j* in stage *i* at period *t* based on inventory position control chart

$CL_{t,D}^{i,j}$ - Centre line for a member *j* in stage *i* at period *t* based on demand control chart

$\sigma_{t,IP}^{i,j}$ - Standard deviation for a member *j* in stage *i* at period *t* based on inventory position control chart

$k^{i,j}$ - Order lead time of member *j* in stage *i*

$L^{i,j}$ - Delivery lead time of member *j* in stage *i*

$L_s^{i,j}$ - Safety lead time of member *j* in stage *i*

Figure 4. Various inventory rules based on inventory position control chart

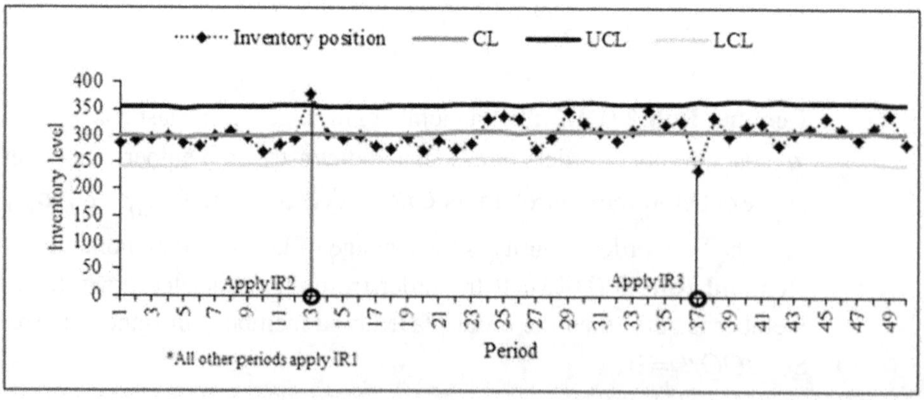

For simplicity, it is assumed that $\sigma_{t,IP}^{i,j} = \sigma_{t,D}^{i,j}$ (Costantino, Di Gravio, Shaban, & Tronci, 2014a, 2014b, 2015a, 2015b).

- **Inventory Rule 1 (IR1):** For a member j in stage i, if the inventory position at period t ($IP_t^{i,j}$) is within in the control limits then the inventory balance at period t ($IB_t^{i,j}$) is zero.
- **Inventory Rule 2 (IR2):** For a member j in stage i, if the last observation in the inventory position control chart is above the upper control limit then a negative inventory balance is determined using Equation (9).

$$IB_t^{i,j} = \delta \times \left(CL_{t,IP}^{i,j} + K_{IP}^{i,j} \sigma_{t,IP}^{i,j} - IP_t^{i,j} \right) \tag{9}$$

where,

δ - Order smoothing parameter

$K_{IP}^{i,j}$ - Number of $\tilde{A}_{t,IP}^{i,j}$ taken to define control limits in inventory position of member j in stage i

- **Inventory Rule 3 (IR3):** For a member j in stage i, if the last observation in the inventory position control chart is below the lower control limit then a positive inventory balance is determined using Equation (10).

$$IB_t^{i,j} = \delta \times \left(CL_{t,IP}^{i,j} - K_{IP}^{i,j} \sigma_{t,IP}^{i,j} - IP_t^{i,j} \right) \tag{10}$$

3. **Order Quantity Determination:** The quantity of order placed at period t can be estimated as the sum of base order quantity and inventory balance, and negative orders are not allowed. So the order quantity determination procedure is given in Equation (11).

$$O_t^{i,j} = \text{Max}\left\{ BOQ_t^{i,j} + IB_t^{i,j}, 0 \right\} \tag{11}$$

Development of Simulation Models for Comparative Study

Two simulation models are developed in Scilab 5.5.0, and the models are capable of simulating supply chain systems. The first and second models describe the serial and divergent supply chain systems, respectively. The performance measures diagrams are plotted using MS Excel. To develop the simulation models of the supply chain operations, some assumptions are considered, and these assumptions are given below:

- Customer order arises for a single item and is faced by the retailer(s) alone.
- All members of the supply chain follow the same inventory control policy.
- In the divergent supply chain, transhipments among retailers or wholesalers are not permitted, and the retailers are facing independent demand.
- There are no capacity constraints and holding space constraints at each member in the supply chain.
- The production capacity of the factory is infinite, and enough raw materials are available for the production.

Based on the above assumptions, each simulation is carried out for a length of 2400 periods. The first 1200 periods are not considered for the performance measurement to reduce the effect of initialization. The performances of supply chains in terms of order variance ratio of each stage and bullwhip slope are evaluated by collecting the data from periods 1201 to 2400. For this study, each simulation experiment is carried out with 100 replications to reduce the impact of random variation, and the average value of the performance measure over these replications is considered.

Validation of Simulation Models

To validate the developed simulation model for serial supply chain, the simulation results are compared with the analytical works of Chen, Drezner, Ryan, & Simchi-Levi (2000) and simulation works of Costantino, Di Gravio, Shaban, & Tronci (2014a, 2015b). For a supply chain where the members following OUT policy, the closed form expression for order rate variance ratio calculation under moving average forecast proposed by Chen, Drezner, Ryan, & Simchi-Levi (2000) is as follows:

$$\frac{Var(O^i)}{Var(D)} \geq \prod_i^{m^s} \left(1 + \frac{2L_{Ti}}{MAP} + \frac{2L_{Ti}^{\ 2}}{MAP^2}\right) \quad \forall i \tag{12}$$

In Equation (12), L_{Ti} and MAP represent the total lead time and the number of periods considered to calculate the moving average, respectively. The L_T includes review period (T), order lead time (k), delivery lead time (L), and safety lead time (L_s). In the proposed model, when $K_{IP} = 0$, $a = p$, and $\delta = 1$, the SPC-based policy is equivalent to OUT policy. The comparison of simulation results is given in *Table 2*, which shows that the results of the proposed simulation model are matching with benchmark studies. Hence, the simulation model for the serial supply chain is validated, and this validation also holds good for the divergent supply chain model as suggested by (Dominguez, Cannella, & Framinan, 2015).

Table 2. Performance comparison for validation of the simulation model for the serial supply chain

Supply chain stage	OUT, $L_T = 4$, $MAP = 50$, N (30,3)		Oder rate variance ratio			
			SPC, $a = 100$, $K_D = 1.5$, $K_{IP} = 0.25$, $q = 4$, $L_T = 4$, $\delta = 1$, N (30,3)		SPC, $a = 30$, $K_D = 2$, $K_{IP} = 0.5$, $q = 15$, $L_T = 4$, $\delta = 1$, N (30,3), *Season* =5, *Cycle* = 7	
	Chen, Drezner, Ryan, & Simchi-Levi (2000)	Proposed model	Costantino, Di Gravio, Shaban, & Tronci (2014a)	Proposed model	Costantino, Di Gravio, Shaban, & Tronci (2015a)	Proposed model
Retailer	1.17	1.17	0.78	0.78	0.88	0.88
Wholesaler	1.37	1.39	0.69	0.68	0.83	0.82
Distributor	1.61	1.67	0.64	0.63	0.83	0.81
Factory	1.89	2.02	0.63	0.61	0.85	0.87

Customer Demand Models

For this study, the demand pattern is generated from a demand generator equation (Equation (13)) adapted from (Zhao & Xie, 2002).

$$D_t = base + slope \times t + season \times \sin\left(\frac{2\pi}{season\ cycle} \times t\right) + noise \times snormal(\ ) \tag{13}$$

The details of different customer demand models faced by the retailer(s) are given in *Table 3*. Under the normal demand, each customer follows the same normal distribution, N(40,5) for the entire simulation period. Under normal with a sudden change in mean, the step-up pattern of demand model is used. The demand level is changing suddenly from one level to another level in one step. For the first 1200 periods, each customer follows a normal distribution, N(40,5). From 1201 period onwards the mean demand level is increased to 80. However, the standard deviation remains the same. In normal demand with seasonality, the demand pattern consists of a seasonal component.

The parameters for the demand pattern generator are as follows: *base* = 40, *slope* = 0, *season* = 5, *cycle* = 7 and *noise* =5. The fourth demand model is a combination of the second and third models. So, the model comprises both step-up and seasonality components. For the first 1200 periods, the parameters for the demand pattern generator are: *base* = 40, *slope* = 0, *season* = 5, *cycle* = 7, and *noise* =5. From period 1201 onwards, the mean demand level is increased to 80. However, other parameters remain the same.

Table 3. Different customer demand models

Model	Parameters settings	Pattern nature
Normal	$D_t = \mathrm{N}(40,5) \quad t \in [1, 2400]$	
Normal with a sudden change in mean	$D_t = \begin{cases} \mathrm{N}(40,5) & t \in [1, 1200] \\ \mathrm{N}(80,5) & t \in [1201, 2400] \end{cases}$	
Normal with seasonality	$D_t = 40 + 5 \times \sin(2\pi t/7) + \mathrm{N}(40,5) \quad t \in [1, 2400]$	
Normal with seasonality and a sudden change in mean	$D_t = \begin{cases} 40 + 5 \times \sin(2\pi t/7) + \mathrm{N}(40,5) & t \in [1, 1200] \\ 80 + 5 \times \sin(2\pi t/7) + \mathrm{N}(40,5) & t \in [1201, 2400] \end{cases}$	

For the present study, the length of review is one period ($T = 1$) and the lead time parameters are: $k = 0$, $L = 2$ and $L_S = 1$. The other parameters are set as follows: $a = 50$, $K_D = 2$, $K_{IP} = 0.5$, $q = 4$, $\delta = 1$ and 0.25. When the order smoothing parameter (δ) is set at 1, then there is no smoothing applied to the OUT and SPC-based policies. The order smoothing parameter (δ) is set at 0.25 when smoothing applied to the policies. Then the policies are become smoothed OUT and SPC-based policies. Under information sharing, the real-time customer demand is shared among the members of the supply chain.

Bullwhip Effect Quantification

The bullwhip effect can be quantified as a stage-wise measure or supply chain network measure. Order rate variance ratio is a metric for the stage-wise measure and bullwhip slope is a metric for the supply chain network measure.

- Order rate Variance Ratio of stage i (OVR^i) is calculated using Equation (14) (Chen, Drezner, Ryan, & Simchi-Levi, 2000).

$$OVR^i = \frac{\text{Sum of the order variance of all the members in stage } i}{\text{Sum of the order variance of all the customers}} \tag{14}$$

- Bullwhip Slope (BwSl): Order rate variance ratio is the most commonly used performance measure of bullwhip effect. However, it is not a representative measure considering the entire supply chain. BwSl is a measure of the presence of bullwhip effect considering the entire supply chain. A high value of the slope means a fast propagation of bullwhip through the supply chain while a low value means a smooth propagation. BwSl is calculated using Equation (15) (Dominguez, Cannella, & Framinan, 2013).

$$\text{BwSl} = \frac{m^S \sum_{i=1}^{m^S} E^i OVR^i - \left(\left(\sum_{i=1}^{m^S} E^i \right) \left(\sum_{i=1}^{m^S} OVR^i \right) \right)}{m^S \sum_{i=1}^{m^S} \left(E^i \right)^2 - \left(\sum_{i=1}^{m^S} E^i \right)^2} \tag{15}$$

where,

i - Stage index

m^S - Number of stages in a supply chain

E^i - Position of stage i in supply chain

OVR^i - Order rate variance ratio of stage i

SOLUTIONS AND RECOMMENDATIONS

The bullwhip effect performance of the supply chains is analysed under four customer demand models and the simulation results obtained are explained in this section.

Comparison of Performances under Normal Demand

The order rate variance ratio and the bullwhip slope obtained for both supply chains are given in *Figure 5* and *Table 4* respectively. It is observed that for both serial and divergent supply chains, the order variance ratios for all stages are less for the SPC-based policy compared to OUT policy. Also, the order variance ratios obtained are similar for both serial and divergent supply chains. The order rate variance ratio is further less in both supply chains under smoothing OUT and SPC-based policies. The smoothing is achieved by changing the order smoothing parameter (δ) from 1 to 0.25. For both serial and divergent supply chains, as the bullwhip slope value obtained for all scenarios is very less (<1), the propagation rate of bullwhip through the supply chains is very slow. The negative value of bullwhip slope indicates the presence of de-whip effect within the supply chains, which results in more stable production planning and scheduling at the factory stage. The sharing of customer demand and smoothing of policy further reduces the order variance ratio at each stage.

Figure 5. Order rate variance ratio for serial and divergent supply chains under normal demand

(a) Order rate variance ratio for serial supply chain

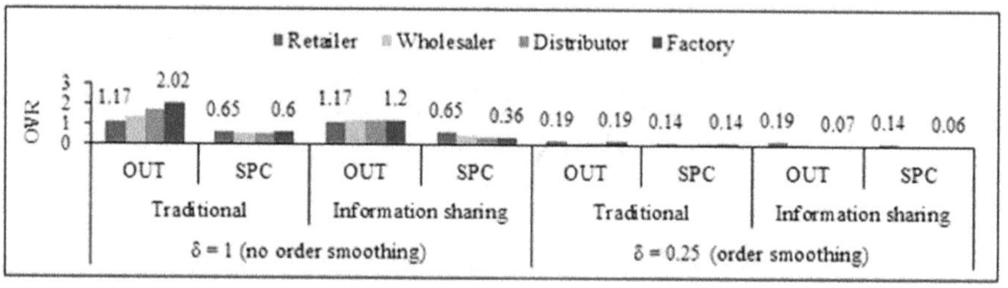

(b) Order rate variance ratio for divergent supply chain

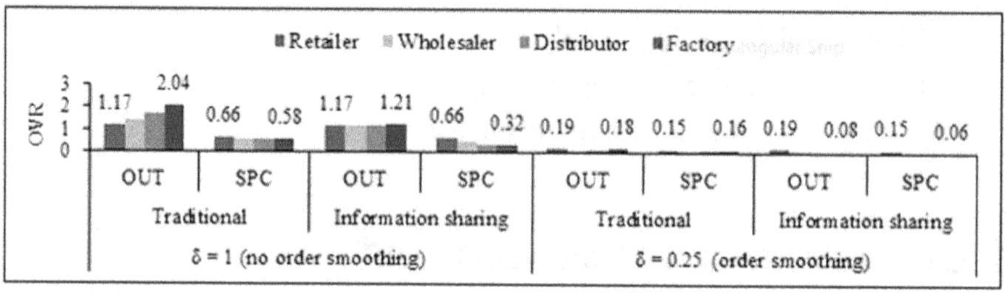

Table 4. Comparison of bullwhip slope under normal demand

Supply chain structure	$\delta = 1$				$\delta = 0.25$			
	Traditional		Information sharing		Traditional		Information sharing	
	OUT	SPC	OUT	SPC	OUT	SPC	OUT	SPC
Serial	0.283	-0.015	0.010	-0.097	0.002	0.006	-0.038	-0.025
Divergent	0.290	-0.024	0.013	-0.111	0.001	0.008	-0.035	-0.028

Comparison of Performances under Normal with a Sudden Change in Mean

The order variance ratio obtained for both supply chains under normal with a sudden change in mean is shown in *Figure 6*. The bullwhip slope estimated for the evaluation periods for both supply chains, are given in *Table 5*. The results show that the order rate variance ratios obtained for the stages of the divergent supply chain are different from that of the serial supply chain. For each stage of the divergent supply chain, the order rate variance ratio is higher compared to the serial supply chain. So, under step-up demand pattern, the structure of the supply chain influences the bullwhip effect. The step-up present in the end customer demand causes an increase in the stock-out at retailers. This stock-out is propagated and amplified through the supply chain networks that cause more stock-out at upper stages of supply chains. In the case of the serial supply chain, the factory manages the stock-out due to the step-up in demand faced by a single retailer. However, in the case of the divergent supply chain, the number of retailers is eight which create more stock-out at factory compared to the serial supply chain. The effect of order smoothing parameter is also observed in the graphical results. When the order smoothing parameter is changed from 1 to 0.25 the order rate variance ratio is further reduced in both supply chains.

Figure 6. Order rate variance ratio for serial and divergent supply chains under normal with a sudden change in mean

(a) Order rate variance ratio for serial supply chain

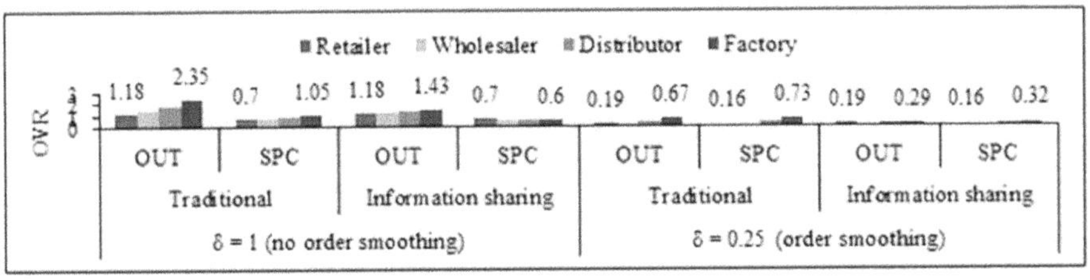

(b) Order rate variance ratio for divergent supply chain

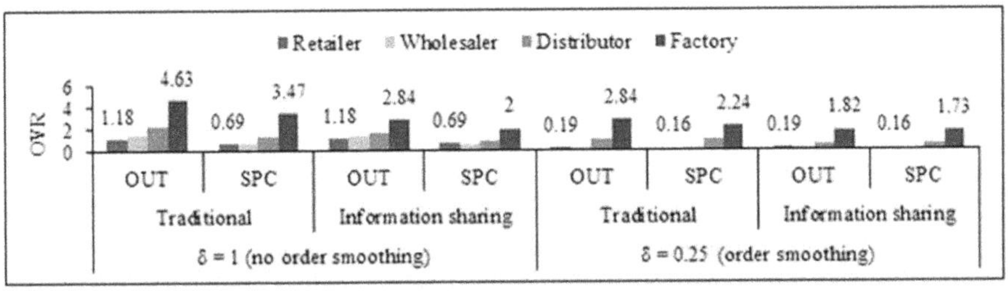

Table 5. Comparison of bullwhip slope under normal with a sudden change in mean

Supply chain structure	$\delta = 1$				$\delta = 0.25$			
	Traditional		Information sharing		Traditional		Information sharing	
	OUT	SPC	OUT	SPC	OUT	SPC	OUT	SPC
Serial	0.389	0.127	0.084	-0.032	0.159	0.189	0.035	0.055
Divergent	1.114	0.890	0.536	0.420	0.866	0.704	0.522	0.510

Comparison of Performances under Normal with Seasonality

Both supply chains are analysed under normal with seasonality, and the obtained results are shown in *Figure 7* and *Table 6*. It is noticed that the presence of seasonal components in the demand pattern controls the amplification of order variance through the supply chains. For $\delta = 1$ (no order smoothing), the order rate variance ratio obtained is different for both supply chains. However, when $\delta = 0.25$ (order smoothing), the order variance ratio obtained for the supply chains is similar. The bullwhip slope value shows that the propagation rates of bullwhip effect through the supply chains is also the same and in all experimental scenarios de-bullwhip effect present in the supply chains. So, in the divergent supply chain under smoothed inventory control policy, the effect of seasonal components on bullwhip is cancelled out and, the amplification of order variance is restricted.

Figure 7. Order rate variance ratio for serial and divergent supply chains under normal with seasonality

(a) Order rate variance ratio for serial supply chain

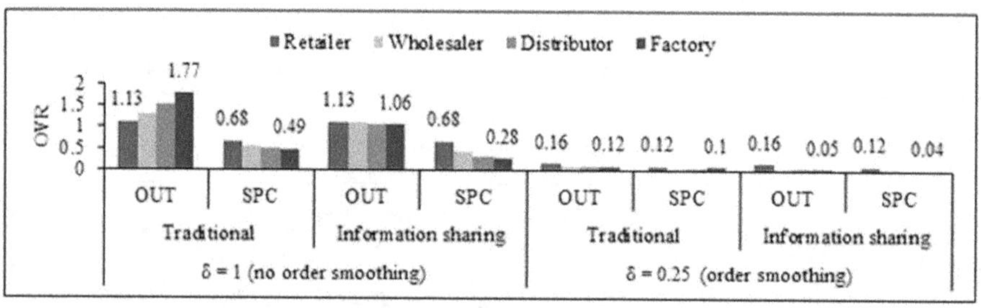

(b) Order rate variance ratio for divergent supply chain

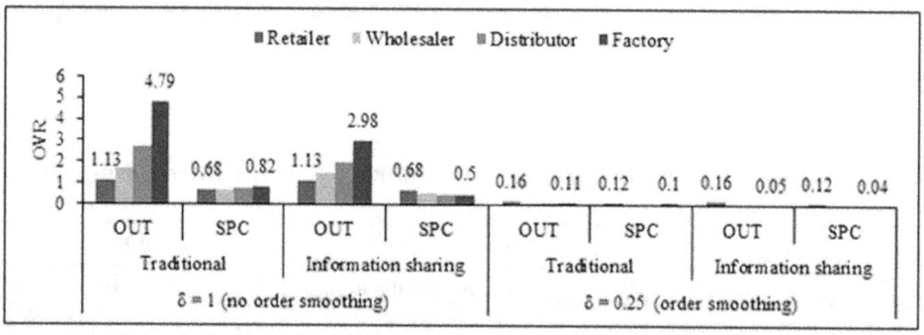

Table 6. Comparison of bullwhip slope under normal with seasonality demand pattern

Supply chain structure	$\delta = 1$				$\delta = 0.25$			
	Traditional		Information sharing		Traditional		Information sharing	
	OUT	SPC	OUT	SPC	OUT	SPC	OUT	SPC
Serial	0.213	-0.062	-0.024	-0.132	-0.010	-0.005	-0.034	-0.025
Divergent	1.210	0.047	0.609	-0.603	-0.013	-0.004	-0.032	-0.022

Comparison of Performances under Normal with Seasonality and a Sudden Change in Mean

The fourth customer demand model is the combination of the second and the third models. The obtained results are given in *Figure 8* and *Table 7*. The combined effect of seasonality, and sudden change in mean results in the order variance increase in both serial and divergent supply chains. The order rate variance ratio is further less in both supply chains under smoothing OUT and SPC-based policies. However, in most of the scenarios, the bullwhip effect propagation rate is reduced as compared to normal with a sudden change in mean model, which is due to the presence of seasonal components in the demand model.

Z-Statistical Test

This test is used to compare the bullwhip effect performance of supply chains under OUT/OUT smoothing policy and SPC-based policy with different demand patterns. In the present study, *z*-test is conducted to compare the bullwhip slope under both policies in serial and divergent supply chains. In this test, *z*-value is calculated using Equation (16), and should be compared with the *z*-critical value for the fixed significance value from the statistical table. The hypothesis must be rejected when calculated *z*-value is higher than the *z*-critical value from the statistical table. In the present study, the hypotheses are tested at 5% significance level.

Figure 8. Order rate variance ratio for serial and divergent supply chains under normal with seasonality and a sudden change in mean

(a) Order rate variance ratio for serial supply chain

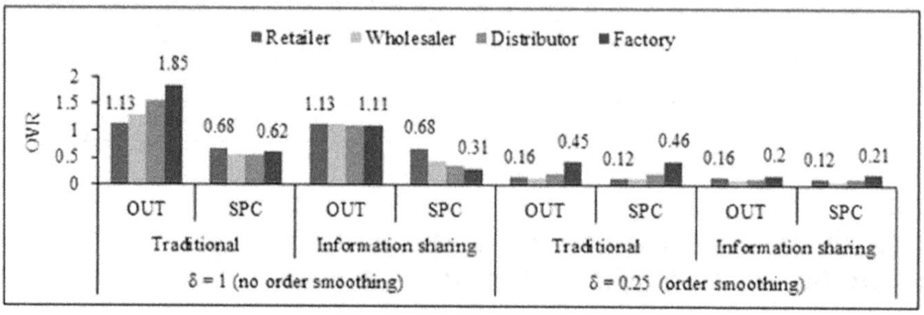

(b) Order rate variance ratio for divergent supply chain

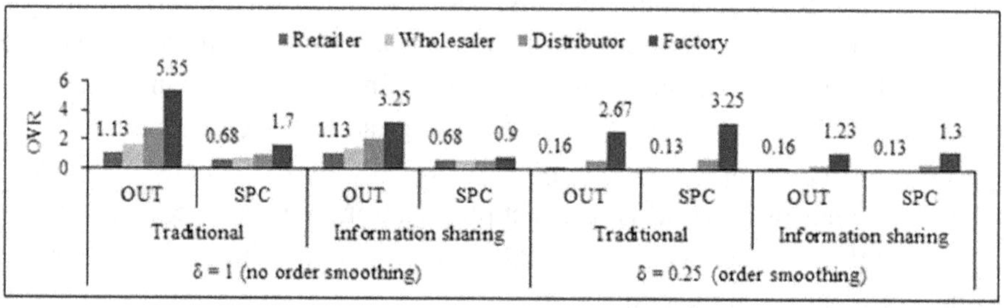

Table 7. Comparison of bullwhip slope under normal with seasonality and sudden change in mean

Supply chain structure	$\delta = 1$				$\delta = 0.25$			
	Traditional		Information sharing		Traditional		Information sharing	
	OUT	SPC	OUT	SPC	OUT	SPC	OUT	SPC
Serial	0.239	-0.019	-0.008	-0.122	0.097	0.113	0.015	0.031
Divergent	1.379	0.328	0.696	0.067	0.798	0.991	0.344	0.377

$$z_{calculated} = \frac{(\overline{x_1} - \overline{x_2}) - (\mu_1 - \mu_2)}{\sqrt{\frac{s_1^2}{n_1} + \frac{s_2^2}{n_2}}} \quad (16)$$

where,

$\overline{x}_1$ - Sample mean value of bullwhip effect under OUT/ OUT smoothing policy

$\overline{x}_2$ - Sample mean value of bullwhip effect under SPC-based policy

μ_1 - Population mean value of bullwhip effect under OUT/ OUT smoothing policy

μ_2 - Population mean value of bullwhip effect under SPC-based policy

s_1 - Sample standard deviation of bullwhip effect under OUT/ OUT smoothing policy

s_2 - Sample standard deviation of bullwhip effect under SPC-based policy

Z-Test for Comparing the Bullwhip Slope Under OUT and SPC-Based Policies with Different Demand Patterns

Hypothesis One: There is no difference in bullwhip slope of supply chains under OUT and SPC-based policies in normal demand pattern.

Hypothesis Two: There is no difference in bullwhip slope of supply chains under OUT and SPC-based policies in normal with a sudden change in mean demand pattern.

Hypothesis Three: There is no difference in bullwhip slope of supply chains under OUT and SPC-based policies in normal with seasonality demand pattern.

Hypothesis Four: There is no difference in bullwhip slope of supply chains under OUT and SPC-based policies in normal with seasonality and a sudden change in mean demand pattern.

From *Table 8*, it is found that the *z*-calculated is greater than $z_{0.05}$(table) = 1.96 under all demand patterns for both supply chains. Hence, all the hypothesis must be rejected and concludes that for both supply chains the bullwhip slope under OUT policy is significantly differing from the bullwhip slope under the SPC-based policy.

Table 8. The z-test parameters and z-critical value for bullwhip slope under OUT and SPC-based policies

Demand pattern	Parameter	Serial supply chain			Divergent supply chain		
		OUT policy	SPC-based policy	z-value	OUT policy	SPC-based policy	z-value
Normal	Mean	0.283	-0.015	z-calculated = 201.63 $z_{0.05}$(table) = 1.96	0.291	-0.024	z-calculated = 84.55 $z_{0.05}$(table) = 1.96
	Standard deviation	0.009	0.011		0.034	0.013	
	Sample size	100	100		100	100	
Normal with a sudden change in mean	Mean	0.389	0.127	z-calculated = 105.24 $z_{0.05}$(table) = 1.96	1.11	0.89	z-calculated = 37.58 $z_{0.05}$(table) = 1.96
	Standard deviation	0.018	0.017		0.044	0.039	
	Sample size	100	100		100	100	
Normal with seasonality	Mean	0.213	-0.062	z-calculated = 202.78 $z_{0.05}$(table) = 1.96	1.21	0.047	z-calculated = 331.41 $z_{0.05}$(table) = 1.96
	Standard deviation	0.009	0.01		0.033	0.013	
	Sample size	100	100		100	100	
Normal with seasonality and a sudden change in mean	Mean	0.239	-0.019	z-calculated = 151.81 $z_{0.05}$(table) = 1.96	1.379	0.328	z-calculated = 235.24 $z_{0.05}$(table) = 1.96
	Standard deviation	0.011	0.012		0.037	0.024	
	Sample size	100	100		100	100	

Z-Test for Comparing the Bullwhip Slope Under OUT and SPC-Based Policies with Order Smoothing with Different Demand Patterns

Hypothesis One: There is no difference in bullwhip slope of supply chains under OUT and SPC-based policies with order smoothing in normal demand pattern.

Hypothesis Two: There is no difference in bullwhip slope of supply chains under OUT and SPC-based policies with order smoothing in normal with a sudden change in mean demand pattern.

Hypothesis Three: There is no difference in bullwhip slope of supply chains under OUT and SPC-based policies with order smoothing in normal with seasonality demand pattern.

Hypothesis Four: There is no difference in bullwhip slope of supply chains under OUT and SPC-based policies with order smoothing in normal with seasonality and a sudden change in mean demand pattern.

Table 9. The z-test parameters and z-critical value for bullwhip slope under OUT and SPC-based policies with order smoothing

Demand pattern	Parameter	Serial supply chain			Divergent supply chain		
		OUT policy with order smoothing	SPC-based policy with order smoothing	z-value	OUT policy with order smoothing	SPC-based policy with order smoothing	z-value
Normal	Mean	0.002	0.006	z-calculated = -3.54 $z_{0.05}$(table) = -1.96	0.001	0.008	z-calculated = -4.54 $z_{0.05}$(table) = -1.96
	Standard deviation	0.008	0.008		0.010	0.011	
	Sample size	100	100		100	100	
Normal with a sudden change in mean	Mean	0.159	0.189	z-calculated = -7.86 $z_{0.05}$(table) = -1.96	0.866	0.704	z -calculated = 25.07 $z_{0.05}$(table) = 1.96
	Standard deviation	0.027	0.027		0.044	0.047	
	Sample size	100	100		100	100	
Normal with seasonality	Mean	-0.01	-0.005	z-calculated = -6.48 $z_{0.05}$(table) = -1.96	-0.013	-0.004	z-calculated = -9.04 $z_{0.05}$(table) = -1.96
	Standard deviation	0.005	0.005		0.007	0.007	
	Sample size	100	100		100	100	
Normal with seasonality and a sudden change in mean	Mean	0.097	0.113	z-calculated = -6.44 $z_{0.05}$(table) = -1.96	0.798	0.991	z-calculated = -26.77 $z_{0.05}$(table) = -1.96
	Standard deviation	0.017	0.017		0.049	0.052	
	Sample size	100	100		100	100	

From *Table 9*, it is found that the calculated z-calculated is less than $z_{0.05}$(table) = -1.96 under all demand patterns for both supply chains, except under the normal with a sudden change in mean demand pattern for the divergent supply chain. Hence, all these hypotheses must be rejected and conclude that for both supply chains the bullwhip slope under OUT policy with order smoothing is significantly differing from the bullwhip slope under the SPC-based policy with order smoothing, except under the normal with a sudden change in mean demand pattern and the divergent supply chain. Reason for the better performance of the smoothed OUT policy is the following. When order smoothing applied to the OUT policy, the entire gap between order-up-to level and inventory position is not filled, i.e. the smoothing applied to the net difference of order-up-to level and inventory position. However, in the case of order smoothing of SPC-based policy, the smoothing applied to the inventory balance, which is determined using inventory position chart only.

MANAGERIAL IMPLICATIONS AND FUTURE RESEARCH DIRECTIONS

Useful managerial findings are derived based on the simulation study. In a real supply chain scenario, the implementation of right inventory control policies at organisations improves the bullwhip effect performance. One of the most difficult decision makings is the selection of the right inventory control policy. If the supply chain system is large and more complex, then the selection of the inventory control policy becomes challenging. The present study addresses the impact of SPC-based policy on the bullwhip effect of serial and divergent supply chain networks. If the supply chain manager wants to make a decision based on the bullwhip effect performance of the SPC-based policy, then the findings of this study provide proper guidelines. The customer demand models are more realistic as this take into account the shock and seasonal components. As suggested by the simulation study, the SPC-based policy adopts suitably with these uncertainties in customer demand and so this policy performs better than the OUT policy. However, the performance under OUT smoothing policy is significantly better than the SPC-based policy. In a supply chain network, for the products having stable demand pattern the minor variations do not take into account. However, the products having significant variability in customer demand the serial and divergent supply chains performance are found to be differing. The SPC-based policy absorbs the amplification up to some level. Information sharing among the stages in a supply chain reduces uncertainties, coordinates various activities and improves the performance of supply chain.

This study can be further extended by comparing the performance of supply chains by considering other performance measures such as supply chain fill rate, inventory variance ratio, and total cost. Also, strategies can be prepared for the mitigation of the bullwhip effect in supply chains. The effect of divergence of supply chain on the bullwhip performance is another area that can be explored. It may be noted that in practice a second stage member has large number of downstream members which shows large level divergence of the supply chain.

CONCLUSION

The chapter addresses the impact of SPC-based policy on the bullwhip effect of serial and divergent supply chain networks. If the supply chain manager wants to take a decision based on the bullwhip effect performance of the SPC-based policy, then the findings of this study provide proper guidelines. The customer demand models are more realistic as this take into account the shock (jump in mean demand) and seasonal components. As suggested by the simulation study, the SPC-based policy adopts suitably with these uncertainties in customer demand and thus this policy performs better than the OUT policy. However, when smoothing is applied to the order quantity, the impact of policies on bullwhip slope is changed. The performance under OUT policy with order smoothing is significantly differing from the performance under SPC-based policy with order smoothing. The performance of serial and divergent supply chains is found to be differing when the products have significant variability in customer demand. It is found that the SPC-based policy absorbs the amplification up to a certain level.

REFERENCES

Bottani, E., Montanari, R., & Volpi, A. (2010). The impact of RFID and EPC network on the bullwhip effect in the Italian FMCG supply chain. *International Journal of Production Economics*, *124*(2), 426–432. doi:10.1016/j.ijpe.2009.12.005

Boute, R. N., Disney, S. M., Lambrecht, M. R., & Van Houdt, B. (2007). An integrated production and inventory model to dampen upstream demand variability in the supply chain. *European Journal of Operational Research*, *178*(1), 121–142. doi:10.1016/j.ejor.2006.01.023

Chatfield, D. C., Kim, J. G., Harrison, T. P., & Hayya, J. C. (2004). The bullwhip effect-impact of stochastic lead time, information quality, and information sharing: A simulation study. *Production and Operations Management*, *13*(4), 340–353. doi:10.1111/j.1937-5956.2004.tb00222.x

Chen, F., Drezner, Z., Ryan, J. K., & Simchi-Levi, D. (2000). Quantifying the bullwhip effect in a simple supply chain: The impact of forecasting, lead times, and information. *Management Science*, *46*(3), 436–443. doi:10.1287/mnsc.46.3.436.12069

Cheng, J.-C., & Chou, C.-Y. (2008). A real-time inventory decision system using Western Electric run rules and ARMA control chart. *Expert Systems with Applications*, *35*(3), 755–761. doi:10.1016/j.eswa.2007.07.019

Costantino, F., Di Gravio, G., Shaban, A., & Tronci, M. (2014b). SPC-based inventory control policy to improve supply chain dynamics. *IACSIT International Journal of Engineering and Technology*, *6*(1), 418–426.

Costantino, F., Di Gravio, G., Shaban, A., & Tronci, M. (2014a). Inventory control system based on control charts to improve supply chain performances. *International Journal of Simulation Modelling*, *13*(3), 263–275. doi:10.2507/IJSIMM13(3)1.263

Costantino, F., Di Gravio, G., Shaban, A., & Tronci, M. (2015a). A real-time SPC inventory replenishment system to improve supply chain performances. *Expert Systems with Applications*, *42*(3), 1665–1683. doi:10.1016/j.eswa.2014.09.028

Costantino, F., Di Gravio, G., Shaban, A., & Tronci, M. (2015b). SPC forecasting system to mitigate the bullwhip effect and inventory variance in supply chains. *Expert Systems with Applications*, *42*(3), 1773–1787. doi:10.1016/j.eswa.2014.09.039

Dejonckheere, J., Disney, S. M., Lambrecht, M. R., & Towill, D. R. (2003). Measuring and avoiding the bullwhip effect: A control theoretic approach. *European Journal of Operational Research*, *147*(3), 567–590. doi:10.1016/S0377-2217(02)00369-7

Dejonckheere, J., Disney, S. M., Lambrecht, M. R., & Towill, D. R. (2004). The impact of information enrichment on the bullwhip effect in supply chains: A control engineering perspective. *European Journal of Operational Research*, *153*(3), 727–750. doi:10.1016/S0377-2217(02)00808-1

Disney, S. M., Lambrecht, M., Towill, D. R., & Van de Velde, W. (2008). The value of coordination in a two-echelon supply chain. *IIE Transactions*, *40*(3), 341–355. doi:10.1080/07408170701488003

Dominguez, R., Cannella, S., & Framinan, J. M. (2014). On bullwhip-limiting strategies in divergent supply chain networks. *Computers & Industrial Engineering*, *73*(1), 85–95. doi:10.1016/j.cie.2014.04.008

Dominguez, R., Cannella, S., & Framinan, J. M. (2015). The impact of the supply chain structure on bullwhip effect. *Applied Mathematical Modelling*, *39*(23–24), 7309–7325. doi:10.1016/j.apm.2015.03.012

Dominguez, R., Framinan, J. M., & Cannella, S. (2013). Serial vs. divergent supply chain networks: A comparative analysis of the bullwhip effect. *International Journal of Production Research*, *52*(7), 2194–2210. doi:10.1080/00207543.2013.860495

Duan, Q., & Liao, T. W. (2013). A new age-based replenishment policy for supply chain inventory optimization of highly perishable products. *International Journal of Production Economics*, *145*(2), 658–671. doi:10.1016/j.ijpe.2013.05.020

Gaalman, G. (2006). Bullwhip reduction for ARMA demand: The proportional order-up-to policy versus the full-state-feedback policy. *Automatica*, *42*(8), 1283–1290. doi:10.1016/j.automatica.2006.04.017

Kim, I., & Springer, M. (2008). Measuring endogenous supply chain volatility: Beyond the bullwhip effect. *European Journal of Operational Research*, *189*(1), 172–193. doi:10.1016/j.ejor.2007.05.012

Kurano, T., McKay, K. N., & Black, G. W. (2014). Proactive inventory policy intervention to mitigate risk within cooperative supply chains. *International Journal of Industrial Engineering Computations*, *5*(2), 249–264. doi:10.5267/j.ijiec.2013.11.006

Lee, H. L., Padmanabhan, V., & Whang, S. (1997). Information Distortion in a Supply Chain: The Bullwhip Effect. *Management Science*, *43*(4), 546–558. doi:10.1287/mnsc.43.4.546

Lee, H. T., & Wu, J. C. (2006). A study on inventory replenishment policies in a two-echelon supply chain system. *Computers & Industrial Engineering*, *51*(2), 257–263. doi:10.1016/j.cie.2006.01.005

Paik, S.-K., & Bagchi, P. K. (2007). Understanding the causes of the bullwhip effect in a supply chain. *International Journal of Retail & Distribution Management*, *35*(4), 308–324. doi:10.1108/09590550710736229

Pamulety, T. C., & Pillai, V. M. (2011). Impact of information sharing in supply chain performance. *Technology Systems and Management*, *145*, 327–332. doi:10.1007/978-3-642-20209-4_47

Pfohl, H.-C., Cullmann, O., & Stolzle, W. (1999). Inventory management with statistical process control: Simulation and evaluation. *Journal of Business Logistics*, *20*(1), 101–120.

Pillai, M., Talari, P. C., & Elluri, P. V. (2013). Performance analysis of some supply chain replenishment strategies. *International Journal of Logistics Research and Applications*, *17*(5), 357–376. doi:10.1080/13675567.2013.862227

Towill, D. R., Zhou, L., & Disney, S. M. (2007). Reducing the bullwhip effect: Looking through the appropriate lens. *International Journal of Production Economics*, *108*(1–2), 444–453. doi:10.1016/j.ijpe.2006.12.024

Watts, C., Hahn, C. K., & Sohn, B.-K. (1994). Monitoring the Performance of a Reorder Point System: A Control Chart Approach. *International Journal of Operations & Production Management*, *14*(2), 51–61. doi:10.1108/01443579410053211

Wright, D., & Yuan, X. (2008). Mitigating the bullwhip effect by ordering policies and forecasting methods. *International Journal of Production Economics*, *113*(2), 587–597. doi:10.1016/j.ijpe.2007.10.022

Zhao, X., & Xie, J. (2002). Forecasting errors and the value of information sharing in a supply chain. *International Journal of Production Research*, *40*(2), 311–335. doi:10.1080/00207540110079121

ADDITIONAL READING

Banks, J., Carson, J. S., Nelson, B. L., Nicol, D. M., & Shahabudeen, P. (2005). Discrete-event system simulation (4th ed.). Pearson Education.

Bhattacharya, R., & Bandyopadhyay, S. (2011). A review of the causes of bullwhip effect in a supply chain. *International Journal of Advanced Manufacturing Technology*, *54*(9–12), 1245–1261. doi:10.100700170-010-2987-6

Chen, F., Ryan, J. K., & Simchi-Levi, D. (2000). The impact of exponential smoothing forecasts on the bullwhip effect. *Naval Research Logistics*, *47*(1), 269–286. doi:10.1002/(SICI)1520-6750(200006)47:4<269::AID-NAV1>3.0.CO;2-Q

Costantino, F., Di Gravio, G., Shaban, A., & Tronci, M. (2015). The impact of information sharing on ordering policies to improve supply chain performances. *Computers & Industrial Engineering*, *82*, 127–142. doi:10.1016/j.cie.2015.01.024

Lau, R., Xie, J., & Zhao, X. (2008). Effects of inventory policy on supply chain performance : A simulation study of critical decision parameters. *Computers & Industrial Engineering*, *55*(3), 620–633. doi:10.1016/j.cie.2008.02.002

Li, Q., Disney, S. M., & Gaalman, G. (2014). Avoiding the bullwhip effect using damped trend forecasting and the order-up-to replenishment policy. *International Journal of Production Economics*, *149*, 3–16. doi:10.1016/j.ijpe.2013.11.010

Metters, R. (1997). Quantifying the bullwhip effect in supply chains. *Journal of Operations Management*, *15*(2), 89–100. doi:10.1016/S0272-6963(96)00098-8

Pamulety, T. C., George, J., & Pillai, V. M. (2017). An inventory position-based policy for better supply chain performance. *Journal of Industrial and Production Engineering*, *34*(3), 180–198. doi:10.1080/21681015.2016.1243166

Sensi, G. D., Longo, F., & Mirabelli, G. (2008). Inventory policies analysis under demand patterns and lead times constraints in a real supply chain. *International Journal of Production Research*, *46*(24), 6997–7016. doi:10.1080/00207540701528776

KEY TERMS AND DEFINITIONS

Back Order: Demand (past due) against an item whose current stock level is insufficient to satisfy demand. A customer order that cannot be filled when arose, and for which the customer has to wait for some time.

Bullwhip Effect: Increase in order variability from the downstream stage to upstream in a supply chain.

Inventory Policy: Rule followed by a member to make decisions on when and how much to order.

Inventory Position: It is the sum of on-hand inventory and on-order inventory.

Lead Time: Time gap between placing and receiving an order. The lead time of a member is the sum of order lead time and replenishment or delivery lead time.

Order Rate Variance Ratio: Ratio of order variance of a particular member/stage relative to the customer order variance.

Serial vs. Divergent Supply Chain: Cascading of several dyadic structures (which comprises of two business entities) forms a serial supply chain structure. While divergent supply chain has a tree-like structure, where each facility has at most one predecessor, but any number of successors.

Chapter 10
Supply Chain Manufacturing Practices (SCMP):
An Approach to Become Global Dairy Leader

Rajeev Kumar
https://orcid.org/0000-0002-1115-3403
Rajiv Gandhi South Campus (RGSC), Banaras Hindu University, India

ABSTRACT

The chapter attempts to find out the relationship between the supply chain manufacturing practices (SCMP) and organizational performance, which are identified as financial and market performance. In the context of SCM, the financial and market performance factor is operationalized in terms of market share, return of total assets to firms, profit margin annuals sales growth, frequency of stock out, backorder rate, etc. Multiple regression analysis statistical technique has been used for the analysis of the adoption continuum questions in order to find the predictor variables for various performance measuring variables. The findings suggest that of supply chain manufacturing practices (SCMP) play a crucial role in enhancing the performance of the dairies companies in the form of increase in performance matrix indicators (i.e., level of supplier's defect-free deliveries, inventory turnover, frequency of stock out, backorder rate, sales growth, profit margin, return on investment, return on assets to firm).

DOI: 10.4018/978-1-7998-2867-9.ch010

INTRODUCTION

Dairying in India has played a key role in solidification India's rural economy. It has been recognized as an instrument to bring about socio economic transformation. Small and marginal farmers and landless labourers, who derive a substantial part of their livelihood from safe of milk, own about 70 percent of cattle in the rural areas. The vast potential of dairying in employment generation and poverty alleviation is well recognized. In addition to this, dairy farming' production systems worldwide must be able to combine profitability with the responsibility of protecting human health, animal health, animal welfare and the environment. They, as the primary producers in the supply chain, must be given the opportunity to add value to their product by adopting methods of production that satisfy the demands of processors and customers. In order to do this, individual dairy farmer need a single guide on how to achieve this at a practical farm level.

The white revolution has transformed India dairy industry. It has increased the availability of milk as well as provided a reliable source of income and employment to the millions of our rural families which also help in doubling the income of farmers, thus improving the quality and raising the standard of the rural families. India today has the distinction of being the largest producer of milk in the world, the credit goes to Operation flood that has linked rural farmers to the urban cities. But in spite of being number one milk producing country in the world, quality remains the same problems in today 21 century as said by the late father of white revolution Dr. Vergies Kurien, and AMUL (Anand Milk Union Limited) is the only brand from India who is representing to the world in dairy market. So, to maintain the quality of the milk and milk products there comes the role of supply chain manufacturing practices who aim at to ensure the safety of milk and milk products which further satisfy the highest expectation of the dairy industry as well as their consumers. Dairy plant should ensure that processing of milk from farmers to the dairy processing plants must follows good supply chain manufacturing practices. The basic principles for production, processing and handling of milk and milk products are (i) all dairy products from raw material production to the point of consumption should be subject to good supply chain manufacturing practices (SCMP) and good agricultural practices (GAP), and should meet the appropriate level of the public health protection (ii) Good hygienic practices should be implemented throughout the production and processing of milk and milk products because these practices ensure the marketing of safe, quality assured milk and milk products.

That why the purpose of this paper is to create awareness about the significant role of good manufacturing practices for the dairy companies specially the small companies who didn't know its importance and assure it implementation at their workplace so that they can also improve their organization performance in term of sales growth, profit margin, return on investment (ROI) to name a few and provide the satisfaction to their stakeholders.

ROLE OF SUPPLY CHAIN MANUFACTURING PRACTICES (SCMP) IN THE INDIAN DAIRY INDUSTRY

In the dairy industry, supply chain manufacturing practices (SCMP) play a significant role as they set the guidelines to assure that food products are manufactured and stored under safe and sanitary conditions. Good manufacturing practices (GMP) guidelines are established to satisfy regulatory requirements as well as maintain high quality standards of the products supplied to your customers. Good manufacturing practices should be followed by dairy plant owners, operators and employees in order to maximally assure the production of safe and sanitary products at all times. In order to maintain high quality of milk and milk products, the Indian dairy industry needs good manufacturing practices (GMP's), so that it can assure that milk and milk products are manufactured and stored under safe and sanitary conditions. There are some guidelines of GMP which offer suggestions for measures and precautions that should be taken regarding employee health, food handling practices, appearance, personal hygiene, plant procedures, plant and equipment design, maintenance, and sanitation. It is important that every employee be made knowledgeable and aware of the necessity of adhering to these guidelines at all times, that the guidelines be re-emphasized on a regular basis and that regular assessment and review of how well the guidelines are being followed is conducted by management. There are various guidelines for good supply chain manufacturing practices (GMPs) given by Smith et al (1995) for dairy processing plants, which help in enhancing organizational performance, which are categorized into six factors briefed below:

1. **Personal Practices**: Personal cleanliness is of utmost importance in order to maintain the quality and safety of milk and milk products. Poor personal practices can cause contamination of products resulting in spoilage of product or illness of consumers.
2. **Sanitary Operations and Production**: It is the second most important guideline which dairy plants should take care of in order to maintain the quality of the milk and milk products. It includes various parameters like floors, drains, periodic cleaning schedule, hand dips, sanitary utensils, trash storage and disposal, lubricants etc.
3. **Building and Facilities**: This is the third guideline which dairy plants should adhere to in order to maintain the quality of the milk and milk products,

because it comprises of the place where production and storage of milk and milk product take place.

4. **Warehouse Areas:** This is the fourth guideline which dairy plants should take care off in order to maintain the quality of the milk and milk products, because due to its perishable nature these require a special type of cold chain which maintains their temperature in order to keep them in good a condition.
5. **Equipment and Utensil Design:** This is the fifth guideline which dairy plant should take care of in order to maintain the quality of the milk and milk products. It includes various parameters like 3A, USPH/FDA, and USDA Standards, approved materials, utensil construction etc.
6. **Training:** This is the sixth guideline which dairy plants should take care of in order to maintain the quality of the milk and milk products. In this, all new and/or temporary employees need to be introduced to the GMP program prior to entering the job site. Continual training and reinforcement of GMP's for all employees should be done on a regular basis. These are some guidelines of GMPs which offer suggestions for measures and precautions that should be taken regarding employee health, food handling practices, appearance, personal hygiene, plant procedures, plant and equipment design, maintenance, and sanitation.

CRITICAL LITERATURE REVIEW ON SUPPLY CHAIN MANUFACTURING PRACTICES AND ORGANIZATIONAL PERFORMANCE

A crux of literature review from various research paper on good manufacturing practices and organization through supply chain management practices involving its methodology, key findings and key learning is described in *table 1*.

Table 1. Critical literature review on supply chain manufacturing practices (SCMP) and organizational performance

Authors and Year	Objective of the study and Methodology	Key Findings	Key Learning
Babatunde et al (2016)	· Researcher carried out a study to examine the impact of supply chain management practices on market performance of the selected major marketers of petroleum products in Nigeria. · The survey method was used to collect primary data through administration of questionnaires on 126 respondents from the selected seven major marketers of petroleum using convenience and stratified sampling technique, respectively. Standardized Multiple Regression and Pearson Correlation Analysis were used to analyses the data obtained.	The findings of the study revealed that Supply Chain Management Practices (SCMP) have significant impact on market performance of the organization. Also, Supplier and Customer Relationship Management have very strong positive relationship with organizational performance.	The study illustrates that adopting supply chain management practices in which good manufacturing practices is a part will help in enhancing the organizational performance of the firm.
Muhammad et al (2012)	· Author carried out a research work in order to find the impact supply chain on overall performance of an organization. · Data was collected through questionnaires in the month of May 2012, approximately 30 questionnaires were distributed among the managers of the two organizations expected to have the best knowledge about the supply chain operations and its impact on the overall performance of the organization.	The key finding reveals various important dimensions which are associated with SCM methods as well as explains the connection amongst SCM methods, aggressive benefit, as well as organizational overall performance.	The actual study focuses on the causal associations between SCM exercise, aggressive benefit and organizational overall performance.
Singh et al (2012)	· The researcher carried out a study to show the important role of carbon dioxide modified atmosphere packing (MAP) in the processing and packaging of milk and dairy products. · The methodology used is an extensive literature review on the role of carbon dioxide (CO_2) and modified atmosphere packing (MAP) in increasing the shelf life and quality of raw milk.	The key finding revealed the important role of modified atmosphere packing (MAP) which is being used with high carbon dioxide (CO2) concentration as well as CO2/N2 gas mixes. Researchers also find that modified atmosphere packaging or 'gas flushing' has become a popular technique which is used to extend the shelf life (both quality and safety) of a number of dairy products.	· This study shows how modified atmosphere packaging (MAP) plays an important role in preserving the freshness of fresh produces, meats and fish by controlling their biochemical metabolism. It also revealed that MAP dramatically extends the shelf life of packaged food products, and in some cases, food does not require any further treatments or any special care during distribution. · Researchers also show that MAP has found application in milk and milk products with the use of CO2 injection technique, which is a unique natural antimicrobial and processing aid that has several potential uses in the dairy industry. It is unique because it can be added to and removed from dairy products with no deleterious effects.
Anuar & Yusuff (2011)	· The research paper investigated the current level of best manufacturing practices in Malaysian ISO 9000 certified small and medium enterprises (SMEs). · The authors conducted a survey on 270 ISO 9000 certified manufacturing SMEs. The questionnaire only covered eight areas of benchmarking and was analyzed using descriptive statistics. Data was analyzed using the SPSS software.	The results showed that the level of best manufacturing practices can be improved further, especially in the area of technology and product innovation.	· The paper provides knowledge in assisting the SMEs to identify the areas that they have to improve to achieve best manufacturing practices. Based on an extensive search of literature on performance requirements, eight areas were identified. Thus, the questionnaire was designed consisting of the eight areas which are management, human resources development (HRD), technology and product innovation, marketing strategy, quality, production process, supply chain management (SCM) and customer focus. · The paper also provides some useful insights and can help Malaysian manufacturing companies to implement best practices and benchmarking to improve their practices.

continued on following page

Table 1. Continued

Authors and Year	Objective of the study and Methodology	Key Findings	Key Learning
Bigllardi and Bottani (2010)	· Researcher developed a balance scorecard (BSC) model that is designed and delimited for performance measurement in food supply chain. · The research methodology is a combination of literature analysis, Delphi technique and case study research.	Researchers had provided a structured performance measurement system tailored for the food supply. Researchers' case study shows that the company examined has a similar view on three of the four perspectives of the BSC, which can be thus considered as validation, which includes: customer perspective, internal processes perspective, learning and growth perspective and lastly financial perspective.	Researchers have developed a balanced score card (BSC) model which included four perspectives i.e. · First one is customer which involves parameters like customer query time, order lead time, distribution lead time, delivery reliability, effectiveness of distribution planning schedule, quality of delivery goods, customer perceived value of product, flexibility in service system to meet particular customer need and responsiveness to urgent delivery. · Second perspective is internal processes whose indicators are accuracy of forecasting techniques, purchase order cycle time, planned process cycle time total inventory cost etc. · Third perspective is financial, which includes cost per operation hour, return on investment, supplier cost saving activities and fourth perspective is learning and growth whose indicators are order entry method and level of information sharing etc. which is expected to help in judging the performance measurement in food supply chain.
Nordin et al (2010)	· The researcher presented an exploratory study of lean manufacturing implementation in Malaysian automotive industries and also examines the drivers and barriers that influence the implementation of lean manufacturing. · The survey was performed on 60 Malaysian automotive components manufacturing firms. A questionnaire survey is used to explore the extent of lean manufacturing implementation. The respondents were chosen from those who are directly involved with lean manufacturing practices such as production and quality personnel.	· The key findings show that most of the respondent firms are classified as in-transition towards lean manufacturing practice. These firms believe that the factors that drive the implementation of lean manufacturing are the desire to focus on customers and to achieve the organization's continuous improvement. · The paper also shows the main barriers to implement lean manufacturing system are the lack of understanding lean concepts and shop floor employees' attitude.	· Lean manufacturing system helps in improving and enhancing the performance of the firms. · The study also focuses on the various lean manufacturing practices, namely 5S, preventive maintenance, training, visual control, daily schedule adherence, employee involvement, equipment layout, supplier quality level, customer involvement in quality, cross functional teams, Kanban/ pull production, workforce commitment, setup time reduction, group problem solving, continuous flow, customer involvement in product design, small lot size, JIT link with customers, supplier involvement in quality, "Error proof" equipment, levelled production, JIT delivery by suppliers, long term contract, product design – simplicity, supplier involvement in product design, cellular manufacturing etc. which are essential for every organization in order to get competitive edge over the others.
Costa & Lima (2009)	· The research paper presented the rationality for the organizational design development related to advanced manufacturing design (AMT) adoption. · The theoretical development was illustrated by some empirical data, particularly in the cases of competences, capabilities and manufacturing vision statements formulation.	The contribution of this paper is to the development of rationality for integration of AMT adoption to the required organizational design, within the scope of the manufacturing function, intended to represent the best solution towards the cohesion assurance between the technology to be introduced and the current organizational change.	This paper is a theoretical construction that organizes and synthesizes the issues that are being studied in the main theme: "The adoption of the automated systems," focusing the discussion on the manufacturing strategy and organizational design domains.

continued on following page

Table 1. Continued

Authors and Year	Objective of the study and Methodology	Key Findings	Key Learning
Chandan (2007)	Researcher in his research paper shows the important role played by hazard analysis critical control point (HACCP) in dairy industry, which is a management tool that provides a structured and scientific approach to the control of identified hazards. The researchers revealed that HACCP has international recognition as an effective means of controlling food safety hazards and is endorsed as such by the Food and Agricultural Organization (FAO) and by World Health Organization (WHO) Codex Alimentarius Commission.	The key findings revealed that the factors like plant conditions, manufacturing practices, housekeeping, sanitary standards, personal hygiene and work habits of employees and visitors assumes critical importance in plant control of quality, product safety, personal safety, and financial integrity etc. play a significant role in making a food plant successful.	Importance of HACCP is being highlighted in food plants and also defined various guidelines which include plant standards like clean floors, walls and ceiling maintenance, good condition of doors and window, lighting and ventilation separate room for production and non-production area, toilet facilities- sewage disposal, water supply, plant cleanliness, hand washing facilities, locker and lunchroom disposal of wastes, personnel practice, training and standardization and HACCP audit and follow-up actions etc. which make the dairy plant in good condition.
Narang (2007)	Researcher in his paper talks about the different new technologies which are being used in order to improve the quality of and achieve food safety by adopting more and more stringent measures in terms of hygiene in the entire food chain starting from primary production to the final consumption point.	The key findings revealed the important part played by MMPO, which provides for: Standards of hygiene and sanitation to be observed by dairies, inspection of dairy units before commercial production/commissioning and also on an annual basis for sanitary & hygienic products, as per schedule V of MMPO. Milk and milk products to compulsorily conform to quality standard prescribed by the government.	Important provision for hygiene under the MMPO which are the requirement of the surroundings of buildings housing the dairy units, the requirement of dairy plant building which includes raw milk receiving section, chill room/storage, processing section, tables, utensils and equipment's, general condition for all sections etc., cleaning and sanitation, changing room for workers, the requirement of plant and equipment, packaging and storage, inspection, testing and supervision, raw material, requirement for personal hygiene, water, statutory requirement, desirable attributes- HACCP/ISO certification, additional information on set-up of the plant etc.
Punjrath (2007)	Author in his work, revealed the role of packaging of milk which is the first thing that attracts the customer. The researchers also revealed that many new products could see the light of the day only because of availability of appropriate technologies.	· The key findings show how the high-tech packaging technology helps in extending the shelf life and also distribution of paneer to remote area. · The findings also revealed that good packaging lowers product cost' reduces product waste, helps consumers make informed purchase decisions, protects against tampering and spoilage, and is essential for human health, safety and comfort.	Packaging of milk is important in order to maintain quality and freshness of the milk and milk products. The study also shows the increasing role of various technologies which are used for packaging of milk and milk products like: 'Modified Atmosphere Packaging' (MAP), also called Controlled Atmosphere Packaging (CAP), which is known for increasing the shelf life of milk and milk products. 'Oxygen absorbers/Scavenger' which have the great potential for extending the shelf life of whole milk powder/ infant foods, cheese, peda, ghee and many Indian sweets. 'Poly clip system' which is based on a new packaging concept. The UHT (ultra-heat treatment) technology combined with aseptic packaging which is being already used in packing a variety of fresh milk and products like lassi and various others milk products in order to increase their shelf-life and facilitate their national and international marketing.
Goyal and Alam (2007)	Researcher in their paper talk about the various technologies used for semi-automatic packaging of milk and milk products which are believed to maintain the quality and freshness of dairy products.	The paper revealed the importance of a whole range of automatic, semi-automatic packaging and sealing machines, which are pouch/sachet form fill and seal (FFS) machines, tube filling machines, cup filling and packaging machines, cup filling and sealing machine, cartooning machine, can filling machines, shrink wrapping machines etc.	This paper emphasizes the importance of various automatic, semi-automatic packaging and sealing machines which play a very important role in packaging of milk and milk product which helps in maintaining the quality and freshness of dairy products.

continued on following page

Table 1. Continued

Authors and Year	Objective of the study and Methodology	Key Findings	Key Learning
National Bureau of Agricultural Commodity and Food Standards (NBACFS) (2005)	· Author established standards for Good Manufacturing Practices (GPs) for milk collection center in order to control the milk production, increase the milk quality management to be effective and conformed to the standards as well as enhance the ability in competitiveness to the international market in the future. · This is the Agricultural Standards Committee report prepared by National Bureau of Agricultural Commodity and Food Standards Ministry of Agriculture and Cooperatives on good manufacturing practices for milk collection center in 2005.	This report revealed the various important guidelines for the good manufacturing practices for milk collection center, which are milk collection center management, management of machines and equipment and tools for raw milk receiving, raw milk cooling system management, storage tank management, cleaning-in-place (CIP), maintenance of machines and equipment, utility management which involves electricity, water supply etc., management of transportation and transport vehicles which involves transportation, raw milk transport vehicle etc., management of raw milk purchasing system, personnel management, safety measures and environment management and management of raw milk quality control.	Good supply manufacturing practices (SCMP) play a crucial role in providing upper edge and enhancing performance of the company. It also helps in raising the quality and freshness of dairy products.
Smith et al (1995)	· Researcher in his research paper has given the various guidelines that have been developed to highlight good manufacturing practices that should be followed by dairy plant owners, operators and employees to maximally assure the production of safe and sanitary products at all times. · This is the dairy practice council report prepared by plant equipment and procedure task force on good manufacturing practices for dairy processing plants in 1995.	This report revealed the various important guidelines for the good manufacturing practices for dairy processing plants which are (i) Personal practices is related to maintain the personal hygiene of the employee working in the dairy plant (ii) Sanitary Operations and Production which take care of in order to maintain the quality of the milk and milk products (iii) Building and Facilities which involve the dairy plants who should adhere to in order to maintain the quality of the milk and milk products, because it comprises of the place where production and storage of milk and milk product take place (iv) Warehouse Areas where dairy plants should take care of storage of milk and milk products, because due to its perishable nature these require a special type of cold chain which maintains their temperature in order to keep them in good a condition. Equipment and Utensil Design is the next guideline.	· This report revealed how various good manufacturing practices i.e. Personal Practices, Sanitary operation and production, Buildings and facilities, Warehousing areas practices, Equipment and utensil design practices play a significant role in improving and enhancing the quality and freshness of dairy products. · The guideline offers suggestions for measures and precautions that should be taken regarding employee health, food handling practices, appearance, personal hygiene, plant procedures, plant and equipment design, maintenance, and sanitation. · The researcher also revealed that implementing various good manufacturing practices (GMP) at the workplace is linked to enhancing the organizational performance also.

RESEARCH METHODOLOGY

Research Problem

Apart from India's enormous potential to become global dairy leader, food safety has always been an important issue in Indian scenario specially in dairy market. Indian dairy product has to compete not only globally but with the imported product in the domestic market as well. The domestic dairy industry needs to be competitive in, beside price, product safety and quality. It is therefore imperative that India strengthens its national food safety control systems and programme. Producing safe food is now not a matter of choice, it is a necessity.

Food borne diseases caused by microbial logically contaminated food is a huge and leading to the public health problem. There have been reports of significant increase over the past few decades in the incident of diseases caused by pathogens in food. According to the WHO report, adulteration the biggest problem in the dairy industry and if it is not check immediately, 87 percent of the Indian citizen by year 2020 would be suffering from the serious disease like cancer.

Thus, creating an alarming situation for the country and demanding for the effective and efficient adoption and implementation of good supply chain management practices at their workplace. For efficient utilization of available resources, the key areas that the dairy industry need to focus on are the products, the process and the people. The primary concern for any dairy companies relates to three inter-related sub-systems, namely: milk production, processing and marketing.

In such situation supply chain manufacturing practices (SCMP) can play an important role in improving organizational performance and achieving competitive advantage. Through implementing good supply chain manufacturing practices (SCMP), dairy industry can minimize their system wide costs and also provide maximum value to their customers. In such scenario the problem is to how strategize and manage the supply chain manufacturing practices (SCMP) so that the Indian dairy industry can improve their organizational performance and achieve competitive advantage in highly competitive Indian Dairy market?

Objectives of Study

The study has been carried out with following objectives:

- To critically analyze the impact of adopted supply chain manufacturing practices (SCMP) on the organization's performance.
- To suggest a roadmap for improving the performance of the Indian dairy industry through supply chain manufacturing practices (SCMP).

Research Hypotheses

The study has been carried out with following alternate hypotheses:

- **H1:** Supply chain manufacturing practices (SCMP) would serve as an enabler to improve organizational performance.

RESEARCH DESIGN

The research study was a kind of exploratory study which aimed at finding out the nitty-gritty of the Indian dairy supply chain management, followed by a descriptive research design, which helped in evaluating the impact of Supply chain manufacturing practices (SCMP) on the dairy industry performance matrices.

Sampling of Indian Dairy Industry

The research is carried out with one identified group of respondents, which are basically the supply chain members of dairy industry which is elaborated in *table 2*.

- Milk Processing Unit (Chilling, Processing, Packaging and Transportation).

Table 2. Sampling of Indian dairy industry

Category of Respondent	Population	Sampling Frame	Sampling Unit	Sampling Technique and Sample Size
Milk Processing Unit (Chilling, Processing, Packaging and Transportation).	All milk processing units operating in UP and New Delhi-NCR.	All registered milk processing units situated in UP and New Delhi-NCR i.e. 59.	Individual registered milk processing unit's three top executives, i.e., Head of the unit, Operational Head and Marketing Head.	First group of respondents (Milk Processing Unit) – Judgmental sampling based on the market position of the organization and plant production capacity (i.e. one lakh liter per day), has been opted for to select the various milk processing units. Ten dairy plants have been taken and from each dairy plant three respondents, i.e., head of dairy company, operations head and marketing head were targeted for the study, which rendors the sample size of thirty respondents.

DATA COLLECTION

Primary Data

Primary data was collected through survey method using structures questionnaire for one category of respondents i.e. 10 dairy plants operating in UP and New Delhi-NCR region, and from each dairy plant 3 respondents has been taken i.e. head of the dairy plant, marketing head of dairy plant and operation head of the dairy plant, so total sample size was 30.

Secondary Data

Reports and documents will be taken from different magazines, journals, newspaper, central government agencies as well as of state government agencies.

QUESTIONNAIRE DESIGN

The study used various variables. The study identified variables according to research objectives. As per the research sample plan, there are two groups of respondents for whom two categories of the structured questionnaire were developed. The dairy plant questionnaire consisted of two separate groups of variables, which are listed below:

Supply Chain Manufacturing Practices (SCMP)
Organizational Performance Factors

DATA ANALYSIS

Cronbach's alpha for adoption continuum questionnaire was calculated as .827 which was found more than 0.6 showing a high correlation, which indicated high reliability of scale. Multiple regression analysis has been used for the analysis of the adoption continuum questions in order to find the predictor variables for various performance measuring variables which is given below in *table 3*.

FINDINGS

Objective 1: To critically analyse the impact of adopted supply chain manufacturing practices (SCMP) on the dairy organization's performance.

Table 3. Types of questions and data analysis techniques used

S. No.	Types of Questions	Data Analysis Technique	Remarks
1.	Range of performance measurement questions.	Multiple Regression analysis	To find the predictor variables for various performance measuring variables.

Multiple Regression Analysis (Dairy Plant)

Summary of Multiple Regression Analysis of dependent variable, "Level of Supplier's Defect Free Deliveries", is given in the *table 4.*

Table 4. Multiple regression analysis summary table

Step No.	Predictor Variables Entered	Standardized Beta Coefficients	t	Sig. (p)	R	Adjusted R^2	F	Sig. (p)
I	SCMP	.592	-3.887	.001	.351	.327	15.110	.000

For dependent variable 'Level of Supplier's Defect Free Deliveries', one variable supply chain manufacturing practices (SCMP) is found significant predictors as verified by F- value (F=15.110, p=0.000).

At step I, "supply chain manufacturing practices (SCMP)", entered into the regression analysis. The value of adjusted R^2 (=.327) indicates that 32.7 percent of variance in response has been attributable to supply chain manufacturing practices (SCMP). The value of Standardized Beta coefficients of one predictor variable is .592. The value is showing the impact on the dependent variable i.e., Level of Supplier's Defect Free Deliveries.

Summary of Multiple Regression Analysis of dependent variable, "Inventory Turnover", is given in the *table 5.*

Table 5. Multiple Regression Analysis Summary Table

Step No.	Predictor Variables Entered	Standardized Beta Coefficients	t	Sig. (p)	R	Adjusted R^2	F	Sig. (p)
I	SCMP	.329	-3.274	.000	.313	.291	27.707	.000

For dependent variable 'Inventory Turnover', one variable supply chain manufacturing practices (SCMP) is found significant predictor as verified by F-value (F=27.707, p=0.000).

At step I, "supply chain manufacturing practices (SCMP)", entered into the regression analysis. The value of adjusted R^2 (=.291) indicates that 29.1 percent of variance in response has been attributable to supply chain manufacturing practices (SCMP). The values of Standardized Beta coefficients of one predictor variable is .329. The value is showing the impact on the dependent variable i.e., Inventory Turnover.

Summary of Multiple Regression Analysis of dependent variable, "Frequency of Stock Out" is given in the *table 6.*

Table 6. Multiple Regression Analysis Summary Table

Step No.	Predictor Variables Entered	Standardized Beta Coefficients	T	Sig. (p)	R	Adjusted R^2	F	Sig. (p)
I	SCMP	.685	6.579	.000	.617	.584	21.902	.000

For dependent variable 'Frequency of Stock Out', one variable supply chain manufacturing practices (SCMP) is found significant predictors as verified by F-value (F=21.902, p=0.000).

At step I, "supply chain manufacturing practices (SCMP)", entered into the regression analysis. The value of adjusted R^2 (=.584) indicates that 58.4 percent of variance in response has been attributable to supply chain manufacturing practices (SCMP). The value of Standardized Beta coefficients of one predictor variable is .685. The value is showing the impact on the dependent variable i.e., Frequency of Stock Out.

Summary of Multiple Regression Analysis of dependent variable, "Backorder Rate", is given in the *table 7.*

Table 7. Multiple Regression Analysis Summary Table

Step No.	Predictor Variables Entered	Standardized Beta Coefficients	t	Sig. (p)	R	Adjusted R^2	F	Sig. (p)
I	SCMP	-.707	-5.289	.000	.500	.483	27.968	.000

For dependent variable 'Backorder Rate', one variable supply chain manufacturing practices (SCMP) is found significant predictor as verified by F- value (F=27.968, p=0.000).

At step I, "supply chain manufacturing practices (SCMP)", entered into the regression analysis. The value of adjusted R^2 (=.483) indicates that 48.3 percent of variance in response has been attributable to supply chain manufacturing practices (SCMP). The value of Standardized Beta coefficients of one predictor variables is -.707 respectively. These values are showing the impact on the dependent variable i.e., Backorder Rate.

Summary of Multiple Regression Analysis of dependent variable, "Sales Growth", is given in the *table 8*.

Table 8. Multiple regression analysis summary table

Step No.	Predictor Variables Entered	Standardized Beta Coefficients	t	Sig. (p)	R	Adjusted R^2	F	Sig. (p)
I	SCMP	.620	4.186	.000	.385	.363	17.521	.000

For dependent variable 'Sales Growth, "supply chain manufacturing practices (SCMP)", was found a significant predictor as verified by F- value (F=17.521, p=0.000).

The value of adjusted R^2 (=.363) indicates that 36.3 percent of variance in responses has been attributable to (SCMP). The value of Standardized Beta coefficients for predictor variable is .620. The value is showing the impact on the dependent variable i.e., Sales Growth.

Summary of Multiple Regression Analysis of dependent variable, "Return on Investment (ROI)", is given in the *table 9*.

Table 9. Multiple regression analysis summary table

Step No.	Predictor Variables Entered	Standardized Beta Coefficients	t	Sig. (p)	R	Adjusted R^2	F	Sig. (p)
I	SCMP	.789	6.797	.000	.623	.609	38.004	.000

For dependent variable 'Return on Investment (ROI)', one variable supply chain manufacturing practices (SCMP) is found significant predictors as verified by F-value (F=38.004, p=0.000).

At step I, "supply chain manufacturing practices (SCMP)", entered into the regression analysis. The value of adjusted R^2 (=.609) indicates that 60.9 percent of variance in response has been attributable to supply chain manufacturing practices (SCMP). The value of Standardized Beta coefficients of one predictor variable is .789. The value is showing the impact on the dependent variable i.e., Return on Investment (ROI).

Summary of Multiple Regression Analysis of dependent variable, "Profit Margin", is given in the *table 10.*

Table 10. Multiple regression analysis summary table

Step No.	Predictor Variables Entered	Standardized Beta Coefficients	t	Sig. (p)	R	Adjusted R^2	F	Sig. (p)
I	SCMP	.776	4.445	.000	.414	.393	19.757	.000

For dependent variable 'Profit Margin', one variable supply chain manufacturing practices (SCMP) is found significant predictor as verified by F- value (F=19.757, p=0.000).

At step I, "supply chain manufacturing practices (SCMP) entered into the regression analysis. The value of adjusted R^2 (=.393) indicates that 39.3 percent of variance in response has been attributable to supply chain manufacturing practices (SCMP). The value of Standardized Beta coefficients of one predictor variable are .776. The value is showing the impact on the dependent variable i.e., Profit Margin.

Summary of Multiple Regression Analysis of dependent variable, "Return on Assets to Firm", is given in the *table 11.*

Table 11. Multiple regression analysis summary table

Step No.	Predictor Variables Entered	Standardized Beta Coefficients	t	Sig. (p)	R	Adjusted R^2	F	Sig. (p)
I	SCMP	-.462	-2.756	.010	.213	.185	7.593	.010

For dependent variable 'Return on Assets to Firm', "supply chain manufacturing practices (SCMP)", was found a significant predictor as verified by F- value (F=7.593, p=0.000).

The value of adjusted R^2 (=.185) indicates that 18.5 percent of variance in responses has been attributable to supply chain manufacturing practices (SCMP). The value of Standardized Beta coefficients for predictor variable is -.462. The value is showing the impact on the dependent variable i.e., Return on Assets to Firm.

H1: Supply Chain Manufacturing Practices (SCMP) would serve as an enabler to improve organizational performance.

Multiple regression analysis was performed to check the proposed hypothesis on DP. As per the analysis findings, supply chain manufacturing practices (SCMP) emerged as predictor for organization performance variables such as level of supplier's defect free deliveries, inventory turnover, frequency of stock out, backorder rate, sales growth, profit margin, return on investment, return on assets to firm.

In conclusion, the alternate hypothesis (H1) is being accepted for the dairy plants i.e., DP.

Objective 2: To suggest a roadmap for improving the performance of the Indian dairy industry through Supply Chain Manufacturing practices (SCMP).

Based on the analysis performed on the questionnaires, a comprehensive conclusion and recommendation for different stakeholders of dairy industry were coined with suitable logic. Those recommendations will definitely improve the performance of Indian dairy industry through implementing of supply chain manufacturing practices (SCMP) which is given below:

CONCLUSION AND RECOMMENDATION

The above findings suggest that of supply chain manufacturing practices (SCMP) play a crucial role in enhancing the performance the dairies companies in the form of increase in performance matrix indicators i.e., level of supplier's defect free deliveries, inventory turnover, frequency of stock out, backorder rate, sales growth, profit margin, return on investment, return on assets to firm. The following section briefly focuses and explores the relationship between various supply chain manufacturing practices and organizational performance.

Subsequently, the above findings highlighting or sending a signal to all dairy companies of India specially the small dairies companies to adopt the good supply chain manufacturing practices (GMP's) in order to get increase in performance matrix indicators which is said in the above paragraph. The implementation of good supply chain manufacturing practices (GMP's) at the workplace assure that milk and milk products are manufactured and stored under safe and sanitary conditions which maintain the quality of the product because in the dairy market, consumers prefer only quality products and they will not compromise it with any cost which will only come through practicing good manufacturing practices followed by dairy plant owners, operators and employees in order to maximally assure the production of safe and sanitary products at all times. There are some guidelines of GMP which offer suggestions for measures and precautions that should be taken regarding employee health, food handling practices, appearance, personal hygiene, plant procedures, plant and equipment design, maintenance, and sanitation. By their maintaining quality the consumer will definitely buy their milk and milk products, which will increase their sales growth. Secondly, sales growth increases through the timely arrival of products in the market. Dairy companies must focus on maintaining quality standards through adoption of Hazard Analysis and Critical Control Point (HACCP) at their workplace because it prioritizes and controls potential hazards in food production. By controlling major food risks such as microbiological, chemical and physical contaminants, the dairy industry can better assure consumers that its products are safe and healthy. Adulteration and food safety are another issue which received attention in the research. The most important aspect of milk processing is the challenge to ensure its purity and wholesomeness. There have been instances of substitution with cheap skimmed milk powder which is hazardous to health. Even though there are Food Safety Acts in force, still every other day we get to hear about tankers of spurious milk being apprehended. Hence, the rule-implementation agencies need to be strengthened. Training & Development programmes for the industry's unskilled and semiskilled workers should be made mandatory because there is a lack of trained and skilled workers who can handle the milk processing operations hygienically and safely.

Good manufacturing practices (GMP) guidelines are established to satisfy regulatory requirements as well as maintain high quality standards of the products supplied to your customers. Good manufacturing practices should be followed by dairy plant owners, operators and employees in order to maximally assure the production of safe and sanitary products at all times. In order to maintain high quality of milk and milk products, the Indian dairy industry needs good manufacturing practices (GMP's), so that it can assure that milk and milk products are manufactured and stored under safe and sanitary conditions which will surely result in providing profit to the organization.

In order to become global leader in world dairy market all the Indian dairy companies specially the small dairy companies should develop the strategy for implementing or make it mandatory to follow the following activities which is defined above at their workplace so that the organization and its stakeholders get the benefits in the form of getting or consuming quality milk and milk products which will surely coming from incorporating those practices at their workplace.

LIMITATION OF THE STUDY

Since it was a descriptive study, its accuracy depends on correct information given by the respondents, i.e., the managers and executives of dairy companies, milk retailers and their employees, and the customers who are actually consuming the milk and milk products. Respondents might have been reluctant to express their honest opinions on the attributes pertaining to the functioning of their respective departments. The questionnaire method has been used for the survey in the present study. Though every effort was made to make the questionnaire as simple as possible, with all possible definitions of the terms, still some respondents may not have been able to comprehend it fully. Resource constraint in terms of money, manpower and other resources to cover all the possible respondents. Even though the study included the responses of dairy supply chain members i.e. dairy plant (DP), operating in UP and Delhi NCR, its finding can't be generalized for pan India.

SCOPE OF FUTURE RESEARCH

As the present research study is only limited to one specific geographical area i.e. Uttar Pradesh and Delhi-NCR and that, too, only registered dairy plants. In future research it could be interesting for any researcher to conduct research on a pan-India basis that too with the inclusion of time and small dairies also. Future research can expand the domain of SCM practices by considering additional dimensions such as geographical proximity, cross-functional coordination, logistics integration, green practices and agreed supply chain leadership, which have not been covered extensively in the present research. This kind of research not only provides a geographical comparison, but also provides intra-industry comparison between registered and non-registered milk processing units.

REFERENCES

Anuar, A., & Yusuff, R. M. (2011). Manufacturing best practices in Malaysian small and medium enterprises (SMEs). *Benchmarking*, *18*(3), 324–341. doi:10.1108/14635771111137750

Babatunde, B. O., Gbadeyan, R. A., & Bamiduro, J. A. (2015). Supply Chain Management Practices and Market Performance: Evidence from Selected Major Marketers of Petroleum Products in Nigeria. *Pacific Journal of Science and Technology*, *7*(1), 129–139.

Bigliardi, B., & Bottani, E. (2010). Performance measurement in the food supply chain: A balanced scorecard approach. *Facilities*, *28*(5/6), 249–260. doi:10.1108/02632771011031493

Chandan, R. C. (2007). *Implementing HACCP* (6th ed.). Dairy India.

Da Costa, S. E. G., & De Lima, E. P. (2009). Advanced manufacturing technology adoption: An integrated approach. *Journal of Manufacturing Technology Management*, *20*(1), 74–96. doi:10.1108/17410380910925415

Goyal, G. K., & Alam, T. (2007). *Semi automatic packaging of milk and milk products* (6th ed.). Dairy India.

Muhammad, Q., N., Ali, M., & Shazad, K. (2012). The Impact of Supply Chain Management Practices on the Overall Performance of the Organization, *Proceedings of 3rd International Conference on Business Management*, *1*, 1–23.

Narang, I. K. (2007). *Check list for dairy plant's MMPO certification* (6th ed.). Dairy India.

NBACFS. (2005). Good manufacturing practices for milk collection center. *Royal Gazette, 122*, 1-20.

Nordin, N., Deros, B. M., & Wahab, D. A. (2010). A study on lean manufacturing implementation in Malaysian automotive component industry. *International Journal of Innovation, Management and Technology*, *1*(4), 374–380.

Punjrath, J. S. (2007). *Packaging innovation* (6th ed.). Dairy India.

Singh, P., Wani, A. L. I. A., Karim, A. A., & Langowski, H. (2012). The use of carbon dioxide in the processing and packaging of milk and dairy products. *International Journal of Dairy Technology*, *65*(2), 161–177. doi:10.1111/j.1471-0307.2011.00744.x

Smith, G.B. (1995). Good manufacturing practices for dairy processing plant. *The Dairy Practice Council*, 1-16.

Tan, K. C., Kannan, V. R., & Handfield, R. B. (1998). Supply chain management: Supplier performance and firm performance. *International Journal of Purchasing and Materials Management, 34*(3), 2–9.

Chapter 11
Key Success Factors Facilitating SME E-Commerce in Developing Countries:
Literature Review

Hijrah Saputra
https://orcid.org/0000-0003-1843-1741
University of Hull, UK

ABSTRACT

This chapter presents a systematic literature review and research agenda regarding key success factors (KSFs) facilitating SME e-commerce in developing countries. Previous studies had mainly pre-adoption when the internet and e-commerce were new. However, SMEs have largely been ignored, and now that attention has turned to post-adoption issues research, which is required in SME and developing country contexts due to the worldwide growth of e-commerce. This chapter comprises a structured literature review using Denyer and Tranfield's context, intervention, mechanisms, and outcome (CIMO) criteria for critical analysis to enable the development of future empirical research areas. The KSFs are considered significant and of concern to stakeholders, including inter alia SMEs and governments to encourage SME growth in e-commerce and positively influence SME and overall business performance to meet customer demand.

DOI: 10.4018/978-1-7998-2867-9.ch011

INTRODUCTION

E-commerce provides a lot of advantages as a platform for conducting business. It supports business transaction effectiveness, potential '24/7' sources of income, international sales, and easy showcasing of bestselling items as well as buying encouragement (Einav et al., 2014). Further, e-commerce technologies enable both small and large enterprises to progress their business practices and communications, both within the organization and with external business associates (Chong and Pervan, 2009).

E-commerce has also encouraged emerging countries which have the potential to attain fast and sustainable economic and social development by building e-commerce economies where small and medium sized enterprises (SMEs) are truly networked with the system (UNDP, 2004). SMEs have grown in prominence in the world's economy during the last several decades and some theoretical and practical business development literature acknowledges the strategic contributions of SMEs to the development of both domestic and global economic growth. This reality is not simply defined by the number of SMEs, which constitutes approximately 90% of all business establishments around the world, but also their important role in generating employment prospects (Hall, 2002).

In many developing countries Internet practices and e-commerce applications have yet to attain a critical mass in network performance to sufficiently motivate SMEs to select e-commerce developments (Rahayu and Day, 2017, Hatten, 2015). Notwithstanding, governments are enabling development of, and enacting regulation in, e-commerce which is an important aspect to support SMEs effectively and positively affect the aggregate economy in developed countries (Triandini et al., 2015). However, government support for SME e-commerce has been a serious problem in developing countries which has affected growth (Rahayu and Day, 2017, Kapurubandara and Lawson, 2006).

Previous research concerning e-commerce application for SMEs has been mostly conducted in developed countries (Daniel, et.al., 2002) with only a few concerned about SMEs in emerging countries. Research relating to e-commerce last mile delivery and distribution (e.g. Lim et al., 2018, Melacini et al., 2018, Mangiaracina et al., 2019) has encouraged the importance of logistics operation on e-commerce applications, however those studies are based in developed countries which has different circumstances compared to developing countries. Likewise, the few empirical investigations concerning additional logistics activities such as reverse logistics for e-commerce (e.g. Sorkun, 2019, Hjort et al., 2019) were also focussed on developed countries instead of emerging countries. Further, the limitations on infrastructure, information and communication technology (ICT), payment systems, customer behaviour and other conditions, has provided our motivation to investigate how SMEs should adopt e-commerce in developing countries (Kurnia et al., 2015, Williams et al., 2009, Parker and Castleman, 2007).

Additionally, most of the earlier studies focussed on pre-adoption problems as the e-commerce growth stage was at an initial phase in the early 2000s (MacGregor et al., 2002, Dwivedi et al., 2009). The pre-adoption stage is when e-commerce is first applied in business applications and research has focused here on identifying issues and difficulties in pre-adoption of ICT related to business e-commerce. However, the rapid growth of ICT has already led to a post-adoption focus categorising the specific effects and problems that happen after the adoption stage has been well established and investigated. Earlier studies had a tendency to investigate the issues that enable (or consider the obstacles that challenge) e-commerce adoption rather than adoption or implementation benefits and advantages and post-adoption issues (Molla and Heeks, 2007, Alyoubi, 2015, Sukasame et al., 2008, Intan Salwani et al., 2009, Kurnia et al., 2015, Kabango and Asa, 2015, Rahayu and Day, 2017).

Additionally, there are few studies concerned with KSFs (Key Success Factors) for SME e-commerce implementation which has not provided for motivation SMEs, especially in developing countries, to devote to e-commerce applications. Moreover, different stages have different concerns and considerations. Hence, considering those conditions our research objective is to provide an improved understanding about the application of e-commerce by SMEs in developing countries, especially in the post-adoption phase for the improvement of their business transaction. This chapter's purpose therefore is to conduct a systematic literature review (SLR) to identify KSFs supporting and facilitating SME e-commerce in developing countries and set-out a research agenda for SMEs to improve business transactions through effective e-commerce implementation.

There have been several SLRs conducted regarding e-commerce and omnichannel, e.g. Saghiri et al. (2017), Galipoglu et al. (2018), Melacini et al. (2018) and Mangiaracina et al. (2019), but they are very generic. In fact, Saghiri et al. (2017) present a conceptual framework for omni-channel systems, discussing also a set of enablers including integration and visibility; Galipoglu et al. (2018) discuss the intellectual foundation of e-commerce and omni-channel retailing research, highlighting a focus on the Western retail context; Mangiaracina et al. (2019) attempted to investigate particular solutions concerning the efficiency of last-mile delivery in business to consumer (B2C) e-commerce however this likely focusing generally on the large company in developed countries. Meanwhile, still in the area of ecommerce logistics, Melacini et al. (2018) tried to identify the major issues relating to e-fulfilment and distribution. But likewise, their study was remaining broad for business in general, and not specific to developing countries. Therefore, we believe a deeper and concentrated approach is required for the three e-commerce themes of KSFs, SMEs and developing countries. The determination of such KSFs will likely be significant for SMEs, governments and stakeholders in developing countries to encourage awareness of them and enable the effective development and improvement of SME e-commerce. In that regard this chapter also contributes to the UN's sustainable development goals (SDGs) 8 – Good Jobs and Economic Growth and 9 – Innovation and Infrastructure.

After this introduction, which has explained the background and the significance of the study, the remaining structure of this chapter is as follows. First, the SLR process in general and pertaining to the study is described. Then, the thematic findings related to KSFs for SME e-commerce implementation in developing countries are summarised. Finally, conclusions are drawn based on the findings and a further research agenda are proposed.

LITERATURE REVIEW METHOD

Fundamentally, a literature analysis is a key contribution within research development as it considers a broad historic viewpoint of the relevant research topic and explanation of self-directed ad important research challenges. It is crucial to systematically review and analyse literature for a critical assessment to attain a credible understanding and knowledge on which to develop robust philosophies and conceptions (Mentzer and Kahn, 1995). Thus, the focus for the review is on identifying pertinent discussions of KSFs facilitating the growth of SME e-commerce in developing countries. Hence, to achieve a solid and organised literature analysis, we adopted the intensive investigation technique of a systematic literature review (SLR) as practised by Denyer and Tranfield (2009), Ali et al. (2017) and Strozzi et al. (2017).

The SLR technique enables an improved understanding in this study area by means of a systematic, logical and reasonable method compared to conventional expressive analyses. It expands the references compared to many studies that fail to cover the evolutionary period of an area of research and depend on subjectivity as the basis for choosing literature and categorise research according to pre-determined coding structures. The SLR process, originally set-out by Denyer and Tranfield (2009), provides guidance for the delineation of research literature through four stages shown in Figure 1.

Figure 1.Stages of the systematic literature review (SLR) process
Source: Adapted by Author from Denyer and Tranfield (2009)

Firstly, it is necessary to outline the scope of the literature study in order to formulate research questions and it suggested this is done through consideration of a piece of literature's context, intervention, mechanism and outcome or CIMO (Denyer and Tranfield, 2009, Colicchia and Strozzi, 2012). The CIMO approach is shown in Table 1 and enabled us to effectively identify attributes for the study's topic areas in the four significant CIMO sections to be further examined.

The second stage comprises locating studies connected to keywords, period, category of papers and language. In the locating studies process for further analysis, the string of keywords shown in Table 2 were applied as searching parameters within the Scopus and Web of Science (WoS) websites with the purpose of selecting papers possessing the relationship with aspects of SME e-commerce adoption in developing countries. The selected keywords and strings were identified from the most keywords related to prior research noted in the introduction: ICT, logistics capability, customer demand, human resources, payment system, and regulation. Moreover, the keywords selection was also agreed through a process of scientific consultation with a panel of experts. Four experts were from industry sectors of e-commerce and logistics service providers, three experts were from academia, and one expert was from a government ministry for economic affairs.

The last stage before analysis is study selection and evaluation. The result of this stage was a collection of nominated papers. With the aim of including only applicable and significant papers, it was critical to determine inclusion and exclusion criteria recommended by Newbert (2007) and shown in Table 3. This stage effectively drove the literature selection process shown in Figure 2. The final stage in the process is a synthesis and analysis of the literature to provide a review of the literature development, gaps and conclusions.

Table 1. The CIMO approach in SLR

<table>
<tr><th colspan="2">[C] CONTEXT</th></tr>
<tr><td>Which individuals, relationships, institutional settings or wider systems are being studied?
Who are the individuals of interest?</td><td>SME (Seller): Owner, Manager, and Worker
Customer/online shopper (Buyer): Direct buyer
Government (Facilitator): President / Ministry
3PL of LSP (Logistics Service Provider):
Private Logistics/Courier Service Company
State Owned Enterprise (Logistics Service and Support):
State company of Logistics/Courier Service
Financial Agent (Payment System):
Banks, Postal Financial Agent/channel
IT & Network Provider:
Private and State IT and Network Provider</td></tr>
<tr><td>Which interpersonal relationship are of interest?
Which aspect of the institutional setting are of interest?</td><td>Operation including logistics, Financial/Economic, Environment, Social, Country Economic Development, SMEs Empowerment.</td></tr>
<tr><td>Which aspect of wider infrastructural systems are of interest?</td><td>Other Context: Type of products (cloth/fashion, handy craft, food, agriculture, etc.), ICT infrastructure and system, HR.</td></tr>
<tr><th colspan="2">[I] INTERVENTION</th></tr>
<tr><td>The effects of what event, action or activity are being studied?
What is the intervention of interest? (Leadership style, planning and control systems, training, performance management, etc.)</td><td>Key Success Factors of SMEs e-commerce in developing country due to the improvement of business transaction. In which focusing the potential factors of logistics capability. Logistics capability would embrace the entire capability of logistics in term of scope and activities such as the planning and control system, operation design of logistics operations (warehouse, transportation, distribution and delivery)</td></tr>
<tr><th colspan="2">[M] MECHANISM</th></tr>
<tr><td>What are the mechanisms that explain the relationship between interventions and outcomes?
Under what circumstances are these mechanisms activated or not activated?</td><td>The improvement of logistics capability; internally in the application of self-operated logistics and externally in the collaboration with 3PL. This potentially manage through a good internal business management of SMEs. In addition, regional logistics capability would be potentially considered as this influence the quality among the logistics capabilities.</td></tr>
<tr><th colspan="2">[O] OUTCOMES</th></tr>
<tr><td>What are the effects of the intervention?
How will the outcomes be measured?
What are the intended and unintended effects?</td><td>1. Increase SMEs e-commerce transaction
2. Speed the products delivery of SMEs e-commerce transaction
3. Provide up to date report of delivery
4. Lower cost of transportation and delivery
5. Effective delivery point
6. Effective and speed the reverse/return delivery
7. Improve the postal code system
8. Increase customer satisfaction of products delivery
9. Increase customer trust
10. Develop a trusty and easy payment of e-commerce</td></tr>
</table>

Source: Adapted by Author from Denyer and Tranfield (2009) and Colicchia and Strozzi (2012)

Table 2. String of keywords in the literature investigation

No.	String of keywords	Databases
1	"E-commerce" + SME*	Scopus and Web of Science
2	"E-commerce" + SME* + "Developing Country*"	
3	"E-commerce" + SME* + "Customer Demand"	
4	"E-commerce" + "Customer Demand"	
5	"E-commerce" + "Demand"	
6	"E-commerce" + SME* + Logistics	
7	"E-commerce" + SME* + "Logistics Capability"	
8	"E-commerce Logistics"	
9	"E-commerce" + SME* + "ICT"	
10	"E-commerce" + SME* + "IT"	
11	"E-commerce" + SME* + "Payment System"	
12	"E-commerce" + "Payment System"	
13	"E-commerce" + SME* + "Online Transaction"	
14	"E-commerce" + SME* + "Internet Regulation"	
15	"E-commerce" + "Internet Regulation"	
16	"E-commerce" + SME* + "Electronic Commerce Regulation"	
17	"E-Commerce Regulation"	
19	"E-commerce" + SME* + "Human Resources Management"	
20	"E-commerce" AND "HRM"	
21	"E-commerce" + SME* + "Marketing"	
22	"E-commerce" + SME* + "Marketplace"	

Source: Author

From the second stage using the string of keywords in Table 2 we found 6,485 pieces of literature which consists of journal articles, conference proceedings, and books or books section. The first level filtering criteria excluded 4,677 items that were inappropriate areas business and management for this study's objectives, reducing the amount to 1808. The next filtering of the criteria used relevant studies and abstracts as well as language and 1,636 papers which deemed not applicable to the research. That left a final number of 178 pieces of literatures as resources to analyse and developed the fundamental aspects and substance for research as shown in Table 4. A full bibliographic list of the 178 sources noted in Table 4 is available from the authors upon request. Only references cited in this paper are included in the reference list for space considerations.

Table 3. Inclusion criteria

No.	Inclusion criteria	Rationale
1	Papers containing at least one of the identified keywords in title or abstracts	Two key words; E-commerce and SMEs will be the set of key words to ensure gaining the relevant topic of discussion
2	Appropriate area of business and management	Some papers of e-commerce are related to other area such as engineering, technology and computer science. Business and Management will be the relevant one to be considered.
3	Relevant studies/abstracts	The relevant area should be followed by relevant studies/abstract since many topics in business and management doesn't discuss about SMEs e-commerce
4	English is the preferred language	English is the dominant language in the field of Logistics and SCM research
5	Selection of papers published 1999-2017	The year 1999 was chosen as the earliest point of studies and application on e-commerce to identify a broader and comprehensive view on how e-commerce grows and give impact to the business activities.

Source: Developed by Author from Newbert (2007)

RESULTS AND FINDINGS

Figure 2. Literature study selection process
Source: Author

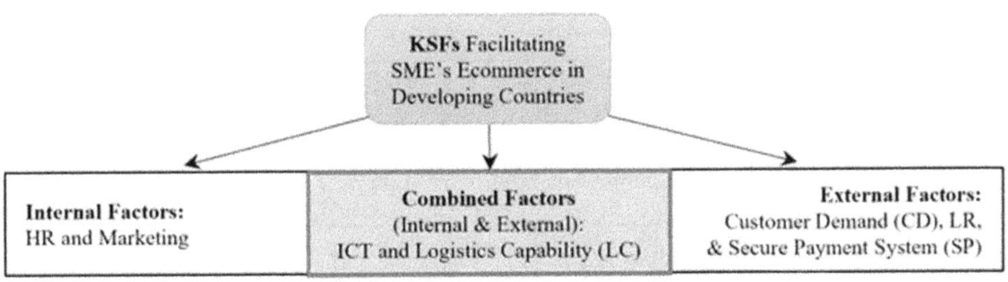

KSFs for SME E-Commerce

Table 4. Final 178 literature sources for KSFs of SME E-commerce in developing countries

No.	Issue Under Investigation	Sources
1	E-commerce and SME	(Grandon & Pearson, 2004), (Subba Rao et al., 2003), (Tan et al., 2007), (Drew, 2003), (Quayle, 2002), (Jeffcoate et al., 2002), (Feindt et al., 2002), (Tiessen et al., 2001), (Rowe et al., 2012), (Saffu et al., 2008), (Chong & Pervan, 2009), (MacGregor & Kartiwi, 2010), (Pham et al., 2011), (Wymer & Regan, 2013), (Rahayu & Day, 2015), (Kurnia et al., 2015), (Afshar Jahanshahi et al., 2013), (Rahayu & Day, 2013), (Kartiwi, 2006), (Eikebrokk & Olsen, 2003), (Kurnia, 2006), (As'ad, 2012), (Humphrey et al., 2003), (Lawrence & Tar, 2010), (Payne, 2002), (Singapore Post, 2014), (Taylor & Murphy, 2004), (Triandini et al., 2015), (Wilson et al., 2008), (Dwivedi et al., 2009), (Pradana, 2016), (Scupola et al., 2009), (Corbitt et al., 2003), (Melnik & Alm, 2002), (Gefen, 2000), (Grabner-Kraeuter, 2002), (Molla & Licker, 2005), (Wang & Ahmed, 2009), (Wickramasinghe, 2003), (Boerhanoeddin, 2005), (Ngai & Gunasekaran, 2007), (Rillo & dela Cruz, 2016), (Mahadevan, 2000)
2	E-commerce and SME and Customer Demand	(Koufaris & Hampton-Sosa, 2004), (Pang, 2016), (Hong et al., 2004), (Dennis et al., 2009), (Zhang et al., 2002), (Andersen et al., 2003), (Changchit & Klaus, 2015), (Ward & Lee, 2000), (Lin et al., 2014), (Yuan et al., 2014)
3	E-commerce and SME and Logistics Capability	(Joong-Kun Cho et al., 2008), (XiaoYan et al., 2012), (Fernie et al., 2010), (Gligor & Holcomb, 2012), (Shang & Marlow, 2005), (Lu & Yang, 2010), (Yu, 2017), (Daly & Cui, 2003), (Ghezzi et al., 2012), (Weltevreden, 2008), (Ying & Dayong, 2005), (Ramanathan, 2010), (Delfmann et al., 2002), (Xu et al., 2011), (Roberts & Thomas, 2003), (Fernie et al., 2010), (Ji & Zhang, 2015), (Klumpp & Jasper, 2008), (Lee & Whang, 2001), (Mahindru, 2014), (Żurek, 2015), (Gunasekaran et al., 2002), (Ji & Liu, 2011), (Xu & Yao, 2010), (Zhang et al., 2017), (Xu & Huang, 2017), (Wang et al., 2015), (Mangiaracina et al., 2015), (Kuang et al., 2014), (Liu, 2011), (Shihua, 2010), (Li et al., 2010), (Yong-mei et al., 2010), (Hao & Zhang, 2010), (Murfield et al., 2017) (Wollenburg et al., 2018) (Galipoglu et al., 2018) (Xing & Grant, 2006) (Xing et al., 2010) (Bourlakis et al., 2011)
4	E-commerce and SME and ICT	(Walker et al., 2016), (Ghobakhloo et al., 2011), (Lihua, 2013), (Zaidan, 2017), (Chen et al., 2013), (Lim & Baharudin, 2013), (Nejadirani et al., 2011), (Kapurubandara & Lawson, 2007), (Gide & Wu, 2006), (Lertwongsatien & Wongpinunwatana, 2003), (Astuti & Nasution, 2014), (Spiridon & Dichiu, 2008), (Qing-bian et al., 2003), (Einav et al., 2014), (Liang & Wei, 2004), (Luthfihadi & Dhewanto, 2013), (Varshney & Vetter, 2002), (Yaakub, 2010), (Huang et al., 2015), (Hameed et al., 2014)
5	E-commerce and SME and Payment System	(Madan et al., 2016), (Rouibah et al., 2016), (Walczak & Borkan, 2016), (Roy & Sahoo, 2016), (Lee & Lin, 2005), (Zhang et al., 2011), (Jing & Peng, 2010), (Beng & Eze, 2010), (Jiang, 2008), (Ling et al., 2007), (Ally & Toleman, 2006), (He et al., 2006), (Fariselli et al., 1999), (Mohmed et al., 2016), (Hsu, 2016), (Xuewen & Jinlong, 2010), (Morgan-Thomas, 2009), (Mark et al., 2007), (Ng-Kruelle et al., 2002)
6	E-commerce and SME and E-commerce Regulation	(Taylor et al., 2005), (Ward et al., 2016), (Mueller, 2003), (Hoeren, 2000), (Chun et al., 2006), (Van Cleynenbreugel, 2017), (Kyobe, 2010), (Endeshaw, 2002), (Braga, 2005), (Krosch, 2002), (Shalmont, 2016), (Taylor et al., 2005b)
7	E-commerce and SME and HRM	(Sukasame et al., 2008), (Blount et al., 2005), (Wang, 2005), (Khatri et al., 2010), (Tsai, 2010), (Ding et al., 2015), (Li et al., 2012; Galperin & Lituchy, 2014), (Jehangir et al., 2012), (Ping, 2010), (Dietz et al., 2006), (Li et al., 2017), (Govindaraju et al., 2012), (Qiang, 2011), (Xi ping & Ming qiang, 2011), (Yu, 2011), (Fazhu et al., 2010), (Liu, 2010), (Yunping, 2010), (Shani & Tesone, 2010), (Power, 2004), (Blount et al., 2003), (Hallowell, 2001)
8	E-commerce and SME and Marketing and Marketplace	(Chaffey & Ellis-Chadwick, 2016), (Ström et al., 2014), (Wirtz & Lovelock, 2016), (Armstrong et al., 2014), (Strauss, 2016), (Armstrong et al., 2015), (El-Gohary, 2010) (Kleindl, 2000) (Stockdale & Standing, 2004) (Nielson et al., 2005) (Khan et al.) (Lekhanya, 2016)

Source: Author

The common factors in various research in this area were considered into four contexts; technological, organisational, environmental and personal (Rahayu and Day, 2015, Kabango and Asa, 2015, Ghobakhloo et al., 2011). These contexts were categorised based on the nature of the growth of ecommerce for business in general. Previous research investigated contexts according to what and who would be influenced by e-commerce. Technological aspects for instance, are the most essential aspects for e-commerce when generating the platform at the initial stage. Other aspects include organisational and personal regarding the institution and person who will implement e-commerce, and the organisational environment that will benefit from the impact of e-commerce. However, there are also other factors essential for consideration at the post-adoption stage once an initial stage has been completed.

We investigated whether e-commerce in post-adoption stage also has any relationship with other aspects observed in the literature in Table 4 and identified other different factors we consider KSFs. Some of those factors reflecting the previous i.e. pre-adoption context but further review aspects such as of ICT reflected from the technological aspect; human resources which flowed from the personal aspect; SME context was considered from the organizational aspect; and law and regulation were related to an environmental aspect. Moreover, the emerging factors also include other aspects not previously considered as essential factors, but which are important especially for SME e-commerce implementation in developing countries. Those factors are customer demand, marketing and marketplace, payment system, and logistics capability as a reflection of a logistical aspect. These KSFs, shown in Figure 3, are classified as internal, external and combined (both internal and external) factors.

Internal factors from of an SME includes human resources related to personnel qualification (HR) and marketing. External factors outside management control of an SME comprise customer demand (CD), law and regulation (LR), and a secure payment system (SP). Finally, combined factors (both internal and external) involve information and communication technology (ICT) and logistics capabilities (LC). Principally, these influencing factors were identified at the post-adoption stage of an SME's e-commerce implementation, i.e. once they have adopted e-commerce in their business activities due to the improvement of business transaction volumes. SMEs should recognise and understand these influencing factors, if they have not already done so, to improve these particular aspects of their business. For example, in term of marketing and marketplace, it would be very important for SME to apply an effective marketing and utilising well-known marketplace to promote their products and business. These KSFs should provide insights and attention for SMEs as an applicable guidance to improve the SMEs' business through the effective implementation of e-commerce and are discussed in turn next.

Figure 3. Key success factors for SME E-commerce in developing countries
Source: Author

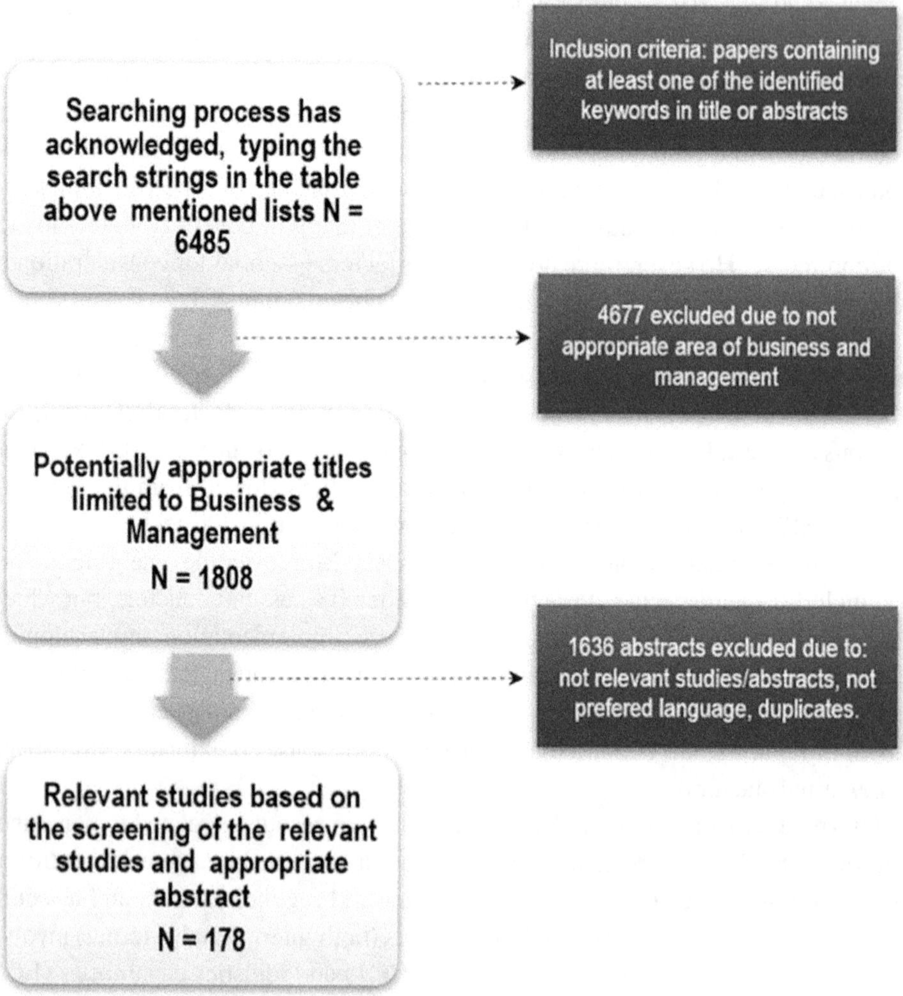

Internal Factors

Several factors were identified from the internal side of the SMEs itself, which are considered significant to influence the development of SMEs. Obviously, these internal factors should be under the control of the SME itself, these are conditions within the SME's control that should be considered seriously to support their business improvement.

Human Resources

In this study human resources (HR) related to personnel or manpower aspect are also considered as an influencing factor of SMEs' e-commerce implementation in developing countries. This is because generally, in SMEs, a strategic business decision is greatly reliant on the manager or owner and afterwards implemented by employees as the part of HR. Therefore, HR including both the manager/owner and workers, would be a significant factor in SMEs' e-commerce implementation, since HR runs all through an SME's business activities. Related to the SME's owner, Cloete et al. (2002) discovered that e-commerce implementation by SMEs is comprehensively influenced by the approval of e-commerce technology of the SMEs owner. This is reasonable since operationally, SMEs adapt a centralized approach, therefore the owner/manager has a significant role in every single business decision (H. Nguyen and S. Waring, 2013).

Marketing and Marketplace

Additional KSFs for an SME's e-commerce initiatives are effective marketing and the development of prospective marketplace. These activities are considered and internal factors their management should be addressed internally by the SME. Simply, marketing in this context is the activity of promoting and selling products or services, as well as market research and advertising where the marketplace is the place either onsite or online to do business transaction both buying and selling. Nowadays, the easiest approach to marketing activities and the development of marketplace would be through utilizing online media. The Internet would simply enable online marketing and marketplace development (Chaffey and Ellis-Chadwick, 2016). For example, promoting a certain products and service online through an online advertising such Facebook, YouTube, and many other social media could be considered as a marketing activity. However, to sell products and services using an effective marketplace such as Amazon, eBay, Alibaba, etc. would be consider as a marketplace utilisation.

Moreover, marketing and marketplace of SMEs' e-commerce, especially in developing countries, could potentially get support from government through supportive laws and regulations as a driver to facilitate SMEs effectively. In fact, various limitations of SMEs especially in developing countries, due to their limited capability, resources and finance, oblige governments to support their business activities. However, the poor bureaucracy system of government in developing countries might be a potential challenge for SMEs to achieve support from the government. Therefore, SMEs should resolve these problems by themselves at the beginning, while the government has a particular policy to facilitate the business of SMEs, especially on e-commerce implementation. (Ström et al., 2014)

External Factors

Several factors were also identified from outside the SME's structure i.e. in their external environment that would potentially influence the achievement of improvement through conducting business transactions by e-commerce. These external factors are important influences on the development of SMEs' e-commerce but are not under control of the SME itself.

Customer Demand

Business will always deal with customer demand (CD) related to the quality and quantity of products or services that customer would buy. It is more likely to investigate the needs and wants of customers both in term of quality and quantity (Pang, 2016, Thompson, 1998). The SME as a business should consider the aspect of customer's needs and wants especially in the implementation of e-commerce in business operations, and a business that does so would effectively satisfy the customer. Consumers as the end users of products and services occasionally have different or unique needs and wants, which can influence the production of the product offered to the consumer (Thompson, 1998). The identification and analysis of customer demands would confidently encourage business to have an effective product to offer to the market. Obviously, it will help companies to understand the exact need and wants of the customer and further, it will effectively assist companies to target the market precisely (Mohmed et al., 2016). Moreover, customer needs and wants would potentially relate to price, product, and services (Lee and Lin, 2005, Pang, 2016).

The investigation of customer demand in SME e-commerce should identify the needs and wants of the e-commerce online shopper, according to the services they expect. Customer demands might vary in practice, due to a great number of customers requiring particular products or services, especially in e-commerce which is a new approach to buying and selling and utilising the Internet as the bridge between seller and buyer. To investigate these customer needs and wants, various relevant approaches could be used, such as surveys, interview, experiments, investigations and observations (Pang, 2016). For instance, in online shopping through a marketplace such as eBay, Amazon, etc. customers are usually requested to give a review from one to five stars if they are satisfied by the products and service of the seller, and they also can give their comments (Lee and Lin, 2005). The approach of customer relationship management (CRM) could also be utilised for the investigation of customer demand related to the needs and wants of the customers (H. Nguyen and

S. Waring, 2013). The fundamental foundation of the consumer demand concept is a specific observation of individuals' manner and action in managing their limited resources amongst the products that offer them customer satisfaction (Samuelson and Nordhaus, 2005).

Law and Regulation

Law and regulation (LR) are sets of guidelines to manage various matters and conditions in a certain area or country, to achieve effective standardization. Legally, law and regulation are arranged and legitimated by the authorities of a country such as government, council, and official congress or institutions (Van Cleynenbreugel, 2017, Braga, 2005). Various problems in a country can be effectively managed by utilising the power and authority of the government. In fact, every country has its own rules and policy to regulate the economy and businesses according to its development in various aspects (Kyobe, 2010). The business of SMEs is under the law and regulation of government in both developed and developing countries. Numerous policies and regulations of government (such as taxation, funding, licensing and others) would standardise the operation and activities of SMEs as enterprises (Braga, 2005, Kyobe, 2010). Moreover, the application of SME e-commerce in business would also be under the regulation of government since e-commerce is a contemporary approach to business transactions (Van Cleynenbreugel, 2017).

Security and Payment System

It is generally recognised by both government and business organizations that, from a consumer perspective, the problems of the information security and payment systems (SP) are a critical problem regarding e-commerce growth. The sensitivity to risk concerning Internet security has also been acknowledged as a concern for both skilled and unskilled users of Internet technologies (Miyazaki and Fernandez, 2001). Further, Miyazaki and Fernandez (2001) have identified fraudulent actions by online sellers as a crucial concern for Internet users. Therefore, e-commerce users recognise hackers as a serious security risk to e-commerce (Rose et al., 1999). Such behaviour occurs as online availability and accessibility of warehoused data for many businesses provides opportunities to any hacker on the Internet to steal data from these commercial archives. These risks have been recognised in numerous recent studies (Aleid et al., 2009, Al-Ghaith et al., 2010).

Another study among Indian customers indicates that various influence factors such as security and confidentiality, reliability, easiness, innovativeness, and responsiveness level have increased the approval of e-banking services as a part of e-commerce services (Dixit and Datta, 2010). Therefore, official institutions that ensure the development of business transactional integrity (through law and policies, and technology infrastructure) have a critical role towards the development of e-commerce in emerging countries (Oxley and Yeung, 2001).

Combined Factors

Factors considered here are a combination of internal factors and external factors, since they are related to internal conditions and external circumstances as well. Hence, these combined factors should be considered seriously by companies internally, and stakeholders externally (government and private sectors).

Information and Communication Technology (ICT)

Information communication and technology (ICT) performs an essential activity in any organisation (Brock, 2000). The implementation of ICT, which ranges from laptops to personal computers and word processing to sophisticated applications and systems, has achieved considerable progress in large, medium and even small organisations (Doukidis et al., 1996). Research has discovered constructive signs that SMEs are positively able to gain the benefits of e-commerce as a category of ICT, in facilitating the growth of their business activities (MacGregor et al., 2002). At both the stage of pre-implementation and at the time of e-commerce implementation, such technological factors refer to conditions such as perceived advantage, compatibility and budget, which encourage the implementation of e-commerce technology. The perceived advantages relate to the level of proof of the potential benefits that e-commerce methods can offer for the business (Oliveira and Martins, 2010, Iacovou et al., 1995). SMEs should understand that ICT implementation in SMEs' business is a vital requirement to enter the greater e-commerce market and would bring numerous advantages due to the business improvement, especially in sales and transactions.

Logistics Capabilities

E-commerce and marketing networks generated by the Internet, will have a deep influence on how enterprises do business and manage logistical support operations, i.e. their logistical capabilities (LC) (Brooksher, 1999, Karpinski, 1999, Copacino, 1997). E-commerce as well as online order fulfilment completely depends upon an effective logistics infrastructure within a country (Song, 2011). In many developing countries, logistical innovations and improvement need to be a priority in order to generate an excellent operation for effective contribution in e-commerce growth (Joong-Kun Cho et al., 2008). Ineffectiveness in vital services such as postal and logistics services as well as delivery operation, especially international transactions can tremendously discourage the achievement of the business itself.

Transportation (forward and reverse), collection, distribution, delivery systems and networks are the strategic aspects in developing e-commerce, especially including the optimisation of e-commerce itself within the SMEs' business environment (Joong-Kun Cho et al., 2008). Due to the size of their business in e-commerce, the simplest approach for SMEs to manage logistics operations is through a domestic or international postal or courier service. These are simple 3PL services that SMEs can utilise to support their business. SMEs should select the best 3PL companies to support their business process, to ensure that SMEs get the best service performance to achieve customer satisfaction (Joong-Kun Cho et al., 2008, Sezhiyan et al., 2011).

Explanations of logistics capability regularly emphasize the operation within organizations and businesses, or amongst various partners within the supply chain (Ballou, 2007). Moreover, Bowersox et al. (2002) argued that logistics capability is an informed judgement of an organization's capability to provide excellent logistics service as cost-effectively as possible. However, the type of organization would objectively depend on the size of the organization itself; a small size organization would obviously be relevant for companies and a bigger size organisation would be applicable in the context of a country which is regulated, managed and controlled by government. In relation to the resource-based view (RBV) (Yang et al., 2009), the logistics capability organized by an enterprise internally is a significant part of the enterprises' strategic resources, and enables any enterprise to plan and apply some strategies for improving its operational efficiency and performance.

In the case of utilising the external resources as the outsourced logistics or third-party logistics service (3PL) provider, the company's logistics capability would consequently depend on the 3PL's capability and performance. Broadly, the logistics capability of a country would influence the effectiveness of the entire logistics capability of companies within the country. Therefore, the type of logistics capability in this study comprises three type of logistics capability which are internal corporate logistics capability, outsourced corporate logistics capability, and country logistics capability (Joong-Kun Cho et al., 2008, Song, 2011). These three kinds of logistics capability based on each application has given positive implications on the business of SME as it supports the business process and logistical operation of SME. Directly and indirectly, logistics capability has a significant role supporting the SME's growth (Joong-Kun Cho et al., 2008).

DISCUSSION AND RESEARCH PROPOSITIONS

The result of the investigation on the literature in this study has determined the identification of four research gaps shown in Table 5 which reflect issues missing from previous studies of SME e-commerce in developing countries. Correspondingly, it is acknowledged that the initial stage of pre-adoption in e-commerce are now fairly developed however the post-adoption stage is now becoming more important for investigation to understand how this stage impacts e-commerce implementation.

Likewise, e-commerce is nowadays a commonly applied approach for many businesses in general and particularly for larger enterprises in developed countries, but its application for SMEs especially in developing countries still lags. Therefore, further study is needed to understand its applicability, and relevancy, and influence in this context, including logistical aspects that are important and essential processes within e-commerce practice. In addition, it also contributes to the clarification of the questions within the study.

Table 5. Summary of gaps

Topic of Interest	Author	Previous Studies	Gaps
E-commerce Adoption	Molla & Heeks, 2007; Sukasame et al., 2008; Intan Salwani et al., 2009; Alyoubi, 2015; Kabango & Asa, 2015; Kurnia et al., 2015; Rahayu & Day, 2017	Pre-adoption	Post-adoption
Enterprise Types	(Andersen et al., 2003, Krosch, 2002, Blount et al., 2005, MacGregor and Kartiwi, 2010)	Business in general, large business, some concern on SMEs	Focus contribution toward SMEs especially in developing countries
Country	(Wilson et al., 2008, Alyoubi, 2015, Dwivedi et al., 2009, Rillo and dela Cruz, 2016, Xuewen and Jinlong, 2010)	Concentrated in developed and some in developing countries	Increase the number of researches in developing countries
Concerned Area	Molla & Heeks, 2007; Sukasame et al., 2008; Intan Salwani et al., 2009; Alyoubi, 2015; Kabango & Asa, 2015; Kurnia et al., 2015; Rahayu & Day, 2017	Organisational, Technological and Environmental	Logistical Aspect: Logistics capabilities for E-commerce

Source: Author

As noted, previous literature was focused on the pre-adoption stage within a business and in general for large enterprises, with less study focused on SMEs. Further, previous studies mostly related to developed countries and appear reasonable since the e-commerce applications were first invented and applied in developed countries usually by large enterprises as they had the potential and ability to adopt the e-commerce then due to financial capability. Since then conditions and circumstances have dramatically changed as technology and business have fostered rapid and massive growth in e-commerce. Nowadays, e-commerce applications have reached a post-adoption stage and their growth have driven SMEs in developing countries to implement and embrace e-commerce.

The post-adoption stage for e-commerce has shown different conditions and circumstances, especially for SME in emerging countries based on the nature of those countries' economic conditions. Such conditions include inter alia infrastructure, technology, resources, market, and customer behaviour in developing countries compare to developed countries. Further, previous studies on e-commerce application generally shows the area of concerned on the aspect of technological, organisational and environmental. However, this research of literature on e-commerce application has clarified another aspect that has not been considered as an essential factor on e-commerce adoption which is logistical aspect. Meanwhile, the logistical aspects of e-commerce applications nowadays are clearly showing an importance, example the returns in the fashion sector (Fernie and Grant, 2019). Accordingly, logistical aspects are considered a primary KSF in terms of logistics capabilities.

Therefore, the literature review findings in this chapter suggest the following research propositions (RP):

RP1: Which KSFs of SME e-commerce in developing countries are the most important and are best understood?

RP2: What other aspects of e-commerce might be important in developing countries and which are specific to them, i.e. geography, culture, security, unique delivery platforms, etc.?

RP3: What problems related to SME e-commerce are faced by domestic logistics systems?

RP4: What is the current level of a country's logistics capabilities related to e-commerce logistics?

KSFs were identified from the LSR process but have not been empirically tested to determine their veracity, thus suggesting research to address RP1. Overall general factors are categorised into four contexts; technological, organisational, environmental (i.e. customer demand) and personal. The resultant KSFs also added several new aspects of context which are logistical, marketing, payment system, and governmental (law and regulations).

These 'a priori' KSFs were developed from a lack evidence and information in the e-commerce studies reviewed, particularly in the post-adoption stage concerning SMEs and emerging countries. Consequently, while the resultant KSFs have provided new information on e-commerce research and reflect recent conditions and situations of SMEs in developing countries they require testing to assess their importance and usefulness in different contexts and circumstances. Investigating these contexts and circumstances is also important as they may change dynamically due to e-commerce being related to the rapid growth of technology. This may provide new or alternative KSFs hitherto not considered. For example, there may be cultural or geographical conditions that may affect logistical or distribution operations for fulfilment. Also, there may be aspects of e-commerce security related to fraud-buyers or fraud-sellers which is occurring in developing countries. Additionally, delivery security also an issue in developing countries where the e-commerce delivery function might utilize the platform of online services such as Uber and local companies like Grab or other start-ups focusing delivery using motorbikes. Correspondingly, this will effectively address RP2.

The KSFs from this review, and any emerging from further research, may provide applicable guidance for stakeholders and business entities regarding e-commerce. This guidance would be significant for planning and strategies that comprise planning of regulations, investment, resources, education, etc. The planning and policies might be arranged by government to support SMEs achieving their business objectives considering this identified KSFs which is applicable for the circumstances of developing countries. Correspondingly, the KSF of logistics capabilities is important and suggests the final two propositions.

Findings identified there are issues of a lack of knowledge how logistics capabilities would determine the success of SME e-commerce systems in their business operations, especially in developing countries. As previously noted, logistics capabilities are a significant aspect in business processes as their role is to ensure efficient and effective e-commerce logistical operations for product distribution from suppliers through manufacturers and wholesalers/ retailers to end customers or consumers. However, knowledge of potential problems between extant logistics capabilities and SME e-commerce applications remains lacking. RP3 suggest the major problems in logistics sectors related to SMEs e-commerce need to be identified and investigated to determine, measure and monitor logistics performance, for example by an index score.

This activity can also be investigated relative to a country's logistics capability in facilitating SME e-commerce operations, for example a country's national logistics index, thus addressing RP4. Recognizing major problems in a country's logistics sector will be instructive intended for accurate and effective improvement and planning of national strategy. Acknowledging the problems will also be beneficial for relevant applied policy and regulation arrangements to support logistics improvements related especially to SME business transactions. Furthermore, identifying a national logistics index will effectively provide understanding for stakeholders in the country.

CONCLUSION

This chapter has provided an SLR of key, influencing factors of SME e-commerce in developing countries. The findings contribute to both theory and practice and the subsequent research propositions provide guidance including stakeholders in academia, companies and government. The theoretical contributions and research propositions should motivate other researchers to conduct empirical studies of SME e-commerce as a dynamic process and business activity in order to verify and validate the KSFs identified. Moreover, the KSFs identified also will be useful for companies and governments, especially in developing countries as initial key foci for the effective development of SME e-commerce. In addition, it would also encourage awareness of, and drivers for, arranging effective policies and strategies related to investment, resources, finance, education, and other aspects concerning the improvement of SME e-commerce business transactions. More widely it will be an effective trigger towards domestic economic growth. To that end, we believe this review will also enable developing countries to address and meet, and thus contribute, to the UN's sustainable development goals (SDGs) 8 – Good Jobs and Economic Growth and 9 – Innovation and Infrastructure.

REFERENCES

Al-Ghaith, W., Sanzogni, L., & Sandhu, K. (2010). Factors influencing the adoption and usage of online services in Saudi Arabia. *The Electronic Journal on Information Systems in Developing Countries*, *40*(1), 1–32. doi:10.1002/j.1681-4835.2010.tb00283.x

Aleid, F., Rogerson, S., & Fairweather, B. (2009). Factors affecting consumers adoption of ecommerce in Saudi Arabia from a consumers' perspective. *IADIS International Conference e-Commerce*, 11-18.

Ali, A., Mahfouz, A., & Arisha, A. (2017). Analysing supply chain resilience: Integrating the constructs in a concept mapping framework via a systematic literature review. *Supply Chain Management*, *22*(1), 16–39. doi:10.1108/SCM-06-2016-0197

Alyoubi, A. A. (2015). E-commerce in Developing Countries and how to Develop them during the Introduction of Modern Systems. *Procedia Computer Science*, *65*, 479–483. doi:10.1016/j.procs.2015.09.127

Andersen, K. V., Bjorn-Andersen, N., & Dedrick, J. (2003). Governance initiatives creating a demand-driven e-commerce approach: The case of Denmark. *The Information Society*, *19*(1), 95–105. doi:10.1080/01972240309475

Ballou, R. H. (2007). *Business Logistics/Supply Chain Management, 5/E (With Cd)*. Pearson Education.

Blount, Y., Castleman, T., & Swatman, P. M. (2005). E-commerce, human resource strategies, and competitive advantage: Two Australian banking case studies. *International Journal of Electronic Commerce*, *9*(3), 74–89. doi:10.1080/10864415.2005.11044335

Bowersox, D. J., Closs, D. J., & Cooper, M. B. (2002). *Supply Chain Logistics Management*. McGraw-Hill.

Braga, C. A. P. (2005). E-commerce regulation: New game, new rules? *The Quarterly Review of Economics and Finance*, *45*(2-3), 541–558. doi:10.1016/j.qref.2004.12.019

Brock, J. (2000). Information and communication technology in the small firm. *Enterprise and small business: Principles, practice and policy*, 384-408.

Brooksher, D. (1999). E-commerce and Logistics. *Traffic World*, *260*, 31.

Chaffey, D., & Ellis-Chadwick, F. (2016). *Digital Marketing*. Prentice Hall.

Chong, S., & Pervan, G. (2009). *Factors influencing the extent of deployment of electronic commerce for small-and medium-sized enterprises*. IGI Global. doi:10.4018/978-1-60566-126-1.ch013

Cloete, E., Courtney, S., & Fintz, J. (2002). Small Businesses' Acceptance and Adoption of e-Commerce in the Western-Cape Province of South-Africa. *The Electronic Journal on Information Systems in Developing Countries*, *10*(1), 1–13. doi:10.1002/j.1681-4835.2002.tb00062.x

Colicchia, C., & Strozzi, F. (2012). Supply chain risk management: A new methodology for a systematic literature review. *Supply Chain Management*, *17*(4), 403–418. doi:10.1108/13598541211246558

Copacino, W. C. (1997). Electronic commerce: How it will affect logistics. *Logistics Management*, *36*, 39.

Daniel, E., Wilson, H., & Myers, A. (2002). Adoption of e-commerce by SMEs in the UK: Towards a stage model. *International Small Business Journal, 20*(3), 253–270. doi:10.1177/0266242602203002

Denyer, D., & Tranfield, D. (2009). Producing a systematic review. In D. A. Buchanan & A. Bryman (Eds.), *The Sage handbook of organizational research methods* (pp. 671–689). Sage Publications Ltd.

Dixit, N., & Datta, S. K. (2010). Customer's perception on internet banking and their impact on customer satisfaction and loyalty: A study in Indian context. *Journal of Computing*, *2*, 131–135.

Doukidis, G. I., Lybereas, P., & Galliers, R. D. (1996). Information systems planning in small business: A stages of growth analysis. *Journal of Systems and Software, 33*(2), 189–201. doi:10.1016/0164-1212(95)00183-2

Dwivedi, Y. K., Papazafeiropoulo, A., & Scupola, A. (2009). SMEs'e-commerce adoption: Perspectives from Denmark and Australia. *Journal of Enterprise Information Management*, *22*(1/2), 152–166. doi:10.1108/17410390910932803

Einav, L., Levin, J., Popov, I., & Sundaresan, N. (2014). Growth, adoption, and use of mobile e-commerce. *The American Economic Review*, *104*(5), 489–494. doi:10.1257/aer.104.5.489

Fernie, J. & Grant, D. B. (2019), *Fashion Logistics: Insights into the Fashion Retail Supply Chain*. Kogan Page Publishers.

Galipoglu, E., Kotzab, H., Teller, C., Yumurtaci Huseyinoglu, I. Ö., & Popelbub, J. (2018). Omni-channel retailing research–state of the art and intellectual foundation. *International Journal of Physical Distribution & Logistics Management*, *48*(4), 365–390. doi:10.1108/IJPDLM-10-2016-0292

Ghobakhloo, M., Arias-Aranda, D., & Benitez-Amado, J. (2011). Adoption of e-commerce applications in SMEs. *Industrial Management & Data Systems, 111*(8), 1238–1269. doi:10.1108/02635571111170785

Hall, C. (2002). *Profile of SMEs and SME Issues in APEC, 1990-2000*. Academic Press.

Hatten, T. S. (2015). *Small business management: Entrepreneurship and beyond.* Nelson Education.

Hjort, K., Hellström, D., Karlsson, S., & Oghazi, P. (2019). Typology of practices for managing consumer returns in internet retailing. *International Journal of Physical Distribution & Logistics Management, 49*(7), 767–790. doi:10.1108/IJPDLM-12-2017-0368

Iacovou, C. L., Benbasat, I., & Dexter, A. S. (1995). Electronic data interchange and small organizations: Adoption and impact of technology. *Management Information Systems Quarterly, 19*(4), 465–485. doi:10.2307/249629

Intan Salwani, M., Marthandan, G., Daud Norzaidi, M., & Choy Chong, S. (2009). E-commerce usage and business performance in the Malaysian tourism sector: Empirical analysis. *Information Management & Computer Security, 17*(2), 166–185. doi:10.1108/09685220910964027

Joong-Kun Cho, J., Ozment, J., & Sink, H. (2008). Logistics capability, logistics outsourcing and firm performance in an e-commerce market. *International Journal of Physical Distribution & Logistics Management, 38*(5), 336–359. doi:10.1108/09600030810882825

Kabango, C. M., & Asa, A. R. (2015). Factors influencing e-commerce development: Implications for the developing countries. *International Journal of Innovation and Economics Development, 1*(1), 64–72. doi:10.18775/ijied.1849-7551-7020.2015.11.2006

Kapurubandara, M., & Lawson, R. (2006). Barriers to Adopting ICT and e-commerce with SMEs in developing countries: an Exploratory study in Sri Lanka. University of Western Sydney.

Karpinski, R. (1999). The Logistics Of E-Business. *InternetWeek*, 1-3.

Krosch, L. (2002). E-Commerce Regulations 2002— UK. *Computer Law & Security Review, 18*(4), 252–258. doi:10.1016/S0267-3649(02)00705-7

Kurnia, S., Choudrie, J., Mahbubur, R. M., & Alzougool, B. (2015). E-commerce technology adoption: A Malaysian grocery SME retail sector study. *Journal of Business Research, 68*(9), 1906–1918. doi:10.1016/j.jbusres.2014.12.010

Kyobe, M. E. (2010). E-Crime and Non-Compliance with Government Regulations on E-Commerce: Barriers to E-Commerce Optimization in South African SMEs. In *E-Commerce Adoption and Small Business in the Global Marketplace: Tools for Optimization* (pp. 47–66). IGI Global. doi:10.4018/978-1-60566-998-4.ch003

Lee, G.-G., & Lin, H.-F. (2005). Customer perceptions of e-service quality in online shopping. *International Journal of Retail & Distribution Management, 33*(2), 161–176. doi:10.1108/09590550510581485

Lim, S. F. W., Jin, X., & Srai, J. S. (2018). Consumer-driven e-commerce. *International Journal of Physical Distribution & Logistics Management, 48*(3), 308–332. doi:10.1108/IJPDLM-02-2017-0081

Macgregor, R., Vrazalic, L., Carlsson, S., Bunker, D., & Magnusson, M. (2002). The impact of business size and business type on small business investment in electronic commerce: A study of swedish small businesses. *AJIS. Australasian Journal of Information Systems, 9*(2). doi:10.3127/ajis.v9i2.189

Macgregor, R. C., & Kartiwi, M. (2010). Perception of barriers to e-commerce adoption in SMEs in a developed and developing country: A comparison between Australia and Indonesia. *Journal of Electronic Commerce in Organizations, 8*(1), 61–82. doi:10.4018/jeco.2010103004

Mangiaracina, R., Perego, A., Seghezzi, A., & Tumino, A. (2019). Innovative solutions to increase last-mile delivery efficiency in B2C e-commerce: A literature review. *International Journal of Physical Distribution & Logistics Management, 49*(9), 901–920. doi:10.1108/IJPDLM-02-2019-0048

Melacini, M., Perotti, S., Rasini, M., & Tappia, E. (2018). E-fulfilment and distribution in omni-channel retailing: A systematic literature review. *International Journal of Physical Distribution & Logistics Management, 48*(4), 391–414. doi:10.1108/IJPDLM-02-2017-0101

Mentzer, J. T., & Kahn, K. B. (1995). A framework of logistics research. *Journal of Business Logistics, 16*, 231.

Miyazaki, A. D., & Fernandez, A. (2001). Consumer perceptions of privacy and security risks for online shopping. *The Journal of Consumer Affairs, 35*(1), 27–44. doi:10.1111/j.1745-6606.2001.tb00101.x

Mohmed, A. S. I., Azizan, N. B., & Jali, M. Z. (2016). Factors Affecting Purchase Intention of Customers to Accept E-Commerce Transaction: A Conceptual Framework. *Research Journal of Applied Sciences, 11*, 1188–1194.

Molla, A., & Heeks, R. (2007). Exploring e-commerce benefits for businesses in a developing country. *The Information Society, 23*(2), 95–108. doi:10.1080/01972240701224028

Newbert, S. L. (2007). Empirical research on the resource-based view of the firm: An assessment and suggestions for future research. *Strategic Management Journal, 28*(2), 121–146. doi:10.1002mj.573

Nguyen, H., & Waring, T. S. (2013). The adoption of customer relationship management (CRM) technology in SMEs: An empirical study. *Journal of Small Business and Enterprise Development, 20*(4), 824–848. doi:10.1108/JSBED-01-2012-0013

Oliveira, T., & Martins, M. F. (2010). Understanding e-business adoption across industries in European countries. *Industrial Management & Data Systems, 110*(9), 1337–1354. doi:10.1108/02635571011087428

Oxley, J. E., & Yeung, B. (2001). E-commerce readiness: Institutional environment and international competitiveness. *Journal of International Business Studies, 32*(4), 705–723. doi:10.1057/palgrave.jibs.8490991

Pang, H. (2016). Research on Optimization of B2C E-commerce Service Quality Oriented by Customer Demand. *Revista de la Facultad de Ingeniería, 31*(6), 103–113.

Parker, C., & Castleman, T. (2007). New directions for research on SME-eBusiness: Insights from an analysis of journal articles from 2003-2006. *Journal of Information Systems and Small Business, 1*, 21–40.

Rahayu, R., & Day, J. (2015). Determinant factors of e-commerce adoption by SMEs in developing country: Evidence from Indonesia. *Procedia: Social and Behavioral Sciences, 195*, 142–150. doi:10.1016/j.sbspro.2015.06.423

Rahayu, R., & Day, J. (2017). E-commerce adoption by SMEs in developing countries: Evidence from Indonesia. *Eurasian Business Review, 7*(1), 25–41. doi:10.100740821-016-0044-6

Rillo, A. D., & Dela Cruz, V. (2016). The Development Dimension of E-Commerce in Asia: Opportunities and Challenges. *Asian Development Bank Institute*. http://hdl.handle.net /11540/6484

Rose, G., Khoo, H., & Straub, D. W. (1999). Current technological impediments to business-to-consumer electronic commerce. *Communications of the AIS, 1*, 1. doi:10.17705/1CAIS.00116

Saghiri, S., Wilding, R., Mena, C., & Bourlakis, M. (2017). Toward a three-dimensional framework for omni-channel. *Journal of Business Research, 77*, 53–67. doi:10.1016/j.jbusres.2017.03.025

Samuelson, P., & Nordhaus, W. (2005). *Economics*. McGraw-Hill.

Sezhiyan, D., Page, T., & Iskanius, P. (2011). The impact of supply effort management, logistics capability, and supply chain management strategies on firm performance. *International Journal of Electronic Transport*, *1*(1), 26–44. doi:10.1504/IJET.2011.043114

Song, J. (2011). *Regional logistics capability and economic development of the regions in Great Britain*. University of Hull.

Sorkun, M. F. (2019). The impact of product variety on LSQ in e-marketplaces. *International Journal of Physical Distribution & Logistics Management*, *49*(7), 749–766. doi:10.1108/IJPDLM-06-2018-0223

Strom, R., Vendel, M., & Bredican, J. (2014). Mobile marketing: A literature review on its value for consumers and retailers. *Journal of Retailing and Consumer Services*, *21*(6), 1001–1012. doi:10.1016/j.jretconser.2013.12.003

Strozzi, F., Colicchia, C., Creazza, A., & Noe, C. (2017). Literature review on the 'Smart Factory' concept using bibliometric tools. *International Journal of Production Research*, *55*(22), 6572–6591. doi:10.1080/00207543.2017.1326643

Sukasame, N., Sebora, T. C., & Mohedano-Suanes, A. (2008). E-commerce entrepreneurship as a national priority: The case of Thailand. *Service Industries Journal*, *28*(7), 989–1001. doi:10.1080/02642060701861357

Thompson, H. (1998). Marketing strategies: What do your customers really want? *The Journal of Business Strategy*, *19*(4), 16–21. doi:10.1108/eb039946

Triandini, E., Djunaidy, A., & Siahaan, D. (2015). Factors Influencing E-Commerce Adoption by SMES Indonesia: A Conceptual Model. Lontar Komputer: Jurnal Ilmiah Teknologi Informasi, 4(2).

UNDP. (2004). UNCTAD E-Commerce and Development Report 2004. *United Nations Conference on Trade and Development.*

Van Cleynenbreugel, P. (2017). The European Commission's Geo-Blocking Proposals and the Future of EU E-Commerce Regulation. *Masaryk UJL & Tech.*, *11*(1), 39. doi:10.5817/MUJLT2017-1-3

Williams, M. D., Dwivedi, Y. K., Lal, B., & Schwarz, A. (2009). Contemporary trends and issues in IT adoption and diffusion research. *Journal of Information Technology*, *24*(1), 1–10. doi:10.1057/jit.2008.30

Wilson, H., Daniel, E., & Davies, I. A. (2008). The diffusion of e-commerce in UK SMEs. *Journal of Marketing Management*, *24*(5-6), 489–516. doi:10.1362/026725708X325968

Xuewen, S., & Jinlong, B. (2010). Research on the innovation and development of the third-party B2B e-commerce model of China. *2010 3rd International Conference on Advanced Computer Theory and Engineering (ICACTE),* V4-317-V4-319. 10.1109/ICACTE.2010.5579506

Yang, C.-C., Marlow, P. B., & Lu, C.-S. (2009). Assessing resources, logistics service capabilities, innovation capabilities and the performance of container shipping services in Taiwan. *International Journal of Production Economics*, *122*(1), 4–20. doi:10.1016/j.ijpe.2009.03.016

Chapter 12
Returns Management:
An Instrument for Enhancing Customer Service for the Indian E-Retail Industry

Nikhil Singh
Ecom Express Private Limited, India

Smriti Asthana
https://orcid.org/0000-0001-5730-6260
Confederation of Indian Industry School of Logistics, Amity University, Noida, India

ABSTRACT

The e-retail sector of the Indian e-commerce industry being a price-sensitive market has witnessed an increase in customer interest and flexibility to compare a product while making a purchase decision through e-commerce platforms. The increase in internet penetration and users in India has been facilitated by a boost of the telecom industry and data penetration from 34% in 2017 to 60% in 2022. While some players like Flipkart and Amazon have disrupted the sector with their customer acquisition ratio in the market, other new players, Jio Mart and Paytm Mall, are merely surviving or gearing up to the competition. The cost factors like marketing, forward logistics, inventory, and reverse logistics are associated with customer acquisition, which the organizations are not able to recover because of low average gross merchandise value (GMV) and high logistics cost to serve the customer. This chapter depicts the returns management process, which, while integrating the forward and the reverse logistics in a supply chain, is productive financially and logistically.

DOI: 10.4018/978-1-7998-2867-9.ch012

INTRODUCTION

The e-retail sector has witnessed big mergers of Jabong and Myntra, a failed merger of Snapdeal and Flipkart and latest one is of Flipkart itself which has been acquired by Walmart for a big billion deal of $16 billion for 77% stake in 2019. To expand their respective portfolios, the organizations have entered in the e-grocery market, with Amazon acquiring Aditya Birla's 'more' and Flipkart planning to follow the trend to sustain in competition. There is cost associated with customer acquisition which the organizations are not able to recover despite having high growth rate because of low average gross merchandise value (GMV) and high logistics cost to serve the customer which is around $2 for an average GMV of around $24 as compared to China where the figures are $2.2 for an average GMV nearly three times to that Indian market. The computation further gets affected with the delay in cash flow as around 60% -70% of the customers in India prefer cash on delivery on products. The current market curve is in growing stage but the investors like Goldman Sachs, Softbank are eagerly eyeing upon the break-even point and profits to be posted for their huge investment in the e-retail sector.

The major cost parameters involve marketing, forward logistics, inventory and reverse logistics. While first two parameters are inevitable and are directly linked with customer acquisition and service levels. The third aspect of inventory optimization is dealt through marketplace model[1] to avoid cost of obsolete products and reducing carrying cost by e-retail organizations. Reverse Logistics, the fourth parameter is a grey area and the returns process is also an unorganized and unstructured part of the whole supply chain. The resultant increase in the cost of reverse logistics is due to various factors like lose control over quality of products; high quantity of returns and some other inherited traits like absence of physical verification of products on virtual platforms elaborated under the limitation of marketplace model.

The rate of goods or merchandise returns on an average is 15% compared to the total forward shipments but can be as high as 40% in apparel category (KPMG, 2018). The organizations where monthly transaction is in millions, managing and controlling the reverse logistics cost itself is massive area which needs recovery on immediate basis to push down the operational cost and squeeze the incurring losses to a minimum level. One of the drawbacks of the current reverse logistics involves place and time restriction for customers to be available at their respective premises and delays in replacement or monetary refund processes of over 30 hours which hampers the customer retention(Bureau F, 2016).To improve visibility of inventory of the returned products, e- retailers are opting to reduce the replacement or return tenure to a specific amount, which is adversely affecting the preference to be a top choice for customers. In fact, 92% of customers have reported that they would shop on virtual platforms if the return processes are flexible and agile (Saleh K, 2018).

The other side of the bottleneck is the cost involved, borne either by the customer or the seller, which both the parties are not in support to pay for the logistics.

This chapter depicts the management & process of product return system in Indian market by application of a solution which while integrating the forward and the reverse logistics in a supply chain is also productive both financially and logistically. The solution is akin to introducing the brick and motor model (B & M) facility in the supply chain of the e- retail segment of the eCommerce industry.

A B & M facility that would be easily accessible to the customers and can be aligned with their respective daily commutation or travel track to return or replace the product is the need of the hour. The location for the facility can be identified based on analysis of transportation zones of a study area and examining the mass movement patterns. The deployment of such model will not only eliminate the restriction of customers to be present on their premises but also create a responsive return or refund management process to cater to the demand of customers. Since the Indian demographic conditions are much oriented towards brick and mortar model involving the trust factor as a major parameter, the success of attaining an organized management system to effectively manage returns are on higher side.

As far as the benefit for e-retailers are concerned, it will also act as a first level screening platform to control the nuances of fraud trades and fake returned products with appropriate integration of IT systems at the facility for inspecting the products returned by customers. In addition to reducing the cost, apart from last mile pick up and deliveries which are completely eliminated under this model, utilization of economies of scale function for transportation of products to the e-retail organization's warehouse or seller's storage location by implication of Charles Wright heuristics, where each facility will act as node and warehouse as depot will be a crucial measure.

The internet penetration level is projected to reach 829 million by 2020 in the world's seventh largest economy, benefiting Indian e-commerce sector to scale up their operations and acquire the emerging market which will stretch to $107 billion by 2020 (RedSeer, 2018).The data usage increase from 34% in 2017 to an 60% in 2022 (E) (PwC, 2018) leads to more accessibility to customers to browse, compare and evaluate products leading to e-retail growth as well as increased pressure on reverse logistics by virtue of product return due to availability of multiple choice options, price range and demographics. The e-retail category unfolding as backbone of the sector, has administered large investments and decent acquisitions of small players to sustain in the competitive market.

While e-retail will account for around 5% in the total retail market in India in next two years (KPMG, 2018), in lieu of that, companies are positioning best of the efforts to attract customers without much focus and evaluation of the operational cost they incur, to serve them. The big sale events to woo customers in a price sensitive economy, to membership schemes for continuous regulation of buyer's interest, are few of the strategies that keep customers always active on the virtual platforms of these organizations.

The basic supply chain for e-retail involves a verified supplier enlisting their products on a virtual market. When a customer requests for the product, the order management initiates at organization's end, either by intimating supplier regarding the request and shipping directly from the supplier (drop shipment) or processing the order from the integral distribution center and fulfilling the requirement through logistics partner. While the first alternative enables agile and lean process than the latter one, but the quality assurance issue prevails with the case. The major revenue generating commodities are mobile phones and apparels including accessories section that comprise of a hefty share of gross merchandise value for the organizations.

The acquisition of Flipkart by Walmart has been a turning point in the e-retail market. Earlier present is business to business segment (B2B), the American giant was eyeing to enter in business to customer(B2C) segment but the country's legal measures has refrained the firm from deploying its vision on the field. With Flipkart acting as a subsidiary, Walmart can rationalize the whole value chain with its expertise to operate at optimal cost and pass on the savings to its customers. Another side of the account is Amazon which also is closing the market share deficit to Flipkart by small margin and is eager to operate in revealing e-grocery market by acquiring Aditya Birla Company owned 'more' supermarket chain and pitching the competition from American markets to the Indian streets.

The growth stage of the sector although making investors like Soft Bank, Goldman Sachs and others to continue capital flow through the organizations but the losses occurring due to high operational cost and contribution of low average gross merchandise value will affect the funds eventually. The prime motive of the organizations is to acquire customers for which burning few more dollars for their satisfaction is the only way out as far as the operations and sales economies advance to the maturity phase. Flipkart took a forward step with enabling credit system directly through their platform which will burden the liability statement of the organization.

The pertinent cause for the high operation cost is not only the growth stage but few of the nuances in the demography as well. There is an increase in the number of fake orders for which the sale value is nullified against the operating cost. On an average a delivery attempt is more than once for each order to be delivered in addition to road infrastructure and connectivity issues of the last mile locations and the emerging trend of "wear today and return next day" for the apparels has tested the strategies of the organizations to work hard for securing margins for every value addition they make to fulfil the requirement of each consumer. Since, the forward shipment cost cannot be contained due to serviceability and customer satisfaction issues, measures like restructuring the replacement policies from 30 days to 10 days and providing refunds on selected products will only hamper the relationship with customer, which the organizations are thriving to build for a while now.

The companies are aware of the fact that the reverse logistic cost can cumulatively cause a huge dent in the P& L Statement of the company caused by milk run scenario where a product movement increases almost upto 3 times and also including the administration and last end delivery cost. The entity in turn are investing into financial platforms and online wallet offerings to enable the money stay with the service provider to facilitate repeat and secondary sales example amazon pay

LITERATURE REVIEW

The e-commerce sector comprises of various categories ticketing, taxi services, retailing, pharmacy, food delivery and groceries. The major share is composed of retail sector which was around $18 billion out of $53 billion market in 2017 i.e. approximately 33% contributing to the industry (RedSeer, 2018).

Propelled by rising smartphone penetration, the launch of 4G networks and increasing consumer wealth, the Indian e-commerce market is expected to grow to US$ 200 billion by 2026 from US$ 38.5 billion in 2017. Online retail sales in India are expected to grow by 31 per cent to touch US$ 32.70 billion in 2018, led by Flipkart, Amazon India and Paytm Mall and is expected to continue its strong growth, by registering a CAGR of over 35 per cent and to reach Rs 1.8 trillion (US$ 25.75 billion) by FY20.(IBEF, 2020)

The demand distribution is also asymmetrical across regions of India. The south region accord for 41% of the total order value with major metro cities like Bangalore, Hyderabad and Chennai contributing to 14%, 5% and 4% respectively while north region share is around 32% contributed by Delhi at 11%, Gurgaon at 3%, Noida at 3% and Ghaziabad at 1.5% (Browntape, 2014) . While organizations have achieved the market of tier-1 cities, the mission is to reach out to tier-2 and tier-3 cities.

The expanding market with low order value of products has created imbalance considering cost of logistics closing around $2 on average order value depending largely on cash on delivery payments as compared to other countries like China which has three times average order value with logistics cost of $2.2 (Kola V, 2017). With the mindset to operate in such conditions, e-retail organizations are functioning through partial fulfilment through integral logistics arms while others through third party logistics providers to attain economies of scale especially for tier-2 and tier-3 cities where currently the presence of the organizations are at limited scale. Partnering with Delhivery, Ecom Express, FedEx, BLUE DART and GATI is a move to lean asset model where the e-retail can focus on their operations without distractions of logistics.

The issue arises when the lean asset model rebounds to its very cause particularly in the case of marketplace model which is now a trend in the sector. Consider a situation where a direct delivery from supplier is required to be made through drop shipment to customer through a 3PL logistics partner. The scenario involves a very low-level control for e-retail organizations to track and assure quality of the product to be delivered to the right customer, within the committed time duration. And if the customer returns the product the whole process repeats itself without generating any revenue and adding extra 50% cost to normal operating cost of the delivery.

The net margin in the categories of mobile phones and apparels is around 3.5% and 15% but the cost of returns diminishes the margins for both seller and the e-retail organizations. In 2016, Flipkart and Amazon reported a total revenue of ₹ 1952 crores and ₹ 2275 crores but also incurred a net loss of ₹ 2306 crores and ₹ 3572 crores respectively due to high operations cost (ETRetail, 2016). The financial figures in the FY2019, however, changed to Rs 4,234.5 crore revenue while losses were at Rs 1,625.7 crore for Flipkart and to the revenue of Rs 7,594 crore and losses at Rs 5,685.4 crore for

Figure 1. Return process in an e-retail organization (Jayaraman R. et al. 2013)

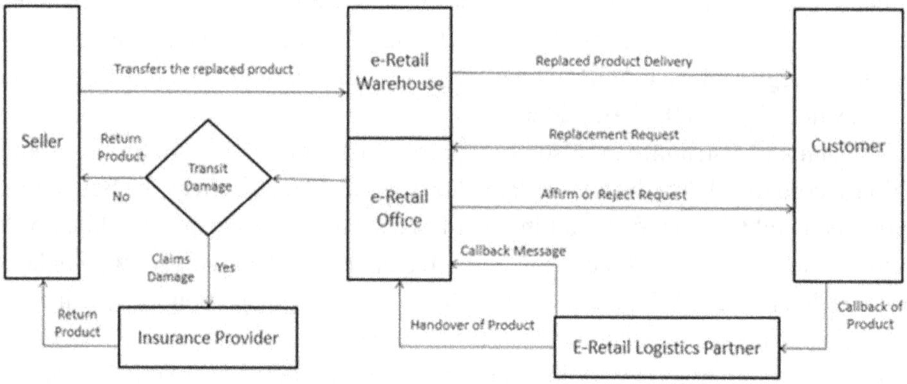

Amazon India (Yourstory, 2019). The factors that affect the operational cost involves marketing, forward logistics, salaries, inventory and reverse logistics. The prior four cost involved in the value chain are inevitable for every business but can be contained with appropriate strategies involving qualitative and quantitative methods. But the latter cost is the one pinching the e-retail industry, the cost of return of products which is measured around 15-20% of total forward shipments and varying with categories of apparels which induce 40% and mobile phones with 20% (Mukul P, 2018). The process of handling returns is also largely unorganized in the system and it takes a longer time process the return as the product flows from the point of sale to

logistics partner handed over to e-retailer and then reaches to supplier and cost of this process is on shared basis or borne by the seller all together.

The brick and mortar model incurs a return rate of 8.8% without incorporating the return process cost, primarily the reverse logistics cost which is quite high for virtual platforms(Saleh K). The category of apparels require a touch and feel parameter before decision for purchase of the product and Marketplace model of the e-retail further degrades the experience with quality issues due to unsteady control over process like return policy (Singh 2017), time range acceptability, return goods collection and checklist, refund, turnaround time and last but not the least inclusion of ethical and moral aspect in every stage of the reverse logistic cycle. Similarly, mobile phones which require features or functionality tests and sometimes physical assurance, because of the status symbol which is now associated with Mobiles, cannot fulfill all the evaluation requirements on the virtual platform provided by the e-retailers.

The endeavors by all the upstream and downstream channel partners is to facilitate best experience to consumers, hence the loop holes present in the system affect not only e-retailers but suppliers and customers as well in some or the other way. The majority of e-shoppers' purchasing experience is directly linked to the quality of the delivery service that the ecommerce players provides them making the last mile delivery a key step in the online shopper's satisfaction (Jose, 2018).

As per a survey conducted on the return handling process of e-retail sector, 92% respondents agreed to buy more if the return process is minimalistic while 79% of respondents require free shipping, a cost borne by either seller or the e-retail organizations in the current scenario. In addition to that, 62% of the respondents are certain to shop online if they can return products in a store facility. (Saleh K).

Reverse Logistics in Indian E-Commerce Industry

The case studies, research papers, reports and articles mentioned in the section are thoroughly read to establish the business scope within reverse logistics segment in e-retail sector under Indian e-commerce industry. The classification of the study has been identified as following:

Table 1.

SNo	Author	Publisher	Articles/ Research Papers
1	PTI	ETRetail	E-tailers exploring ways to improve reverse logistics costs: study (2018)
2	Murthy D and Sumanth K	Case Centre	Reverse Logistics of e-commerce in India - control, cost and clearance (2017)
3	Manoj SN	Linkedin	Barriers to reverse logistics in e-commerce industry in India (2015)
4	Krishna V	Vccircle	How heavy is the reverse logistics burden for top e-com players in India (2014)
5	Mukherjee R	The Hacker Street	The unsolved problem of E-Commerce Industries: Reverse Logistics (2016)
6	Guest	Trak	'Return Guaranteed' – Indian e-commerce and the issue of reverse logistics (2017)
7	Shah N	Shiprocket	Reverse Logistics for Ecommerce: Understanding The Basics (2014)
8	Richer S	Industrytoday	Nimble reverse logistics in e-commerce (2017)
9	Samad S and Chowdary N	Etcases	Cash on delivery and reverse logistics (2014)
10	Sekar R	The International Journal	E-commerce support on reverse logistics in India
11	Bhargava R	ISB	The growing relevance of reverse logistics in India (2017)
12	Ali S and Thiyagarajan G	Indian Journal of Science and Technology	Analysis of Reverse Logistics Implementation Barriers in Online Retail Industry (2016)
13	KPMG	KPMG	India's e-commerce retail logistics growth story (2016)
14	BI Intelligence	Business Insider	The reverse logistics report: How retailers can save money by making returns smoother in the e-commerce age (2016)
15	Krishna V	Yourstory	Why the units of Flipkart (and competitors) will not work for another decade (2017)
16	FT Bureau	The Financial Express	Snapdeal fastest in refunds, beats Flipkart, Amazon (2016)
17	Jayaraman R et al	Journal of Supply Chain Management Systems	A Study of Operating Practices and Supply Chains in the e-Commerce Online Retail Businesses in India (2013)
18	J Jolly	ETPrime	Last mile intra-city logistics: The key to e-commerce customer satisfaction (2018)
19	RedSeer	RedSeer	E-commerce industry in India (2018)
20	KPMG	KPMG	E-commerce retail logistics in India (2018)
21	Bhaskar A	Times of India	Product return remains a key challenge for online customers (2018)

Table 2.

Secondary Sources	Frequency	Percentage (%)
Articles	13	65
Research Papers	1	5
Case Studies	3	15
Reports	3	15
Total	20	100

METHODOLOGY

The approach adopted for the solution accommodates analysis of market and environmental conditions through various secondary sources and examine the published data for organization benefits and customer satisfaction at optimal cost of operations and better service levels respectively in e-retail sector of e-commerce industry in India.

DATA ANALYSIS

The growth of Indian e-retail sector amplified revenue streams for two major organizations i.e. Flipkart and Amazon. With Flipkart enhancing its portfolio proposition by acquiring Myntra and Jabong to own the fashion segment, simultaneously Amazon which is also a contender for top spot pushed its entitlement under the electronics and white goods segments. Considering the recent reports which claim that the combined market share for both the organization account for more than 75% of the total e-retail sector with average transaction rate of 10 million per month (Krishna V, 2014). In addition to this fact, the return rate of 11% is dependent on customer initiation and the rest 4% is the outcome of logistics inefficiencies and pilferage constituting 15%as mentioned in Section 3 of the report. The return transactions account for 1.5 million per month. The cost of returns is comparatively higher for Tier II and Tier III markets, which currently are feasible target markets for the e-retail organizations, due to growth in data and internet penetration levels and high competition in Tier I cities to acquire and retain customers. The average cost of returns is $2 per transaction for Tier I cities, this value computes to be around $3 million per month or $36 million in a year. With 45% of cost engaged in last mile delivery or pick up, the annual cost turns out to be $16.2 million.

The fix adopted by due diligence, by most of the organizations is to screen and evaluate their suppliers before partnering with them on the virtual portal. this solution turns out to be on temporal basis and with growing base of suppliers as well as customers on a marketplace model restrains a better control over returns management. Addressing the very cause to the root of its origin to minimize cost, a hybrid model of brick mortar and virtual platform is required to be adopted to cater the e-retail organizations in returns management.

MODEL

A project to outsource reverse shipment channel by deploying a physical facility where a customer can reach out to the nearest store to deliver their returnable product in due course of their respective journeys and isolate it from forward shipment system. The location of the B & M facility can be based on data analysis of historical data of returns and at areas of high contact or commutation pattern of the customers from one transportation analysis zone to other in a study area like from home to work or from home to college or vice-versa, majorly targeting vicinity of an office or college or market hub area. Hence, extracting the advantage of economies of scale for the vehicle to optimize transportation cost as per Clarke Wright heuristics to deliver products back to the warehouse as well as eliminating cost of last mile pick up.

The facility can also function as a replacement center and can deliver the right product if customer intimates the e-retail organization beforehand for replacement thus providing a better customer experience and eliminating repeated cost of last mile delivery. The objectives of the model are:

Customer Satisfaction

1. Ability to minimize the restrictions of availability of customer at their premises for return/ replacement of bought product as customer can choose a location nearby to their respective journey and can return the product on the go.
2. Facilitating a faster return process, the current system operates at around 30 hours for reverse pick up and another 12 hours to deliver the product to the e-retail's warehouse while refunds are clocked at 2-3 days (Bureau F, 2016).

With the hybrid model, the reverse pick time will be reduced to only 24 hours as customers will deliver the returnable product to the facility and by the end of the day product will be delivered to the e-retail's warehouse. Also, the refund process can be initiated with immediate effect as soon as the return order is punched into the system at the facility.

Figure 2. Current model of return process in an e-retail organization

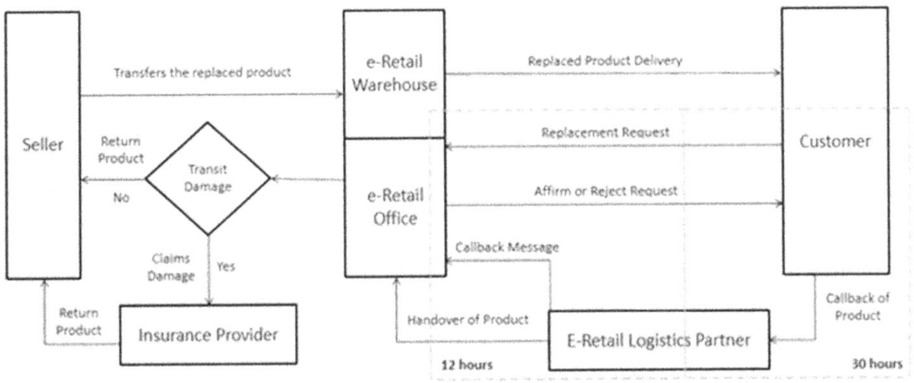

Figure 3. Hybrid model of return process in an e-retail organization

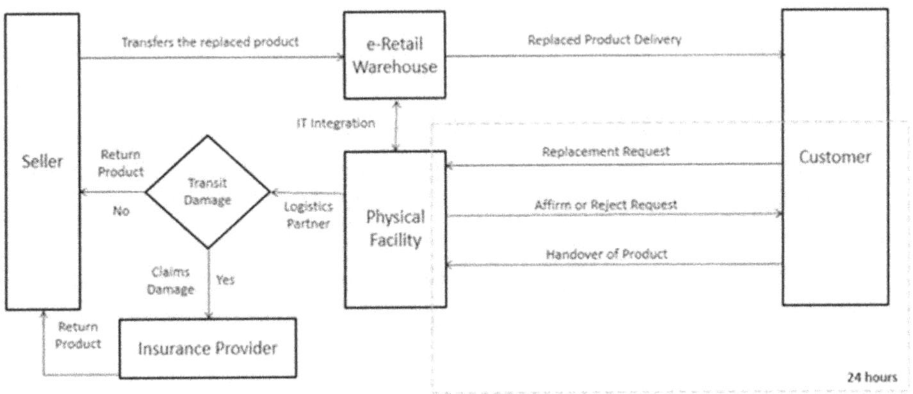

Responsiveness

1. The enhanced reduction in processing time will enable a better flow of products from customer to seller reducing locked capital load in the system.
2. A better inventory visibility can be attained through the process, especially in case of such returned products which require just re-packaging to resell them on the virtual platform.

FUTURE SCOPE

- The model can be deployed for an alpha test in a tier I city location where the returns are high to examine the response of the customers towards the model.
- An initial strategy to provide a proportional virtual currency based on the returned product cost can be adopted to lure the customers for promotion of the model, this will enable them not only to return product at the facility but also to buy more from the respective virtual platform.
- Further with success of the model in a study area, the priority delivery option can be availed through the hybrid model, reducing the cost of forward shipments as well and hence passing the benefit to customers by providing optimal priority delivery charges.
- As we move towards the concept of contactless deliveries, this model can provide customers a safe and transparent last mile delivery experience.

LIMITATIONS

- The best scenario to attain success of the model is dependent on the customer adoption but also relies on outsourcing the reverse channel to a third party as handling returns on individual basis will lead to inability to attain economies of scale benefit which is the core parameter of the model.
- To attain the benefit strictly on individual basis, the return order transactions should be quite high to overcome the operational and setup cost of the number of facility units to be deployed in the study area.

CONCLUSION

The e-retail market lost 30% of total gross merchandise value due to returns in 2017 (Mukul P, 2017). This is a considerable amount of revenue for investors supporting the organizations which are losing on the concerned part just toacquire and retain customers for the sake of survival in the market.

Current system to manage the return channel is not quite organized and organizations in the sector are handling returns with their vested strategies to reduce the extra and inevitable cost as much as possible. The hybrid model seems to minimize the problem but require support of the customers and organizations willing to adopt it by partnering with other organizations for the benefit of complete value chain in the e-retail sector.

REFERENCES

Bhargava, R. (2017, December). *The Growing Relevance of Reverse Logistics in India.* Retrieved September 5, 2018, from https://www.isb.edu/newsletters/almamatters/oct-dec-2017/relevanceofreverselogistics

Bhaskar, A. (2018, July 5). Product return remains a key challenge for online customers: Study. *Times of India.* Retrieved September 23, 2018, from https://timesofindia.indiatimes.com/business/india-business/product-return-remains-a-key-challenge-for-online-customers-study/articleshow/64873757.cms

Browntape. (2014, December 18). *Which Part of India is Contributing The Most to E-Commerce Growth?* Retrieved August 13, 2018, from http://www.iamwire.com/2014/12/part-india-contributing-e-commerce-growth/106607

Bureau, F. (2016, July 26). *Snapdeal fastest in refunds, beats Flipkart, Amazon.* Retrieved September 16, 2018, from https://www.financialexpress.com/industry/snapdeal-fastest-in-refunds-beats-flipkart-amazon/328761/

ETRetail. (2016, November 26). Flipkart report losses of Rs 2,306 crores in FY 16. *ET Retail.* Retrieved August 21, 2018, from https://retail.economictimes.indiatimes.com/news/e-commerce/e-tailing/flipkart-report-losses-of-rs-2306-crores-in-fy-16/55631416

IBEF. (2020). *Indian ecommerce Industry Report, February 2020.* India Brand Equity Foundation.

Intelligence, B. I. (2016, October 10). *The Reverse Logistics Report: How retailers can save money by making returns smoother in the e-commerce age.* Retrieved September 13, 2018, from https://www.businessinsider.com/reverse-logistics-and-reverse-supply-chain-research-returns-recalls-repairs-and-end-of-life-returns-2016-10

Jayaraman, R. (2013). *A Study of Operating Practices and Supply Chains in the e-Commerce Online Retail Businesses in India.* Retrieved September 16, 2018, from http://www.publishingindia.com/jscms/41/a-study-of-operating-practices-and-supply-chains-in-the-e-commerce-online-retail-businesses-in-india/236/1781/

Jose, J. (2018, February 16). Last mile intra-city logistics: The key to e-commerce customer satisfaction - Re-Tales by Jolly Jose. *ET Retail.* Retrieved September 18, 2018, from https://retail.economictimes.indiatimes.com/re-tales/last-mile-intra-city-logistics-the-key-to-e-commerce-customer-satisfaction/2900

Kola, V. (2017, August 2). *E-commerce-focused logistics companies riding the wave in India*. Retrieved September 18, 2018, from https://yourstory.com/2017/08/e-commerce-focussed-logistics-companies-riding-the-wave-in-india/

KPMG. (2016, August). *India's e-commerce retail logistics growth story*. Retrieved September 12, 2018, from KPMG website: https://assets.kpmg.com/content/dam/kpmg/in/pdf/2016/08/E-commerce-retail-logistics-India.pdf

KPMG. (2018, May). *e-Commerce retail logistics in India*. Retrieved September 25, 2018, from KPMG website: https://assets.kpmg.com/content/dam/kpmg/in/pdf/2018/05/e-commerce-retail-logistics.pdf

Krishna, V. (2014, November 17). *How heavy is the reverse logistics burden for top e-com players in India*. Retrieved August 21, 2018, from https://www.vccircle.com/how-heavy-reverse-logistics-burden-top-e-com-players-india/

Krishna, V. (2017, February 27). *Why the unit economics of Flipkart (and competitors) will not work for another decade*. Retrieved August 4, 2018, from https://yourstory.com/2017/02/unit-economics-flipkart/

Manoj, S. N. K. (2015, April 22). *Barriers to Reverse Logistics in E-Commerce industry in India*. Retrieved August 19, 2018, from https://www.linkedin.com/pulse/barriers-reverse-logistics-e-commerce-industry-india-k/

Mukherjee, R. (2016, November 10). *The unsolved problem of E-Commerce Industries: Reverse Logistics!* Retrieved August 8, 2018, from https://in.thehackerstreet.com/problem-e-commerce-reverse-logistics/

Mukul, P. (2018, April 6). *E-commerce firms losing over 30 per cent of GMV due to cancellations/returns*. Retrieved September 28, 2018, from https://indianexpress.com/article/business/business-others/e-commerce-firms-losing-over-30-per-cent-of-gmv-due-to-cancellations-returns-5125471/

PTI. (2018, July 6). E-tailers exploring ways to improve reverse logistics costs: Study. *ET Retail*. Retrieved August 10, 2018, from https://retail.economictimes.indiatimes.com/news/e-commerce/e-tailing/e-tailers-exploring-ways-to-improve-reverse-logistics-costs-study/64878780

PwC India. (2020). *Research & insights, 2018, Propelling India towards global leadership in e-commerce*. Author.

RedSeer. (2018, May). *Ecommerce industry in India*. Retrieved September 21, 2018, from https://redseer.com/reports/ecommerce-industry-in-india/

'Return Guaranteed' – Indian E-commerce and the issue of Reverse Logistics! (2017, August 22). Retrieved August 20, 2018, from https://trak.in/tags/business/2012/06/22/indian-ecommerce-return-policy-logistics/

Richer, S. (2017, March 27). *Nimble Reverse Logistics in e-Commerce*. Retrieved August 23, 2018, from https://industrytoday.com/article/nimble-reverse-logistics-in-e-commerce/

Saleh, K. (n.d.). *E-commerce Product Return Rate – Statistics and Trends* [Infographic]. Retrieved September 9, 2018, from https://www.invespcro.com/blog/ecommerce-product-return-rate-statistics/

Samad & Chowdhary. (n.d.). *Cash-On-Delivery and Reverse Logistics*. Retrieved September 4, 2018, from https://www.etcases.com/cash-delivery-reverse-logistics-marketing-case-study.html

Sekar. (n.d.). *eCommerce Support On Reverse Logistics In India*. Retrieved August 21, 2018, from http://www.theinternationaljournal.org/ojs/index.php?journal=rjebs&page=article&op=view&path[]=1378

Shah, N. (2018, June 22). *Reverse Logistics for Ecommerce: Understanding The Basics*. Retrieved September 1, 2018, from https://www.shiprocket.in/blog/reverse-logistics-for-ecommerce/

Singh, S. (2017, September 12). *Is a 30-day return policy still necessary in ecommerce? Sellers answer*. Retrieved August 16, 2018, from https://indianonlineseller.com/2017/09/30-day-return-policy-in-ecommerce/

Thiyagarajan, G., & Ali, S. (2016, May). *Reverse Logistics of e-Commerce in India - Controls, Cost and Clearance*. Retrieved August 15, 2018, from https://www.thecasecentre.org/programmeAdmin/products/view&&id=144830

Thiyagarajan, G., & Ali, S. (2016, May 19). *Analysis of Reverse Logistics Implementation Barriers in Online Retail Industry*. Retrieved September 8, 2018, from https://www.indjst.org/index.php/indjst/article/view/94193

Yourstory. (2019, Nov.). *Ecommerce paradox: Flipkart and Amazon India continue to make losses, but there's a silver lining*. https://yourstory.com/2019/11/flipkart-amazon-india-losses-ecommerce-walmart

ENDNOTE

1 Marketplace Model is an online store (marketplace) where multiple sellers/ vendors come together to sell their products to customers. The store is owned by the administrator, who invites multiple sellers/vendors in the exchange of a commission or a fixed listing fee (https://vinsol.com/blog/2019/05/10/marketplace-model/).

Compilation of References

Adjei-Nsiah, S., Owurak, S. D., & Kuyper, T. W. (2012). Exploring opportunities for enhancing innovation in agriculture: The case of oil palm production in Ghana. *The Journal of Agricultural Science*, *4*(10), 212–223.

AGROINLOG. (2020). *AGROINLOG, Integrated Biomass Logistics Centres for the agro industry*. Retrieved from http://agroinlog-h2020.eu/en/home/

Ajam, M., Alshawi, M., & Mezher, T. (2010). Augmented process model for e-tendering: Towards integrating object models with document management systems. *Automation in Construction*, *19*(6), 762–778. doi:10.1016/j.autcon.2010.04.001

Akhtar, P., Tse, Y.K., Khan, Z., & Rao-Nicholson, R. (2016). Data-driven and adaptive leadership contributing to sustainability: global agri-food supply chains connected with emerging markets. *International Journal of Production Economics*. doi:10.1016/j.ijpe.2015.11.013

Akintola Akintoye, G. M. (2000). A survey of supply chain collaboration and management in construction industry. *European Journal of Purchasing & Supply Management*, 159-168.

Akintoye, A., McIntosh, G., & Fitzgerald, E. (2000). A survey of supply chain collaboration and management in the UK construction industry. *European Journal of Purchasing & Supply Management, 6*(3-4), 159-168.

Akintoye, A., McIntosh, G., & Fitzgerald, E. (2000). A survey of supply chain collaboration and management in the UK construction industry. *European Journal of Purchasing & Supply Management*, *6*(3), 159–168. doi:10.1016/S0969-7012(00)00012-5

Al Rostamani Group. (2019). http://www.alrostamanigroup.ae/sites/en/Pages/SubCompanyDetails.aspx?ItemID=10

Albayrak, E., & Erensal, Y. C. (2004). Using analytic hierarchy process (AHP) to improve human performance: An application of multiple criteria decision making problem. *Journal of Intelligent Manufacturing*, *15*(4), 491–503. doi:10.1023/B:JIMS.0000034112.00652.4c

Aleid, F., Rogerson, S., & Fairweather, B. (2009). Factors affecting consumers adoption of ecommerce in Saudi Arabia from a consumers' perspective. *IADIS International Conference e-Commerce*, 11-18.

Alfredo Serpell, B. H. (2004). Supply chain management in construction: Diagnosis and application issues. *Globalisation and Construction*, 455-466.

Al-Futtaim Carillion. (2019). Available at http://www.afcarillion.ae/

Al-Ghaith, W., Sanzogni, L., & Sandhu, K. (2010). Factors influencing the adoption and usage of online services in Saudi Arabia. *The Electronic Journal on Information Systems in Developing Countries*, *40*(1), 1–32. doi:10.1002/j.1681-4835.2010.tb00283.x

Ali, A. S., Mohd-Don, Z., Alias, A., Kamaruzzaman, S. N., & Pitt, M. (2010). The performance of construction partnering projects in Malaysia. *International Journal of Physical Sciences*, *5*(4), 327–333.

Ali, A., Mahfouz, A., & Arisha, A. (2017). Analysing supply chain resilience: Integrating the constructs in a concept mapping framework via a systematic literature review. *Supply Chain Management*, *22*(1), 16–39. doi:10.1108/SCM-06-2016-0197

Alma Spaho, T. M. (2012). Supply Chain Management in Albania: An Empirical Study. *EuroEconomica*, (1), 17-24.

Almog-Bareket, G. (2012). Visionary leadership in business schools: An institutional framework. *Journal of Management Development*, *31*(4), 431–440. doi:10.1108/02621711211219086

Al-Werikat, G. (2017, March). Supply Chain Management in Construction; Revealed. *International Journal of Scientific & Technology Research*, *6*(3), 106–110.

Alyoubi, A. A. (2015). E-commerce in Developing Countries and how to Develop them during the Introduction of Modern Systems. *Procedia Computer Science*, *65*, 479–483. doi:10.1016/j.procs.2015.09.127

Amit, R., & Zott, C. (2001). Value creation in e-business. *Strategic Management Journal*, *22*(6-7), 493–520. doi:10.1002mj.187

Andersen, K. V., Bjorn-Andersen, N., & Dedrick, J. (2003). Governance initiatives creating a demand-driven e-commerce approach: The case of Denmark. *The Information Society*, *19*(1), 95–105. doi:10.1080/01972240309475

Anderson, J. C., & Narus, J. A. (1990). A model of distributor firm and manufacturer firm working partnerships. *The Journal of Marketing*, 42-58.

Andrew, R. J., & Dainty, G. H. (2001). Subcontractor perspectives on supply chain alliances. *Construction Management and Economics*, *19*(8), 841–848. doi:10.1080/01446190110089727

Ang, D., Griffin, T., Goodson, J., & Ho, J. (2010). Enterprise System Education through Supply Chain Management. *Contemporary Management Research*, *6*(1), 3–10. doi:10.7903/cmr.2666

An, H. J., & Searcy, S. W. (2012). Economic and energy evaluation of a logistics system based on biomass modules. *Biomass and Bioenergy*, *46*, 190–202. doi:10.1016/j.biombioe.2012.09.002

Anitha, P., & Patil, M. M. (2018) A Review on Data Analytics for Supply Chain Management A Case study. *International Journal of Information Engineering and Electronic Business, 5*, 30-39. Available at https://business.fiu.edu/centers/ryder/pdf/SCM_in_Emerging_Mkts-Mexico.pdf

Annevelink, E., van Gogh, B., Nogués, F. S., Espatolero, S., De la Cruz, T., Luzzini, D., . . . Olsson, J. (2017). *Conceptual description of an Integrated Biomass Logistics Centre (IBLC).* Paper presented at the European Biomass Conference & Exhibition 2017, Stockholm, Sweden.

Anuar, A., & Yusuff, R. M. (2011). Manufacturing best practices in Malaysian small and medium enterprises (SMEs). *Benchmarking, 18*(3), 324–341. doi:10.1108/14635771111137750

APICS. (2015). *Next Generation Supply Chain Leader.* APICS SCC Report.

Arabian Business. (2018). *Abu Dhabi deploys drones to inspect construction sites.* Available at https://www.arabianbusiness.com/technology/401936-wkd-abu-dhabi-deploys-drones-to-inspect-construction-sites

Arabian Industry. (2015). *UAE construction to grow by 9.3% in 2015.* Available at https://www.arabianindustry.com/construction/news/2015/may/11/uae-construction-to-grow-by-93-in-2015-5036161/

Arayici, Y., & Coates, P. (2012). A system engineering perspective to knowledge transfer: a case study approach of BIM adoption. In *Virtual Reality-Human Computer Interaction.* InTech. doi:10.5772/51052

Armstrong, E. (2006). Buying–and selling–transportation. *Paperboard Packaging, 91*(9), 40–42.

Azambuja, M., Alves, T., Leite, F., & Gong, J. (2012). Leveraging building information models to support supply chain decisions in construction projects. In *Construction Research Congress: Construction Challenges in a Flat World* (pp. 747-756). 10.1061/9780784412329.076

Aziz, N. A., Ahmad, R., & Durai, D. D. (2012, January). B2B collaboration method through trust values for e-supply chain integrator: a case study of Malaysian construction industry. In *Fourth International Conference on Machine Vision (ICMV 2011): Computer Vision and Image Analysis; Pattern Recognition and Basic Technologies* (Vol. 8350, p. 835031). International Society for Optics and Photonics. 10.1117/12.920549

Babatunde, B. O., Gbadeyan, R. A., & Bamiduro, J. A. (2015). Supply Chain Management Practices and Market Performance: Evidence from Selected Major Marketers of Petroleum Products in Nigeria. *Pacific Journal of Science and Technology, 7*(1), 129–139.

Badi, S., & Murtagh, N. (2019). Green supply chain management in construction: A systematic literature review and future research agenda. *Journal of Cleaner Production, 223*, 312–322. doi:10.1016/j.jclepro.2019.03.132

Balasubramanian, S., & Shukla, V. (2017). Green supply chain management: The case of the construction sector in the United Arab Emirates (UAE). *Production Planning and Control, 28*(14), 1116–1138. doi:10.1080/09537287.2017.1341651

Ballou, R. H. (2007). *Business Logistics/Supply Chain Management, 5/E (With Cd)*. Pearson Education.

Baltacioglu, K., Yurt, O., & Kaplan, C. (2007). A New Framework for Service Supply Chain. *Service Industries Journal, 27*(2), 105–124. doi:10.1080/02642060601122629

Bao, J., Su, Z., & Jin, S. (2014). Building and Operation of Construction Supply Chain Information Integration Management Mode Based on Building Information Model. In *Proceedings of the 18th International Symposium on Advancement of Construction Management and Real Estate* (pp. 467-476). Springer. 10.1007/978-3-642-44916-1_46

Barlow Rick Dana. (2015). What ignites a progressive supply chain leader? *Healthcare Purchasing News, 39*(7), 10-13.

Basu, & Jeyasingam, & Habib. (2016). Education Supply Chain Management Model to Achieve Sustainability in Private Universities in Malaysia: A Review. *International Journal of Supply Chain Management, 5*(4), 24–37.

Batidzirai, B., Valk, M., Wicke, B., Junginger, M., Daioglou, V., Euler, W., & Faaij, A. P. C. (2016). Current and future technical, economic and environmental feasibility of maize and wheat residues supply for biomass energy application: Illustrated for South Africa. *Biomass and Bioenergy, 92*, 106–129.

Bayut. (2019). *What's the difference between freehold and free zone areas in Dubai?* Available at https://www.bayut.com/mybayut/freezone-vs-freehold-property-dubai/

Behneke, K., & Janssen, M. F. W. H. A. (2019). Boundary conditions for traceability in food supply chains using blockchain technology. *International Journal of Information Management*. Advance online publication. doi:10.1016/j.ijinfomgt.2019.05.025

Benton, J. A. (2010). *Construction Purchasing & Supply Chain Management*. McGraw-Hill.

Bergen, M., Dutta, S., & Walker, O. C. Jr. (1992). Agency Relationships in Marketing: A review of the Implications and Applications of Agency and Related Theories. *Journal of Marketing, 56*(July), 1–24. doi:10.1177/002224299205600301

Bergmann, R., & Rawlings, C. (1998). Transport management. In J. Gattoma (Ed.), *Strategic supply chain alignment: best practice in supply chain management* (Vol. 1, pp. 369–380). Gower.

Beske, P. (2012). Dynamic capabilities and sustainable supply chain management. *International Journal of Physical Distribution & Logistics Management, 42*(4), 372–387. doi:10.1108/09600031211231344

Bhargava, R. (2017, December). *The Growing Relevance of Reverse Logistics in India*. Retrieved September 5, 2018, from https://www.isb.edu/newsletters/almamatters/oct-dec-2017/relevanceofreverselogistics

Bhaskar, A. (2018, July 5). Product return remains a key challenge for online customers: Study. *Times of India*. Retrieved September 23, 2018, from https://timesofindia.indiatimes.com/business/india-business/product-return-remains-a-key-challenge-for-online-customers-study/articleshow/64873757.cms

Bigliardi, B., & Bottani, E. (2010). Performance measurement in the food supply chain: A balanced scorecard approach. *Facilities*, *28*(5/6), 249–260. doi:10.1108/02632771011031493

Birasnav, M., Mittal, R., & Loughlin, S. (2015). Linking Leadership Behaviors and Information Exchange to Improve Supply Chain Performance: A Conceptual Model. *Global Journal of Flexible Systems Managment*, *16*(2), 205–217. doi:10.100740171-015-0092-2

Blackburn, R., Lurz, K., Priesea, B., G¨ob, R., & Darkowa, I. L. (2015). A predictive analytics approach for demand forecasting in the process industry. *International Transactions in Operational Research*, *22*(3), 407–428. doi:10.1111/itor.12122

Blount, Y., Castleman, T., & Swatman, P. M. (2005). E-commerce, human resource strategies, and competitive advantage: Two Australian banking case studies. *International Journal of Electronic Commerce*, *9*(3), 74–89. doi:10.1080/10864415.2005.11044335

Bø, E., & Grønland, S. E. (2012). Increased cooperation in the supply chains: how to reduce the need for transportation? In H. C. Dreyer & T. Foss (Eds.), Intelligent goods in transport systems. Trondheim: NTNU, Faculty of Engineering Science and Technology: Akademika Publishing.

Bø, E., & Hammervoll, T. (2010). Cost-based pricing of transportation servies in a wholesaler-carrier relationship: an MS Excel spreadsheet decision tool. *International Journal of Logistics: Research and Applications, 13*(3), 197-210.

Boone, T., Ganeshan, R., Jain, A., & Sanders, N. R. (2019). Forecasting sales in the Supply Chain: Consumer analytics in the big data era. *International Journal of Forecasting*, *35*(1), 170–180. doi:10.1016/j.ijforecast.2018.09.003

Bottani, E., Montanari, R., & Volpi, A. (2010). The impact of RFID and EPC network on the bullwhip effect in the Italian FMCG supply chain. *International Journal of Production Economics*, *124*(2), 426–432. doi:10.1016/j.ijpe.2009.12.005

Boute, R. N., Disney, S. M., Lambrecht, M. R., & Van Houdt, B. (2007). An integrated production and inventory model to dampen upstream demand variability in the supply chain. *European Journal of Operational Research*, *178*(1), 121–142. doi:10.1016/j.ejor.2006.01.023

Bowersox, D. J., Closs, D. J., & Cooper, M. B. (2002). *Supply Chain Logistics Management*. McGraw-Hill.

Bowman, R. (1994). *Rookie transportation buyers*. Distribution.

Braga, C. A. P. (2005). E-commerce regulation: New game, new rules? *The Quarterly Review of Economics and Finance*, *45*(2-3), 541–558. doi:10.1016/j.qref.2004.12.019

Bresnen, M. J., & Haslam, C. O. (1991). Construction industry clients: A survey of their attributes and project management practices. *Construction Management and Economics*, *9*(4), 327–342. doi:10.1080/01446199100000026

Briscoe, G. H., Dainty, A. R., Millett, S. J., & Neale, R. H. (2004). Client-led strategies for construction supply chain improvement. *Construction Management and Economics*, *22*(2), 193–201. doi:10.1080/0144619042000201394

Briscoe, G., Dainty, A. R., & Millett, S. (2001). Construction supply chain partnerships: Skills, knowledge and attitudinal requirements. *European Journal of Purchasing & Supply Management*, *7*(4), 243–255. doi:10.1016/S0969-7012(01)00005-3

Brock, J. (2000). Information and communication technology in the small firm. *Enterprise and small business: Principles, practice and policy*, 384-408.

Brooksher, D. (1999). E-commerce and Logistics. *Traffic World*, *260*, 31.

Browntape. (2014, December 18). *Which Part of India is Contributing The Most to E-Commerce Growth?* Retrieved August 13, 2018, from http://www.iamwire.com/2014/12/part-india-contributing-e-commerce-growth/106607

Bureau, F. (2016, July 26). *Snapdeal fastest in refunds, beats Flipkart, Amazon*. Retrieved September 16, 2018, from https://www.financialexpress.com/industry/snapdeal-fastest-in-refunds-beats-flipkart-amazon/328761/

Burkert, M., Ivens, B. S., & Shan, J. (2012). Governance mechanisms in domestic and international buyer-supplier relationships: An empirical study. *Industrial Marketing Management*, *41*(3), 544–556. doi:10.1016/j.indmarman.2011.06.019

Burtonshaw-Gunn, S. A. R. L. (2004). Developments in Construction Supply Chain Management and Prime Contracting. In *1st International SCRI Symposium*, (pp. 334-347). Academic Press.

Bystriakova, N., Kapos, V., & Lysenko, I. (2004). *Bamboo Biodiversity*. UNEP-WCMC/INBAR.

Cagliano, R., Caniato, F., & Spina, G. (2006). The Linkage between Supply Chain Integration and Manufacturing Improvement Programs. *International Journal of Operations & Production Management*, *26*(3), 282–299. doi:10.1108/01443570610646201

Cao, Z., & Lumineau, F. (2015). Revisiting the interplay between contractual and relational governance: A qualitative and meta-analytic investigation. *Journal of Operations Management*, *33-34*(1), 15–42. doi:10.1016/j.jom.2014.09.009

Capaldo, A., & Giannoccaro, I. (2015). Interdependence and network-level trust in supply chain networks. A computational study. *Industrial Marketing Management*, *44*(1), 180–195. doi:10.1016/j.indmarman.2014.10.001

Chaffey, D., & Ellis-Chadwick, F. (2016). *Digital Marketing*. Prentice Hall.

Chakravarthy, B., & Lorange, P. (2008). Driving renewal: The entrepreneur-manager. *Journal of Business Strategy, 29*(2), 14-21. doi:10.1108%2F02756660810858116

Chandan, R. C. (2007). *Implementing HACCP* (6th ed.). Dairy India.

Chatfield, D. C., Kim, J. G., Harrison, T. P., & Hayya, J. C. (2004). The bullwhip effect-impact of stochastic lead time, information quality, and information sharing: A simulation study. *Production and Operations Management, 13*(4), 340–353. doi:10.1111/j.1937-5956.2004.tb00222.x

Chen, F., Drezner, Z., Ryan, J. K., & Simchi-Levi, D. (2000). Quantifying the bullwhip effect in a simple supply chain: The impact of forecasting, lead times, and information. *Management Science, 46*(3), 436–443. doi:10.1287/mnsc.46.3.436.12069

Chenga, J. C. (2011). A web service framework for measuring and monitoring environmental and carbon footprint in construction supply chains. *Procedia Engineering, 14*, 141–147. doi:10.1016/j.proeng.2011.07.016

Cheng, J. C., Law, K. H., Bjornsson, H., Jones, A., & Sriram, R. (2010). A service oriented framework for construction supply chain integration. *Automation in Construction, 19*(2), 245–260. doi:10.1016/j.autcon.2009.10.003

Cheng, J.-C., & Chou, C.-Y. (2008). A real-time inventory decision system using Western Electric run rules and ARMA control chart. *Expert Systems with Applications, 35*(3), 755–761. doi:10.1016/j.eswa.2007.07.019

Chen, J. V., Yen, D. C., Rajkumar, T. M., & Tomochko, N. A. (2011). The antecedent factors on trust and commitment in supply chain relationships. *Computer Standards & Interfaces, 33*(3), 262–270. doi:10.1016/j.csi.2010.05.003

Chen, P. H., Ong, C. F., & Hsu, S. C. (2016). The linkages between internationalization and environmental strategies of multinational construction firms. *Journal of Cleaner Production, 116*, 207–216. doi:10.1016/j.jclepro.2015.12.105

Child, J., & Tsai, T. (2005). The Dynamic Between Firms' Environmental Strategies and Institutional Constraints in Emerging Economies: Evidence from China and Taiwan. *Journal of Management Studies, 42*(1), 95–125. doi:10.1111/j.1467-6486.2005.00490.x

Chong, S., & Pervan, G. (2009). *Factors influencing the extent of deployment of electronic commerce for small-and medium-sized enterprises.* IGI Global. doi:10.4018/978-1-60566-126-1.ch013

Christopher, M. (2005). *Logistics and Supply Chain Management: Creating Value-Adding Networks* (3rd ed.). Pearson Education.

Christopher, M. (2012). Managing Supply Chain Complexity: Identifying the Requisite Skills. *Supply chain Forum. International Journal (Toronto, Ont.), 13*(2), 4–9.

Christopher, M., & Towill, D. R. (2002). Developing Market Specific Supply Chain Strategies. *International Journal of Logistics Management, 13*(1), 1–14. doi:10.1108/09574090210806324

CIPS. (2019). *Chartered Institute of Procurement and Supply*. Available at https://www.cips.org/en-ME/knowledge/procurement-topics-and-skills/srm-and-sc-management/global-supply-chains/

Cloete, E., Courtney, S., & Fintz, J. (2002). Small Businesses' Acceptance and Adoption of e-Commerce in the Western-Cape Province of South-Africa. *The Electronic Journal on Information Systems in Developing Countries*, *10*(1), 1–13. doi:10.1002/j.1681-4835.2002.tb00062.x

Colicchia, C., & Strozzi, F. (2012). Supply chain risk management: A new methodology for a systematic literature review. *Supply Chain Management*, *17*(4), 403–418. doi:10.1108/13598541211246558

Connect and Construct. (2019). *Top 10 Benefits of BIM in Construction*. Available at https://connect.bim360.autodesk.com/benefits-of-bim-in-construction

Construction Week Online. (2015). *UAE construction to grow by 9.3% in 2015*. Available at https://www.constructionweekonline.com/article-33629-uae-construction-to-grow-by-93-in-2015

Construction Week Online. (2017). *ECC awarded joint-venture project with McLaren Construction*. Available at https://www.constructionweekonline.com/article-45480-ecc-awarded-joint-venture-project-with-mclaren-construction

Construction Week Online. (2018). *Acciona unit wins Expo 2020 Dubai Sustainability Pavilion contract*. Available at https://www.constructionweekonline.com/article-50793-acciona-unit-wins-expo-2020-dubai-sustainability-pavilion-contract

Construction Week Online. (2019a). *Construction, building contribute $1.6bn to Abu Dhabi FDI in 2018*. Available at https://www.constructionweekonline.com/business/180938-construction-adds-16bn-to-abu-dhabi-fdi-in-2018

Construction Week Online. (2019b). *How has technology disrupted the Middle East's construction sector?* Available at https://www.constructionweekonline.com/products-services/180835-large-uae-contractors-opt-for-3d-printing-new-tech-to-implement-construction

Construction Week Online. (2019c). *ALEC deploys robotics to build Dubai's $1bn Marina Gate*. Available at https://www.constructionweekonline.com/projects-tenders/168633-uae-contractor-alec-uses-robotics-to-build-dubai-marina-gate-by-select-group

Construction Week Online. (2019d). *Inside a Dubai MEP company's modular design factory in Jebel Ali*. Available at https://www.constructionweekonline.com/products-services/168757-a-look-inside-bk-gulfs-game-changing-modular-construction-mep-factory-in-jebel-ali

Copacino, W. C. (1997). Electronic commerce: How it will affect logistics. *Logistics Management*, *36*, 39.

Costantino, F., Di Gravio, G., Shaban, A., & Tronci, M. (2014b). SPC-based inventory control policy to improve supply chain dynamics. *IACSIT International Journal of Engineering and Technology*, *6*(1), 418–426.

Costantino, F., Di Gravio, G., Shaban, A., & Tronci, M. (2014a). Inventory control system based on control charts to improve supply chain performances. *International Journal of Simulation Modelling, 13*(3), 263–275. doi:10.2507/IJSIMM13(3)1.263

Costantino, F., Di Gravio, G., Shaban, A., & Tronci, M. (2015a). A real-time SPC inventory replenishment system to improve supply chain performances. *Expert Systems with Applications, 42*(3), 1665–1683. doi:10.1016/j.eswa.2014.09.028

Costantino, F., Di Gravio, G., Shaban, A., & Tronci, M. (2015b). SPC forecasting system to mitigate the bullwhip effect and inventory variance in supply chains. *Expert Systems with Applications, 42*(3), 1773–1787. doi:10.1016/j.eswa.2014.09.039

Cox, A. W., Ireland, P., & Townsend, M. (2006). *Managing in Construction Supply Chains and Markets: Reactive and Proactive Options for Improving Performance and Relationship Management.* Thomas Telford.

CSCMP. (2019). Retrieved from Council of Supply Chain Management Professionals: https://cscmp.org/CSCMP/Academia/SCM_Definitions_and_Glossary_of_Terms/CSCMP/Educate/SCM_Definitions_and_Glossary_of_Terms.aspx?hkey=60879588-f65f-4ab5-8c4b-6878815ef921

Da Costa, S. E. G., & De Lima, E. P. (2009). Advanced manufacturing technology adoption: An integrated approach. *Journal of Manufacturing Technology Management, 20*(1), 74–96. doi:10.1108/17410380910925415

Dağdeviren, M., Yavuz, S., & Kılınç, N. (2009). Weapon selection using the AHP and TOPSIS methods under fuzzy environment. *Expert Systems with Applications, 36*(4), 8143–8151. doi:10.1016/j.eswa.2008.10.016

Dallasega, P., Marcher, C., Marengo, E., Rauch, E., Matt, D. T., & Nutt, W. (2016). *A decentralized and pull-based control loop for on-demand delivery in ETO construction supply chains.* International Group for Lean Construction.

Daniel, E., Wilson, H., & Myers, A. (2002). Adoption of e-commerce by SMEs in the UK: Towards a stage model. *International Small Business Journal, 20*(3), 253–270. doi:10.1177/0266242602203002

Danish, M., & Senjyu, T., MatinIbrahimi, A., Ahmadi, M., & Howlader, A. (2018). A Managed Framework for Energy-efficient Building. *Journal of Building Engineering.*

Danneels, E. (2002). The Dynamics of Product Innovation and Firm Competences. *Strategic Management Journal, 23*(12), 1095–1121. doi:10.1002mj.275

Das, M., Cheng, J. C., & Law, K. H. (2015). An ontology-based web service framework for construction supply chain collaboration and management. *Engineering, Construction, and Architectural Management, 22*(5), 551–572. doi:10.1108/ECAM-07-2014-0089

Davide Aloini, R. D. (2012). Supply chain management: A review of implementation risks in the construction industry. *Business Process Management Journal, 18*(5), 753–761. doi:10.1108/14637151211270135

Davis, T. (1993). Effective Supply Chain Management. *Sloan Management Review*, •••, 35–46.

de Man, J. C., & Strandhagen, J. O. (2017). An Industry 4.0 research agenda for sustainable business models. *Procedia CIRP*, *63*, 721–726. doi:10.1016/j.procir.2017.03.315

Defee, C. C., Esper, T., & Mollenkopf, D. (2009). Leveraging Closed-Loop Orientation and Leadership for Environmental Sustainability. *Supply Chain Management*, *14*(2), 87–98. doi:10.1108/13598540910941957

Dejonckheere, J., Disney, S. M., Lambrecht, M. R., & Towill, D. R. (2003). Measuring and avoiding the bullwhip effect: A control theoretic approach. *European Journal of Operational Research*, *147*(3), 567–590. doi:10.1016/S0377-2217(02)00369-7

Dejonckheere, J., Disney, S. M., Lambrecht, M. R., & Towill, D. R. (2004). The impact of information enrichment on the bullwhip effect in supply chains: A control engineering perspective. *European Journal of Operational Research*, *153*(3), 727–750. doi:10.1016/S0377-2217(02)00808-1

Denyer, D., & Tranfield, D. (2009). Producing a systematic review. In D. A. Buchanan & A. Bryman (Eds.), *The Sage handbook of organizational research methods* (pp. 671–689). Sage Publications Ltd.

Denyer, D., & Tranfield, D. (2009). Producing a systematic review. In D. A. Buchanan & A. Bryman (Eds.), *The SAGE handbook of organizational research methods* (pp. 671–689). Sage Publications Ltd.

Deokar, A., Raj, S., Jayakrishna, K., & Abdul Zubar, H. (2019). *Implementation of Lean Concepts Using Value Stream Mapping in Automotive Firm*. Advances in Manufacturing Technology. doi:10.1007/978-981-13-6374-0_17

DER. (2018). *Dubai Economic Report 2018*. Available at http://www.dubaided.ae/StudiesAndResearchDocument/Dubai-Economic-Report-2018-Full-Report.pdf

Deshpande, A. (2012). Supply chain management dimensions, supply chain performance and organizational performance: An integrated framework. *International Journal of Business and Management*, *7*(8), 2–19. doi:10.5539/ijbm.v7n8p2

DEWA. (2017). *3D-Printed Lab at Mohammed bin Rashid Al Maktoum Solar Park*. Available at https://www.dewa.gov.ae/en/about-us/media-publications/latest-news/2017/07/he-saeed-mohammed-al-tayer-visits-3d-printed-lab-at-mohammed-bin-rashid-al-maktoum-solar-park

Dhingra, A., Kumar, S., & Singh, B. (2019). Cost reduction and quality improvement through Lean-Kaizen concept using value stream map in Indian manufacturing firms. *International Journal of Systems Assurance & Engineering Management*.

Dike, I. U., & Kapogiannis, G. (2014). A conceptual model for improving construction supply chain performance. *Proceedings of the 30th Annual Association of Researchers in Construction Management Conference (ARCOM 2014)*.

DiMaggio, P., & Powell, W. W. (1983). The iron cage revisited: Collective rationality and institutional isomorphism in organizational fields. *American Sociological Review*, *48*(2), 147–160. doi:10.2307/2095101

Disney, S. M., Lambrecht, M., Towill, D. R., & Van de Velde, W. (2008). The value of coordination in a two-echelon supply chain. *IIE Transactions*, *40*(3), 341–355. doi:10.1080/07408170701488003

Dixit, N., & Datta, S. K. (2010). Customer's perception on internet banking and their impact on customer satisfaction and loyalty: A study in Indian context. *Journal of Computing*, *2*, 131–135.

Dominguez, R., Cannella, S., & Framinan, J. M. (2014). On bullwhip-limiting strategies in divergent supply chain networks. *Computers & Industrial Engineering*, *73*(1), 85–95. doi:10.1016/j.cie.2014.04.008

Dominguez, R., Cannella, S., & Framinan, J. M. (2015). The impact of the supply chain structure on bullwhip effect. *Applied Mathematical Modelling*, *39*(23–24), 7309–7325. doi:10.1016/j.apm.2015.03.012

Dominguez, R., Framinan, J. M., & Cannella, S. (2013). Serial vs. divergent supply chain networks: A comparative analysis of the bullwhip effect. *International Journal of Production Research*, *52*(7), 2194–2210. doi:10.1080/00207543.2013.860495

Doukidis, G. I., Lybereas, P., & Galliers, R. D. (1996). Information systems planning in small business: A stages of growth analysis. *Journal of Systems and Software*, *33*(2), 189–201. doi:10.1016/0164-1212(95)00183-2

Doukidis, G. L., Matopoulos, A., Vlachopoulou, M., Manthou, V., & Manos, B. (2007). A conceptual framework for supply chain collaboration: Empirical evidence from the agri-food industry. *Supply Chain Management*, *12*(3), 177–186. doi:10.1108/13598540710742491

Duan, Q., & Liao, T. W. (2013). A new age-based replenishment policy for supply chain inventory optimization of highly perishable products. *International Journal of Production Economics*, *145*(2), 658–671. doi:10.1016/j.ijpe.2013.05.020

Dubai Future Foundation. (2019a). *Office of the Future. The World's First 3D Printed Office*. Available at https://www.dubaifuture.gov.ae/our-initiatives/office-of-the-future/

Dubai Future Foundation. (2019b). *Dubai 3D printing strategy*. Available at https://www.dubaifuture.gov.ae/our-initiatives/dubai-3d-printing-strategy/

Dubai Metro. (2013). *UAE leads GCC with USD1.38trn projects; awaits Expo 2020 win*. Available at http://www.dubaimetro.eu/uae-leads-gcc-with-usd1-38trn-projects-awaits-expo-2020-win/

Dubey, R., Gunasekaran, A., & Samar Ali, S. (2015). Exploring the relationship between leadership, operational practices, institutional pressures and environmental performance: A framework for green supply chain. trajectories. *International Journal of Production Economics*, *160*, 120–132. doi:10.1016/j.ijpe.2014.10.001

Dubois, A., & Gadde, L. E. (2000). Supply strategy and network effects—purchasing behaviour in the construction industry. *European Journal of Purchasing & Supply Management*, *6*(3-4), 207-215.

Dubois, A., & Gadde, L. E. (2002). The construction industry as a loosely coupled system: Implications for productivity and innovation. *Construction Management and Economics*, *20*(7), 621–631. doi:10.1080/01446190210163543

DuBox. (2019). Available at https://www.dubox.me/

Duriau, V. J., Reger, R. K., & Pfarrer, M. D. (2007). A content analysis of the content analysis literature in organization studies: Research themes, data sources and methodological refinements. *Organizational Research Methods*, *10*(1), 5–34. doi:10.1177/1094428106289252

Dwivedi, Y. K., Papazafeiropoulo, A., & Scupola, A. (2009). SMEs'e-commerce adoption: Perspectives from Denmark and Australia. *Journal of Enterprise Information Management*, *22*(1/2), 152–166. doi:10.1108/17410390910932803

Dyer, J. H., & Chu, W. (2003). The role of trustworthiness in reducing cost of improving performance: Empirical evidence from the United States, Japan and Korea. *Organization Science*, *14*(1), 57–68. doi:10.1287/orsc.14.1.57.12806

Earnhart, D. H., Khanna, M., & Lyon, T. P. (2014). Corporate environmental strategies in emerging economies. *Review of Environmental Economics and Policy*, *8*(2), 164–185. doi:10.1093/reep/reu001

Ebadian, M., Sowlati, T., Sokhansanj, S., Stumborg, M., & Townley-Smith, L. (2011). A new simulation model for multi-agricultural biomass logistics system in bioenergy production. *Biosystems Engineering*, *110*(3), 280–290. doi:10.1016/j.biosystemseng.2011.08.008

Edarabia. (2019). *45 Free Zones in UAE (All Emirates).* Available at https://www.edarabia.com/45-free-zones-uae/

Ehrgott, M., Reimann, F., Kaufmann, L., & Crater, C. R. (2013). Environmental Development of Emerging Economy Suppliers: Antecedents and Outcomes. *Journal of Business Logistics*, *34*(2), 131–147. doi:10.1111/jbl.12015

Einav, L., Levin, J., Popov, I., & Sundaresan, N. (2014). Growth, adoption, and use of mobile e-commerce. *The American Economic Review*, *104*(5), 489–494. doi:10.1257/aer.104.5.489

Eisenhardt, K. E. (1989). Agency Theory: An Assessment and Review. *Academy of Management Review*, *14*(1), 57–74. doi:10.5465/amr.1989.4279003

Ellram, L. M., & Cooper, M. C. (1990). Supply chain management, partnership, and the shipper-third party relationship. *International Journal of Logistics Management*, *1*(2), 1–10.

Ellram, L. M., Tate, W. L., & Billington, C. (2004). Understanding and managing the services supply chain. *The Journal of Supply Chain Management*, *40*(4), 17–32. doi:10.1111/j.1745-493X.2004.tb00176.x

ETRetail. (2016, November 26). Flipkart report losses of Rs 2,306 crores in FY 16. *ET Retail.* Retrieved August 21, 2018, from https://retail.economictimes.indiatimes.com/news/e-commerce/e-tailing/flipkart-report-losses-of-rs-2306-crores-in-fy-16/55631416

Faaij, A. P., & Domac, J. (2006). Emerging international bio-energy markets and opportunities for socio-economic development. *Energy for Sustainable Development, 10*(1), 7–19.

FAO. (2017). *Faostat Crops.* Retrieved from http://www.fao.org/faostat/en/#data/QC/visualize

FCSA. (2019). *Federal Competitiveness and Statistics Authority.* Available at https://fcsa.gov.ae/ar-ae/Pages/home.aspx

FDI. (2014). *The Foreign Direct Investment Report 2014. Global Greenfield investment trends.* The Financial Times Limited.

Feizpour, M. A., & Mehrjardi, A. S. (2014). Comparative Advantages and Sustainable Development in Iranian Manufacturing Industries. *Indian Economic Review, 18*(1), 33–52.

Fernie, J. & Grant, D. B. (2019), *Fashion Logistics: Insights into the Fashion Retail Supply Chain.* Kogan Page Publishers.

Gaalman, G. (2006). Bullwhip reduction for ARMA demand: The proportional order-up-to policy versus the full-state-feedback policy. *Automatica, 42*(8), 1283–1290. doi:10.1016/j.automatica.2006.04.017

Galipoglu, E., Kotzab, H., Teller, C., Yumurtaci Huseyinoglu, I. Ö., & Popelbub, J. (2018). Omni-channel retailing research–state of the art and intellectual foundation. *International Journal of Physical Distribution & Logistics Management, 48*(4), 365–390. doi:10.1108/IJPDLM-10-2016-0292

Geissdoerfer, M., Savaget, P., Bocken, N. M., & Hultink, E. J. (2017). The Circular Economy–A new sustainability paradigm? *Journal of Cleaner Production, 143*, 757–768.

Geng, Y., Sarkis, J., Ulgiati, S., & Zhang, P. (2013). Measuring China's circular economy. *Science, 339*(6127), 1526–1527. doi:10.1126cience.1227059 PMID:23539584

Gertler, M. S. (2003). Tacit knowledge and the economic geography of context, or the undefinable tacitness of being (there). *Journal of Economic Geography, 3*(1), 75–99. doi:10.1093/jeg/3.1.75

Getuli, V., Ventura, S. M., Capone, P., & Ciribini, A. L. (2016). A BIM-based construction supply chain framework for monitoring progress and coordination of site activities. *Procedia Engineering, 164*, 542–549. doi:10.1016/j.proeng.2016.11.656

Ghobakhloo, M., Arias-Aranda, D., & Benitez-Amado, J. (2011). Adoption of e-commerce applications in SMEs. *Industrial Management & Data Systems, 111*(8), 1238–1269. doi:10.1108/02635571111170785

Ghosh, A., & Fedorowicz, J. (2008). The role of trust in supply chain governance. *Business Process Management Journal, 14*(4), 453–470. doi:10.1108/14637150810888019

Giang, D. T., & Pheng, L. S. (2011). Role of construction in economic development: Review of key concepts in the past 40 years. *Habitat International*, *35*(1), 118–125. doi:10.1016/j.habitatint.2010.06.003

Global Data. (2017). *Global Construction Outlook 2021*. Available at https://www.globaldata.com/store/report/gd-cn0004go--global-construction-outlook-2021/

Goffnett, S. P., & Goswami, A. (2016). Supply chain transformational leadership, supply chain innovation performance, and satisfaction with relationships and results: Moderating role of supply chain innovativeness. *International Journal of Logistics Systems & Management*, *24*(3), 356–382.

Gong, J., & Azambuja, M. (2013). Visualizing construction supply chains with google cloud computing tools. In *ICSDEC 2012: Developing the Frontier of Sustainable Design* (pp. 671–678). Engineering, and Construction.

Gong, Y., Jia, F., Brown, S., & Koh, S. C. L. (2018). Supply chain learning of sustainability in multi-tier supply chains: A resource orchestration perspective. *International Journal of Operations & Production Management*, *38*(4), 1061–1090. doi:10.1108/IJOPM-05-2017-0306

Gopalakrishnan. (2015). How to apply academic supply chain management: The Case of an International University. *Management*, *20*(1), 207-221.

Gosling, J., Jia, F., Gong, Y., & Brown, S. (2016). The role of supply chain leadership in the learning of sustainable practice: Toward an integrated framework. *Journal of Cleaner Production*, *137*, 1458–1469. doi:10.1016/j.jclepro.2014.10.029

Government.ae. (2019). *Crowdfunding*. Available at https://government.ae/en/information-and-services/business/crowdfunding

Goyal, G. K., & Alam, T. (2007). *Semi automatic packaging of milk and milk products* (6th ed.). Dairy India.

Green, K. (2007). *Analytics and Assessment: A New Imperative for Campus and IT Services*. Edu Connection, Sun Microsystems.

Guajardo, J. A., Cohen, M. A., Kim, S.-H., & Netessine, S. (2011). Impact of performance-based contracting on product reliability: An empirical analysis. guimaraes, T., Igbaria,M. (2008). characteristics of the research on reverse logistics. *International Journal of Production Research*.

Gulf News. (2019a). *Foreign direct investments to UAE expected to rise by 20% in 2019*. Available at https://gulfnews.com/business/foreign-direct-investments-to-uae-expected-to-rise-by-20-in-2019-1.63143316

Gulfnews. (2019b). *Partial title deeds law opens up investor pools for Dubai*. Available at https://gulfnews.com/business/property/partial-title-deeds-law-opens-up-investor-pools-for-dubai-1.65030251

Gulfnews. (2019c). *UAE is most advanced drones market in Middle East*. Available at https://gulfnews.com/technology/uae-is-most-advanced-drones-market-in-middle-east-1.2104797

Gunasekaran, A., Reichhart, A., & Holweg, M. (2007). Creating the customer-responsive supply chain: A reconciliation of concepts. *International Journal of Operations & Production Management, 27*(11), 1144–1172. doi:10.1108/01443570710830575

Habib, M., & Jungthirapanich, C. (2009). Research framework of education supply chain, research supply chain and educational management for the universities. *International Journal of the Computer, the Internet and Management, 17*(24), 1-8.

Habib, M. M., & Jungthirapanich, C. (2008). An integrated framework for research and education supply chain for the universities. *Proceedings of 4th IEEE International Conference on Management of Innovation and Technology*, 1027-1032. 10.1109/ICMIT.2008.4654509

Hall, C. (2002). *Profile of SMEs and SME Issues in APEC, 1990-2000.* Academic Press.

Halldórsson, A., & Skjøtt-Larsen, T. (2004). Developing logistics competencies through third party logistics relationships. *International Journal of Operations & Production Management, 24*(2), 192–206. doi:10.1108/01443570410514885

Hammervoll, T., & Bø, E. (2010). Shipper- Carrier Integration - overcomming the transparency problem through trust and collaboration. *European Journal of Marketing, 44*(7/8), 1121–1139. doi:10.1108/03090561011047553

Hampson, K., Kraatz, J. A., & Sanchez, A. X. (2014). The global construction industry and R&D. In *R&D Investment and Impact in the Global Construction Industry* (pp. 42–61). Routledge. doi:10.4324/9781315774916

Hannon, D. (2005a). *Negotiating skills a must for logistics buyers.* Purchasing.

Harland, C. M., Caldwell, N. D., Powell, P., & Zheng, J. (2007). Barriers to supply chain information integration: SMEs adrift of eLands. *Journal of Operations Management, 25*(6), 1234–1254. doi:10.1016/j.jom.2007.01.004

Harrington, L. H. (1997). *The ABC's of Motor Carrier Economics.* Transportation & Distribution.

Hartmut Stadtler, C. K. (2005). *Supply Chian Management and Advanced Planning* (3rd ed.). Springer. doi:10.1007/b106298

Hatmoko, J. U. D. (2008). *The impact of supply chain management practice on construction project performance* (Doctoral dissertation). Newcastle University.

Hatten, T. S. (2015). *Small business management: Entrepreneurship and beyond.* Nelson Education.

Heidelberg.Bassioni, H. A., Price, A. D., & Hassan, T. M. (2004). Performance measurement in construction. *Journal of Management Engineering, 20*(2), 42–50. doi:10.1061/(ASCE)0742-597X(2004)20:2(42)

Hjort, K., Hellström, D., Karlsson, S., & Oghazi, P. (2019). Typology of practices for managing consumer returns in internet retailing. *International Journal of Physical Distribution & Logistics Management, 49*(7), 767–790. doi:10.1108/IJPDLM-12-2017-0368

Horvat, A., Behdani, B., Fogliano, V., & Luning, P. (2019). A systems approach to dynamic performance assessment in new food product development. *Trends in Food Science & Technology*, *91*, 330–338. doi:10.1016/j.tifs.2019.07.036

Ho, W., Hashim, H., & Lim, J. (2014). Integrated biomass and solar town concept for a smart eco-village in Iskandar Malaysia (IM). *Renewable Energy*, *69*, 190–201.

How, B. S., Tan, K. Y., & Lam, H. L. (2016). Transportation decision tool for optimisation of integrated biomass flow with vehicle capacity constraints. *Journal of Cleaner Production*, *136*, 197–223.

Hsu, C., Tan, K., & Mohamad Zailani, S. (2016). Strategic orientations, sustainable supply chain initiatives, and reverse logistics. *International Journal of Operations & Production Management*, *36*(1), 86–110. doi:10.1108/IJOPM-06-2014-0252

Hult, G. T. M., Ketchen, D. J., & Arrfelt, M. (2007). Strategic supply chain management: Improving performance through a culture of competitiveness and knowledge development. *Strategic Management Journal*, *28*(10), 1035–1052. doi:10.1002mj.627

Iacovou, C. L., Benbasat, I., & Dexter, A. S. (1995). Electronic data interchange and small organizations: Adoption and impact of technology. *Management Information Systems Quarterly*, *19*(4), 465–485. doi:10.2307/249629

IBEF. (2020). *Indian ecommerce Industry Report, February 2020*. India Brand Equity Foundation.

Immensa Technology Labs. (2019). *How 3D printing is impacting the construction industry in UAE and globally*. Available at https://www.immensalabs.com/how-3d-printing-is-impacting-the-construction-industry-in-uae-and-globally/

Instat. (2019). Retrieved from Instituti i Statistikes: http://www.instat.gov.al/al/temat/industria-tregtia-dhe-sh%C3%ABrbimet/nd%C3%ABrtimi/#tab2

Intan Salwani, M., Marthandan, G., Daud Norzaidi, M., & Choy Chong, S. (2009). E-commerce usage and business performance in the Malaysian tourism sector: Empirical analysis. *Information Management & Computer Security*, *17*(2), 166–185. doi:10.1108/09685220910964027

Intelligence, B. I. (2016, October 10). *The Reverse Logistics Report: How retailers can save money by making returns smoother in the e-commerce age*. Retrieved September 13, 2018, from https://www.businessinsider.com/reverse-logistics-and-reverse-supply-chain-research-returns-recalls-repairs-and-end-of-life-returns-2016-10

Ireland, R. D., & Webb, J. W. (2007). A multi-theoretic perspective on trust and power in strategic supply chains. *Journal of Operations Management*, *25*(2), 482–497. doi:10.1016/j.jom.2006.05.004

Irizarry, J., Karan, E. P., & Jalaei, F. (2013). Integrating BIM and GIS to improve the visual monitoring of construction supply chain management. *Automation in Construction*, *31*, 241–254. doi:10.1016/j.autcon.2012.12.005

Jayaraman, R. (2013). *A Study of Operating Practices and Supply Chains in the e-Commerce Online Retail Businesses in India*. Retrieved September 16, 2018, from http://www.publishingindia.com/jscms/41/a-study-of-operating-practices-and-supply-chains-in-the-e-commerce-online-retail-businesses-in-india/236/1781/

Jingura, R. M., & Matengaifa, R. (2008). The potential for energy production from crop residues in Zimbabwe. *Biomass and Bioenergy*, *32*(12), 1287–1292.

John, T., & Mentzer, W. D. (2001). Defining Supply Chain Management. *Journal of Business Logistics*, *22*(2), 1–24. doi:10.1002/j.2158-1592.2001.tb00001.x

Jones, G. R. (1983). Transaction costs, property rights, and organizational culture: An exchange perspective. *Administrative Science Quarterly*, *28*(3), 454–467. doi:10.2307/2392252

Joong-Kun Cho, J., Ozment, J., & Sink, H. (2008). Logistics capability, logistics outsourcing and firm performance in an e-commerce market. *International Journal of Physical Distribution & Logistics Management*, *38*(5), 336–359. doi:10.1108/09600030810882825

Jose, J. (2018, February 16). Last mile intra-city logistics: The key to e-commerce customer satisfaction - Re-Tales by Jolly Jose. *ET Retail*. Retrieved September 18, 2018, from https://retail.economictimes.indiatimes.com/re-tales/last-mile-intra-city-logistics-the-key-to-e-commerce-customer-satisfaction/2900

Kabango, C. M., & Asa, A. R. (2015). Factors influencing e-commerce development: Implications for the developing countries. *International Journal of Innovation and Economics Development*, *1*(1), 64–72. doi:10.18775/ijied.1849-7551-7020.2015.11.2006

Kagermann, H., Helbig, J., Hellinger, A., & Wahlster, W. (2013). *Recommendations for Implementing the Strategic Initiative INDUSTRIE 4.0: Securing the Future of German Manufacturing Industry, acatech*. Irizarry.

Kapurubandara, M., & Lawson, R. (2006). Barriers to Adopting ICT and e-commerce with SMEs in developing countries: an Exploratory study in Sri Lanka. University of Western Sydney.

Karpinski, R. (1999). The Logistics Of E-Business. *InternetWeek*, 1-3.

Keikha, A., Hoveida, R., & Yaghoubi, N. M. (2017). The Development of an Intelligent Leadership Model for State Universities. *Foresight and STI Governance*, *11*(1), 66–74. doi:10.17323/2500-2597.2017.1.66.74.

Kets de Vries, M. (2006). *The Leadership Mystique*. Pearson.

Khanna, T., Palepu, K. G., & Sinha, J. (2005, June). Strategies That Fit Emerging Markets. *Harvard Business Review*, 4–18. PMID:15938439

Kim, D., Jean, R. J. B., & Sinkovics, R. R. (2018). Drivers of virtual interfirm integration and its impact on performance in international customer esupplier relationships. *Management International Review*, *58*(3), 495–522. doi:10.100711575-018-0344-4

Kim, I., & Springer, M. (2008). Measuring endogenous supply chain volatility: Beyond the bullwhip effect. *European Journal of Operational Research, 189*(1), 172–193. doi:10.1016/j.ejor.2007.05.012

Kim, N., Moon, J. J., & Yin, H. (2016). Environmental pressure and the performance of foreign firms in an emerging economy. *Journal of Business Ethics, 137*(3), 475–490. doi:10.100710551-015-2568-6

Kisperska-Moroń, D. (2013). Required Skill Set for the Supply Chain Manager in Changing Economic Reality. *Journal of Economics & Management, 11*, 34–48.

Kola, V. (2017, August 2). *E-commerce-focused logistics companies riding the wave in India.* Retrieved September 18, 2018, from https://yourstory.com/2017/08/e-commerce-focussed-logistics-companies-riding-the-wave-in-india/

Korczynski, M. (1996). The low-trust route to economic development: Inter-firm relations in the UK engineering construction industry in the 1980s and 1990s. *Journal of Management Studies, 33*(6), 787–808. doi:10.1111/j.1467-6486.1996.tb00172.x

Kothman, I., & Faber, N. (2016). How 3D printing technology changes the rules of the game: Insights from the construction sector. *Journal of Manufacturing Technology Management, 27*(7), 932–943. doi:10.1108/JMTM-01-2016-0010

KPMG. (2016, August). *India's e-commerce retail logistics growth story*. Retrieved September 12, 2018, from KPMG website: https://assets.kpmg.com/content/dam/kpmg/in/pdf/2016/08/E-commerce-retail-logistics-India.pdf

KPMG. (2018, May). *e-Commerce retail logistics in India*. Retrieved September 25, 2018, from KPMG website: https://assets.kpmg.com/content/dam/kpmg/in/pdf/2018/05/e-commerce-retail-logistics.pdf

Kraatz, J. A., & Sanchez, A. X. (2014). R&D Investment and Impact in the Global Construction Industry. Routledge.

Krishna, V. (2014, November 17). *How heavy is the reverse logistics burden for top e-com players in India*. Retrieved August 21, 2018, from https://www.vccircle.com/how-heavy-reverse-logistics-burden-top-e-com-players-india/

Krishna, V. (2017, February 27). *Why the unit economics of Flipkart (and competitors) will not work for another decade*. Retrieved August 4, 2018, from https://yourstory.com/2017/02/unit-economics-flipkart/

Krishnan, R. T., & Jha, S. K. (2011). Innovation Strategies in Emerging Markets: What Can We Learn from Indian Market Leaders. *ASCI Journal of Management, 41*(1), 21–45.

Krosch, L. (2002). E-Commerce Regulations 2002— UK. *Computer Law & Security Review, 18*(4), 252–258. doi:10.1016/S0267-3649(02)00705-7

Kruja, A. (2013). Entrepreneurship and knowledge-based economies. *Revista Românească pentru Educaţie Multidimensională, 5*(1), 7-17.

Kruja, A. D. (2020). *Enterprise Investments, Innovation and Performance: Evidence from Albania* (Vol. 11). International Journal of Innovation in the Digital Economy.

Kumar, V. A., & Rai, S. (2017). Role of human resource flexibility in Organizational performance: A study of Indian IT firms. *International Journal of Indian Culture and Business Management, 14*(3), 306–325. doi:10.1504/IJICBM.2017.083236

Kurano, T., McKay, K. N., & Black, G. W. (2014). Proactive inventory policy intervention to mitigate risk within cooperative supply chains. *International Journal of Industrial Engineering Computations, 5*(2), 249–264. doi:10.5267/j.ijiec.2013.11.006

Kurnia, S., Choudrie, J., Mahbubur, R. M., & Alzougool, B. (2015). E-commerce technology adoption: A Malaysian grocery SME retail sector study. *Journal of Business Research, 68*(9), 1906–1918. doi:10.1016/j.jbusres.2014.12.010

Kyobe, M. E. (2010). E-Crime and Non-Compliance with Government Regulations on E-Commerce: Barriers to E-Commerce Optimization in South African SMEs. In *E-Commerce Adoption and Small Business in the Global Marketplace: Tools for Optimization* (pp. 47–66). IGI Global. doi:10.4018/978-1-60566-998-4.ch003

Laaksonen, T., Pajunen, K., & Kulmala, H. I. (2008). Co-evolution of trust and dependence in customer-supplier relationships. *Industrial Marketing Management, 37*(8), 910–920. doi:10.1016/j.indmarman.2007.06.007

Lamers, P., Tan, E. C. D., Searcy, E. M., Scarlata, C. J., Cafferty, K. G., & Jacobson, J. J. (2015). Strategic supply system design–a holistic evaluation of operational and production cost for a biorefinery supply chain. *Biofuels, Bioproducts and Biorefining, 9*(6), 648-660.

Lamming, R. C., Caldwell, N. D., Harrison, D. A., & Phillips, W. (2001). Transparency in supply relationships: Concept and practice. *The Journal of Supply Chain Management, 37*(3), 4–10. doi:10.1111/j.1745-493X.2001.tb00107.x

Lange, E. (2018). The Supply Chain leader of the future. *Anaplan blog*. https://www.anaplan.com/blog/supply-chain-leader-future/

Langley, C. J. J. (2007). Collaboration: the only way forward. Capgemini, 2007 Third-Party Logistics. Results and Findings of the 12th Annual Study, 44.

Latham, S. M. (1994). *Constructing the team: Final report of the government/industry review of procurement and contractual arrangements in the UK construction industry. HM Stationery Office*. HMSO.

Leal, M. R. L. V., Galdos, M. V., Scarpare, F. V., Seabra, J. E. A., Walter, A., & Oliveira, C. O. F. (2013). Sugarcane straw availability, quality, recovery and energy use: A literature review. *Biomass and Bioenergy, 53*, 11–19.

LEED. (2015). *Top 10 countries for LEED in 2015*. Retrieved January 21, 2016, from https://www.usgbc.org/2015top10countries

Lee, G.-G., & Lin, H.-F. (2005). Customer perceptions of e-service quality in online shopping. *International Journal of Retail & Distribution Management*, *33*(2), 161–176. doi:10.1108/09590550510581485

Lee, H. L., Padmanabhan, V., & Whang, S. (1997). Information Distortion in a Supply Chain: The Bullwhip Effect. *Management Science*, *43*(4), 546–558. doi:10.1287/mnsc.43.4.546

Lee, H. T., & Wu, J. C. (2006). A study on inventory replenishment policies in a two-echelon supply chain system. *Computers & Industrial Engineering*, *51*(2), 257–263. doi:10.1016/j.cie.2006.01.005

Lim, S. F. W., Jin, X., & Srai, J. S. (2018). Consumer-driven e-commerce. *International Journal of Physical Distribution & Logistics Management*, *48*(3), 308–332. doi:10.1108/IJPDLM-02-2017-0081

Lindley, D. V., & Lindley, D. V. (1985). *Making decisions*. Wiley.

Linton, J., Klassen, R., & Jayaraman, V. (2007). Sustainable supply chains: An introduction. *Journal of Operations Management*, *25*(6), 1075–1082. doi:10.1016/j.jom.2007.01.012

Li, S., Ragu-Nathan, B., Ragu-Nathan, T. S., & Rao, S. S. (2006). The impact of supply chain management practices on competitive advantage and organizational performance. *Omega*, *34*(2), 107–124. doi:10.1016/j.omega.2004.08.002 PMID:17876965

Liu, W., Bai, E., Liu, L., & Wei, W. (2017). A Framework of Sustainable Service Supply Chain Management: A Literature Review and Research Agenda. *Sustainability*, *9*(3), 421. doi:10.3390u9030421

Li, Y., Li, G., & Feng, T. (2015). Effects of suppliers' trust and commitment on customer involvement. *Industrial Management & Data Systems*, *115*(6), 1041–1066. doi:10.1108/IMDS-11-2014-0351

Lockström, M., & Lei, L. (2013). Antecedents to supplier integration in China: A partial least squares analysis. *International Journal of Production Economics*, *141*(1), 295–306. doi:10.1016/j.ijpe.2012.08.007

Lockström, M., Schadel, J., Harrison, N., Moser, R., & Malhotra, M. K. (2010). Antecedents to supplier integration in the automotive industry: A multiple-case study of foreign subsidiaries in China. *Journal of Operations Management*, *28*(3), 240–256. doi:10.1016/j.jom.2009.11.004

Logan, M. S. (2000). Using Agency Theory to Design Successful Outsourcing Relationships. *International Journal of Logistics Management*, *11*(2), 21–32. doi:10.1108/09574090010806137

London, K. (2004). *Construction Supply Chain Procurement Modelling* (PhD thesis). The University of Melbourne.

Lorange, P. (2002). *New Vision for Management Education: Leadership Challenges*. Elsevier.

Macgregor, R. C., & Kartiwi, M. (2010). Perception of barriers to e-commerce adoption in SMEs in a developed and developing country: A comparison between Australia and Indonesia. *Journal of Electronic Commerce in Organizations*, *8*(1), 61–82. doi:10.4018/jeco.2010103004

Macgregor, R., Vrazalic, L., Carlsson, S., Bunker, D., & Magnusson, M. (2002). The impact of business size and business type on small business investment in electronic commerce: A study of swedish small businesses. *AJIS. Australasian Journal of Information Systems*, *9*(2). doi:10.3127/ajis.v9i2.189

Madas, M. (2014). *Building on ICT to Connect SMEs in the Digital Construction Supply Chain, Information Systems & e-Business Lab*. Available: http:// www.iseb.gr/blog/building-ict-connect-smes-digital-construction-supply-chain

Madhukar, B. A. (2017). *Construction Supply Chain Management. For Reeingeneering Construction Industry*. Available: http://www. builtconstructions.in/OnlineMagazine/Bangalore/Pages/Construction-Supply-Chain-Management-0114.aspx

Mahmoudi, M., Sowlati, T., & Sokhansanj, S. (2009). Logistics of supplying biomass from a mountain pine beetle-infested forest to a power plant in British Columbia. *Scandinavian Journal of Forest Research*, *24*(1), 76–86.

MajrouhiSardroud, J., & Limbachiya, M. C. (2010). *Integrated advance data storage technology for effective construction logistics management*. Academic Press.

Maku, T. C., Collins, T. R., & Beruvides, M. G. (2005). The impact of human interaction on supply chain management practices. *Performance Improvement*, *44*(7), 26–33. doi:10.1002/pfi.4140440708

Mangan, J., & Christopher, M. (2005). Management development and the supply chain manager of the future. *International Journal of Logistics Management*, *16*(2), 178–191. doi:10.1108/09574090510634494

Mangiaracina, R., Perego, A., Seghezzi, A., & Tumino, A. (2019). Innovative solutions to increase last-mile delivery efficiency in B2C e-commerce: A literature review. *International Journal of Physical Distribution & Logistics Management*, *49*(9), 901–920. doi:10.1108/IJPDLM-02-2019-0048

Mani, V., Agrawal, R., & Sharma, V. (2015). Supply chain social sustainability: A comparative case analysis in Indian manufacturing industries. *Procedia: Social and Behavioral Sciences*, *189*, 234–251. doi:10.1016/j.sbspro.2015.03.219

Manoj, S. N. K. (2015, April 22). *Barriers to Reverse Logistics in E-Commerce industry in India*. Retrieved August 19, 2018, from https://www.linkedin.com/pulse/barriers-reverse-logistics-e-commerce-industry-india-k/

Manuj, I., & Sahin, F. (2011). A model of supply chain and supply chain decision-making complexity. *International Journal of Physical Distribution & Logistics Management*, *41*(5), 511–549. doi:10.1108/09600031111138844

March, J. G., & Shapira, Z. (1987). Managerial perspectives on risk and risk taking. *Management Science*, *33*(11), 1404–1418. doi:10.1287/mnsc.33.11.1404

Markets and Markets. (2018). *3D Concrete Printing Market*. Available at https://www.marketsandmarkets.com/Market-Reports/3d-concrete-printing-market-10362292.html

Marshall, M. N. (1996). Sampling for qualitative research. *Family Practice*, *13*(6), 522–525. doi:10.1093/fampra/13.6.522 PMID:9023528

Martha, C., & Cooper, D. M. (1997). Supply Chain Management: More Than a New Name for Logistics. *International Journal of Logistics Management*, *8*(1), 1–13. doi:10.1108/09574099710805556

Mason, M. (Ed.). (2008). *Complexity Theory and the Philosophy of Education*. Wiley-Blackwell. doi:10.1002/9781444307351

Matthews, J., Pellew, L., Phua, F., & Rowlinson, S. (2000). Quality relationships: Partnering in the construction supply chain. *International Journal of Quality & Reliability Management*, *17*(4/5), 493–510. doi:10.1108/02656710010371191

ME Construction News. (2019a). *Over half of construction leaders expect 6-10% growth over the next year*. Available at https://meconstructionnews.com/36353/over-half-of-construction-leaders-expect-6-10-growth-over-the-next-year

ME Construction News. (2019b). *Trends in offsite modular construction*. Available at https://meconstructionnews.com/34495/trends-in-offsite-modular-construction

MEED. (2019). *3D printing to take over construction*. Available at https://www.meed.com/3d-printing-take-construction/

Melacini, M., Perotti, S., Rasini, M., & Tappia, E. (2018). E-fulfilment and distribution in omni-channel retailing: A systematic literature review. *International Journal of Physical Distribution & Logistics Management*, *48*(4), 391–414. doi:10.1108/IJPDLM-02-2017-0101

Melnyk, S. A. (2017). The emergence of the strategic leader. *Supply Chain Management Review*. https://www.scmr.com/article/the_emergence_of_the_strategic_leader

Melnyk, S. A., Lummus, R. R., Vokurka, R. J., Burns, L. J., & Sandor, J. (2009). Mapping the future of supply chain management: A Delphi study. *International Journal of Production Research*, *47*(16), 4629–4653. doi:10.1080/00207540802014700

MENA Herald. (2019). *Dubai Land Department launches Rent-to-Own Title Deed, first of its kind in the region*. Available at https://www.menaherald.com/en/economy/real-estate-construction/dubai-land-department-launches-rent-own-title-deed-first-its-kind

Mentzer, J. T., DeWitt, W., Keebler, J. S., Min, S., Nix, N. W., Smith, C. D., & Zacharia, Z. G. (2001). Defining supply chain management. *Journal of Business Logistics*, *22*(2), 1–25.

Mentzer, J. T., & Kahn, K. B. (1995). A framework of logistics research. *Journal of Business Logistics*, *16*, 231.

Mikles, S. (2016). Characteristics of a Supply Chain Leader. *Flash Global Blog*. https://flashglobal.com/blog/characteristics-supply-chain-leader/

Ming, C. H., Ghi, F. Y., & Tzu, C. L. (2014). Re-examining supply chain integration and the supplier's performance relationships under uncertainty. *Supply Chain Management*, *19*(1), 64–78. doi:10.1108/SCM-04-2013-0114

Min, J. U., & Bjornsson, H. C. (2008). Agent-based construction supply chain simulator (CS 2) for measuring the value of real-time information sharing in construction. *Journal of Management Engineering*, *24*(4), 245–254. doi:10.1061/(ASCE)0742-597X(2008)24:4(245)

Min, S., & Mentzer, J. T. (2004). Developing and measuring supply chain management concepts. *Journal of Business Logistics*, *25*(1), 63–99. doi:10.1002/j.2158-1592.2004.tb00170.x

Mitchell, C., Bridgwater, A., Stevens, D., Toft, A. J., & Watters, M., & Bioenergy. (1995). Technoeconomic assessment of biomass to energy. *Biomass*, *9*(1-5), 205–226.

Miyazaki, A. D., & Fernandez, A. (2001). Consumer perceptions of privacy and security risks for online shopping. *The Journal of Consumer Affairs*, *35*(1), 27–44. doi:10.1111/j.1745-6606.2001.tb00101.x

Mkoma, S. L., Kawamura, K., & Fu, P. Q. (2013). Contributions of biomass/biofuel burning to organic aerosols and particulate matter in Tanzania, East Africa, based on analyses of ionic species, organic and elemental carbon, levoglucosan and mannosan. *Atmospheric Chemistry and Physics*, *13*(20), 10325–10338.

Mohanty, R. P. (1992). Project selection by a multiple-criteria decision-making method: An example from a developing country. *International Journal of Project Management*, *10*(1), 31–38. doi:10.1016/0263-7863(92)90070-P

Mohmed, A. S. I., Azizan, N. B., & Jali, M. Z. (2016). Factors Affecting Purchase Intention of Customers to Accept E-Commerce Transaction: A Conceptual Framework. *Research Journal of Applied Sciences*, *11*, 1188–1194.

Mokhtar, A. R. M., Genovese, A., Brint, A., & Kumar, N. (2019). Supply chain leadership: A systematic literature review and a research agenda. *International Journal of Production Economics*, *216*, 255–273. doi:10.1016/j.ijpe.2019.04.001

Molla, A., & Heeks, R. (2007). Exploring e-commerce benefits for businesses in a developing country. *The Information Society*, *23*(2), 95–108. doi:10.1080/01972240701224028

Mongelluzzo, B. (1999). Choose service over lower rates, exporters told. *Journal of Commerce*, (11), 12.

Moon, S., Han, S., Zekavat, P. R., Bernold, L. E., & Wang, X. (2017). Process-waste reduction in the construction supply chain using proactive information network. *Concurrent Engineering*, *25*(2), 123–135. doi:10.1177/1063293X16667451

Morais, D. O. C., & Silvestre, B. S. (2018). Advancing social sustainability in supply chain management: Lessons from multiple case studies in an emerging economy. *Journal of Cleaner Production*, *199*, 222–235. doi:10.1016/j.jclepro.2018.07.097

Morash, E. A. (1987). Using transportation intermediaries for industrial purchasing decisions. *Journal of Business and Industrial Marketing*, *2*(4), 15–27. doi:10.1108/eb006039

Morrison, O. (2019). *Seven ways business leaders can transform the food system.* Retrieved from https://www.foodnavigator.com/Article/2019/10/16/7-ways-business-leaders-can-transform-the-food-system

Mourshed, M., Farrell, D., & Barton, D. (2012). Education to Employment: Designing a System that Works. *McKinsey Centre for Government.* Available at: www.mckinsey.com/mcg

Muerza, V., De la Cruz, M. T., & Urciuoli, L. (2019). La logística como factor de éxito en los centros logísticos integrados de biomasa. *Revista de Economía Aragonesa*, *67*, 107–120.

Muhammad, Q., N., Ali, M., & Shazad, K. (2012). The Impact of Supply Chain Management Practices on the Overall Performance of the Organization, *Proceedings of 3rd International Conference on Business Management*, *1*, 1–23.

Mukherjee, R. (2016, November 10). *The unsolved problem of E-Commerce Industries: Reverse Logistics!* Retrieved August 8, 2018, from https://in.thehackerstreet.com/problem-e-commerce-reverse-logistics/

Mukul, P. (2018, April 6). *E-commerce firms losing over 30 per cent of GMV due to cancellations/returns.* Retrieved September 28, 2018, from https://indianexpress.com/article/business/business-others/e-commerce-firms-losing-over-30-per-cent-of-gmv-due-to-cancellations-returns-5125471/

Mulatu, Y., & Kindu, M. (2010). Status of bamboo resource development, utilisation and research in Ethiopia: A review. *Ethiopian Journal of Natural Resources*, *1*, 79–98.

Mulla Aneesa, I. A. K. (2015, March). Supply Chain Management: Effective Tool in Construction Industry. *International Journal of Novel Research in Engineering and Science*, *2*(1), 35–40.

Müller-Seitz, G., & Sydow, J. (2012). Manoeuvring between networks to lead: A longitudinal case study in the semiconductor industry. *Long Range Planning*, *45*(2/3), 105–135. doi:10.1016/j.lrp.2012.02.001

Nakheel. (2015). *Nakheel and Engel & Völkers sign joint venture agreement.* Available at https://www.nakheel.com/en/media/news/nakheel-and-engel-and-volkers-sign-joint-venture-agreement

Narang, I. K. (2007). *Check list for dairy plant's MMPO certification* (6th ed.). Dairy India.

NBACFS. (2005). Good manufacturing practices for milk collection center. *Royal Gazette, 122*, 1-20.

Newbert, S. L. (2007). Empirical research on the resource-based view of the firm: An assessment and suggestions for future research. *Strategic Management Journal*, *28*(2), 121–146. doi:10.1002mj.573

Nguyen, H., & Waring, T. S. (2013). The adoption of customer relationship management (CRM) technology in SMEs: An empirical study. *Journal of Small Business and Enterprise Development*, *20*(4), 824–848. doi:10.1108/JSBED-01-2012-0013

Nordin, N., Deros, B. M., & Wahab, D. A. (2010). A study on lean manufacturing implementation in Malaysian automotive component industry. *International Journal of Innovation, Management and Technology*, *1*(4), 374–380.

NRC. (2006). Shea. In Lost Crops of Africa (Vol. 2). Washington, DC: The National Academies Press.

Nyaga, G. N., Whipple, J. M., & Lynch, D. F. (2010). Examining supply chain relationships: Do buyer and supplier perspectives on collaborative relationships differ? *Journal of Operations Management*, *28*(2), 101–114. doi:10.1016/j.jom.2009.07.005

O'Brien, E. M., & Deans, K. R. (1996). Educational supply chain: A tool for strategic planning in tertiary education? *Marketing Intelligence & Planning*, *14*(2), 33–40. doi:10.1108/02634509610110787

O'Brien, T., Nedelkoska, L., & Frasheri, E. (2017). *What is the Binding Constraint to Growth in Albania*. Center for International Development at Harvard University.

O'Byrne. (2016). 6 Key Supply Chain Leaders Skills and why you need them? *Logistics Bureau Blog*. https://www.logisticsbureau.com/6-key-supply-chain-leaders-skills-and-why-you-need-them

O'Marah. (2018). Lessons in Excellence from Five Supply Chain Leaders, SCM world learning engine. *SCM World*. https://www.forbes.com/sites/kevinomarah/2018/05/30/lessons-in-excellence-from-five-supply-chain-leaders/#403559551545

O'Rourke, D. (2005). Market movements: Nongovernmental organization strategies to influence global production and consumption. *Journal of Industrial Ecology*, *9*(1-2), 115–128. doi:10.1162/1088198054084608

O'Brien, W. J. (1999). *Construction Supply-Chain Management: A Vision for Advanced Coordination, Costing, and Control*. NSF Berkley - Stanford Construction Research Workshop 6.

Oesterreich, T. D., & Teuteberg, F. (2016). Understanding the implications of digitisation and automation in the context of Industry 4.0: A triangulation approach and elements of a research agenda for the construction industry. *Computers in Industry*, *83*, 121–139. doi:10.1016/j.compind.2016.09.006

Ofori, G. (2000). Greening the construction supply chain in Singapore. *European Journal of Purchasing & Supply Management*, *6*(3-4), 195–206. doi:10.1016/S0969-7012(00)00015-0

Ojha, D., Acharya, C., & Cooper, D. (2018). Transformational leadership and supply chain ambidexterity: Mediating role of supply chain organizational learning and moderating role of uncertainty. *International Journal of Production Economics*, *197*, 215–231. doi:10.1016/j.ijpe.2018.01.001

Olatz, P., Beatriz, R., & Javier, N. (2019). Life cycle thinking toward sustainable development policy-making:The Example of energy retrofits. *Journal of Cleaner Production*, 267–281.

Oliveira, T., & Martins, M. F. (2010). Understanding e-business adoption across industries in European countries. *Industrial Management & Data Systems*, *110*(9), 1337–1354. doi:10.1108/02635571011087428

Ou, C. S., Liu, F. C., Hung, Y. C., & Yen, D. C. (2010). A structural model of supply chain management on firm performance. *International Journal of Operations & Production Management*, *30*(5), 526–545.

Oxley, J. E., & Yeung, B. (2001). E-commerce readiness: Institutional environment and international competitiveness. *Journal of International Business Studies*, *32*(4), 705–723. doi:10.1057/palgrave.jibs.8490991

Pagell, M., & Wu, Z. (2009). Building a more complete theory of sustainable supply chain management using case studies of 10 exemplars. *The Journal of Supply Chain Management*, *45*(2), 37–56. doi:10.1111/j.1745-493X.2009.03162.x

Paik, S.-K., & Bagchi, P. K. (2007). Understanding the causes of the bullwhip effect in a supply chain. *International Journal of Retail & Distribution Management*, *35*(4), 308–324. doi:10.1108/09590550710736229

Pala, M., Edum-Fotwe, F., Ruikar, K., Peters, C., & Doughty, N. (2016). Implementing commercial information exchange: A construction supply chain case study. *Construction Management and Economics*, *34*(12), 898–918. doi:10.1080/01446193.2016.1211718

Pamulety, T. C., & Pillai, V. M. (2011). Impact of information sharing in supply chain performance. *Technology Systems and Management*, *145*, 327–332. doi:10.1007/978-3-642-20209-4_47

Panayides, P. M., & Lun, V. Y. H. (2009). The impact of trust on innovativeness and supply chain performance. *International Journal of Production Economics*, *122*(1), 35–46. doi:10.1016/j.ijpe.2008.12.025

Pang, H. (2016). Research on Optimization of B2C E-commerce Service Quality Oriented by Customer Demand. *Revista de la Facultad de Ingeniería*, *31*(6), 103–113.

Parker, C., & Castleman, T. (2007). New directions for research on SME-eBusiness: Insights from an analysis of journal articles from 2003-2006. *Journal of Information Systems and Small Business*, *1*, 21–40.

Park, Y. W. (2014). Integration of Supply and Demand Chain in Emerging Markets. *Journal of Business and Economics*, *5*(12), 2282–2293. doi:10.15341/jbe(2155-7950)/12.05.2014/009

Partida, B. (2019). Using Dynamic Leadership to Prepare for the Future. *Supply Chain Management Review*. https://www.scmr.com/article/using_dynamic_leadership_to_prepare_for_the_future

Pérez-Salazar, M. R., Lasserre, A. A. A., Cedillo-Campos, M. G., & González, J. C. H. (2017). The Role of Knowledge Management in Supply Chain Management: A Literature Review. *Journal of Industrial Engineering and Management*, *10*(4), 711–788. doi:10.3926/jiem.2144

Pfeiffer. (2014). *Lessons learned in Supply Chain Leadership: A Delphi Study* (PhD dissertation). University of Phoenix.

Pfohl, H.-C., Cullmann, O., & Stolzle, W. (1999). Inventory management with statistical process control: Simulation and evaluation. *Journal of Business Logistics*, *20*(1), 101–120.

Pillai, M., Talari, P. C., & Elluri, P. V. (2013). Performance analysis of some supply chain replenishment strategies. *International Journal of Logistics Research and Applications*, *17*(5), 357–376. doi:10.1080/13675567.2013.862227

Poppo, L., & Zenger, T. (2002). Do formal contracts and relational governance function as substitutes or complements? *Strategic Management Journal*, *23*(8), 707–725. doi:10.1002mj.249

Powell, J. M., Pearson, R. A., & Hiernaux, P. H. (2004). Crop–livestock interactions in the West African drylands. *Agronomy Journal*, *96*(2), 469–483.

Prajogo, D., & Jan, O. (2012). Supply chain integration and performance: The effects of longterm relationships, information technology and sharing, and logistics integration. *International Journal of Production Economics*, *135*(1), 514–522. doi:10.1016/j.ijpe.2011.09.001

Prakash, A., & Mohanty, R. P. (2015). Understanding construction supply chain management for road projects. *International Journal of Logistics Systems and Management*, *22*(4), 414–435. doi:10.1504/IJLSM.2015.072747

Pryke, S. (Ed.). (2009). *Construction Suply Chain Management: Concepts and Case Studys*. Wiley-Blackwell. doi:10.1002/9781444320916

PTI. (2018, July 6). E-tailers exploring ways to improve reverse logistics costs: Study. *ET Retail*. Retrieved August 10, 2018, from https://retail.economictimes.indiatimes.com/news/e-commerce/e-tailing/e-tailers-exploring-ways-to-improve-reverse-logistics-costs-study/64878780

Punjrath, J. S. (2007). *Packaging innovation* (6th ed.). Dairy India.

PwC India. (2020). *Research & insights, 2018, Propelling India towards global leadership in e-commerce*. Author.

Rahayu, R., & Day, J. (2015). Determinant factors of e-commerce adoption by SMEs in developing country: Evidence from Indonesia. *Procedia: Social and Behavioral Sciences*, *195*, 142–150. doi:10.1016/j.sbspro.2015.06.423

Rahayu, R., & Day, J. (2017). E-commerce adoption by SMEs in developing countries: Evidence from Indonesia. *Eurasian Business Review*, *7*(1), 25–41. doi:10.100740821-016-0044-6

Rai, A., Patnayakuni, R., & Patnayakuni, N. (2006). Firm Performance Impacts of Digitally-enabled Supply Chain Integration Capabilities. *Management Information Systems Quarterly*, *30*(2), 225–246. doi:10.2307/25148729

Rajagopalan, P., Andamon, M., & Moore, T. (2019). Energy Performance in the Australian Built Environment. In P. Rajagopalan, M. Andamon, & T. Moore (Eds.), *Green Energy and Technology*. Springer.

Ramakrishna, Y. (2016). Supply Chain Management: Large vs. Small and Medium Enterprises (SMEs). In A. Dwivedi (Ed.), *Innovative Solutions for Implementing Global Supply Chains in Emerging Markets* (pp. 141–151). IGI Global. doi:10.4018/978-1-4666-9795-9.ch009

Ramon-Jeronimo, J.M., Florez-Lopez, R. & Ramon-Jeronimo, M.A. (2017). Understanding the generation of value along supply chains: balancing control information and relational governance mechanisms in downstream and upstream relationships. *Sustainability, 9*(8).

Randall, L. M., & Lori, A. (2007). Applying adaptive leadership to successful change initiatives in academia. *Leadership and Organization Development Journal*, *28*(4), 325–335. doi:10.1108/01437730710752201

Razali, N., & Afthanorhan, W. (2014). Improving Energy Conservavtion Using Six Sigma Methodology at Faculty of Computer & Mathematical Sciences (FSKM), Universiti Teknologi Mara Shah Alam. *Asian Journal of Economic Modelling*, 52-68.

RedSeer. (2018, May). *Ecommerce industry in India*. Retrieved September 21, 2018, from https://redseer.com/reports/ecommerce-industry-in-india/

'Return Guaranteed' – Indian E-commerce and the issue of Reverse Logistics! (2017, August 22). Retrieved August 20, 2018, from https://trak.in/tags/business/2012/06/22/indian-ecommerce-return-policy-logistics/

Rezgui, Y., & Miles, J. (2009). Exploring the potential of SME alliances in the construction sector. *Journal of Construction Engineering and Management*, *136*(5), 558–567. doi:10.1061/(ASCE)CO.1943-7862.0000150

Richer, S. (2017, March 27). *Nimble Reverse Logistics in e-Commerce*. Retrieved August 23, 2018, from https://industrytoday.com/article/nimble-reverse-logistics-in-e-commerce/

Riddell, T. (2016). *Top 5 issues facing the construction industry in 2017*. Available at: https://esub.com/top-issues-facing-the-construction-industry-2017/

Rillo, A. D., & Dela Cruz, V. (2016). The Development Dimension of E-Commerce in Asia: Opportunities and Challenges. *Asian Development Bank Institute*. http://hdl.handle.net/11540/6484

Robinson, C. J., & Malhotra, M. K. (2005). Defining the concept of supply chain quality management and its relevance to academic and industrial practice. *International Journal of Production Economics*, *96*(3), 315–377. doi:10.1016/j.ijpe.2004.06.055

Rogers, E. M. (1962). *Diffusion of Innovations*. The Free Press of Glencoe.

Rojko, A. (2017). Industry 4.0 concept: Background and overview. *International Journal of Interactive Mobile Technologies*, *11*(5), 77–90. doi:10.3991/ijim.v11i5.7072

Rose, G., Khoo, H., & Straub, D. W. (1999). Current technological impediments to business-to-consumer electronic commerce. *Communications of the AIS*, *1*, 1. doi:10.17705/1CAIS.00116

Rother, M. (1999). *Learning to See: Value Stream Mapping to Create Value and Eliminate Muda*. The Lean Enterprise Institute.

Ruben Vrijhoev, L. K. (2000, December). Roles of Supply Chain Management in Construction. *European Journal of Purchasing & Supply Management*, *6*(3-4), 69–178. doi:10.1016/S0969-7012(00)00013-7

Rushton, A., Croucher, P., & Baker, P. (2006). *The Handbook of Logistics and Distribution Management* (3rd ed.).

Saaty, T. (1980). *The Analytic Hierarchy Process*. McGraw-Hill.

Saaty, T. (1982). *Decision-Making for Leaders*. Wadsworth.

Saaty, T. L. (2008). Decision making with the analytic hierarchy process. *International Journal of Services Sciences*, *1*(1), 83–98. doi:10.1504/IJSSCI.2008.017590

Saghiri, S., Wilding, R., Mena, C., & Bourlakis, M. (2017). Toward a three-dimensional framework for omni-channel. *Journal of Business Research*, *77*, 53–67. doi:10.1016/j.jbusres.2017.03.025

Sahay, B., Halldórsson, Á., & Skjøtt-Larsen, T. (2006). Dynamics of relationship governance in TPL arrangements-a dyadic perspective. *International Journal of Physical Distribution & Logistics Management*, *36*(7), 490–506. doi:10.1108/09600030610684944

Salamon, S. D., & Robinson, S. L. (2008). Trust that binds: The impact of collective felt trust on organizational performance. *The Journal of Applied Psychology*, *93*(3), 593–601. doi:10.1037/0021-9010.93.3.593 PMID:18457488

Saleh, K. (n.d.). *E-commerce Product Return Rate – Statistics and Trends* [Infographic]. Retrieved September 9, 2018, from https://www.invespcro.com/blog/ecommerce-product-return-rate-statistics/

Samad & Chowdhary. (n.d.). *Cash-On-Delivery and Reverse Logistics*. Retrieved September 4, 2018, from https://www.etcases.com/cash-delivery-reverse-logistics-marketing-case-study.html

Sampson. (2000). Customer-supplier duality and bidirectional supply chains in service organizations. *International Journal of Service Industry Management*, *11*(4), 348-364.

Samuelson, P., & Nordhaus, W. (2005). *Economics*. McGraw-Hill.

Sanders, R. N., & Premus, R. (2005). Modeling the relationship between firm IT capability, collaboration and performance. *Journal of Business Logistics*, *26*(1), 1–23. doi:10.1002/j.2158-1592.2005.tb00192.x

Sardroud, J. M. (2012). Influence of RFID technology on automated management of construction materials and components. *Scientia Iranica*, *19*(3), 381–392. doi:10.1016/j.scient.2012.02.023

Sarkar & Sharma. (2015), Challenges Faced by Educators in Management Education. *Parikalpana, KIIT Journal of Management*, *11*(1), 74-87.

Sarrico, C. S., & Rosa, M. J. (2016). Supply chain quality management in education. *International Journal of Quality & Reliability Management*, *33*(4), 499–517. doi:10.1108/IJQRM-11-2014-0181

SCC. (1999). *Supply-Chain Operations Reference-Model: Overview of SCOR Version 3.0*. Pittsburgh, PA: Supply-Chain Council Inc.

Schiller, M. (2017). Looking beyond cost control – a new role for strategic supply chain leaders. *Healthcare Financial Management*. https://www.hfma.org/topics/article/55362.html

Schoemaker, P. J., Krupp, S., & Howland, S. (2013). Strategic leadership: The essential skills. *Harvard Business Review*, *91*(1), 131–134. PMID:23390746

Sekar. (n.d.). *eCommerce Support On Reverse Logistics In India*. Retrieved August 21, 2018, from http://www.theinternationaljournal.org/ojs/index.php?journal=rjebs&page=article&op=view&path[]=1378

Serpell, A., & Heredia, B. (2004). Supply chain management in construction: Diagnosis and application issues. *Globalisation and Construction*, 455-466.

Sezhiyan, D., Page, T., & Iskanius, P. (2011). The impact of supply effort management, logistics capability, and supply chain management strategies on firm performance. *International Journal of Electronic Transport*, *1*(1), 26–44. doi:10.1504/IJET.2011.043114

SGER. (2015). *State of Green Economy Report.* World Green Economy Submit, Dubai, UAE. Available at https://dcce.ae/state-of-green-economy-report-2015/

SGER. (2016). *State of Green Economy Report. United Arab Emirates Ministry of Climate Change and Environment, Second Edition*. Available at www.moccae.gov.ae/assets/download/40a8d3c1/green-economy-report-2016.aspx

Shah, N. (2018, June 22). *Reverse Logistics for Ecommerce: Understanding The Basics*. Retrieved September 1, 2018, from https://www.shiprocket.in/blog/reverse-logistics-for-ecommerce/

Shahzad, K., Ali, T., Takala, J., Helo, P., & Zaefarian, G. (2018). The varying roles of governance mechanisms on ex-post transaction costs and relationship commitment in buyer-supplier relationships. *Industrial Marketing Management*, *71*, 135–146. doi:10.1016/j.indmarman.2017.12.012

Sharfman, M. P., Shaft, T. M., & Anex, R. P. Jr. (2009). The road to cooperative supply-chain environmental management: Trust and uncertainty among pro-active firms. *Business Strategy and the Environment*, *18*(1), 1–13. doi:10.1002/bse.580

Sharif, A. M., & Irani, Z. (2012). Supply Chain Leadership. *International Journal of Production Economics*, *14*(1), 57–68. doi:10.1016/j.ijpe.2012.01.041

Shi, Q., Ding, X., Zuo, J., & Zillante, G. (2016). Mobile Internet based construction supply chain management: A critical review. *Automation in Construction*, *72*(82016), 143–154. doi:10.1016/j.autcon.2016.08.020

Silvestre, B. S. (2015a). A hard nut to crack! Implementing supply chain sustainability in an emerging economy. *Journal of Cleaner Production*, *96*, 171–181. doi:10.1016/j.jclepro.2014.01.009

Silvestre, B. S. (2015b). Sustainable supply chain management in emerging economies: Environmental turbulence, institutional voids and sustainability trajectories. *International Journal of Production Economics*, *67*, 56–169. doi:10.1016/j.ijpe.2015.05.025

Singh, S. (2017, September 12). *Is a 30-day return policy still necessary in ecommerce? Sellers answer*. Retrieved August 16, 2018, from https://indianonlineseller.com/2017/09/30-day-return-policy-in-ecommerce/

Singh, A., Shukla, N., & Mishra, N. (2018). Social media data analytics to improve supply chain management in food industries. *Transportation Research Part E, Logistics and Transportation Review*, *114*, 398–415. doi:10.1016/j.tre.2017.05.008

Singh, P., Wani, A. L. I. A., Karim, A. A., & Langowski, H. (2012). The use of carbon dioxide in the processing and packaging of milk and dairy products. *International Journal of Dairy Technology*, *65*(2), 161–177. doi:10.1111/j.1471-0307.2011.00744.x

Singleton, T., & Cormican, K. (2013). The influence of technology on the development of partnership relationships in the Irish construction industry. *International Journal of Computer Integrated Manufacturing*, *26*(1-2), 19–28. doi:10.1080/0951192X.2012.681907

Sinkovics, R., & Roath, A. (2004). Strategic orientation, capabilities, and performance in manufacturers – 3PL relationships. *Journal of Business Logistics*, *25*(2), 43–55. doi:10.1002/j.2158-1592.2004.tb00181.x

Sithole, B., Sergio, G. S., & Kavelj, M. (2016). Supply chain optimization: Enhancing end-to-end visibility. *Procedia Engineering*, *159*, 12–18. doi:10.1016/j.proeng.2016.08.058

Sivakumara, K., & Fengb, C. (2019). Patterns of product improvements and customer response. *Journal of Business Research*, *104*, 27–43. doi:10.1016/j.jbusres.2019.06.044

Smith, G.B. (1995). Good manufacturing practices for dairy processing plant. *The Dairy Practice Council*, 1-16.

Smyrlis, L. (2005). Are you employing the right strategies to control rising truck rates? *Canadian Transportation Logistics*, *208*(4), 4.

Snyder, S. (2013). *The Simple, the Complicated, and the Complex: Educational Reform Through the Lens of Complexity Theory*. OECD.

Sokhansanj, S., Kumar, A., & Turhollow, A. F., & Bioenergy. (2006). Development and implementation of integrated biomass supply analysis and logistics model (IBSAL). *Biomass*, *30*(10), 838–847.

Somapa, S., Cools, M., & Dullaert, W. (2012). Unlocking the potential of time-driven activity-based costing for small logistics companies. *International Journal of Logistics Research and Applications*, *15*(5), 303–322. doi:10.1080/13675567.2012.742043

Song, J. (2011). *Regional logistics capability and economic development of the regions in Great Britain*. University of Hull.

Soosay, C. A., Hyland, P. W., & Ferrer, M. (2008). Supply chain collaboration: Capabilities for continuous innovation. *Supply Chain Management*, *31*(2), 160–169. doi:10.1108/13598540810860994

Sorkun, M. F. (2019). The impact of product variety on LSQ in e-marketplaces. *International Journal of Physical Distribution & Logistics Management*, *49*(7), 749–766. doi:10.1108/IJPDLM-06-2018-0223

Spekman, R. E., Spear, J., & Kamauff, J. (2002). Supply chain competency: Learning as a key component. *Supply Chain Management*, *7*(1), 41–55. doi:10.1108/13598540210414373

SpencerStuart. (2015). *Agribusiness leadership of the future. A Snapshot of Strategic Priorities and Talent Needs in Asia Pacific*. Retrieved from https://www.spencerstuart.com/-/media/pdf-files/research-and-insight-pdfs/agribusiness-leadership-of-the-future_080216.pdf

Spendlove, M. (2007). Competencies for effective leadership in higher education. *International Journal of Educational Management*, *21*(5), 407–417. doi:10.1108/09513540710760183

Srivastava, S. K. (2007). Green supply-chain management: A state-of-the-art literature review. *International Journal of Management Reviews*, *9*(1), 53–80. doi:10.1111/j.1468-2370.2007.00202.x

Stank, T. P., Keller, S. B., & Daugherty, P. J. (2001). Supply chain collaboration and logistical service performance. *Journal of Business Logistics*, *22*(1), 29–48. doi:10.1002/j.2158-1592.2001.tb00158.x

Stock, J. R., & Lambert, D. M. (2001). *Strategic logistics management* (Vol. 4). McGraw-Hill.

Stokoe, J. (2017). *The construction industry – a leader or a follower in the fourth industrial revolution?* Available at: https://blogs.3ds.com/uk/construction-industry-revolution/

Stratman. (2010). Are Supply Chain leaders ready for Supply Chain Management Review? *Supply Chain Management Review*. https://www.scmr.com/article/are_supply_chain_leaders_ready_for_the_top1

Strom, R., Vendel, M., & Bredican, J. (2014). Mobile marketing: A literature review on its value for consumers and retailers. *Journal of Retailing and Consumer Services*, *21*(6), 1001–1012. doi:10.1016/j.jretconser.2013.12.003

Strozzi, F., Colicchia, C., Creazza, A., & Noe, C. (2017). Literature review on the 'Smart Factory'concept using bibliometric tools. *International Journal of Production Research*, *55*(22), 6572–6591. doi:10.1080/00207543.2017.1326643

Stukhart, G. (1995). *Construction materials management*. Marcel Dekker Inc.

Sucellog. (2017). *Project deliverables*. Retrieved from www.sucellog.eu/en/publications-reports.html

Sukasame, N., Sebora, T. C., & Mohedano-Suanes, A. (2008). E-commerce entrepreneurship as a national priority: The case of Thailand. *Service Industries Journal*, *28*(7), 989–1001. doi:10.1080/02642060701861357

Svensson, G. (2002). A conceptual framework of vulnerability in firms' inbound and outbound logistics flows. *International Journal of Physical Distribution & Logistics Management*, *32*(2), 110–134. doi:10.1108/09600030210421723

Tan, K. C., Kannan, V. R., & Handfield, R. B. (1998). Supply chain management: Supplier performance and firm performance. *International Journal of Purchasing and Materials Management*, *34*(3), 2–9.

Tate, W. L., Dooley, K. J., & Ellram, L. M. (2011). Transaction cost and institutional drivers of supplier adoption of environmental practices. *Journal of Business Logistics*, *32*(1), 6–16. doi:10.1111/j.2158-1592.2011.01001.x

Thiyagarajan, G., & Ali, S. (2016, May 19). *Analysis of Reverse Logistics Implementation Barriers in Online Retail Industry*. Retrieved September 8, 2018, from https://www.indjst.org/index.php/indjst/article/view/94193

Thiyagarajan, G., & Ali, S. (2016, May). *Reverse Logistics of e-Commerce in India - Controls, Cost and Clearance*. Retrieved August 15, 2018, from https://www.thecasecentre.org/programmeAdmin/products/view&&id=144830

Thomas, H., & Thomas, L. (2011). Perspectives on leadership in business schools. *Journal of Management Development*, *30*(5), 526–540. doi:10.1108/02621711111133037

Thompson, H. (1998). Marketing strategies: What do your customers really want? *The Journal of Business Strategy*, *19*(4), 16–21. doi:10.1108/eb039946

Thornton, L. M., Autry, C. W., Gligor, D. M., & Brik, A. B. (2013). Does Socially Responsible Supplier Selection Pay Off for Customer Firms? A Cross-Cultural Comparison. *The Journal of Supply Chain Management*, *49*(3), 66–89. doi:10.1111/jscm.12014

Thornton, S., Henneberg, S., Leischnig, A., & Naudé, P. (2019). It's in the Mix: How Firms Configure Resource Mobilization for New Product Success. *Journal of Product Innovation Management, 36*(4), 513–531. doi:10.1111/jpim.12489

Thunberg, M. (2016). *Developing a Framework for Supply Chain Planning in Construction* (Doctoral thesis). Linkoping Studies in Science and Technology, Linkoping.

Towill, D. R., Zhou, L., & Disney, S. M. (2007). Reducing the bullwhip effect: Looking through the appropriate lens. *International Journal of Production Economics, 108*(1–2), 444–453. doi:10.1016/j.ijpe.2006.12.024

Triandini, E., Djunaidy, A., & Siahaan, D. (2015). Factors Influencing E-Commerce Adoption by SMES Indonesia: A Conceptual Model. Lontar Komputer: Jurnal Ilmiah Teknologi Informasi, 4(2).

Trunic, P. A. (2006, Dec.). Price matters. *Logistics Today,* 24–25.

Tumpa, T. J., Ali, S. M., Rahman, M. H., Paul, S. K., Chowdhury, P., & Khan, S. A. R. (2019). Barriers to green supply chain management: An emerging economy context. *Journal of Cleaner Production, 236*, 117617. doi:10.1016/j.jclepro.2019.117617

UAE NIS. (2015). *UAE National Innovation Strategy.* Available at https://government.ae/en/about-the-uae/strategies-initiatives-and-awards/federal-governments-strategies-and-plans/national-innovation-strategy

UNCTAD. (2017). *World Investment Report. United Nations Conference on Trade and Development.* United Nations. Available at https://unctad.org/en/PublicationsLibrary/wir2017_en.pdf

UN-DESA. (2019). *World Urbanization Prospects 2019: Highlights.* Department of Economic and Social Affairs. Available at: https://population.un.org/wup/Publications/Files/WUP2018-Highlights.pdf

UNDP. (2004). UNCTAD E-Commerce and Development Report 2004. *United Nations Conference on Trade and Development.*

Urciuoli, L., & Muerza, V. (2018). *An integrated Framework for Evaluating Costs of IBLCs' supply chains.* Paper presented at the International Conference on Information Systems, Logistics and Supply Chain, Lyon, France.

Utterback, J. M., & Abernathy, W. J. (1975). A dynamic model of process and product innovation. *Omega, 3*(6), 639–656. doi:10.1016/0305-0483(75)90068-7

Vachon, S., & Klassen, R. D. (2006). Green project partnership in the supply chain: The case of package printing industry. *Journal of Cleaner Production, 14*(6), 661–671. doi:10.1016/j.jclepro.2005.07.014

Van Cleynenbreugel, P. (2017). The European Commission's Geo-Blocking Proposals and the Future of EU E-Commerce Regulation. *Masaryk UJL & Tech., 11*(1), 39. doi:10.5817/MUJLT2017-1-3 van Dam, J. E. G., Elbersen, H. W., & Daza Montaño, C. M. (2018). Bamboo production for industrial utilisation. In E. Alexoupoulo (Ed.), *Perennial grasses for bioenergy and bioproducts* (pp. 175–216). Academic Press.

Venkataraman, R. (2007). Project Supply Chain Management: Optimizing Value: The way we manage the total supply chain. *The Wiley Guide to Managing Projects*, 621-642.

Verma, D., Gope, P. C., Maheshwari, M. K., & Sharma, R. K. (2012). Bagasse fiber composites-A review. *J. Mater. Environ. Sci*, *3*(6), 1079–1092.

Watts, C., Hahn, C. K., & Sohn, B.-K. (1994). Monitoring the Performance of a Reorder Point System: A Control Chart Approach. *International Journal of Operations & Production Management*, *14*(2), 51–61. doi:10.1108/01443579410053211

WBG. (2017). *Doing Business 2017*. World Bank Group Flagship Report, 14th Edition. Available at https://www.doingbusiness.org/~/media/WBG/DoingBusiness/Documents/Annual-Reports/English/DB17-Full-Report.pdf

Westbrook, R., & Frohlich, M. (2001). Arcs of integration: An international study of supply chain strategies. *Journal of Operations Management*, *19*(2), 185–200. doi:10.1016/S0272-6963(00)00055-3

Wilding, R., Wagner, B., Fayezi, S., O'Loughlin, A., & Zutshi, A. (2012). Agency theory and supply chain management: A structured literature review. *Supply Chain Management*, *17*(5), 556–570. doi:10.1108/13598541211258618

William, J., & O'Brien, K. L. (2004). Construction Supply Chain Modeling: a research review and interdisciplinary research agenda. *ICAF Journal of Operations Management, 3*(3), 64-84.

Williams, M. D., Dwivedi, Y. K., Lal, B., & Schwarz, A. (2009). Contemporary trends and issues in IT adoption and diffusion research. *Journal of Information Technology*, *24*(1), 1–10. doi:10.1057/jit.2008.30

Wilson, H., Daniel, E., & Davies, I. A. (2008). The diffusion of e-commerce in UK SMEs. *Journal of Marketing Management*, *24*(5-6), 489–516. doi:10.1362/026725708X325968

Witkowski, K. (2017). Internet of Things, Big Data, Industry 4.0 – Innovative Solutions in Logistics and Supply Chains Management. *Procedia Engineering*, *182*, 763–769. doi:10.1016/j.proeng.2017.03.197

World Bank Data. (2019). *United Arab Emirates*. Available at https://data.worldbank.org/country/united-arab-emirates?view=chart

Wright, D., & Yuan, X. (2008). Mitigating the bullwhip effect by ordering policies and forecasting methods. *International Journal of Production Economics*, *113*(2), 587–597. doi:10.1016/j.ijpe.2007.10.022

Wu, P. J., & Huang, P. C. (2018). Business analytics for systematically investigating sustainable food supply chains. *Journal of Cleaner Production*, *203*, 968–976. doi:10.1016/j.jclepro.2018.08.178

Xie, X., Lu, Y., & Gou, Z. (2017). Green building pro-environment behaviors: Are green users also green buyers? *Sustainability*, *9*(10), 1703. doi:10.3390u9101703

Xperiencegroup. (2016). *Five Ways to Improve Construction Supply Chain Management.* Available: http://xperiencedynamics.com/blog/30/five-ways-toimprove- construction-supply-chain-management/

Xuewen, S., & Jinlong, B. (2010). Research on the innovation and development of the third-party B2B e-commerce model of China. *2010 3rd International Conference on Advanced Computer Theory and Engineering (ICACTE),* V4-317-V4-319. 10.1109/ICACTE.2010.5579506

Yanamandra, R. (2018). Development of an integrated healthcare supply chain model, *Supply Chain Forum. International Journal (Toronto, Ont.)*, *19*(2), 111–121. doi:10.1080/16258312.2018.1475823

Yang, C.-C., Marlow, P. B., & Lu, C.-S. (2009). Assessing resources, logistics service capabilities, innovation capabilities and the performance of container shipping services in Taiwan. *International Journal of Production Economics*, *122*(1), 4–20. doi:10.1016/j.ijpe.2009.03.016

Yawar, S. A., & Seuring, S. (2017). Management of social issues in supply chains: A literature review exploring social issues, actions and performance outcomes. *Journal of Business Ethics*, *141*(3), 621–643. doi:10.100710551-015-2719-9

Yourstory. (2019, Nov.). *Ecommerce paradox: Flipkart and Amazon India continue to make losses, but there's a silver lining.* https://yourstory.com/2019/11/flipkart-amazon-india-losses-ecommerce-walmart

Yuvamitra, J., Guiberteau, K., & Kozman, T. (2014). Six-Sigma Approach to Energy Management Planning. *Strategic Planning for Energy and the Environment.*

Zacharia, Z. G., Sanders, N. R., & Nix, N. W. (2011). The emerging role of the third party logistics provider (3PL) as an orchestrator. *Journal of Business Logistics*, *32*(1), 40–54. doi:10.1111/j.2158-1592.2011.01004.x

Zaefarian, G., Najafi-Tavani, Z., Henneberg, S. C., & Naude, P. (2016). Do supplier perceptions of buyer fairness lead to supplier sales growth? *Industrial Marketing Management*, *53*, 160–171. doi:10.1016/j.indmarman.2015.07.003

Zailai, S., Jeyaraman, K., Vengadasam, G., & Premkumar, R. (2012). Sustainable supply chain management (SSCM) in Malaysia: A survey. *International Journal of Production Economics*, *140*(1), 330–340. doi:10.1016/j.ijpe.2012.02.008

Zhang, M., Wang, J., & Zhang, J. (2009, October). Research on construction supply chain management in e-business environment. In *Industrial Engineering and Engineering Management, 2009. IE&EM'09. 16th International Conference on* (pp. 1565-1568). IEEE. 10.1109/ICIEEM.2009.5344374

Zhao, X., Pan, J., & Song, Y. (2018). Dependence on supplier, supplier trust and green supplier integration: The moderating role of contract management difficulty. *Sustainability, 10*(5), 1673. doi:10.3390u10051673

Zhao, X., & Xie, J. (2002). Forecasting errors and the value of information sharing in a supply chain. *International Journal of Production Research, 40*(2), 311–335. doi:10.1080/00207540110079121

Zhou, J. (2008, October). The optimization mode for construction supply chain management based on information techniques. In *Service Operations and Logistics, and Informatics, 2008. IEEE/SOLI 2008. IEEE International Conference on* (Vol. 1, pp. 1054-1058). IEEE.

Zhou, H., & Benton, W. Jr. (2007). Supply chain practice and information sharing. *Journal of Operations Management, 25*(6), 1348–1365. doi:10.1016/j.jom.2007.01.009

Zhou, J. (2008). The optimization mode for construction supply chain management based on information techniques. *SOLI 2008, IEEE International Conference on Service Operations and Logistics, and Informatics*, 1054–1058. 10.1109/SOLI.2008.4686554

Zou, P. X., & Seo, Y. (2006). Effective applications of e-commerce technologies in construction supply chain: Current practice and future improvement. *Journal of Information Technology in Construction, 11*(10), 127–147.

About the Contributors

Ashish Dwivedi is a Member of the Centre for Systems Studies at Hull University Business School, UK. Dr Ashish Dwivedi holds a PhD from Coventry University, UK, an MSc in Information Technology for Management from Coventry University, UK. He also has an MBA and BA in Management. His disciplinary research interests lie in the fields of Supply Chain Management and Knowledge Management. His current research focuses on the management and organizational aspects of systems thinking and design science and he leads the development of systems thinking for the MBA programme and for executive development at Hull University Business School.

Mohammed Saad Alshamrani is an experienced lecturer with a demonstrated history of working in the civilian and military industry. Skilled in Data Analysis (Excel, SPSS and Smart-PLS) Editing, Reviewing and Microsoft Office. Strong education professional with a PhD focused in HRM & Leadership and Gender from The University of Hull.

* * *

Anand Mohan Agrawal is serving the GLA University, Mathura as the Pro-Vice-Chancellor and the Director of the Institute of Business Management. He has a doctoral degree from the ISM Dhanbad. He completed his graduation as well as MBA from the BIT, Mesra. He started his career from the ISM Dhanbad where he worked close to a decade at various positions. From there, he moved to AICTE as a Director and subsequently, an advisor. Then on, he changed his workplace once more and came to his alma mater, namely BIT Mesra, where he went on to become a Dean. Next, he worked at the BITIC, Muscat as a Director and Dean. He has published 28 research papers as well as presented 26 research papers in international and national conferences/seminars. He has guided scholars for PhD, some of whom have been awarded their degree and some are currently working under him. He has published a book and another one is in the pipeline.

Vivek Agrawal is an Associate Professor in the Department of Management Studies in GLA University, Mathura (U.P.), India. He has first class degree in MBA. He received his PhD in the area of e-service quality from the Institute of Business Management, GLA University, Mathura (U.P.), India. He has guided many Master level theses in management and published more than 20 research papers in national/ international journals/conferences to his credit. He has more than eight years of teaching experience and his specialisation includes e-service quality and operations management.

Eni Ahmeti graduated from Epoka University with a Bachelor's Degree in International Marketing and Logistics Management. During her academic years she was engaged in volunteering activities with international organisations and summer programs in USA. Because of these engagements, she experienced firsthand the importance of maintaining good relations with other parties in an organisation and how the outcome depended on those relationships. Thus, she was encouraged to write her Graduation Project on Supply Chain Management in Construction Operations.

Raj V. Amonkar is a B.Tech. in chemical engineering from Indian Institute of Technology, Banaras Hindu University with a Post Graduate Diploma in Operations Management from Indira Gandhi National Open University. Raj attended the Process Business Management Programme at University of Warwick, UK and also completed the and Supply Manager Course at Syngenta's Supply Chain Academy. He is pursuing PhD at BITS Pilani, Goa campus. Raj is currently Associate Professor in the area Production & Operations Management at Goa Institute of Management since November 2011. He is additionally charged with the responsibility of the Pots Graduate Diploma in Management program of Goa Institute of Management.. Prior to joining Goa Institute of Management, Raj had over 26 years of industrial experience with reputed organizations in the areas of Global Logistics and Supply Chain (including Production and Supply Chain Planning, Supply Chain Design, Vendor Scheduling, Export-Import, Warehouse/Stores, Inventory Control and Dispatch, Distribution Safety and Compliance) and Manufacturing Operations (encompassing Production, Quality, Technical Services, Projects and Utilities). Raj had also presented papers at several national and international conferences. Raj was Member Logistics Committee, Goa Chamber of Commerce and Industry during 2009-2011 and was nominated as Expert-Chemicals by TUV SUD, Germany during 2003-2004.

E. (Bert) Annevelink is working as senior scientist at WFBR since 2006 and before that, he worked at IMAG, another research institute in Wageningen, since 1986. He holds an MSc Degree in Forestry from Wageningen Agricultural University, and a PhD in Agricultural Mathematics/Operational Research also from Wageningen Agricultural University. His main field of interest is logistics, production planning and scheduling. Since 1996, he has applied his knowledge on these topics to the field of bioenergy and biorefinery research. This has resulted in contributions to several simulation and optimization models on biomass logistics. Managing bioenergy and biorefinery related research at Wageningen UR has always been an important aspect of his work. He was co-founder of the Dutch Biorefinery Knowledge Network, project coordinator of the EU FP6 CSA project BIOPOL (on the assessment of BIOrefinery concepts and the implications for agricultural and forestry POLicy) and member of the editorial board of the Dutch Roadmap Biorefinery, that was produced for the Dutch Government. Furthermore, he participated in the EU FP7 CSA project StarColibri where he was co-author of the Biorefinery vision 2030 and the European Research Roadmap 2020. Recently he was involved in the FP7 S2Biom project as leader of the work package on the logistic organisation of lignocellulosic biomass feedstocks. Currently he is WP-leader in the EU-project AGROinLOG and involved in the EU-projects BECOOL and MAGIC. In 2017-2018, he was coordinator at Wageningen UR of the research theme Circular & biobased Economy. Bert has already been participating in IEA Bioenergy Task42 Biorefinery since the task meeting in Lille in 2010, and acts as active Task Leader for this triennium (2019-2021).

Smriti Asthana is an Assistant Professor at CII School of Logistics, Amity University, Delhi NCR, India. She received her PhD in Management and Certification from IIT Madras in Foundations of Supply Chain Management. Her research and teaching interests are in the area of International Logistics, Supply Chain Management, International Business Operations and Third-Party Logistics with specific focus on Performance Measurement of Third-Party Logistics Organizations in the Indian Logistics Industry. She is a member of the Editorial Advisory Board of Innovative Solutions for Implementing Global Supply Chains in Emerging Markets, IGI Global Journal.

Sreejith Balasubramanian is a Senior Lecturer in Supply Chain Management, and Chair of the Research Committee at Middlesex University, Dubai. His areas of expertise include supply chain, operations management, sustainability, higher education and knowledge management. He is also an expert data analyst with skills in statistical modeling and forecasting. Sreejith completed his PhD from Middlesex University Business School, London. He also holds a Master's degree in International Business from University of Wollongong and a Bachelor's degree in Electronics and Communication Engineering from University of Calicut. He has more than 10 years of experience in teaching, research, consultancy and project management.

His work has been published in leading international journals and conferences in areas of Supply Chain Management, Sustainability, and Knowledge Management.

Eirill Bø is a teaching professor at Norwegian Business School. Teaching and research within the area of supply chain management, logistics, inventory and transportation. Specialized in transport pricing and contracts.

Joby George is Assistant Professor, Department of Mechanical Engineering, Amal Jyothi College of Engineering, Kerala, India. He has completed M.Tech from College of Engineering Trivandrum and PhD from National Institute of Technology Calicut. His research interest includes modelling of problems in supply chain operation simulation, inventory control, and simulation modelling. With more than 13 years of teaching experience and over 13 publications in international journals, book chapter and conferences, he has developed two laboratory software packages in the area of supply chain management and inventory control. He has guided several B. Tech and M.Tech projects.

Smitha Girija is currently a Professor of Marketing at SOIL Scool of Business Design. She received her PhD in Impact of Organised Retail on Unorganised Retail in India. Her primary areas of interest are Qualitative and Quantitative Social Research and Consumer Behaviour. Her current areas of research are marketing strategy and consumer behaviour of social enterprises in rural India, Mobile applications and customer engagement in India, and Gaming Dependency among Indian Adolescents.

Alba Kruja is lecturer at Epoka University in Albania, Department of Business Administration. She holds an MBA degree from Nebraska University, Lincoln, USA and a PhD degree on Entrepreneurship from Agribusiness University of Tirana, Albania. At Epoka she teaches courses of Entrepreneurship and Management Science Research on Bachelor, Master and PhD level. At the same time, she holds the administrative duty of the Academic Coordinator of Business Informatics Program. She is author of many research articles and book chapters. Her main research focus is on Entrepreneurship, Innovation and Business Performance.

Rajeev Kumar is Ph.D. in the area of Marketing and Supply Chain Management from Institute of Management Studies, Banaras Hindu University, Varanasi. He has done his Bachelor Degree in Agriculture from Institute of Agricultural Sciences, Banaras Hindu University in 2008 and MBA Degree with specialization in Marketing from Faculty of Management Studies, Banaras Hindu University, Varanasi in 2010. He is awarded with UGC-NET/JRF/SRF in Management in year 2011 and has total experience of about 4 years in working with different organizations i.e. ICICI

Bank Pvt ltd., as Assistant Manager-II, Department of Agriculture, Uttar Pradesh Government as Technical Officer (Agriculture) and in Directorate of Urban Local Bodies, Uttar Pradesh Government as Food and Sanitary Inspector (FSI). His area of interest includes Marketing, Logistics and Supply Chain Management, Customer Relationship Management, Agribusiness and Rural Development, Agri- Retail Management. He has published several research papers in reputed referred journals and edited books and presented around 8 research papers at various international and national conference like IIM-Ahmedabad, IIIT- Delhi and BIMTECH- New Delhi.

R. P. Mohanty has 29 years experience in Academics in India and Foreign Universities and 10 years in Indian Industry in top management positions. After superannuating, he is engaged in leadership education, management consulting and managerial competency development. He has published 6 Text Books, more than 200 research papers in reputed International Journals, more than 100 papers in Indian Journals and Newspapers. He has guided 12 Ph.D. research scholars and several hundreds of master theses. He has advised more than 25 big companies in India and abroad in the areas of Engineering and Management. He has served as Chairman and President of many Professional associations in India and also as a board member in International Professional Institutions. He represents in the Editorial Board of 10 international journals.

Victoria Muerza is an Assistant Professor at the University of Zaragoza, area of Quantitative Methods for Business and Economy. She holds a BSc in Electronics Engineering, a MSc in Industrial Engineering, and a PhD in Industrial Engineering from the University of Zaragoza. She has been certified as a Risk Management Expert and a Quality Management Expert by the National Distance Education University (UNED). Dr. Muerza's main research interests include multi-criteria decision making, decision-making optimization, Transport and Logistics in the Supply Chain, the analysis and development of industrial and technological diversification processes, the analysis of the technological competitiveness of firms and regions, the management of technology and innovation, and technology evaluation. Dr. Muerza has previously been employed as a research engineer in the "Council for Competitiveness and Industrial and Technological Diversification of the University of Zaragoza", the "Aragon Institute of Engineering Research (i3A)" at the Transport and Logistics area, and as a Postdoctoral researcher at "Zaragoza Logistics Center" in the MIT International Logistics Program. Orcid: 0000-0002-2405-4375.

V. Madhusudanan Pillai is Professor, MED, National Institute of Technology Calicut, Kerala, India. With more than 28 years of teaching experience and over 135 publications in international journals and conferences, and editorship of a book, he has developed several laboratory exercises and software packages in the area of manufacturing management and supply chain management. His expertise in the area of developing the logic for e-learning tools on supply chain operation simulation has resulted in the development of several supply chain operation simulators and he owns copyright for three such software packages. He offers courses on Production planning and control, Inventory and supply chain management, Lean production management, and Group technology & FMS. His research interest includes modelling of problems in supply chain operation simulation, e-learning tools for supply chain operation simulation, sustainable supply chain management, cellular manufacturing systems, material requirements planning, scheduling, facility layout planning, inventory control, lean manufacturing, manpower planning – annualised hours, and ergonomics. He supervised 9 Ph.D. theses, over 76 Master students and he is currently advising 4 Ph.D. scholars and 4 Master students on their research. He is the reviewer for several Science Citation Indexed international journals, and conferences.

Yanamandra Ramakrishna currently works as Assistant Professor and Chair of Quality and Risk Management Committee in Skyline University College, Sharjah, UAE. He possesses around twenty eight years of corporate and academic experience. A PhD in SCM from JNTU, Hyderabad, India, he was a Manager-Operations in a leading Public Sector Undertaking in India and managed large scale projects related to Production, Operations & SCM. He has been teaching in leading business schools in India, pursuing research and conducting workshops for executives in Operations & SCM, Lean, TQM, Six Sigma, Project Management and Service Operations Management areas.

Hijrah Saputra is an Associate Professor in Politeknik Pos Indonesia, and he is now completing the Doctoral Research in University of Hull.

Vinaya Shukla is a Senior Lecturer in Operations and Supply Chain Management at Middlesex University and researches in the areas of Supply Chain Sustainability, supply chain risk management and supply chain systems. He has published in journals such as International Journal of Production Economics, International Journal of Production Research, Supply Chain Management: An International Journal, Production Planning and Control and International Journal of Logistics Research and Applications.

Nikhil Singh is a Data Analyst with Ecom Express Private Limited, India. He is a gold medalist in Masters of Business Administration in Supply Chain Management and an Engineering graduate. His expertise is in the area of inventory optimization and data analytics.

Joost Snels is senior scientist at Wageningen Food & Biobased Research since 2000. He studied Logistics and Business Administration at the University of Applied research at Tilburg. After graduation het studied Business Economics, major in Logistic Management at Tilburg University, The Netherlands. Since 2000 he is working at Wageningen Food & Biobased Research, the R&D organisation for sustainable innovation in the areas of healthy food, sustainable fresh food chains and biobased products. He is senior scientific researcher and project manager with experience in the field of product quality driven international supply chain management. Since 10 years he has been involved in several projects that focus on preventing and reducing food waste and food losses in international food chains.

Vandana Srivastava is a faculty of Information Systems & Management. She is currently associate with CHRIST (Deemed to be University), Bengaluru, India as an Adjunct Faculty in the area of Business Analytics. She obtained her doctoral degree from Jamia Millia Islamia, Delhi, India, and Master of Technology in Computer Applications from Indian Institute of Technology (IIT), Delhi, India. Her areas of research interest include artificial intelligence, information systems, spreadsheet modelling and business analytics. She is presently engaged in research work in the domain of applications of artificial intelligence and allied topics.

Luca Urciuoli is Associate Professor at KTH Royal Institute of Technology, Department of Industrial Economics and Management. Currently, he is also Adjunct Professor at the MIT - Zaragoza Logistics Center (Zaragoza, Spain), and research affiliate at the MIT Center for Transportation and Logistics (Boston, US). He has a MSc degree in Industrial Engineering, from Chalmers University of Technology, Gothenburg, and a PhD from the Engineering university of Lund. In the past, he has been working at the research unit of the Volvo group as a project manager developing telematics services in the areas of transport and logistics optimization, security, and uptime management and diagnostics. He also led the research of the Cross-border Research Association in Switzerland and collaborated in several consultancy and FP7 research projects, with a focus on topics like e-Customs, trade facilitation, supply chain security, waste and postal supply chains. Prior to moving to Stockholm, Dr Urciuoli was Associate Professor at the MIT Global scale center in Zaragoza, Spain, teaching in the MIT master of Engineering in Logistics and Supply Chain Management both in Zaragoza and Boston. In addition, he was doing research in the fields of risk and resilience, network design, biomass supply chains and digital supply chains.

Jan E. G. van Dam is senior scientist at the institute Food and Biobased Research of Wageningen UR, with specialization in the application research for sustainable lignocellulosic fibre in industrial processes. He studied bio-organic chemistry and pharmacognosy at the Utrecht State University. His PhD thesis was on the development of semisynthetic bacterial polysaccharide vaccines. He has been working on chemical and biochemical carbohydrate modification and processing of plant fibres and various polysaccharides for non-food application developments. He was vice-president of the European Polysaccharide network of Excellence (EPNOE 2002-2018). He has been involved in a large number of projects addressing fibre formation, fibre processing and quality, application development in paper and pulp, textiles, composites and building materials. He has been initiating international cooperation (China, Chile, Malaysia, India) for fibre crop innovation and biorefinery processing (flax, hemp, jute, coconut, cotton, kenaf, kapok, sisal, bamboo, sugar beet) and sustainable development of biobased materials including agricultural byproducts use such as palm oil residues, coffee residues and lignin application. He has been advising in several renewable building projects and to the Dutch Government for green building policy and transition of the circular textile. He has been supervisor and co-promotor in several PhD thesis programs.

Seemant Yadav has more than 12 years of teaching and research experience in the field of supply chain management and entrepreneurial marketing.

Index

H

I

L

M

O

P

R

S

T

W

www.ingramcontent.com/pod-product-compliance
Lightning Source LLC
LaVergne TN
LVHW081343300926
849161LV00008B/2050